A Natural Passion

'Such a family harmony'
(*Sir Charles Grandison*, Vol. 1)
Philippe Mercier, *A Music
Party* (Frederick Prince of
Wales and his sisters)

A Natural Passion

A STUDY OF THE NOVELS OF SAMUEL RICHARDSON

By Margaret Anne Doody

Love is a natural Passion
  Sir Charles Grandison, Volume II
Love various minds does variously inspire
  Dryden, Tyrannick Love, Act II

OXFORD
AT THE CLARENDON PRESS
1974

Oxford University Press, Ely House, London W. 1

GLASGOW NEW YORK TORONTO MELBOURNE WELLINGTON
CAPE TOWN IBADAN NAIROBI DAR ES SALAAM LUSAKA ADDIS ABABA
DELHI BOMBAY CALCUTTA MADRAS KARACHI LAHORE DACCA
KUALA LUMPUR SINGAPORE HONG KONG TOKYO

ISBN 0 19 812029 X

© *Oxford University Press 1974*

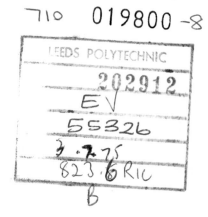
*Printed in Great Britain
at the University Press, Oxford
by Vivian Ridler
Printer to the University*

This book is dedicated to

ANNE AND HUBERT DOODY

Preface

IN this work I have endeavoured to discuss all Richardson's novels, with particular reference to the two greatest, *Clarissa* and the sadly neglected *Sir Charles Grandison*. Literary background, sources, and analogues are discussed in some detail. An examination of such literary background, however, can be illuminating only in the study of works worth the illuminating; the central fact here is that Richardson is a very powerful and profoundly creative novelist. The fullness of his creative powers is nowhere more clearly revealed than in the differences between the novels.

It is not usual to furnish a critical work on novels with visual illustrations, although the practice has become fairly common in discussions of poetry of some periods. It is possible that we pay too little attention to the nature of images in novels of the past: these images may have a significance now partly hidden from us. The iconography of images in prose fiction is worth our study.

Richardson's imagery has always fascinated me, for he is a master of the cumulative and intricate effect made possible by imagery; yet it has received little attention. In *Clarissa*, particularly, the imagery sustains and explains the religious theme which is central to the whole novel—but which does not seem to be well understood by modern critics. Visual images familiar in Richardson's time can clarify the purport of his imagery; and I have therefore taken the opportunity to insert into the present work some photographs of pictures which would have been interesting and useful to me when I first began to read, with great delight, Richardson's novels.

I wish to express my thanks to the Canada Council which gave me a Graduate Fellowship in 1964-5 and thus allowed me to begin graduate studies at Oxford, and to Imperial Oil Ltd. which awarded me a Graduate Fellowship from 1965 to 1968, enabling me to complete the thesis on Richardson for the Oxford D.Phil. I am also grateful to the Canada Council for having given me a post-doctoral research and travel grant for the summer of 1968. The University College of Swansea has also assisted me with a small travel grant in the summer of 1970.

Like every one who enjoys the experience of working in the Bodleian Library, Oxford, I am greatly indebted to the courtesy and kind assistance of the Library staff. I also wish to thank the staff of the Victoria and Albert Museum Library, and the staff of the British Museum Reading Room. Miss I. M. de Groot of the Rijksmuseum, Amsterdam, has also been most helpful.

I am happy to have the opportunity to express my gratitude to Miss Mary Lascelles of Somerville College, who first supervised my work on Richardson, and to Miss Rachel Trickett, of St. Hugh's College, for her unfailing interest in and encouragement of my progress in writing this book. I am also deeply obliged to Dr. Catherine Ing, of St. Hilda's College, who has been a splendid source of witty cheer and scholarly advice.

I should like to say, in addition, how grateful I am to Lady Margaret Hall, where as undergraduate and graduate student I spent six enjoyable years, and in particular to Miss K. M. Lea, until recently Vice-Principal and English Tutor of that College, who has given to me, as to all her students, instruction, example, and kind encouragement.

I am obliged to Mr. N. H. MacMichael, F.S.A., Keeper of the Muniments, Westminster Abbey, for kindly answering my queries about the Carteret Monument. I should also like to thank Mr. Roger Davies, L.R.P.S., of the Photographic Unit, Faculty of Arts, University College of Swansea, who took the photographs, from books in my possession, on which pictures in Plates 1 and 2 are based.

Finally, I am happy to have the opportunity of thanking a number of friends and colleagues who at various times assisted the work in its progress, suggesting points of interest, helping with references, reading sections of the typescript, and (not least in meriting my gratitude) being willing to talk about Richardson and bearing with my persistent enthusiasm on that subject.

Contents

List of Plates

I

Samuel Richardson and the Natural Passion

SAMUEL RICHARDSON's literary career was unusual. It is not often that a creative artist begins his work at the age of fifty. In the eighteenth century it was unusual for a member of the artisan class to turn to literary activity, unless he had previously renounced his craft or trade to pursue fame on the stage, or in Grub Street. Defoe, Richardson's elder, had combined his work as a writer with other pursuits, including trade and spying, but his novels came after a long apprenticeship in journalism, and his tales, unlike Richardson's, were not directed to the upper- and upper-middle-class reading public. The other important English male novelists of the age, Smollett, Fielding, and Sterne, all belonged to the professions, and had been given the benefit of extensive education. That a man in Richardson's situation should become a writer of importance is uncommon, and is the first touch of anomaly to be noticed in the study of works which are themselves anomalous—so embedded in their age in some ways, in others so peculiarly outside the central conventions—and which had a peculiar impact on the literature of the age to come.

Richardson's social position as a middle-class craftsman and tradesman—so prudent, so hard-working, so respectably bourgeois—seems to arouse the contempt of the literary critic who finds the gentleman or the rebel more congenial, while it attracts the interest of the social historian who seeks to understand the 'rise of the middle classes' in the eighteenth century. Richardson was proud of his success as a printer, and of his independence. By the late 1730s he had acquired eminence in his trade, and through his work had made the acquaintance of some of the interesting men of his time without having to beg favours from them. In 1738 he was able to lease The Grange, North End, Fulham, and to enjoy some leisure in surroundings which resembled those of the privileged classes to a much greater extent than did the house over the shop in Salisbury Court. He was not retired from business, and some of the most active years of his life as a printer came during his career as a novelist. He printed the *Journals* of the House of Commons, and was involved as shareholder as well as printer in the publication of the *Universal History*; his importance became increasingly recognized in the Stationers' Company, in which he held various offices until in 1754 he was made Master of the Company.[1] However, it was the decade of the thirties which saw him definitely established in prosperity; he had reached that point of middle age at which a man looks at the progress made in his occupation and feels either downhearted or moderately satisfied. Richardson could afford to feel somewhat elated; even if progress went no further and success remained at this point only, all would be well. At the same time, he was self-employed in a business where his skill and experience were of value, and did not have to fear, as others in less favoured positions might fear, that advancing age would make him redundant. It is probable that the emotional effect of his fortune, an unconscious relaxation of tensions, allowed him to use his mental and emotional energy for new purposes. No one, least of all Richardson himself, could have expected that he was to become a novelist.

The main source of biographical information about Richardson has traditionally been his often quoted letter to Johannes Stinstra of 1753, and many details are curiously vague. Richardson tells Stinstra that his father was a joiner, and that he intended young Samuel to enter the Church, but was unable, because of financial difficulties, to educate him for the ministry, and apprenticed his son to a printer. Richardson himself does not seem to have known where in Derbyshire he was born, and it is only recently that his birthplace has been

---

[1] For a thorough presentation of Richardson's life and business, see Alan Dugald McKillop's *Samuel Richardson: Printer and Novelist*, 1960, and the impressive biography by T. C. Duncan Eaves and Ben D. Kimpel (*Samuel Richardson, A Biography*, 1971); the latter appeared as I was preparing copy for the Press, and I am not indebted to that work for critical opinion or background material relating to the novels.

discovered, after much painstaking research.[1] His date of birth is still uncertain; the year given by Richardson, 1689, is correct, but the day and month recently suggested (31 July) can only be postulated.[2]

Richardson indicates that his father's removal to Derbyshire was the result of his involvement with the Duke of Monmouth and the Earl of Shaftesbury:

> Their known Favour for him, having, on the Duke's attempt on the Crown, subjected him to be looked upon with a jealous Eye . . . he thought proper, on the Decollation of the first-named unhappy Nobleman, to quit his London Business & to retire to Derbyshire; tho' to his great Detriment; & there I, & three other Children out of Nine, were born.[3]

The story may of course be invention; at least in part it seems inaccurate, as Richardson's father seems not to have removed until after the Revolution of 1688.[4] There is a touch of romance in the story of the poor artisan's involvement in great affairs of state, although it is of course not impossible that a man of low rank could be endangered by the political troubles of the period. It has been suggested that there was perhaps something that Richardson wished to conceal about the cause of the flight to Derby.[5] It might have been necessitated

---

[1] T. C. Duncan Eaves and Ben. D. Kimpel have ascertained beyond reasonable doubt that it was the village of Mackworth, outside the city of Derby. See 'Richardson's Immediate Family', Section v of 'Samuel Richardson and His Family Circle', *Notes and Queries*, N.s. xi (Oct. 1964), 364–5.

[2] Ibid. See also the same authors' *Samuel Richardson, A Biography*, p. 5.

[3] Richardson to Johannes Stinstra, 2 June 1753, *Selected Letters of Samuel Richardson*, ed. John Carroll, 1964, pp. 228–9.

[4] Eaves and Kimpel, 'Richardson's Immediate Family', p. 367.

[5] Ibid. See also *Samuel Richardson, A Biography*, pp. 4–5. It would not be surprising if a man of the rank of Richardson's father had Whig sympathies in 1685. Richardson's own political sympathies in earlier life were apparently Tory. He was connected with the Duke of Wharton and the *True Briton* (see McKillop, *Samuel Richardson*, pp. 296–7; also Eaves and Kimpel, *Samuel Richardson, A Biography*, pp. 19–36). In 1724 one Samuel Negus made a list of London printers according to their political persuasion; Richardson is listed under the heading 'Said to be High Flyers' (John Nichols, *Literary Anecdotes of the Eighteenth Century*, 1812–15, i. 311). In 1724 he voted for Tory candidates in an election for sheriff of London and in an election for Member of Parliament (Eaves and Kimpel, *Samuel Richardson, A Biography*, pp. 30–1). Richardson never expressed a sentiment contrary to the principles of the Glorious Revolution; his Tory sympathies seem derived from a distrust of Walpole's administration and its implications. This alone might give pause to those who are so ready to classify Richardson, because of his rank and business, with the money-mad bourgeoisie who are supposed to have arisen in this

by debt, difficulty in obtaining work, or a personal quarrel of some kind, but in any case it would seem more likely that Richardson told Stinstra the story he had heard (or thought he had heard) from his father than that he consciously made up an explanatory tale.

The young Richardson was 'an early Favourite with all the young Women of Taste and Reading in the Neighbourhood', who would ask him to read to them while they did their needle-work.[1] Unfortunately, he does not indicate what books were read; it would be rash to assume that the young ladies' tastes never ran to the more respectable romances and plays. Three of these young women asked the thirteen-year-old boy to write their love-letters for them. This task gave him an insight into the subtleties of the female mind, and into the potential ambi-guities and tensions involved in letter-writing: 'I have been directed to chide, & even repulse, when an Offence was either taken or given, at the very moment when the Heart of the Chider or Repulser was open before me, overflowing with Esteem and Affection; & the fair Repulser dreading to be taken at her Word . . .'[2] The tone of amusement with which Richardson, fifty years later, describes this juvenile activity would seem to indicate that the experience made some im-pression upon him at the time, and that he enjoyed both the detached controlling power of playing with the emotions of both sender and receiver and the imaginative stimulus of adopting a *persona*.

Richardson also achieved popularity through his childhood talent for making up stories:

I recollect, that I was early noted for having Invention. I was not fond of Play, as other Boys: My Schoolfellows used to call me *Serious* and *Gravity*: And five of them particularly delighted to single me out, either for a Walk, or at their Fathers' Houses or at mine, to tell them Stories, as they phrased it. Some I told them from my Reading as true; others from my Head, as mere Invention; of which they would be most fond; & often were affected by them.[3]

period, and to decide that as a representative of the middle class he is entirely on, as it were, the other side of the fence from Pope and Swift.

[1] Richardson to Stinstra, 2 June 1753, *Selected Letters*, p. 231.
[2] Ibid.
[3] Ibid. The school where he knew his first public may have been Merchant Taylors'; see McKillop. *Samuel Richardson*, pp. 287–8.

Many children who are not destined to become writers indulge in this activity, of course, but it is not uncommon to find such a pastime figuring in the early life of those who are later to entertain a wider audience through creative fiction. The juvenile storyteller is not indulging in mere daydreaming; he is communicating something fully formed, rationally judging his effects, maintaining suspense. An audience of other children is brutally critical, unlikely to feign interest; entertainment is a solid achievement.

Richardson, after describing all these early exercises in 'Invention' to Stinstra adds decorously 'I am ashamed of these Puerilities'. Of course he was nothing of the sort. As much puzzled as his friends and admirers about the source of his powers as a novelist he naturally looks back to his earliest years, and is interested in recollections of his first creative essays. These were his last happy years of relative freedom before the shades of the printing-house closed about him. Disappointed of hopes of further schooling and a learned profession, he was doomed to long years of almost unmitigated drudgery at Wilde's establishment. Any pretence to the position of a gentleman had to be relinquished, and any hope of a gentleman's education. Many years later, he still speaks with bitterness about his life as an apprentice:

> I served a diligent Seven Years to it, to a Master who grudged every Hour to me, that tended not to his Profit, even of those Times of Leisure and Diversion, which the Refractoriness of my Fellow-Servants *obliged* him to allow them, and were usually allowed by other Masters to their Apprentices.[1]

The physical proximity of books was no help to the hard-worked apprentice or journeyman. He tells Stinstra 'I stole from the Hours of Rest & Relaxation, my Reading Times for the Improvement of my Mind', taking conscientious care 'that even my Candle was of my own purchasing',[2] but he must have been sadly conscious that no amount of feverish reading between tasks would ever make up the deficiency in formal education. He never lost the defensive tone about his lack of knowledge of Latin and Greek, or even of French; in compensation, all his heroes are proficient in the classics, and his

---

[1] Richardson to Stinstra, 2 June 1753, *Selected Letters*, p. 229. [2] Ibid.

heroines in modern languages. His sense of inferiority on this score may have contributed to his strong antipathy to Fielding. His moral objections to *Tom Jones* were sincere, and shared by some other readers, contemporary and later, but the style and manner probably provided an extra irritant. Richardson's late-flowering talent required the sunshine of applause; not his powers, but his confidence, had been inhibited by the long and arduous struggle in business, and he felt threatened by rivalry. Fielding succeeded in a manner which Richardson could never hope to emulate, with the large easy tone of a confident writer who has all the resources of classical allusion at his command. Perhaps the play upon the epic style and all that that implied touched some over-sensitive nerve in Richardson, exciting extra resentment against one whose position and advantages represented much that he himself had yearned for.

Richardson was bound to the printing-shop, and his creative powers were given a long recess. Probably the ambitious and struggling young journeyman forgot his childish penchant for telling stories, or regarded it as something entirely in the past. Even so, there was an unexpected touch of glamour; he says he was then

engaged in a Correspondence with a Gentleman greatly my superior in Degree, & of ample Fortune, who, had he lived, intended high things for me . . . Multitudes of Letters passed between this Gentleman & me. He wrote well, was a Master of ye Epistolary Style: Our Subjects were various: But his Letters were mostly narrative, giving me an Account of his Proceedings, and what befell him in ye different Nations thro' which he travelled. I could from them, had I been at Liberty, & had I at that time thought of writing as I have done since, have drawn great Helps: But many Years ago, all ye Letters that passed between us by a particular Desire of his (lest they should ever be published) were committed to the Flames.[1]

These letters must have been of considerable importance to the young Richardson, taking him, as they did, into another world, and allowing him to share imaginatively in a position and, experience that were not his by birth or entirely by temperament. His daughters later thought there was a connection between this correspondent and a generous libertine mentioned elsewhere by Richardson, particularly in a passage in the first

---

[1] Richardson to Stinstra, 2 June 1753, *Selected Letters*, pp. 229–30.

edition of the sequel of *Pamela*.[1] Here we find the story of the libertine who loved the beautiful Maria, but was alienated from her by her uncle, 'a Man of a very waspish, positive, and sordid Temper',[2] went on the Continent, married, later contracted a bigamous marriage with his beloved Maria, and died young—how much of this tale is drawn from a true story can probably never be known. It is interesting that in his own random notes and in the later expunged passage in *Pamela* the character of the rake is treated with great sympathy. It is generally accepted that there is a connection between this early friend and the characters of Mr. B. and Lovelace. Certainly the young London apprentice in his emotionally arid surroundings was able to live a vicarious emotional life, in which he could mentally enact the roles both of virtuous and kindly mentor and wayward brilliant youth, though it is not unlikely that the correspondence was of much less importance to the gentleman.

Richardson's own emotional life does not seem to have been devoid of interest and romance. In his mid sixties he gave Lady Bradshaigh a colourful account of proposals of marriage made to him in his youth; a mock-modest third person veils a certain vanity:

He found friends, who thought they saw something of merit in him, through the cloud that his sheepishness threw over him, and, knowing how low his fortune was, laid themselves out to raise him; and most of them by proposals of marriage which, however, had always something impracticable in them. A pretty ideot was once proposed, with very high terms, his circumstances considered; her worthy uncle thought this man would behave compassionately to her. —A violent Roman Catholic lady was another, of a fine fortune, a zealous professor, whose terms were (all her fortune in her own power—a very apron-string tenure!) two years probation, and her confessor's report in favour of his being a true proselyte at the end

---

[1] See McKillop, *Samuel Richardson*, pp. 8, 108–20. The *Pamela* passage, later cancelled, consists of a long poem written by a gentleman to Mr. B, interspersed with Mr. B.'s explanations and Pamela's comments on the narrative (*Pamela* (3rd ed., 1742), iii. 391–403). The poem is poor, but it may have been removed from the novel either because Richardson felt it was indiscreetly close to a real story, or because such an episode could provide material for a novel of its own. There are some slight resemblances between this story and *Clarissa*, but these should not be exaggerated; the fine gentleman in this case is genuinely in love with the lady and wishes to marry her; both hearts are nearly broken because of her family's cruelty.

[2] *Pamela* (3rd ed., 1742), iii. 391.

of them.—Another, a gay, high-spirited, volatile lady, whose next friend offered to be *his* friend, in fear of her becoming the prey (at the public places she constantly frequented) of some vile fortune-hunter. Another there was whom his soul loved; but with a reverence—Hush!—Pen, lie thee down!—

A timely check; where, else, might I have ended?—This lady—how hard to forbear this affecting subject!—But I *will* forbear. This man presumed not . . .[1]

The lady 'whom his soul loved' is the 'Mrs. Beaumont' who figures in *Grandison*, and whose story he may have been planning to amplify.[2] The *History of Mrs. Beaumont* may be treated as Richardson's last and unfinished novel; this last work indicates that at the very end of his career his imagination was still working on some early and first-hand experience, however reshaped and glamorized by memory and a measure of egotism.

From his remarks to Lady Bradshaigh, it is evident that Richardson enjoyed thinking of himself as the hero of an unhappy love story. If this enjoyment is so evident in his old age, it was probably greater in his youth. All the proposals or entanglements mentioned in the letter quoted above are strange, complicated, and unexpected. Richardson either attracted to himself, or wished to think he was attracting, situations of emotional complexity. There is a certain ambiguity in his make-up; on the one hand, we have these bizarre hints, on the other, his prudent and sober marriages to Martha Wilde and Elizabeth Leake. There is no reason to suppose that love did not enter these contracts, but there is no intimation of deep passion or intricate emotion in any of his references to his wives. Like many people, he probably left romance in the outer perimeter of his life, and kept prosaic domestic happiness at its centre. But his youthful emotional life did not appear prosaic to himself, nor did he wish it to be. Perhaps the qualities that in the boy had found an outlet in telling stories and writing young ladies' love-letters, in the youth found expression in experience which was a combination of truth and emotional re-creation of

[1] Richardson to Lady Bradshaigh, 1755, *Selected Letters*, p. 323.
[2] See *The Correspondence of Samuel Richardson*, ed. Anna Lætitia Barbauld, 6 vols., 1804, v. 301–48, for the summary of Mrs. Beaumont's story. A. D. McKillop came into possession of a fragment of the *Beaumont* novel in letters; see *Samuel Richardson*, pp. 9–10.

given facts. That he enjoyed observing women he tells us in his famous portrait of himself at sixty:

Short; rather plump than emaciated, notwithstanding his complaints: about five foot five inches; fair wig; lightish cloth coat, all black besides; one hand generally in his bosom the other a cane in it . . . looking directly foreright, as passers-by would imagine, but observing all that stirs on either hand of him without moving his short neck . . . a regular even pace, stealing away ground, rather than seeming to rid it: a gray eye, too often over-clouded by mistiness from the head: by chance lively; very lively it will be, if he have hope of seeing a lady whom he loves and honours: his eye always on the ladies; if they have very large hoops, he looks down and supercilious, and as if he would be thought wise, but perhaps the sillier for that: as he approaches a lady, his eye is never fixed first upon her face, but upon her feet, and thence he raises it up, pretty quickly for a dull eye; and one would think (if we thought him at all worthy of observation) that from her air and (the last beheld) her face, he sets her down in his mind as *so* or *so*, and then passes on to the next object he meets: only then looking back, if he greatly likes or dislikes, as if he would see if the lady appear to be all of a piece, in the one light or in the other.[1]

This faculty of detached observation and speculation especially about the female sex (speculation finding its chief object in surmise as to character, and tempered by his own kind of moral irony) must have been Richardson's all his life. Sir John Hawkins, who approved of none of the novelists of his time, says slightingly of Richardson: 'He was a man of no learning nor reading, but had a vivid imagination, which he let loose in reflections on human life and manners, till it became so distended with sentiments, that for his own ease, he was necessitated to vent them on paper.'[2]

Imagination was a dominant force in Richardson's mind, and it played upon human life and manners, trying to reach the inner truth of mind and emotion beyond the appearance. The interior life is very important to him; in his 'autobiographical' letters and recollections, he is chary of pedestrian facts, and more concerned with the development of the inner than of the outer life. Hawkins is not intending to be complimentary, but there is some truth in what he says; the imagined became too

[1] Richardson to Lady Bradshaigh, 1749, *Selected Letters*, pp. 135–6.
[2] Sir John Hawkins, *The Life of Samuel Johnson, LL.D.*, 1787, p. 216.

strong not to find expression. All that occurred in the inner life will never be known; it seems unlikely that the young man would entirely relinquish the propensity for making up tales evinced in childhood, and Samuel Richardson, apprentice, journeyman, and master printer, may have been constantly inventing stories that never emerged in any written word.

The love relationship is the focal point of Richardson's imagination. It is far more important in his novels than in any of the works of his great English contemporaries. Even lust is seen as a complicated emotion, which rarely remains in its purely animal state, but attaches itself to other aspects of the personality. The state of being in love fascinated him. He saw it as war, a struggle not only between the male and female principle, but also between various aspects of the character of each individual.

The fragments of autobiography found in the letters reveal that love and its complications played a part in Richardson's life. It is equally interesting that most of these experiences are detached; he was not personally involved in the affections of the three young girls, or the affairs of the interesting libertine. He did not love the 'violent Roman Catholic' or the 'volatile lady' who were, he says, proposed to him. Even in the case of the lady 'whom his soul loved', their acquaintance was brief and the social distance between them was such as not to allow him to 'presume'. Distance gave him room to observe, and to refine upon observation. That passage in the letter to Lady Bradshaigh is an effect of detachment, with a kind of comedy running through it, even to the end, where he is teasing his reader as if he were writing a novel, elaborately stressing the hints that are to be only hints. The distance that allowed him to be spectator was of vital importance to him; it stimulated his imaginative sympathy, and allowed his moral irony to function.

Richardson's perceptions are in some ways intuitively ironic. Love is a major irony. Its effects can be seen in great poetry, or in the wretched lives of seduced serving-girls turned out on the streets. Love worships its object, and wants to devour it. It is not a passive emotion, and because of its energy the whole character is involved. It is recognized as a source of temptation, and it is one which we cannot escape except at the risk of making ourselves less human. An examination of the individual in the complex state of being in love reveals the totality of the character, good or bad, because unconscious as well as conscious powers are at work with unusual force and rapidity. Love requires freedom to work itself out, although this freedom, like all moral freedom, can be disastrous. Freedom is very much at the centre of Richardson's novels. It is the soil from which all authentic actions grow. The other aspect of this freedom is loneliness which love often increases, as the true nature of the beloved cannot be known, and the gulf between male and female views, motives, feelings grows wider because of desire. All Richardson's major characters experience both freedom and loneliness. Their author does not intrude his control over his characters; he is withdrawn, letting them speak for themselves and express more than they know but not more than they feel. Richardson's epistolary form is an image of freedom; the characters are on their own. They are not, like characters in post-Nietzschean works, living in a world which God has abandoned, but they are expressions of a philosophic era from Descartes to Berkeley, in that there is a division between the observer and the observed universe. The inner consciousness is all one can fully know, and the emphasis shifts to the intense personal process. The inner consciousness can include love of God as well as erotic love; God as Consciousness is at least as real as another human psyche. The world of matter is more fragile and evanescent, taking its colour from the individual state of mind; the pleasant and ordinary can appear ugly and preternaturally menacing, as Mr. B.'s mansion does to Pamela. As Clarissa struggles towards liberation, the world of material objects begins to crack and crumble away.

Of course, the fault usually found with Richardson today is that he is too much a moralizer, that his moral views are too intrusive. His reputation has suffered in the climate of two subsequent centuries; the Victorians felt him to be too free on matters of sex, whereas the twentieth century enjoys any description of sex but finds Richardson distasteful because he does not share our more 'liberal' views. There has been a late-romantic tendency to see sexual appetite as divine, a view which Richardson certainly does not hold. There is a counter-tendency to see sexuality as a game in which one is not to be

emotionally involved, a view which Richardson has already
rejected.

In Richardson's novels, love is 'a natural passion', but there
are other passions which are also 'natural'. Some are less
estimable than love or even lust (such as aggressiveness, and
cruelty), others are more admirable (benevolence, devotion to
God). Love tends to attract some of these other strong passions
into, as it were, its own magnetic field. But love has three
meanings—*eros, philia, agape*—and erotic, social, and divine
love are all treated in Richardson's novels as 'natural passions'
which various minds do variously inspire. All three are passions
which have considerable energy, just as all of Richardson's
central characters possess great psychic energy.

The quotation which serves as the title of this book is
ambiguous. It is not so ambiguous in its original context in
Grandison, but it does summarize the ironies of Richardson's
vision. What is love? And what is meant by 'natural'? Is
'nature' good or bad? or partly both? or neutral in the fray?
Each novel provides a slightly different answer to these questions, and each answer is consistent with the characters, action,
and style of the novel—the 'answer' is the novel, in short. The
true morality of a novel emerges only in so far as it can provide
a living experience, Richardson is not merely, or even primarily,
didactic; he can convey a very powerful experience, and he possesses a complex imagination which keeps exploring life's possibilities.

Like all literary works, Richardson's are products of their
own period, in part the result of literary influences. As we shall
see, he drew upon a wealth of material, varying from novel to
novel. A detailed examination of Richardson's treatment of the
natural passion, in the artistic form he discovered and made
his own, takes us into diverse areas of literature. Elements of
the pastoral tradition, the fable, the letter-book, and comic
drama are combined in *Pamela* to produce an original statement about the sexual battle and the individual struggle for
freedom. In *Clarissa*, dramatic tragedy and religious literature
have been grafted upon a slender native stock, the novel of
love, producing a new form and statement. The love novel,
romance, comic drama, and a non-literary tradition of polite
familiar epistles are fused with the themes of Latitudinarian
divines and moralists to produce *Grandison*.

The interest in tracing sources of Richardson's works, in finding analogues and possible influences, lies not in finding and cataloguing but in seeing what the novelist has done with his material. Perhaps above all Richardson's unique use of imagery is one of the greatest manifestations of his creative vision, and hence a subject which demands attention. Images such as he uses are to be found in literature and in pictorial art, as I have endeavoured to illustrate, but it is his particular use of them which evokes the reader's response and the critic's admiration.

In each case, Richardson has used material previously existing to create something new. The novelist has taken only those elements which he needs, and they are fused in the novel as a whole by a force which works with almost ferocious energy through characters and situations controlled by an artistic purpose never disregarded. When sources and conventions are traced, a striking difference in the kind of material used by the author for each novel becomes evident. The relationship between the two major novels, *Clarissa* and *Grandison*, is especially interesting, as they differ so greatly in literary background, theme, and manner. In both works Richardson extends the realm of the novel, making the form serve for tragedy in the one case and domestic comedy in the other. *Pamela* is in a more mixed mode, a prelude to works both more clearly defined and more complex. Yet it is in this work that Richardson first developed the method of epistolary narration, making it convey the inner world of a complex character so completely that the reader is more aware of her total psychological state than she is herself. The first novel is more than an experiment; it stands on its own, although of its sequel the same cannot be said. However, *Pamela I* is mature and complete; it also exhibits the competent and assured use of some devices which are fully effective here and which the author never uses again. Richardson's confidence in refusing to use effects which had been fully successful in previous novels marks his imaginative power. To recognize the variety that Richardson offers is to see how much he accomplished, and how seriously he can claim to be treated as a major novelist.

II

Novels, Fables, and Letter-Books: The Approach to *Pamela*

OF all of Richardson's novels, *Pamela* is the one which is most read, most commented upon, and most adversely criticized. The novel both creates most of Richardson's reputation and obscures it. It is too often seen in the light of *Shamela* and *Joseph Andrews*; Fielding's disparagement of Richardson's first novel is over-emphasized (and sometimes treated as the last word in Richardson criticism) while his consistent admiration of *Clarissa* is forgotten. It is not often that a major writer suffers from the disability of being best remembered by his first and perhaps least excellent major work.

Yet *Pamela* continues to fascinate in its own right. Most modern critics recognize, however grudgingly, the vitality of the heroine, and the interest maintained through the medium of her letters. A re-reading of the novel itself is refreshing, after a perusal of critics old and new. It is also interesting and valuable to see the novel in the context of both general literary background and of Richardson's own literary activity just before he began the story.

Richardson's contemporaries were reluctant to see his work in terms of general literary background, either praising him as an untaught original genius or dismissing him as an uneducated boor producing freakish works in ignorance, even defiance, of any recognizable literary tradition. He is either the free child of fancy, like Shakespeare a warbler of wood-notes (or letters) wild, or the suspect spider, spinning webs out of his own bowels. The questions of literary influence upon him, the tradition and conventions which he represents, and his own education in writing before *Pamela* were largely discounted.

When Sir John Hawkins said that Richardson was 'a man of no learning nor reading' he meant that Richardson had not

relate to Pamela?

had the education of a gentleman, and could not read the classics. As the references scattered through the novels and his personal letters show, Richardson's reading was fairly extensive, including plays, poetry, and didactic and religious literature, but he was limited to works which had appeared in English. Fielding and Smollett could adopt the picaresque novel as it had been developed by Cervantes, Le Sage, and Scarron, and their work is coloured by classical allusion and by the classical theory of comedy. Richardson is outside this frame of reference, and his works are of a more domestic growth. They are related to a tradition of romances and 'inflaming novels', and his constant uncomplimentary references to these show that he was uncomfortably conscious of the relationship. Such novels as Richardson had read must have been almost entirely of native stock. Most of the English novels of his time were written by females, and deal with the question of courtship or seduction from a feminine viewpoint. The attempt to develop the epistolary mode in the English novel is to be found in these stories about the love-affairs of young ladies.[1]

Such novels were regarded by the literary (if regarded at all) as sad trash, hack works dealing with trivial subjects. In Richardson's period, there is something unorthodox, almost something essentially 'low' in a man's bothering to write a novel about a woman. After all, women had, at least in theory, little to do with the real world. Theirs is not the arena in which effective decisions are taken, in which moral choice is important.

The position of women was a subject of debate in the eighteenth century, but there was an accepted theory on the subject to which appeal could readily be made. Richard Allestree (better known for *The Whole Duty of Man*) makes very clear pronouncements about the nature and moral condition of women in his work *The Ladies Calling* (1673). This work, frequently reprinted and widely read in the eighteenth century,

---

[1] For a comprehensive survey of the development of the epistolary mode in the English novel, see R. Adams Day, *Told in Letters: Epistolary Fiction before Richardson*, 1966. I cannot pretend to offer a complete study of early fiction, but only to suggest points at which it anticipates Richardson's work. For a study of various early novels, see J. J. Richetti, *Popular Fiction before Richardson: Narrative Patterns 1700–1739*, 1969. I am not indebted to this useful work which appeared after my own original thesis was completed. Like all students of this early fiction, I am indebted to Bridget G. MacCarthy's *Women Writers, Their Contribution to the English Novel, 1621–1744*, 1944, for listing names and works previously unknown.

is a most succinct and thoughtful statement of the most acceptable views. Woman is man's spiritual equal: 'God . . . gave
the feeblest woman as large and capacious a Soul as that of the
Greatest Hero.'[1] Her exercise of virtue is, however, different
from men's. Her calling removes her from contact with or
influence upon the wider social sphere; her conduct is a household affair. He intimates that virtue is easier for the female sex,
since 'there are many temtations [*sic*] to which men are ex-
posed that are out of their road'.[2] Since God created woman
in subjection to man, her chief virtue (and duty) is obedience,
at first to her father, and, after marriage, to her husband.
Vanity and lightmindedness are her besetting sins, and she
must reject the world's gaudy trifles (although at the same time
she should be capable of managing a household and seeing
that the family lives in fitting style). Female virtue is more
passive than active, and consists more largely in an attitude of
the soul than in action. Modesty, humility, resignation, a
disposition to reject worldly pleasures—these are her glories.
Moral choices are unaggressive, unremarkable. The inner life
blossoms in silence. In the same author's *The Gentleman's Calling*
(1660) masculine virtue is shown as active, powerful in the
world, evoking the world's praise and honour.

The frontispieces to these two works (see Plate 1) serve as
illustrations of the two roles as envisaged according to the
contemporary ideal. They also illustrate the themes of Richardson's novels remarkably well, but Richardson, dramatically
and imaginatively, has reversed their meaning. Sir Charles
Grandison, who is, as we shall see, the epitome of the virtues
described in *The Gentleman's Calling*, the princely character
whose word and actions have great authority, is not the main
character in *Sir Charles Grandison*, although his existence is
central to it. The inward sensitive mental life of the heroines
provides the novel with its interest. The female figure illustrating *The Ladies Calling*, rejecting worldly baubles for a
heavenly crown, could serve as an ironic frontispiece to *Pamela*
and *Clarissa*—ironic because the meaning expressed in this
emblem, urging passive renunciation, is developed in such a
different way in the two novels. The spiritual warfare of inner

[1] Richard Allestree, *The Ladies Calling*, 3rd impression, 1675, c1ᵛ.
[2] Ibid. b4ᵛ.

struggle against the world, of personal endeavour in the name of an integrity of principle which the world does not acknowledge, is presented as more exciting, making more demands upon a whole complex human consciousness, than the assumption of a prepared position of authority. If feminine life is a matter of inner consciousness, then the struggle under various restrictions to understand, to *be*, may be as interesting as, perhaps more significant than, the struggle to be important in the world where authority and success have recognized exterior symbols.

It would seem that Richardson's own personality, his interest in emotional subtleties and the interior life, made it inevitable that he should, when he became a novelist, find himself writing a novel about love, with a woman for the central character. His background, and the focus of his imagination, separated him in many obvious respects from the main concerns of his time. The objective and rational view, the deliberate social comment, broad perspective, and balanced wit of Fielding—who may be taken as representing the best of the central tradition and major concerns—have little to do with Richardson's kind of work. A less obvious tradition Richardson does represent: Locke, Berkeley, and Hume had examined the workings of the mind, stressed inner consciousness and its complexity, indicated the emotional concomitants of rationality. Turning the light inwards, they found flux rather than stability, and an exterior world not merely reflected in the mind but actually created by the knower rather than the known. Richardson himself, more interested in the Christian concept of consciousness as he understood it, was not particularly concerned with such philosophic speculation. Unlike Rousseau, he was not handicapped by considering himself, in any sense, a philosopher. Most immediately, as far as his art is concerned, he was merely taking up certain novelistic conventions established by a number of minor novelists, largely women, who had written about women in love.

After writers like Mrs. Aphra Behn and Mrs. Manley had shown that it was possible for women to write and be read, even to earn money by the exercise of the pen, a host of minor writers had taken up the love novel or novella. The teens and twenties of the century show a proliferation of such works by authors with whose names the veriest dunce of a sorcerer's apprentice would not attempt to conjure: Mrs. Penelope Aubin, Mrs. Jane Barker, Mrs. Mary Davys. Eliza Haywood is the only feminine novelist of the period to achieve any slight degree of lasting fame, and that, the result of Pope's reference in *The Dunciad*, is largely ill repute. Their works have very few claims to recognition, but they are better than one might expect. No English female author achieved a novel of the classic stature of Mme de Lafayette's *La Princesse de Clèves* (1678), although that novel, the French romances, and most notably the *Lettres Portugaises* (1669), had a decided influence upon the English female novel. In the first quarter of the eighteenth century the English writers were moving cautiously away from the more sensational *novella-fabliau* which had been dependably saleable, and were depending more and more upon psychological interest.

Broadly speaking, the female novel of love can be divided into two types: the seduction/rape tale and the courtship novel. The tale of seduction or rape could ostensibly be justified as serving a moral purpose. Mrs. Haywood, who excelled in this genre, says that novels are designed for instruction as well as amusement:

> most of them containing Morals, which if well observed would be of no small Service to those that read 'em.—Certainly if the Passions are well represented, and the Frailties to which Humane Nature is incident . . . it cannot fail to rouze the sleeping Conscience of the guilty Reader . . .[1]

The desire to entertain is more evident than a vocation to instruct; her novels do display something of 'The Frailties of Humane Nature', but whether it is conscience that is roused is not so clear. The novels are heavily sexual, and suspense is built up as the reader awaits the hero's accomplishment of the final act, clasping the heroine's faintly resisting form clad in picturesque *dishabille*. Her heroines are sexually passionate creatures, naturally responsive to a lover's ardour, oppressed by the force of love within as well as by the lover's ruthless importunity. The hero is usually a rake who, while pretending rapturous enslavement, will stop at nothing to get what he wants.

[1] Eliza Haywood, *The Tea-Table: or, A Conversation between some Polite Persons of both Sexes, at a Lady's Visiting Day*, 1725, p. 48.

In *Love in Excess* (1719), *The British Recluse* (1722), and *Idalia* (1723)
the heroine is the victim of treachery or imprisonment. Most of
these heroines submit or are conquered, are rewarded by the
rapture of a brief affair, and are left to endure the agonies of
abandonment and heartbreak, resentment or remorse. It would
be easy enough to say that such novels as Mrs. Haywood's
pretend moral instruction to excuse light pornography, but
this would not be the whole truth. If the hour of consummation
is described at length, so is the loneliness of desertion. The substance of the phrase 'and then he left me' can take up pages in a
Haywood novel. The woman, the agent of feeling, is at the
centre of the stage. The rake-hero is definitely seen by Mrs.
Haywood as fascinating, but the emphasis is almost entirely on
the heroine's emotions and reactions—her story is often told in
the first person. The heroine is the loser in the sex war because
of the ironic difference in the female and male attitudes to love,
but she is victorious in the novel in being perpetual subject, the
centre of the emotional action. The experience of passion as felt
by a female is presented as a full emotional experience, as
something that matters. Socially, in a licit or illicit amour,
woman may be required to be passive, but she is not an object
merely, not psychologically inert or inarticulate. Feeling is
action; indeed, to a novelist like Mrs. Haywood, the experience
of emotion is the only experience that matters.

The heroines of such novels have reactions and emotions
rather than a defined personality, but the flux of emotion is
often, given its context, well described. The development of
female character emerges more fully in the novels of courtship.
Marriage in a recognizable (if not clearly defined) contemporary social situation is the subject, and love is seen in relation
to marriage. These novels place their emphasis, not upon
unbridled passion, but upon correct relationships with the
family and upon proper social behaviour. Although the main
setting is vague, and there is still some lack of vivid detail, the
atmosphere is different from that of the Utopia of gallantry
wherein the heroines of the seduction/rape stories seem to dwell.
The novelists who dealt with courtship did not entirely forsake
the old sensational events of earlier fiction, but the treatment
of emotion is in many respects realistic, and more of the practical
problems of a young lady's life in the Georgian era are taken

into account—problems such as the parental right to choose a daughter's husband, the difficulties in family relationships, problems about money and dowries, the trials of being better educated and more intelligent than is fashionable. Many of the new novels were trying to fulfil some of the functions of the conduct books, by imparting direct or implied advice to women about behaviour. The precepts of the conduct books on duty, obedience, and so on, are examined in relation to the heroine.[1]

Most of these novels intentionally bear out the precepts of the conduct books. In one of the most influential of these novels, Mrs. Mary Davys's *The Reformed Coquet: or, Memoirs of Amoranda* (1724), the spoiled and vain heroine is reformed in a course of surprising adventures which serve to reduce her vanity and instruct her heart. Her guardian, Mentor, who is also in love with her, supervises the process and educates her principles and heart together.[2] The tone of the novel is gentler than its theme might promise; it is the instruction of the heart, the experience of love on the part of a girl who is not very aware of emotion, which makes her a person, not dry precepts. If the courtship novels are conduct books, they are conduct books with a difference, applying judgement and standards with some delicacy. However old the standards of conduct may be, they have to be realized freshly by the young heroine who is, in the most ordinary courtship, dealing with a circumstance new to her. The female novelists' perception, however limited, that the interest of conduct described in fiction must depend on full realization of the exact case in hand led them to particularize more in the courtship novel than in the novel of passion and seduction. In Mrs. Mary Davys's *The Lady's Tale* (1725), which illustrates the trials of filial obedience in a courtship, the domestic setting is credible (although vague as to detail); the heroine is witty enough to be entertaining, and the state of

---

[1] Katherine Hornbeak has pointed out the relation of the conduct books to Richardson's novels in their treatment of family rights and duties ('Richardson's Familiar Letters and the Domestic Conduct Books', *Smith College Studies in Modern Languages*, xix (Jan. 1938)), but she does not mention that such points had already been presented in prose fiction.

[2] The novel is partly a feminine version of *Télémaque*. This is probably the first appearance in English prose fiction of the lover-mentor, a character type to be found in some degree in Sir Charles Grandison, very definitely in Fanny Burney's Edgar Mandlebert in *Camilla* (1796), and (improved beyond recognition) in Jane Austen's Mr. Knightley and Edmund Bertram.

her heart is not uninteresting.[1] The heroine of Mrs. Jane
Barker's *Love's Intrigues; or, The Amours of Bosvil and Galesia*
(1713) and of its sequel, *A Patch Work Screen for the Ladies* (1723),
is a real personality, and in the first part of her story the author
has developed a good novel out of the slightest of plots. Galesia
has fallen in love with a young man who, she fears, may not
return her feeling. The action is mainly interior; Galesia
recounts her own fluctuating emotions, her speculations about
how she should behave in her situation, about the feelings of
Bosvil on the occasion of their various meetings. The main
question, which provides the point of interest, is one which she
is never able, even in retrospect, fully to answer: has she let
her love for Bosvil show too much, or not enough? She is a
consistently drawn character, impetuous, loving, yet reserved
and slightly bookish; she seeks solace in intellectual exercise,
studying her brother's medical texts. She is able to enjoy her
own thoughts, a quality which no English male novelist of the
period would attribute to a young lady of her sort. (It might be
said that Defoe's Moll Flanders and Roxana enjoy thinking,
but these businesslike women enjoy cogitations of strategy, not
thought for its own sake. As for Marivaux's Marianne, 'La
Paysanne Parvenue', her thoughts, if she can be said to have
any, appear to be reflexes of cunning; psychological subtlety is
the attribute of the author, not of his character.) The first-
person narration of Mary Davys's Abaliza or Jane Barker's
Galesia is different from that found in masculine picaresque
novels. The emphasis is placed upon the inner feelings of the
central character in relation to an event; she is no detached
observer, but the centre of emotional conflict, of mental and
emotional life. The female novelist, like Jane Austen a century
later, understood the heroines' need for leisure to think and be
wretched. Even the sensational Mrs. Haywood's Anadea
(heroine of what is really a courtship novel) desires solitude
rather than 'Company, Noise, and Hurry' when shaken by
emotional perplexity.[2]

The female novelists were not attempting to institute a rebellion against masculine domination or the accepted position

[1] See below, chapter vi.
[2] Haywood, *Secret Histories, Novels and Poems*, 2nd ed., 2 vols., 1725, vol. i, *The Fatal Secret*, p. 214.

of women. What they did was quietly to transform the accepted role of woman, not by claiming it should be something else, but by seeing it in a different way. In presenting woman and her reception of experience, her knowledge, her moral choice, her attempt to understand the nuances of situation and her own fluctuation of feeling—her endeavour, in short, to comprehend experience—they implicitly denied an attitude which implicitly held women incapable of important experience. They also brought to the level of literary consciousness material which was to become the stuff of the novel, psychological analysis for which the novel is peculiarly suited, as well as certain modes of presenting this material.

Modes of narration, novelistic devices, had been developed by some of these minor novelists. The first-person narration in the past tense was the best-developed mode, and it is in this kind of narrative, requiring a personal voice, that one is most likely to find attention to style and language, more especially in the courtship novel. Mrs. Davys, for instance, preserves the conversational tone by having Abaliza tell her story to a confidante and interlocutor, and within her retrospective account of her courtship there are lively passages of description and quoted dialogue. The characters occasionally use homely idiom: Abaliza is afraid she might 'make a Botch of my Story'.[1] The language of Mrs. Barker's Galesia is easy without vulgarity, often with a touch of humour: 'the only Syntax I study'd was how to make suitable Answers to my Father and him, when the long'd-for Question should be proposed . . .'[2]

It seems rather a pity that the minor novelists could not do more with what they had. A sense of structure is largely absent; there is rarely an endeavour to sustain a coherent plot, and a novelist's attention to characterization and dialogue almost inevitably entails a slackening of suspense. The novel in letters had, in a sense, been long established, but most English writers of love-novels had used the letter device in a rather slack manner. Books wholly in letters tend to be plotless. In Mrs. Haywood's *Letters from a Lady of Quality to a Chevalier* (1724) the

---

[1] Mary Davys, *The Works of Mrs. Davys*, 2 vols., 1725, vol. ii, *The Lady's Tale*, p. 125.

[2] Jane Barker, *The Entertaining Novels of Mrs. Jane Barker*, 2nd. ed., 2 vols., 1719, vol. ii, *The Amours of Bosvil and Galesia*, p. 19.

letters written 'to the moment' portray the development of the heroine's emotion in the slightest of stories; self-revelation and intensity of passion are all that matters. Mrs. Davys's *Familiar Letters Betwixt a Gentleman and a Lady* (1725) is a witty presentation of an intelligent couple falling in love; letters written to the moment present character without incident or suspense. *Lindamira* (1702; probably by Tom Brown, a Grub Street journalist who was one of the few men to take up the feminine novel) is chatty and amusing, if slight, but the epistolary device here is merely another form of first-person past-tense narration, with no attempt to use the letter's immediacy of effect. The pious Elizabeth Rowe, in *Letters Moral and Entertaining* (1731?), can sometimes create characters through the letter medium; the correspondence between the grave Emilia and her friend, the light-hearted Leticia, foreshadows Richardson's use of Anna Howe and Charlotte Grandison as confidantes of Clarissa and Harriet.[1] Mrs. Rowe can occasionally tell a story, but only in bare outline, in a rapid series of a few epistles.[2]

Since the *Lettres Portugaises* the letter had been recognized as the true voice of feeling. Novelists were slow to exploit the potential of the letter device as a means of conveying authentic personality and experience which the reader himself can recognize without intermediary, while entailing all the ambiguities of self-disguise, fluctuating emotion, conflict in a situation of personal suspense. All these elements can be found, but not together. It is noticeable that two major elements of the novel, detailed characterization and emotional suspense in a vivid situation, are not found in conjunction in the early English epistolary novel. The more credible the character, the less immediate and tense is the work. The most common use of the letter is as an occasional device, as it had been used in the French romances of the previous century.[3] A lover's letter, quoted within a first- or third-person narrative, is used to heighten the

---

[1] Elizabeth Rowe, *Letters Moral and Entertaining*, 1736 ed., part ii, pp. 251–71.

[2] Mrs. Rowe is a precursor of Richardson in her interest in deathbed scenes. One series of letters anticipates Richardson's description of Clarissa's death (ibid., part i, pp. 148–51). The pious tone of her works would have appealed to Richardson. He printed her *Friendship in Death with Letters Moral and Entertaining* in 1740 and 1743. (See William L. Sale, *Samuel Richardson: Master Printer*, 1950, p. 200.)

[3] These romances were still read in Richardson's time. The humour of *The Female Quixote* (1752) by Mrs. Charlotte Lennox depends on the reader's having some knowledge of the works of La Calprenède and Madeleine de Scudéry.

effect of passion—such letters, though not without some dramatic effect, tend to be florid and repetitive. There are momentary
uses of the ironic possibilities of the letter, as when Mrs. Haywood's Anadea writing to her lover gives herself unwittingly
away in one revealing sentence,[1] but such instances are few.

It is quite evident that all three of Richardson's novels are
not an innovation but a development, by an artistic genius,
of a minor tradition established by the writers of love-stories
told in the feminine voice. In Richardson's hands, this type
of fiction becomes more robust and more masculine; male
characters and male points of view balance the central female
interest. In the works of Fielding and Smollett interest is
centred on the hero and the point of view is entirely masculine;
the use of picaresque tale and epic reference precludes the
delicate unfolding of psychological analysis in which their
humbler predecessors in English fiction delighted. In the
picaresque tales attempted seduction is usually treated as
humorous, a point of view radically different from that of the
female novelists. The attitudes to love and to women found in
these earlier feminine novels were to be considered by the picaresque novelists only after Richardson's success with *Clarissa*;
in *Amelia* (1752) and *Ferdinand Count Fathom* (1753) attempted
seduction and the machinations of an intriguing rake are
treated at length, and with a seriousness that originally belonged to the female writers of amatory fiction.

It is fortunate that Richardson did not, when he began his
career as a novelist, consciously undertake to imitate the
feminine love-novels. One could imagine that a man with a
psychological imagination such as Richardson's but without
his particular background and qualities of character would, if
thrown upon Grub Street in his youth, have hacked his way to
some financial success by immediately taking up deliberate
imitation of this minor genre, finding it so congenial that he
would never have gone beyond it. Richardson's sober background, practical business concerns, some snobbery, and a
moral consciousness which is more than mere respectability
saved him from such a literary fate. Had Richardson been a
Bohemian, he might have left us nothing more spectacular than
a Haywoodian novel, or a *Lindamira*.

[1] Haywood, *Secret Histories*, vol. i, *The Fatal Secret*, pp. 219–20.

When Richardson came upon *Pamela*, he came upon it from another direction. Without intending it, he had begun writing by studying style and narrative mode, so that it was not just the story of Pamela but the use of language and the letter form itself which inspired his creative interest. Had he followed directly in the footsteps of the female writers he would either have missed the epistolary mode, concentrating on straight narration which would not have given him the complexity he needed, or he might, before he had learned how to establish character and tone, have written in the thinly febrile manner of the novel in love-letters.

We may be glad that he began his writing career in a modest, practical, and leisurely manner. His first published work is as un-novelistic as could readily be imagined. It appears that he was the author of *The Apprentice's Vade Mecum* (1733), a handbook for printers' apprentices, in which the author is spokesman for the virtues of the honest craftsman and a critic of the vices of the genteel, and of the lower classes who would ape fashionable follies.[1] The sober advice is interspersed with passages of satiric and humorous description, which reveals some of the feeling for caricature that emerges in the delineation of Jackey in *Pamela*, or the fops and beaux in *Clarissa* and *Grandison*.

The next published work by Richardson is his version of *Aesop's Fables* in 1739. Richardson does not pretend to be doing anything more than revising L'Estrange's edition of 1692: 'we confess that it was our Intention, everywhere, except in his *Political Reflections,* to keep that celebrated writer close in our Eye.'[2] To the modern reader, the most entertaining part of Richardson's Fables is the Preface, in which the author, in a sustained satiric vein, defends L'Estrange against the criticism of the Whig Samuel Croxall who had produced his own edition of the *Fables* in which he had denigrated his Royalist predecessor.

We greatly applaud this pompous Declaration of the good Gentleman's Principles: But tho' we might observe, that he has strain'd the natural Import of some of the Fables. near as much

[1] See A. D. McKillop, 'Samuel Richardson's Advice to an Apprentice', *JEGP*, xlii (1943), 40–54.
[2] Richardson, *Fables*, 1739, p. xi.

one way, as Sir *Roger* has done the other . . . Sir *Roger* suffer'd for his Principles, bad as they were: And the Doctor, we hope, for the sake of the *Publick*, as well as for his *own sake*, will never be called upon to such Trials.[1]

Perhaps his own connection with the 'high-flyers' had given the now Whig Richardson some sympathy for the arch-Royalist of the Restoration. Chiefly, however, he is concerned in roundly defending Sir Roger's excellence as a writer.

We presume to hope, that, even in the good Doctor's Opinion, there will not be any Necessity to banish poor *Lestrange* to the barren Desarts of *Arabia*, to the Nurseries of *Turkey, Persia,* and *Morocco* . . . but, for the sake of the excellent Sense contain'd in his other Reflections, where Politicks are not concern'd; for the sake of the Benefit which the *English* Tongue has received from his masterly Hand; for the sake of that fine Humour, apposite Language, accurate and lively Manner, which will always render Sir *Roger* delightful, and which this severe Critick has in some Places so wretchedly endeavour'd to imitate: For all these sakes, I say, let him remain among us still . . . and the rather, if it be only to shew the Difference between a fine Original, and a bungling Imitation; and that no prating *Jays* may strut about in the beautiful Plumage of the *Peacock*.[2]

Richardson omits some of L'Estrange's fables, not only because of their political application but because he considers them as lacking in point, or as in questionable taste, but in those he does use he follows Sir Roger almost word for word. He adopts L'Estrange's method of presentation: Fable followed by Moral followed by Reflection. His admiration of Sir Roger's 'fine Humour, apposite Language, accurate and lively Manner' is evident in almost all of the phrases he preserves.

Sir Roger L'Estrange's style is both lively and easy. His sentence structure is misleadingly careless, although the apparent looseness usually has a good rhetorical structure of its own. At his best, in controversy or exposition, he is the reverse of mannered, and is a master of the colloquial phrase and the concrete image. He has a kind of engaging casualness, a feeling for the good throw-away line. All these qualities appear in his telling of the fables. Take, for instance, his version of the Daw in the borrowed plumage where he uses the phrases of current speech to suggest the Daw as Beau: 'A *Daw* that had a mind to be

---

[1] Richardson, *Fables*, pp. ix–x.   [2] Ibid., pp. vii–viii.

Sparkish, Trick'd himself up with all the *Gay-Feathers* he could Muster together: And upon the Credit of these Stoll'n, or Borrow'd Ornaments, he Valu'd himself above All the Birds in the Air Beside.'[1] Or take the lively realism of his version of 'A City Mouse and a Country Mouse':

> There goes an Old Story of a *Country* Mouse that Invited a *City-Sister* of hers to a Country Collation, where she spar'd for Nothing that the Place afforded; as Mould Crusts, Cheese-Parings, Musty Oatmeal, Rusty Bacon, and the like. Now the *City-Dame* was so well bred, as Seemingly to take All in Good Part: But yet at last, Sister (says she, after the Civilest Fashion) why will you be Miserable when you may be Happy? Why will you lie Pining and Pinching your self in such a Lonesome Starving Course of Life as This is; when tis but going to Town along with Me; to Enjoy all the Pleasures, and Plenty that Your Heart can Wish? This was a Temptation the *Country-Mouse* was not able to Resist; so that away they Trudg'd together, and about Midnight got to their Journeys End. The *City-Mouse* shew'd her Friend the Larder, the Pantry, the Kitchin, and Other Offices where she laid her Stores; and after This, carry'd her into the Parlour, where they found, yet upon the Table, the Reliques of a Mighty Entertainment of That very Night. The *City-Mouse* Carv'd her Companion of what she lik'd Best, and so to't they fell upon a Velvet Couch together. The poor *Bumkin* that had never seen, nor heard of such Doings before, Bless'd her self at the Change of her Condition, when (as ill luck would have it) all on a Sudden, the Doors flew open, and in comes a Crew of Roaring Bullies, with their Wenches, their Dogs, and their Bottles, and put the poor Mice to their Wits End, how to save their Skins.[2]

Pamela has read this fable, probably in L'Estrange's book, and appropriately recollects it: 'I am as much frighted as were the City Mouse and the Country Mouse, in the same Book of Fables at every thing that stirs. Oh! I have a Power of these Things to entertain you with in Winter Evenings, when I come home.'[3]

In producing the *Fables*, Richardson could feel that he had made a contribution to children's literature (of which there was hardly any at the time) that would be both amusing and edifying, but for him the *Fables* were to be, although he did not

[1] L'Estrange, *Fables of Aesop*, 1692, Fable xxxiii, p. 32.
[2] Ibid., Fable xi, p. 10.
[3] *Pamela*, Shakespeare Head edition, 4 vols., 1942, i. 99. All subsequent reference to Richardson's novels will be to this edition, 1929–42.

realize it, an exercise in style. Following in L'Estrange's foot-steps, he could learn to take some of his master's easy strides. This exercise would teach him, almost unconsciously, the art of narration, the uses of certain cadences, the value of the col-loquial or rustic phrase, or the concrete image, at the right moment. Richardson was being prepared for a sustained use of a humorously 'low' and effectively colloquial style.

The *Fables* may have had other influences as well. One can see in such a simple narrative form the beginnings of characteri-zation, and the effect of all fables depends on a manipulation of dramatic irony. Fables also offer a rather pessimistic view of human nature, which Richardson shared; in the beast fable men are traditionally seen as animalistic in much of their behaviour, and his work on the *Fables* would have done nothing to diminish, and much to reinforce, Richardson's somewhat Hobbesian view of man's greed, cruelty, and stupidity. In the novels, Richardson makes frequent references to the fables, among them the following: 'The Ant and the Grasshopper', 'The Country Mouse and the City Mouse', 'The Wolf, Lamb and Vulture', 'The Oak and the Willow' (*Pamela*); 'A Daw and Borrowed Feathers' (*Pamela, Clarissa*); 'The Sun and the Wind', 'The Lady and the Lion', 'Mercury and the Statuary', 'Death and the Old Man' (*Clarissa*); 'The Ass and the two Bundles of Hay' (*Grandison*).

The most varied use of the fable references is found in *Clarissa*, where Lovelace in particular plays with them to suit his own purposes; Lovelace also uses a fable from L'Estrange, 'The Priest and the Pears', which Richardson did not include in his own collection because of its mild indecency. Fables are sported with in *Clarissa*, but it is the tone of the original fable, applied with its original meaning intact, that is most suited to the man-ner of *Pamela*, and to the level of literacy of that heroine. It is also worth noting that in the *Fables* Richardson is working with material very close to emblems (indeed, he refers to one tale as 'this emblem'), and the emblematic had a permanent attraction for him.

Richardson was evidently just finishing the *Fables* when the booksellers Rivington and Osborn asked him to write 'a little Volume of Letters, in a common Style, on such Subjects as might be of Use to those Country Readers who were unable to

indite for themselves'.[1] Such books were common; they performed a service in instructing those of little education in
appropriate forms for business and personal letters, and for
those awkward letters which come between the businesslike
and the friendly (such as applying to a friend for a loan). These
volumes usually contained sample friendly letters and (not
least) various love-letters, and acceptances or rejections of
proposals of marriage. For over a century, such books had fulfilled a second function in affording amusement. Compilers of
such little books delighted in suggesting the character-types of
the various writers, and displaying a variety of styles. In Nicholas
Breton's popular *Poste with a madde Packet of Letters* (1602), which
went through many editions during the seventeenth century,
the second purpose of amusement predominates over instruction. Richardson may have known this old collection; it is
probable that he knew G. F.'s *Secretary's Guide* (which was going
into new editions in the 1740s) and even more likely that he
knew J. Hill's *Young Secretary's Guide*, which his brother-in-law
Allington Wilde brought out in its twenty-second and twenty-
third editions in the 1730s.

In undertaking this unpretentious project, Richardson began
his first creative work. He could, however briefly, imagine
credible, even lively characters, and suggest a whole personality
and mode of life through the tone of one letter. He could range
from the sober ('Advice from a Father to a young Beginner,
what Company to choose, and how to behave in it')[2] to the
light-hearted ('A facetious Young Lady to her Aunt, ridiculing
her Serious Lover').[3] It has entertained critics to see in the
Familiar Letters the future Richardsonian characters in embryo:
the 'facetious Young Lady' anticipates Anna Howe and Charlotte Grandison, while the writer of 'A humorous Epistle of
neighbourly Occurrences and News to a Bottle Companion
abroad' foreshadows Lovelace.[4] The description of the brothel
and its Madam in 'A Young Woman in Town to her Sister in
the Country, recounting her narrow Escape from a Snare laid
for her, on her first Arrival, by a wicked Procuress' suggests
Clarissa's plight at Mrs. Sinclair's, while the country naïveté of

---

[1] Richardson to Stinstra, 2 June 1753, *Selected Letters*, p. 232.
[2] Richardson, *Familiar Letters*, ed. Brian W. Downs, 1928, letter vii, pp. 12–14.
[3] Ibid., letter lxxxiii, pp. 104–6.   [4] Ibid., letter lxxvi, pp. 94–8.

the writer resembles that of Pamela.[1] More directly related to
the story of Pamela are 'A Father to a Daughter in Service, on
hearing of her Master's attempting her Virtue' and 'The Daughter's Answer'.[2] It was while writing these letters 'giving one
or two as cautions to young folk circumstanced as Pamela was'
that Richardson recollected a story about a gentleman who,
after first attempting to seduce his mother's servant-maid, had
then married the virtuous girl, who made him an excellent
wife. This tale from real life was, according to Richardson, told
to him nearly twenty-five years before the novel's appearance,
apparently by the mysterious gentleman and prospective patron
who had been Richardson's friend in youth.[3] The anecdote had
laid dormant in his memory for a long time; it was not until he
started on the actual process of writing which, however limited,
required some originality, that he recollected the tale and
'gave way to enlargement'.[4] Merely creating his own characters
and situations, for even so slight a purpose, seems to have
released Richardson's creative ability. *Familiar Letters* had to
wait until the novel was finished.

Novels in letters, or making extensive use of the letter form,
had become fairly common, but Richardson's first work was
directly inspired by the more homely and prosaic handbook or
'letter-writer'. This was actually a stylistic advantage. Producing a letter-writer is an exercise in style and decorum—an
appropriate manner must be found for each type of writer, and
something of that person's speaking voice must also be repro-
duced. *Pamela* is also an exercise in decorum. The tone of the
country girl must be maintained throughout.

The country writer of the lower class had long been a type-
character in the letter-writers. Usually, the function of the
'country letter' is to provide amusement for the reader. The
country correspondents in the letter-writer have characteristics
in common. They are concerned with the concrete; small
possessions and small sums of money mean a great deal to them,
and they are far less abashed at mentioning such things than
their more sophisticated upper-class neighbours. They also

---

[1] Richardson, *Familiar Letters*, letter lxii, pp. 72–6.
[2] Ibid., letters cxxxviii–cxxxix, pp. 164–5.
[3] Richardson to Hill [1741], *Selected Letters*, pp. 39–41.
[4] Ibid., p. 41.

mention clothes and food with a good deal of practical relish, and on such matters may tend to ramble a bit from the point, as in the letter of Nicholas Breton's Roger to his sweetheart:

The cause of my writing to you at this time, is that, *Margery*, I doe heare since my coming from *Wakefield*, when you know that talke wee had together at the signe of the blew Cuckoe, and how you did giue me your hand, and sweare that you would not forsake me for all the world: and how you made me buy a Ring and a Heart, that cost me eighteene pence, which I left with you, and you gaue me a Napkin to weare in my Hat, I thanke you, which I will weare to my dying day. And I maruel if it be true as I heare, that you haue altered your mind, and are made sure to my neighbour *Hoglins* younger Son.[1]

When these two lovers have made up their quarrel, 'Roger' invites 'Margery' to 'haue a Cake and a Pot, at the Pickerill and spurre',[2] to which she responds with enthusiasm: 'on Friday Ile meet you at ten of the clocke, and bring a peece of Bacon in my pocket, to relish a cup of Ale.'[3]

The country writers do not deal in witty conceits, preferring proverbs and well-tried phrases: 'it shal go hard if all hit right, but some bodie shall wipe their nose for their knauerie';[4] 'as plain as the Prong of a Pitch fork'.[5] They do not write in well-weighed periods; their sentences are unstructured and rambling, following the train of thought without paying too much heed to the restrictions of purely grammatical arrangement:

Your Image is always before my Mind; and, a Dad, I know not what to make on it, for it was never so with me before; but I have lately been rambling among my Thoughts to find out the Reason on't; and, after thinking of one Thing, and thinking of another, the Duce take me if I do not think it Love . . . if my Distemper should happen to be Love, which I am the more ignorant of, because if it be Love, I am sure I never loved before, but this I am very sure, whatever it be, it gives me a great deal of Trouble; for it quite take me off my Business, nay, and off my Sleep, and Victuals too, and still my Mind runs after you, which indeed does make me think it is Love, after all; but if it be, I am sure 'tis time for me to think of a Remedy, or else it will soon undo me.[6]

[1] Nicholas Breton, *A Poste with a Packet of Mad Letters*, 1633 ed., p. 31.
[2] Ibid., p. 38.   [3] Ibid.   [4] Ibid.
[5] G. F., *The Secretary's Guide*, 1734 ed., p. 15.
[6] 'A Plain Country Love-letter from Humphry to Dorothy', ibid., p. 13.

Richardson experiments with this 'low' style in *Familiar Letters,* for light humour, in the sailor's letter to his fiancée and her reply,[1] and for pathos, in the letters of the poor tenant to his landlord's steward, in which the pious and respectable tone anticipates the manner of Pamela's parents.[2]

Pamela's own letters are a *tour de force* in the country manner. She has all the traditional interest in the concrete; her own possessions are of particular interest to her. Like the country correspondents, she is interested in clothes, in food, in small sums of money. What other heroine has burst upon the world with such concern for four guineas, and such consciousness of the physical fact of the coins? 'I send them by *John* our Footman, who goes your Way; but he does not know what he carries; because I seal them up in one of the little Pill-boxes, which my Lady had, wrapp'd close in Paper, that they mayn't chink . . .'[3]

The customarily rambling style of the country writer is used by Richardson to show us Pamela herself, and to let us see the various thoughts and impressions which circulate through her mind. The very first letter is a wonderful jumble (through Pamela's artlessness and Richardson's art) of her real regret for her lady's death, her fear that she will be 'quite destitute again', her practical concern about money, and her admiration for Mr. B.:

Well, but God's will must be done!—and so comes the Comfort, that I shall not be oblig'd to return back to be a Clog upon my dear Parents! For my Master said, I will take care of you all, my good Maidens; and for you, *Pamela,* (and took me by the Hand; yes, he took my Hand before them all) for my dear Mother's sake, I will be a Friend to you, and you shall take care of my Linen. God bless him! and pray with me, my dear Father and Mother, for a Blessing upon him: For he has given Mourning and a Year's Wages to all my Lady's Servants; and I having no Wages as yet, my Lady having said she would do for me as I deserv'd, order'd the House-keeper to give me Mourning with the rest, and gave me with his own Hand Four golden Guineas, and some Silver, which were in my old Lady's Pocket when she dy'd; and said, If I was a good Girl, and faithful and diligent, he would be a Friend to me, for his Mother's sake.[4]

---

[1] *Familiar Letters,* letters cxxvi–cxxvii, pp. 147–50.
[2] Ibid., letters ciii, cvi–cviii, pp. 132–6.
[3] *Pamela,* i. 2–3.   [4] Ibid., p. 2.

The style of the 'country bumpkin' is traditionally comic, and remains so here, although Pamela as a character is raised far above the mere humorous level of the country correspondent. The advantage of her style for an epistolary novel is very great, as the earlier novels in letters had suffered from a lack of definition in milieu and manners, and various characters, often writing in a rather turgid rhetorical style, tend to sound alike. Similar defects dogged the seduction/rape novel; the heroines express the force of their emotions in cloudy purple passages which prevent any individualizing of character. Once a heroine is the centre of such an interesting intrigue, all possibility of treating her in any way with humour is completely lost. Pamela's lowly station makes her a novelty among the heroines of the seduction novel (although not, as we shall see, among the heroines of the attempted seduction story in the drama). Because Richardson started from an unusual point, the homely letter-writer, he was able to solve the problem of presenting a character in a seduction story narrated in letters without falling into the difficulties that hampered his predecessors. Pamela has an individual voice, and because of the nature of that voice (which is also for us her individual character) her inner life is closely connected with a credible outside world.

The novel also resembles both fables and sample letters in being instructive. All Richardson's novels—indeed practically all eighteenth-century English novels, in their divers manners—are didactic, but the overt 'message' is simpler, more closely and succinctly presented than in the later works. *Pamela* is also Richardson's shortest novel, and, considered without the continuation, the most economically (although not the most excellently) developed. The story partakes of the nature of the fable in its rapid and simple development. Like a fable, the story has an indirect bearing on a broader political and social situation. The holder of rank and power over-extends his authority treacherously, until taught a lesson, and those in the pay of the powerful are haughty-minded and foolish counsellors. Sagacious stratagem is allowed to the simple in self-defence, but ambition and false grandeur are despised by the truly humble. Ultimately, the cunning of the wicked and powerful is defeated by the prudence and virtue of the weak and lowly, and the destined victim at the outset becomes the victor in the end. Seen in one light, *Pamela* is an extended fable with human characters. It is also closely related to fairy-tale, folk-tale, and ballad,—*Cinderella, The Goose-Girl, Patient Griselda, King Cophetua and the Beggar Maid, The Beggar's Daughter of Bednall-Green,* and a host of others—which celebrate the union of high and lowly. The ancient roots of the tale give it a strength and simple organic unity of form which the slight works of the new female fiction could not achieve. Another experiment in the epistolary form or in the seduction story could so easily have become another thin and wavering fictional essay, without coherence or the basic strength acquired through a story with universal appeal.

If *Pamela* is a fable, it is a Christian fable. The religious outlook expressed in the novel is no added pious trimming, but essential. The heroine is a country bumpkin, but possesses intelligence and sensibility, and a soul which is as important as that of a princess. Roger Sharrock has suggested that Richardson's novel is an outcome of Christianity, and its transference of the heroic role from the aristocrat to the meek and lowly.[1] Richardson can believe his servant-maid is important enough to be the heroine of a tale, and that a threat against her virtue is as interesting as the attempted seduction of one of the leisured ladies of the novels. Not only so, but the state of her heart is analysed in a manner which in earlier fiction had pertained only to elegant heroines of middle- or upper-class rank. However, he has assurance enough of her central importance to allow her to be, not only of humble birth, but independent-minded, energetic, practical, and funny.

Pamela the heroine is still the country girl, and the comic element, fused with the romantic and religious, is still very much there from the beginning. We are meant both to sympathize and smile, and some of the criticism of Richardson's novel would be allayed if we were to recognize that Richardson adopted a mode of narrative and a type of character which are intentionally features of comedy.

[1] Roger Sharrock, 'Richardson's *Pamela*: the Gospel and the Novel', *Durham University Journal,* lviii (Mar. 1966), 67–74.

III

Pamela: The Pastoral Comedy

THE story of *Pamela* has a given organic unity. It is a comedy, a story of love's vicissitudes which ends happily; ultimately, a wedding is celebrated by which the right partners are united, and the social order enriched. It is not a simple comedy because of its darker, more disturbing elements. The tension in the centre of the tale is real and powerful, and has tragic implications. Pamela feels overwhelmed, her personality threatened. The horror of the imprisonment of one personality by another is strongly suggested in the scenes in the 'awful Mansion', the locked doors, barred windows, high walls—a world in which unforeseen and sudden attacks wait in ambush. These were already part of the machinery of the seduction/rape story which Richardson so imaginatively adapts; he is in *Pamela* anticipating possibilities later developed in *Clarissa*.

There are moments when the intensity and violence of sexual conflict threaten to erupt uncontrollably, completely engulfing all else. *Clarissa* is all eruption—the cheerful, normal, and hopeful are seen as delusions. But in *Clarissa* the author is completely sure of his mood and tone—the novel is tragic from the beginning. Here the author is experimenting, and the experimental nature of the novel is evident, not in the story, which is clear and well shaped, but in the mood, which is somewhat indefinite; suspense and distress almost equal to tragic tension are mingled with the comic treatment.

The scenes of tension are not accidental; Richardson intends to obtain total sympathy for Pamela; the reader should feel threatened. Pamela under stress is the subject, but the quality of that stress menaces the story as a whole. Unlike *Clarissa*, this is not a story in which the victim and the torturer are antitheses, doomed to perpetual separation. In the *Pamela* story, the seducer-hero must be reclaimed and made happy.

It is unlikely that Richardson, when starting to write the story based on the long-remembered anecdote, realized quite where his most powerful effects would lie, and at what point his imagination would be most powerfully stirred. By the time he wrote *Clarissa* he did know, and could use his faculties of darker imagination to their fullest extent.

However, in *Pamela* he possessed the literary skill to keep the central conflict from developing in such a way as to annul the effect of the ending. The vividness with which passion and terror are imagined could be a disintegrating force, considering the novel as a whole. But there are unifying forces at work also, and one of the strongest of these is the consistent motif which Richardson used for this novel alone—the pastoral theme. This theme is in harmony both with the central character and with the fable. The unity of the story is preserved by the fact that it is kept within the bounds of the wide realm of pastoral comedy. In using the style of the country letter-writer, Richardson escaped the nebulousness of the heroines of the established seduction novels; he also allowed scope for comedy, and for the suggestion of a 'natural' world in which threatening passion is redeemable. It is too much to claim that *Pamela* is only a pastoral comedy, if this means claiming that there is nothing in it which could not easily come under this classification; it is not too much to claim that of all literary 'kinds' it most belongs to this. It is not surprising that Richardson chose this mode for his novel. Contemporary dramatists had already dealt romantically with the story of the rakish squire and the virtuous maiden in pastoral comedies. By uniting this story with the downright tone of his country letter-writer, Richardson's imagination had already leaped to originality, and his development of the pastoral comedy in his own manner, with his vigorous characters, consistent atmosphere, and imagery, brought something entirely new to the novel.

The story of the lowly maiden whose virtue is attempted by a man of high degree was very much in the air.[1] In John Leanerd's *The Country Innocence: or, The Chamber-Maid Turn'd Quaker* (1677) (a revision of Anthony Brewer's *The Countrie*

---

[1] Ira Konigsberg, 'The Dramatic Background of Richardson's Plots and Characters', *PMLA*, lxxxiii (Mar. 1968), 42–53; see pp. 42–6. See also his *Samuel Richardson and the Dramatic Novel*, 1968.

Girle, 1647) Margaret, the tenant's daughter, is plagued by the attentions of the lord of the manor, and, in virtuous resistance, kneels to beg his mercy.[1] She is finally victorious, but, as Sir Robert is married, her weakening would be the more heinous, and there is of course no chance of her virtue being rewarded in marriage, or of a *mésalliance* between upper and lower ranks.

Virtue is rewarded in marriage in Charles Johnson's *The Country Lasses* (1715). Heartwell, a town rake temporarily in the country, falls in love with the beautiful village maiden, Flora, and attempts to seduce her. Like Mr. B. he makes handsome offers of financial settlements, and like Pamela, Flora in the name of virtue and piety disdains his offers.

Heart[well]. . . . I will settle 200 *l* a Year upon you for Life, and provide for all our Children . . . Chuse your own Lawyer, take your own Security, make your own Trustees; you shall have an Inheritance in my Heart, and my Land as firm as if you were born to it.

Flora. To be serious then, since you are so; I'll tell you; all the Inheritance I boast or wish for, is this low humble Cottage, and a Mind, I hope a virtuous Mind, that cannot even in this Situation bear Dishonour; take back your worthless Trifle, a Heart, and your more worthless Promises, and know I scorn as much to yield to the mean Bargain of your hireling Passion; as you do to submit to honourable Love.

Heart. Stay; you shall stay—Let me but think a Moment?

Flora. Think then, ungrateful Man, what 'tis you do? My father, whose Prop I am, the Stay of his old Age; taught me with pious Care to tread the Paths of Virtue; how wou'd it tear the Strings of his old Heart to see me fal'n at once to Shame and Infamy?[2]

Flora's virtue shames Hartwell, who yet remains conscious of the social indiscretion of such a marriage:

Heart. Oh thou hast touch'd my Soul; I *feel* thy Words, a conscious Pang starts thro' my Heart, and covers me with Shame, yet *Flora*, yet I hope you will forgive me when you think how strongly we are byass'd to what is wrong, Custom, Family, Fortune, I know not what terrible Words make me fear to suffer in Opinion only.[3]

[1] John Leanerd, *The Country Innocence*, 1677, II. i. p. 15.
[2] Charles Johnson, *The Country Lasses: Or, The Custom of the Manor*, 1727 ed., IV. i. p. 39.
[3] Ibid., p. 40.

He resembles Mr. B. who, even when ashamed of his former
actions, is likewise fearful of marriage: 'But, what can I do?
Consider the Pride of my Condition . . . How then, with the
Distance between us, in the World's Judgment, can I think of
making you my Wife?'[1] Heartwell, like Mr. B., is conquered by
the girl's virtue, and decides he cannot live without marrying
her: 'Thy Words, bright Excelence, charm like thy Beauty . . .
no Family can mend, no Education teach, no habit improve
your Manners . . . In you I see the most perfect Virtue cloath'd
in all the Charms of the most elegant Form . . .'[2] It is, however,
Heartwell who is materially rewarded in his choice of marriage
to Flora, as, after their marriage, she reveals herself as the lady
of the manor, and an heiress. Her appearance as a poor country
maiden has been a masquerade to test her lover's sincerity.

Lillo's *Silvia: or, The Country Burial* (1731) has a similar theme.
The honest country girl is attempted by the rakish Sir John
Freeman, whom she has known since childhood. She is horrified
when he makes insulting proposals:

Sir John. And lest you shou'd think I mean to deceive and to forsake
you, no proud Heiress, that brings a Province for her Portion,
shall be joyntur'd as you shall be. Half my Estate shall be settled
on thee.

Sil[via]. With brutal Force to compel me to hear thy hated Proposals, is such Insolence.—Thy Breath is blasting, and thy touch
infectious. O that my Strength was equal to my Indignation!
I'd give my Hand a Ransom for my Body.

[*Breaks from him*

Sir John. Stay, my charming angry Fair, and hear me speak.

Sil. Wou'd I had never heard you. Oh that 'twere possible to fly
where I might never hear the Voice of Mankind more!—What,
set a Price on my Immortal Soul and Spotless Fame? . . . She,
who capitulates on Terms like these, confesses an Equivalent may
be had for Innocence and Fame, and thereby by forfeits both.[3]

Pamela, like Johnson's Flora and Lillo's Silvia, is offered
handsome settlements (five hundred guineas down, and an
estate in Kent) if she will be her lover's mistress, and she
rejects Mr. B.'s 'Articles' with similar outraged scorn:

I hope, as I can contentedly live at the meanest Rate, and think

[1] *Pamela*, i. 292.
[2] Johnson, *The Country Lasses*, IV. i, p. 40.
[3] George Lillo, *Silvia: or, The Country Burial*. An Opera, 1731, I. iv, pp. 5–6.

not myself above the lowest Condition, that I am also above making an Exchange of my Honesty for all the Riches of the *Indies*. When I come to be proud and vain of gaudy Apparel, and outside Finery; then . . . may I rest my principal Good in such vain Trinkets, and despise for them the more solid Ornaments of a good Fame and a Chastity inviolate![1]

Silvia, telling her honest father, Welford, of Freeman's propositions, confesses "'Twas long before my Heart was taught to love him, and by the Pain his Cruelty gives me I fear 'twill be much longer e're it will learn to hate him,'[2] just as Pamela wonders 'What is the Matter, that, with all his ill Usage of me, I cannot hate him?'[3] Silvia's Sir John, a grosser rake than Mr. B., endeavours to console himself with the simple but far from innocent Lettice, but is eventually brought to propose marriage to his lowly beloved. At the end of the play, it is discovered that their positions are reversed; Sir John is of lowly extraction, and Silvia of noble birth, but despite this Gilbertian revelation they proceed to matrimony.

Similar to both *The Country Lasses* and *Silvia* in its use of the dramatic revelation of the lowly heroine's high birth is Edward Phillips's one-act ballad-opera *The Chamber-Maid* (1730). The hero, Freeman, has fallen in love, not with Rosella, whom his father wishes him to marry, but with her maid, Betty. In order to woo her, he disguises himself as the gardener. Unlike Lillo's Freeman, he makes no attempt at seduction, but decides to marry his humble sweetheart. In declaring his intentions, he draws his father's wrath upon him:

Sir Will[iam Freeman]. What, my Boy! how, marry a Chamber-maid! why thou wout be undone, *Billy*; what, bring a Beggar into the Family! pies on't![4]

Here is a slight attempt to examine the social reaction to such a *mésalliance*, but the course of love is made smooth by Betty's revelation of her true birth.

All three of these eighteenth-century plays make some use of rural background. Lillo uses it chiefly for the country humours of the subplot, but both Johnson and Phillips suggest gardens and flowers, and the delights of country life. Two of the songs in

---

[1] *Pamela*, i. 261–2.   [2] Lillo, *Silvia*, II. ii, p. 32.
[3] *Pamela*, i. 243.
[4] Edward Phillips, *The Chamber-Maid*, 1730, Sc. iv, p. 30.

Phillips's ballad-opera are prettily pastoral ('My Betty is the Snow-drop fair' and 'Thus at the cheerful Dawn of Day') and Johnson's two rakes discuss the pleasures of life in a cottage:

Heart[*well*]. . . . did you observe the sweetness and Purity of this little Dwelling—The Linnen smelt of Lavender and Roses.
Mode[*ly*]. The Honey-suckles hid the Light of our small Casement.[1]

Modely also praises the beauty of 'a wholesome Country Girl, whose Breath is sweeter than the Bloom of Violets, in a Straw Hat, a Kersey Gown, and a white Dimity Wastcoat, with Natural Red and White that innocently flushes over her Face, and shows every motion of her Heart'.[2]

These semi-realistic plays were perhaps influenced by the more exotic pastoral dramas, such as the operatic version of *Il Pastor Fido* (1712), Anthony Aston's *Pastora: or, The Coy Shepherdess* (1712), and Theophilus Cibber's ballad-opera *Patie and Peggy; or, The Fair Foundling* (1730), a dramatic version of Ramsay's *The Gentle Shepherd*. It was the popularity of the pastoral drama that incited Gay to write his 'Newgate Pastoral' ballad-opera, as it had been the popularity of pastoral poetry that inspired his gentle burlesque *The Shepherd's Week* (1714). During this century, the old Renaissance conventions were combined with a relatively new belief in natural landscape, as well as in the simplicity of rustic life, as morally inspiring. Elegant ladies in London drawing-rooms carolled

> Far remote and retir'd from the noise of the town,
> I'll exchange my brocade for a plain russet gown.[3]

The world had acquired a taste, at least aesthetically, for the beauty of the country lass in simple costume. Such a taste had found expression in the novel before Richardson. Mrs. Elizabeth Rowe's Rosalinda forsakes her high station and becomes a servant-girl in order to evade an unwelcome marriage. She is delighted with her service in the farmhouse, and with her new appearance:

A clean Cambrick Cap, and an Holland gown wrought with natural flowers, is the top of my finery; in which I like myself as well, and I think I look as handsome, as when I was dressed in

[1] Johnson, *The Country Lasses*, IV. i, p. 36.   [2] Ibid. p. 2.
[3] Henry Carey, 'Mrs. Stuart's Retirement'; see *The Poems of Henry Carey*, ed. Frederick T. Wood, 1930, p. 121.

brocades and jewels for a birth-night . . . But I have a mind as easy and innocent now, as when burdened with those costly ornaments; a red cross-knot, a glass necklace, and flowers in my bosom, are the only useless parts of my dress; which is either the gift of nature, or honestly paid for; in which I am a thousand times more happy than I should be in borrowed finery, at the expence of some industrious trader's ruin . . .[1]

Pamela, when she changes back to rural costume, typifies country innocence and beauty, and Richardson could be quite sure of his reader's ready response to the famous scene in which she tries on her new clothes:

There I trick'd myself up as well as I could in my new Garb, and put on my round-ear'd ordinary Cap; but with a green Knot, however, and my home-spun Gown and Petticoat, and plain-leather Shoes; but yet they are what they call *Spanish* Leather, and my ordinary Hose, ordinary I mean to what I have been lately used to: tho' I shall think a good Yarn may do very well for every Day, when I come home. A plain Muslin Tucker I put on, and my black Silk Necklace, instead of the *French* Necklace my Lady gave me; and put the Ear-rings out of my Ears; and when I was quite 'quipp'd, I took my Straw Hat in my Hand, with its two blue Strings, and look'd about me in the Glass, as proud as any thing.— To say Truth, I never lik'd myself so well in my Life.[2]

Such clothes are almost a symbol in themselves of beauty and innocence. In *The Country Lasses*, Heartwell registers surprise when he sees Flora enter 'drest very genteely' (as the stage directions remark) and exclaims 'I swear, my Love, thou canst receive no Addition by Dress, but what will injure the Simplicity of thy Charms—But prithee tell me why have you chang'd your Dress? Sure you must be sensible you wanted nothing to make you victorious in your other Habit.'[3] Mr. B. the rake is entranced by the sight of Pamela in her 'new Garb', and Mr. B. the convert to virtue is still proud of her rural dress and appearance. When he warns her to expect visitors, he says:

For since they know of your Condition, and I have told them the Story of your present Dress, and how you came by it, one of·the young Ladies begs it as a Favour, that they may see you just as you

---

[1] Mrs. Elizabeth Rowe, *Letters Moral and Entertaining*, part ii, p. 231.
[2] *Pamela*, i. 67.   [3] Johnson, *The Country Lasses*, v. ii, p. 57.

are: And I am the rather pleased it should be so, because they will perceive you owe nothing to Dress, but make a much better Figure with your own native Stock of Loveliness, than the greatest Ladies, array'd in the most splendid Attire, and adorn'd with the most glittering Jewels.[1]

He introduces her to the company as 'my pretty Rustick'.[2]

Richardson does not make Pamela's parents poor cottagers by birth (this not so much perhaps from snobbery as from the practical difficulty of explaining the Andrews family's degree of literacy) but the better days which they have seen are only moderately bright. We see enough of Pamela's situation at the beginning of the novel to be convinced that she is really a servant, despite the generous care of her former mistress in her upbringing; the rustic beauties in the plays never seem to have done any work. Mrs. Rowe's Rosalinda's position as a servant is an absolute sinecure; she goes rambling about the lush countryside with her master's children, indulging 'some innocent reverie, or pious meditation', or gathering cowslips and daisies.[3] Pamela's world is no such Arcadia. It consists of the servant's hall, the kitchen, the housekeeper's parlour, her attic. The other servants are important in her life, and she often mentions their names. We learn about her through glimpses of life below stairs, such as the footman Harry's offered kiss, which angers her, and her scolding from Mrs. Jervis, or the cook's jealous comments:

Our Cook one Day, who is a little snappish and cross sometimes, said once time, Why this *Pamela* of *ours* goes as fine as a Lady. See what it is to have a fine face!—I wonder what the Girl will come to at last!

She was hot with her Work; and I sneak'd away; for I seldom go down into the Kitchen; and I heard the Butler say, Why, *Jane*, nobody has your good Word: What has Mrs. *Pamela* done to you? . . . And what, said the foolish Wench, have I said to her, *Foolatum*; but that she was pretty?[4]

Pamela is no fine lady seeking to enjoy the contrasting simplicity of the cot; she is a servant-girl for whom service in the great house is relative luxury. She is in a position to appreciate fully, and not without a certain ruefulness, that her chosen life

---

[1] *Pamela*, ii. 42.   [2] Ibid., p. 59.
[3] Rowe, *Letters Moral and Entertaining*, part ii, p. 225.   [4] *Pamela*, i. 48.

of virtuous poverty is going to entail hard and disagreeable work:

> To be sure, I had better, as Things stand, have learn'd to wash and scour, and brew and bake, and such-like. But I hope . . . to learn these soon, if any body will have the Goodness to bear with me, till I am able . . . So I t'other Day, try'd, when *Rachel's* Back was turn'd, if I could not scour a Pewter Plate she had begun. I see I could do't by Degrees: It only blister'd my Hand in two Places.
>
> All the Matter is, if I could get Plain-work enough, I need not spoil my Fingers. But if I can't, I hope to make my Hands as red as a Blood-pudding, and as hard as a Beechen Trencher, to accommodate them to my Condition.[1]

The energy of her final metaphors removes her a good distance from those rural heroines who spent their time inhaling the scent of the jessamines. There is nothing at all romantic about hands 'as red as a Blood-pudding'. She has been used to some rough work in her past life at home, as emerges when she mentions buying 'two Flanel Under-coats' which will 'keep me warm, if any Neighbour should get me to go out to help 'em to milk, now-and-then, as sometimes I used to do formerly'.[2] Had she hoped 'to make the lowing herd her care', or the like, she would have fitted into a romantic landscape, but there is nothing like flannel for bringing us back to the commonplace.

No, there is no hint in this vivid little person of high birth below stairs. She is a respectable servant-girl. The problem of the female servant who finds that her master has designs upon her seemed of sufficient importance for the anonymous author of *A Present for a Servant Maid* (1743) to devote a considerable attention to it.[3] Among injunctions to piety and industry, and recipes for preserves and washing-powders, the writer thinks fit to include advice to the maid about how to cope with attempts on her chastity, under various headings such as 'Temptations from your Master', 'Behaviour to him, if a single Man', 'Temptations

---

[1] Ibid., pp. 98–9.   [2] Ibid., p. 50.

[3] *A Present for a Servant Maid: Or, the Sure Means of gaining Love and Esteem* . . . To which are Added, Directions for going to Market; also, for *Dressing* any *Common Dish*, whether Flesh, Fish, or Fowl. With some *Rules* for Washing, &c. *The Whole calculated for making both the* Mistress *and the* Maid, *happy*, 1743. It has been suggested that this little treatise is the work of Eliza Haywood who, with her publisher T. Gardner, was 'cashing in' on the success of *Pamela*, but the style is not especially Haywoodian. It was in approved use as a servant's vade-mecum.

from your Master's Son', etc. The servant is advised to try to turn her master from his bad design by modest behaviour and remonstrances, but, if his importunate eagerness persists, to 'go directly out of his House'.[1] The servant-girl is also to be suspicious of extravagant offers from a young master, *including* marriage, for even if this offer were faithfully made, the outcome would bring only bitterness:

But there is yet a greater Trial of your Virtue . . . perhaps, if his Circumstances countenance such a Proposal, the Offer of a Settlement for Life, and, it may be, even a Promise of marrying you as soon as he shall be at his own Disposal. This last Bait has seduced some who have been Proof against all the others . . . Suppose he should even keep his Word . . . what you would suffer from the Illusage of his Friends, and 'tis likely from his own Remorse for what he has done, would make you wish, in the greatest Bitterness of Heart, that it were possible for you to loose the indissoluble Knot, which binds you to a Man who no longer loves you, and return to your first humble Station. Such a Disparity of Birth, of Circumstances, and Education can produce no lasting Harmony . . .[2]

The dice were loaded against the servant-maid in any relationship with her master. The master's exercise of a *droit de seigneur* could be condoned, but the girl herself could easily lose her respectable status, with no prospect but that of being eventually thrown upon the town, where life would be nasty, brutish, and short. As Pamela herself sees clearly, the servant-girl is almost powerless within society. Society was extremely careful to preserve distinctions of rank by condemning unequal marriages. Richardson does not advocate the levelling of social classes, but he makes a strong claim for human equality—the equality of souls before God is shown as implying that individual emotional and moral life has an absolute value to which social distinctions are irrelevant. Pamela exclaims, 'My *Soul* is of equal Importance with the Soul of a Princess; though my Quality is inferior to that of the meanest Slave.'[3] The tenor of Richardson's novel is to prove that 'such a Disparity of Birth, of Circumstances, and Education' *can* produce 'lasting Harmony', given the suitability of other more important factors of

[1] *A Present for a Servant-Maid*, p. 46.   [2] Ibid., pp. 47–8.
[3] *Pamela*, i. 213.

heart and mind. But we are meant to see, in the first part of the novel, Pamela's involuntary daring in putting her heart at risk by falling in love without any advantage of birth.

From the beginning Richardson, while stressing the inequality of station between his hero and heroine, is careful to make us aware of their psychological compatibility. Mr. B. is essentially a 'low' character, the masculine conterpart of Pamela herself. He is definitely a country squire, whom one cannot envisage as being much at home in the precincts of St. James's. One has to admit a certain aptness in Fielding's filling in his name as 'Mr. Booby'. The character of Lovelace shows that it was not beyond Richardson's power to draw a subtle and fascinating rake. Here, the woman is given the advantage of subtlety of character, which is her main and unconscious weapon against blunt masculinity. Mr. B.'s interests are not intellectual; his time (when he is not occupied with seducing Pamela) is devoted to hunting, and to caring for his estates. There is not much mental discrepancy between the pair. The conflict between their two separate stations is balanced and made ironic by the refinement of Pamela—a refinement of perception rather than of manner—and the boorishness of Mr. B. His attitude to sex, unlike that of Lovelace, is relatively uncompli-cated, and his sexuality does not seek satisfaction in exquisite mental cruelty. Even his attacks on Pamela, when he uses contrivance, are blundering and grotesque. Lovelace attempt-ing Clarissa never assumes a ridiculous guise, as does Mr. B. when he is present in Pamela's room as the drunken maid with an apron over his face.[1]

Contemporary readers might easily have seen in the two main attempts upon Pamela a resemblance to the exploits of the infamous Colonel Charteris, exploits which had been de-scribed in a coarsely comic and blunt manner.[2] An anonymous pamphlet relating the Colonel's amours describes the case of the 'handsome tall Maid' who is conveyed away from her aged grandmother under promise of finding service by the Colonel's tools '*Trusty Jack* his Man, and *Moll Clapham* his Woman'.[3]

[1] Ibid., p. 272.

[2] A. D. McKillop mentions the Charteris *Memoirs* in connection with *Pamela*; see *Samuel Richardson*, p. 32.

[3] *Some Authentick Memoirs of the Life of Colonel Ch——s, Rape-Master-General of Great Britain.* By an Impartial Hand, 1730, p. 13.

The maid resists the Colonel's first attempts, and Moll pretends to comfort her, allowing the girl to lie with her that night for safety.

> They went to Bed together, and soon after the Colonel enter'd the Room thro' a Trap Door contriv'd for such Purposes: the young Woman shriek'd out, and *Clapham* endeavouring to quit her, the Girl held fast by her Shift, begging for God's sake she would not leave her at that Extremity: but this was all to no purpose, she knew her Master's Resolution, and her own Business too well, to be diverted from it by Tears and Intreaties. The Colonel came into the Bed, *Vi & Armis*, *Clapham* standing by the Side of it, persuading her to reconcile herself to the *Affair in hand*, saying, *she ought to behave like a Woman; for that she was now at Years of Discretion, and not a silly raw Girl*, and such like Expressions.[1]

The Colonel also assumes feminine attire as disguise on another occasion when he plans an attack on a 'Country Wench': 'the Colonel went to Bed dress'd in a Woman's Suit of Night-Cloths; a more engaging Figure *H—d—gg—r* could not have made in a Dishabillé . . .'[2]

There is a resemblance between the Colonel's stratagems and the behaviour of Mr. B. in the two main 'bedroom assaults' upon Pamela. On the first occasion, when Pamela shares the bed of honest Mrs. Jervis, her master is concealed in 'the wicked Closet, that held the worst Heart in the World'.[3] When he rushes out upon her and comes to the bed, Pamela pleads with the housekeeper not to leave her. On the second occasion, in Lincolnshire, Pamela lies with Mrs. Jewkes, who has a family resemblance to the like of 'Moll Clapham'. Mr. B., in the guise of Nan the maid, has been sitting in an elbow-chair 'in a Gown and Petticoat of hers, and her Apron over his Face and Shoulders'.[4] He comes into bed with them, and is assisted by the 'Vile Procuress' who holds Pamela's right arm:

> Now, *Pamela*, said he, is the dreadful Time of Reckoning come, that I have threaten'd—I screamed out in such a manner, as never any body heard the like. But there was nobody to help me: And both my Hands were secured, as I said. Sure never poor Soul was in such Agonies as I. Wicked Man! said I; wicked, abominable Woman! O God! my God! this *Time*, this *one* Time! deliver me from this

---

[1] *Some Authentick Memoirs of the Life of Colonel Ch——s*, p. 14.
[2] Ibid., p. 24.   [3] *Pamela*, i. 75.   [4] Ibid., p. 276.

Distress! or strike me dead this Moment. And then I scream'd again and again . . .

Said she, (O Disgrace of Womankind!) What you do, Sir, do; don't stand dilly-dallying. She cannot exclaim worse than she has done, And she'll be quieter when she knows the worst.[1]

These sections have been called 'the worst parts of Richardson's plot, Mr. B.'s clumsy and brutal attacks on the heroine',[2] but such a reaction misses the full effect of the scenes, which are made viable through a kind of irony. The expected conquest of the villain-rake is not achieved. The heavy braggadocio with which Mr. B. lays his plans is farcical—Richardson has deliberately made it so—but the very clumsiness defeats the assumed brutality. Some of the grotesque humour of the Charteris account, much softened, seems to have been transferred to the novel without detaching the reader from the victim's point of view. Pamela sees Mr. B. as entirely horrifying, but that is not the only way the author and reader see the situation. Part of the irony is of course that Mr. B. is not a psychopathic Charteris. Mr. B.'s attacks are an expression of self-assertion, but he lacks the brutal confidence to proceed. There is an adolescent rawness in his openness of motive, and, while he has the fox-hunter's single-minded ability to pursue his object, he is puzzled and distressed when his real object (Pamela's voluntary offering of herself) eludes him. A manifestation of real revulsion on her part, such as her fainting, puts him off, whereas if he were really a man of unbridled lust (as his masculine ego sometimes makes him think he is) or a sadist like Lovelace, her helplessness would have been his opportunity. Mr. B.'s assumption of the Charteris style is an attempt to assume an aggressive *persona* which he thinks is correctly masculine. When things do not go according to plan, the mask rapidly begins to slip. His *bravura* attempts have a touch of the schoolboy prank which saves them from being really brutal and repellent. Mr. B. partly expected that in circumstances of such theatrical flourish Pamela would enter, at least half-willingly, into the spirit of the piece. When she does not, his well-prepared little dramas are dismal failures. The older, more cynical Mrs. Jewkes makes fun of him (as she evidently feels cheated of a spectacle). 'And will you, Sir, said the wicked

[1] Ibid., p. 278.   [2] McKillop, *Samuel Richardson*, p. 32.

Wretch, for a Fit or two, give up such an Opportunity as this?—I thought you had known the Sex better',[1] but the masculine role is not as simple as all that.

What makes him vulnerable (far weaker than Pamela in her hero-worship suspects) is his desire for affection. We realize from the beginning that he has feelings to be hurt. After she has rejected him, and has decided to return home, she is distressed at his anger, while the reader sees the expression of hurt feelings in the sulks:

> But I believe my Master is fearfully angry with me; for he pass'd by me two or three times, and would not speak to me; and towards Evening he met me in the Passage going into the Garden, and said such a Word to me as I never heard in my Life from him, to Man, Woman or Child; for he first said, This Creature's always in my Way, I think. I said, standing up as close as I could, (and the Entry was wide enough for a Coach too) I hope I shan't be long in your Honour's Way. D—n you! said he (that was the hard Word) for a little Witch; I have no Patience with you.[2]

Such pettishness is pure comedy. Neither of the main protagonists is grand or heroic. Pamela may see Mr. B. as tremendous, in an unconscious attestation of her love and admiration, but both hero and heroine are domestic and ordinary. There is a delightful scene immediately following, in which Mrs. Jervis and Pamela discuss her situation and his behaviour. Mrs. Jervis says:

> I believe he loves my good Maiden, tho' his Servant, better than all the Ladies in the Land; and he has try'd to overcome it, because you are so much his Inferior; and 'tis my Opinion he finds he can't; and that vexes his proud Heart . . . and so he speaks so cross to you, when he sees you by Accident.[3]

It is in scenes like these that we see the forces at work to 'ruin' Mr. B., as he is at work to ruin Pamela. The women analyse situations and people, sift words and actions and motives. A man like Mr. B. is too completely and youthfully masculine to be able, or greatly inclined, to analyse emotional events successfully. (In Lovelace we see a mind which approaches genius, the 'masculine' intelligence combined with 'feminine' perceptiveness.) Pamela, whatever her limitations (and they

---

[1] *Pamela*, i. 279–80.   [2] Ibid., pp. 42–3.   [3] Ibid., p. 44.

are considerable), has 'mother wit', the feminine sensitivity to what is going on beneath the surface, a talent which a person like Mrs. Jervis cultivates in her by her own womanly and instinctive shrewdness. Pamela is far from omniscient, especially about her own feelings, but she is always streets ahead of her lover in total knowledge of the situation. She is able to realize, finally, the situation of her own heart, and, when free, to make the intuitive decision to return to Mr. B. at the turning-point of the story. By coarsening and falsifying this trait into the gross and repugnant habit of calculation, the parodists in *Shamela* and *Anti-Pamela* were able to present the heroine as a caricature of self-interest. But, as a description of Pamela's nature, this is pretty wide of the mark. For one thing, it is not in the interest of a girl in Pamela's position really to fall in love with Mr. B., whatever propositions she might accept for mercenary reasons. Love is a liability to its possessor. Richardson's Pamela is not cold-blooded in her dealings with Mr. B. She is unaware of the force of femininity which is her weapon—the power not only of her youth and beauty but also of her very female cast of mind—because, like most women, she sees the masculine as the powerful. Eventually, it is the force of femininity which defeats Mr. B. or, alternatively, brings him to victory by making him acknowledge the softer side of his own nature, and allowing him, in the completion of happy marriage, to cast off some of the crude hobbledehoy and become civilized. It may be that many of the novel's critics have felt compelled to mock it from a masculine resentment at such a picture of female victory. One may easily feel that the battle of the sexes is here presented in a crude form, with the male, depicted as not over-intelligent, getting the worst of it. However, if Mr. B. is not an imposing representative of his sex, neither does Pamela represent all that is highest in feminine nature. She lacks, almost entirely, Clarissa's beauty of spirit, and the latter loses and suffers so terribly that no man is likely to feel affronted by her. Pamela is practical and bustling enough to be felt as a real threat. Richardson may have recognized how great a victory he had given to the female sex in *Pamela;* certainly in *Grandison* he endeavours to redress the balance by blatantly awarding first-class honours in all qualities, physical, mental and spiritual, to the male. It must be admitted that *Pamela* is a bit harsh, if vigorous, like a rather young wine from a good vineyard. In this novel, the battle of the sexes, which will be subsumed into a higher intellectual and spiritual struggle in *Clarissa*, is fought out almost wholly on the instinctual level. The atmosphere of the novel sustains the instincts.

The atmosphere of the novel is really Pamela's atmosphere; we see everything through her eyes. Richardson constantly uses her 'country style' letters to make us aware of the concrete and physical. Unlike his later heroines, she seldom strays into the abstract, and the world which she shows us is very sharply defined by the five senses. Never again was the author to appeal so much to taste, smell, and touch as well as to sight and hearing. If one pauses to consider the novel in terms of its imagery, something like the following list comes to mind: 'flannel', 'worsted', 'chicken', 'carp', 'elms', 'beans', 'sunflower', 'tiles', 'rose-bush', 'bull', 'grass', 'mould', 'cake', 'Burgundy', 'shoes'. This basic imagery of concrete objects counteracts the higher flights of passion or sensibility and brings us repeatedly back to earth.

One of the most important sets of images pertains to food. There is something definitely earthy, non-romantic indeed, about food, and both hero and heroine are fond of eating. Pamela may declare that in poverty she could 'live like a Bird in Winter upon Hips and Haws, and at other times upon Pig-nuts, and Potatoes, or Turneps'[1] (here the bathos of the second set of phrases is a comic balance to the high flight of her first figure of speech), but when she leaves the Bedfordshire estate she goes provisioned with 'some Plum-cakes, and Diet-bread, made for me over Night, and some Sweet-meats, and Six Bottles of *Canary* Wine'.[2] She eats some of this upon the road, and even in distress at the farm 'made shift to eat a little Bit of boil'd Chicken . . . and drank a Glass of my Sack'.[3] When Mr. B. arrives at the Lincolnshire estate to accomplish his fell purpose, a terrified Pamela listens to his arrival: 'And then I heard his Voice on the Stairs, as he was coming up to me. It was about his Supper; for he said, I shall chuse a boil'd Chicken, with Butter and Parsley.—And up he came!'[4] To

---

[1] *Pamela*, i. 104.   [2] Ibid., p. 133.
[3] Ibid., p. 138.   [4] Ibid., p. 248.

Pamela in her state of fear, these words bode disaster, but they are sure to spell comedy to the reader, and to Richardson. By this point in the novel the author has allowed the reader to appreciate the comic elements in his characters and their situation, at the same time that his sympathy responds to the heroine and to the emotional significance of events.

Mr. B. makes Pamela wait upon him at table, which upsets her (partly because of fright, partly through resentment at having to play the servant's role before him in this false situation), so that she spills some of his Burgundy. Mrs. Jewkes maliciously tells him that Pamela 'eats not so much as will keep Life and Soul together' and that she 'lives upon Love' for Mr. Williams.[1] But after the assault in the bedroom, when Mr. B. is touched by Pamela's distress, he takes an interest in her health, and is solicitous about her eating:

Now, said he, and took a Knife and Fork, and put a Wing upon my Plate, let me see you eat that. O Sir, said I, I have eat a whole Breast of a Chicken already, and cannot eat so much. But he said, I must eat it for his sake, and he would teach me to eat heartily: So I did eat it . . .[2]

Scenes involving eating together are scenes of reconciliation. Once Mr. B. and Pamela are engaged there are feasts with everybody—cake and Canary with Pamela's first guests,[3] a 'boiled Turkey' which Pamela dexterously carves at supper with Mr. B., his guests, and her delighted father.[4] Indeed, this part of the novel would seem to bear out Parson Williams's text 'The liberal Soul shall be made fat' in the most literal manner.[5] Goodman Andrews is packed off with cherry-brandy, cinnaman water, and cake.[6] On the eve of the wedding, Mr. B., observing Pamela's nervousness, urges her to eat: he 'put, now-and-then, a little Bit on my Plate, and guided it to my Mouth.'[7] Pamela records almost every bit and sup she takes on her wedding day: her morning chocolate; the post-nuptial 'Sack, and a Toast, and Nutmeg, and Sugar' which 'chear'd my Heart, I thought for an Hour, after';[8] the dinner with Mrs. Jewkes when she 'made shift to get down a Bit of Apple-pye, and a little Custard';[9] supper, with wine, 'he made me drink

[1] Ibid., p. 250.   [2] Ibid., p. 290.   [3] Ibid., ii. 60.
[4] Ibid., p. 78.   [5] Ibid., p. 102.   [6] Ibid., p. 115.
[7] Ibid., p. 127.   [8] Ibid., p. 146.   [9] Ibid., p. 150.

Two Glasses of Champaign, and afterwards a Glass of Sack'.[1]
It cannot be denied that John Kelly had some justification for
the notorious scene in *Pamela's Conduct in High Life* in which the
pregnant Pamela downs two bottles of Burgundy at a sitting:
'Mr. B. laughing said, well perform'd, my Girl, why thou art a
boon Companion; every Day brings to light some new Virtue
in thee.'[2]

Pamela is the sort of person to whom food and drink are
always of importance. Partly this is because of her background;
she comes from a class to whom the next meal is a subject of
concern, and even in her life as an upper servant dainty food
and the best wines would not have been an every-day affair.
This interest in food is partly an expression of her youth; she is
only sixteen, and children and adolescents usually, like Carroll's
Alice, take great interest in matters of eating and drinking.
It is also a question of constitution; in her natural condition,
when not depressed, she is full of bounce and animal spirits.
Clarissa, even when serene, has an ascetic streak which is not
native to Pamela. She and Mr. B. share a heartiness of disposition; they are both healthy young animals. One of the
pleasures of their marriage will be enjoying good food together.
His feeding her is a gesture quite common to lovers; he is the
sort of young man whose rather awkward new-found tenderness
seeks expression at a level other then the articulate. It is not an
action which one could associate with Clarissa and Lovelace,
even had they been happy, any more than with the courtly
Sir Charles and the elegant, witty Harriet. *Pamela*'s eating
scenes reinforce the lovers' physical and instinctive relationship.
There is nothing approaching this emphasis on food in the two
later novels, where relationships are more sophisticated.

Eating, with its emphasis upon the physical, has a connection
with sex which has often been exploited by suggestion. There
is, for example, the celebrated eating scene between Tom Jones
and Jenny Waters at the inn at Upton. There is a connection
between food and sexuality in *Pamela* in so far as the enjoyment
of eating in both hero and heroine suggests a capacity for
physical love. To some extent, the hints of healthy physicality
in Pamela's interest in food counteract the effect, of which so

---

[1] *Pamela*, p. 154.
[2] [John Kelly], *Pamela's Conduct in High Life*, 1741, p. 126.

many modern readers have complained, of Pamela's over-delicacy, her fears of sex even on her wedding-night, and so on. She is not over-delicate if resistance to being treated as an object is not over-delicate ('And pray, said I . . . how came I to be his Property?').[1] Pamela's fainting at Mr. B.'s rough advances is a non-twentieth-century kind of reaction, and suspicious criticism of her has already been voiced in Mr. B.'s complaint that she can faint at will.[2] It is an easily recognizable unconscious defence mechanism, but if that is her only defence, she is entitled to use it. Although nervous, she doesn't faint on her wedding-night, but displays a timidity considered at that time perfectly natural as well as proper. In Richardson's day, normal young ladies were supposed to be nervous and modest on their wedding-nights. Pamela, once assured that she is the object of love and not of mere lust, enjoys kissing Mr. B. and sitting on his knee. When physical love is a shared pleasure, and not just a male victory, the indications are that she will enjoy it. She is a fully developed and robust female, who has evdently eaten her meals to good purpose; when she makes her escape through the bars of the window, she admits with charming candour to 'sticking a little at my Shoulders and Hips'.[3]

There are a great many jokes about sex scattered throughout the novel, most, of course, at Pamela's expense.

I wish . . . I had thee as *quick another way*, as thou art in thy Re-partees![4]

If a Criminal won't plead . . . we *press* him to Death . . . And so now, Pamela, this is a Punishment shall certainly be yours . . .[5]

Mrs. Jewkes is always, in Pamela's opinion, too ready with coarse remarks, as when Pamela feigns interest in the progress of her beans, and her guardian 'turn'd upon me a most wicked Jest, unbecoming the Mouth of a Woman, about Planting, &c'.[6] Even after the engagement, there are jocular remarks, as when Mr. B. offering Andrews a suit tells Pamela not to come 'for you must not yet see how Men dress and undress them-selves'.[7] Jackey's insulting jest at the unpleasant dinner, at which he and Lady Davers taunt Pamela, directly links eating

---

[1] *Pamela*, i. 167.   [2] Ibid., p. 32.   [3] Ibid., p. 230.
[4] Ibid., p. 89.   [5] Ibid., p. 320.
[6] Ibid., p. 179.   [7] Ibid. ii. 98–9.

and sex: 'But may-be, Child, said he, thou likest the Rump: Shall I bring it thee!'[1] The married Pamela comes out of this encounter very well, and delicacy does not diminish her spirit. There is some truth in Lady Davers's angry remark at Pamela's confidence: 'The Wench could not talk thus, if she had not been her Master's Bed-fellow.'[2] Pamela's happy marriage, in all its aspects, has increased her assurance. She has joined the great freemasonry to which Sir Simon Darnford alludes when he hears she is married: 'Now you are become one of us, I shall be a little less scrupulous than I have been, I'll assure you.'[3] Even at the time of her besieged maidenhood, there is a certain practicality, even humour, in Pamela's view of her master's attempts on her. When, for instance, she is showing Mrs. Jervis the three bundles, she points to those possessions she rejects as the wages of sin and remarks: 'Now I come to the Presents of my dear virtuous Master: Hay! you know, *Closet* for that, Mrs. *Jervis*! She laugh'd, and said, I never saw such a comical Girl in my Life!'[4] Pamela is a 'comical Girl'. It would be impossible to imagine Clarissa making such a flippant summary of her situation as '*Closet* for that!'

The basic idea of sex which the novel upholds is fairly earthy —satisfaction leads to fertility. Mr. B., towards the end of the novel is full of hopes for a child: 'What a sweet Shape is here! It would make one regret to lose it: and yet, my beloved *Pamela*, I shall think nothing but that Loss wanting, to complete my Happiness';[5] and the old steward hopes for a young master's birth 'within this Twelvemonth'.[6] Mrs. Jewkes's remarks about the planting of beans were evidently not so wide of the mark.

Parts of the novel are quite literally earthy. Pamela spends much of her time grubbing in the mould. It has been seen that the story of the virtuous and lowly maiden had become associated with pastoral description, or an idealization of the life of the countryside. Richardson, in his version of the tale of the virtuous country girl, plays upon the pastoral conventions for comic effect. Had Pamela been the usual romantic heroine, we would have expected to see her, imprisoned in her country retreat, decking her hair with wild flowers and warbling

[1] *Pamela*, ii. 205.   [2] Ibid., p. 200.   [3] Ibid., p. 189.
[4] Ibid. i. 100.   [5] Ibid. ii. 186.   [6] Ibid., p. 314.

sadly to grove and stream. Instead, she is placed in a setting of prosaic kitchen-garden, paths, and outbuildings, and she puts her practical mind to work, devising little schemes for her correspondence with Williams: 'I said, Sir, I see Two Tiles upon that Parsly-Bed: Might not one cover them with Mould, with a Note between them, on Occasion?'[1] Pamela herself sees this contrivance as of desperate importance, and speaks of it with swelling rhetoric: 'I say no more, but commit this to the happy Tiles, into the Bosom of that Earth, where I hope my Deliverance will take Root . . .',[2] but her language only points up the trivial homeliness of her little device. There is a homely turn to all her stratagems, as when she gets the maid out of her way by asking her to order a 'sallad' and cucumber from the gardener, and then, when discovered near the sun-flower, covers her shock by explaining: 'I stoop'd to smell at the Sunflower, and a great nasty Worm ran into the Ground, that startled me; for I can't abide Worms. Said she, Sun-flowers don't smell. So I find, reply'd I.'[3]

The 'Sun-flower Correspondence'[4] is of importance to Pamela in keeping up her spirits (albeit her correspondent is a dolefully feeble assistant) and she says, with absurd enthusiasm, 'Of all the Flowers in the Garden, the Sun-flower, sure, is the loveliest!',[5] a remark with which Mr. B. will tease her later.[6] The sunflower is an emblem of hope and steadfastness, but here it is quite definitely a common garden sunflower, cheerful but not fragrant, nor very beautiful—a contrast to the lilies, roses, violets associated with the heroines of romance. It is not a languorous flower, and its sturdy brightness, with its suggestion of optimism, makes the sunflower a fitting emblem of Pamela herself. The sunflower belongs to the kitchen- or cottage-garden, not to the hothouse, and its presence reinforces the fact that Pamela is of truly lowly origin, and not a high-born lady in disguise.

The device of the 'Horse-beans' is a similarly unpoetic means of concealing her secret correspondence: 'this furnishes me with a good Excuse to look after my Garden another time; and if the Mould should look a little freshish, it won't be so much suspected. She mistrusted nothing of this; and I went

---

[1] Ibid i. 161. [2] Ibid., p. 166. [3] Ibid. pp. 170–1.
[4] Ibid., p. 190. [5] Ibid., p. 174. [6] Ibid., ii. 112.

and stuck in here and there my Beans, for about the Length of five Ells . . .'[1] Pamela is not a very good gardener, but we come to associate her with the soil. She hides her papers in the mould under a rosebush,[2] and the pretended gypsy, in the fortune-telling scene, rubs her hand with mould to draw her attention to a letter which she finds when she has 'pull'd up a good Handful of the Grass'.[3] The constant motif gives ironic justifica-tion to the metaphor in Lady Davers's sneer at her brother about 'the dirt you seem so fond of'.[4] We have been led to feel that the 'Dirt' which Pamela represents is good wholesome earth, at any rate.

Pamela's rural surroundings are very ordinary. We learn to know the garden, with its walks and ponds, and about the pasture beyond, which touches the common and leads to the private horseroad—the route along which Pamela maps her escape.[5] She is, for a heroine, an ignominious failure at escape attempts. Her first try is baulked by her fear of the bull, 'an ugly, grim, surly Creature, that hurt the poor Cook-maid',[6] when she thinks she sees him with 'fiery saucer Eyes',[7] and imagination multiplies bulls in the pasture until her spirit is quenched, even after she realizes that what she has seen are only 'two poor Cows, a grazing in distant Places, that my Fears had made all this Rout about'.[8] (She has been an indoor servant too long to have remained completely a country girl.) Her second attempt is baffled by the injuries she receives trying to climb a brick wall. Few heroines have been faced with such prosaic obstacles. The author does, especially in the 'bull' episode, point out Pamela's weakness in that she is to some extent her own prisoner, captured by her own hopes and fears (and Freudians have not been slow to point out connections between the bull and the masculine Mr. B.). But even when we have recognized the strength of Pamela's imagination, the environment is felt as substantial enough to be reckoned with. Few writers have done better at conveying the effects of ordinary objects on the nerves—or on the flesh; the bruises and scratches she receives in trying to climb the wall are unromantic but decidedly believable, and one is constantly impressed with

[1] *Pamela*, i. 175.   [2] Ibid., p. 231.   [3] Ibid., p. 306.
[4] Ibid. ii. 21.   [5] Ibid. i. 190.
[6] Ibid., p. 199.   [7] Ibid., p. 204.   [8] Ibid., p. 205.

the solid physical reality of Pamela herself and of the objects that surround her.

In the first part of the novel there are very few touches of the romantic pastoral, and they are used for special effect. One instance is the mock-pastoral gibe of Mr. B.: 'Then she may be turn'd loose to her evil Destiny, and echo to the Woods and Groves her piteous Lamentations for the Loss of her fantastical Innocence, which the romantick Idiot makes such a work about.'[1] His reference to the 'Woods and Groves' is intended to ridicule Pamela's defence of her chastity as exaggerated and unrealistic (thus anticipating many later critics of the heroine). But Pamela among her beans is quite a different heroine from the usual romantic variety. Another instance of the use of pastoral is found in the second escape scene, when Pamela sitting by the pond considers suicide. When she decides against committing the wicked deed, she exclaims 'Quit with Speed these perilous Banks, and fly from these curling Waters, that seem in their meaning Murmurs, this still Night, to reproach thy Rashness!'[2] These are the tones of the heroine of romance, but such language shows that Pamela's mind is wrought upon. An impression of her own danger, real enough and horrifying to her, leads her to take refuge in traditional hyperbole. She does as much for Mr. B. when she refers to his hunting accident as 'the Peril of perishing in deep Waters'.[3] Pamela's contemplation of suicide is realistically handled, especially when she thinks how sorry everyone will be 'when they see the dead Corpse of the unhappy *Pamela* dragg'd out to these dewy Banks, and lying breathless at their Feet'.[4] The reader sympathizes with her, but knows at the same time that her apostrophe is exaggerated; the 'curling Waters' are only a moderate-sized fishpond. The tone neatly descends to the prosaic again when Pamela limps away to seek shelter in 'the Corner of an Out-house', where she creeps 'behind a Pile of Fire-wood',[5] to be found, scolded, and ministered to with 'old Rum warm'd' and plaster.[6]

In *Pamela* one of Richardson's favourite devices, the use of the emblem, is first apparent, although emblems appear but sparingly compared to their varied and effective use in *Clarissa*. In *Pamela* the images keep, for the most part, to the solidly

---

[1] Ibid., p. 220.   [2] Ibid., p. 236.   [3] Ibid., p. 263.
[4] Ibid., p. 234.   [5] Ibid., p. 237.   [6] Ibid., p. 241.

literal; such images as that of the earth have a cumulative effect, but they are relatively little played upon, although there is a constant metaphorical suggestion. There is one major instance of an emblem used in a complex manner, and this is both unexpected and unobtrusive. The 'fishing scene', in which Mrs. Jewkes and Pamela angle for carp in the pond, has often been admired for its psychological impact:

> She baited the Hook, and I held it, and soon hooked a lovely Carp. Play it, play it, said she. I did, and brought it to the Bank. A sad Thought just then came into my Head; and I took it, and threw it in again; and O the Pleasure it seem'd to have, to flounce in, when at Liberty!—Why this? says she. O *Mrs. Jewkes*! said I, I was thinking this poor Carp was the unhappy *Pamela*. I was likening you and myself to my naughty Master. As *we* hooked and deceived the poor Carp, so was I betrayed by false Baits; and when you said, Play it, Play it, it went to my Heart, to think I should sport with the Destrucion of the poor Fish I had betray'd; and I could not but fling it in again: And did you not see the Joy with which the happy Carp flounc'd from us? O! said I, may some good merciful Body procure me my Liberty in the same manner; for, to be sure, I think my Danger equal![1]

The angling image is fairly old, and had several traditional meanings with which Richardson plays. For one thing, angling is supposed to be a sport calming to the mind, and Pamela's peace of mind is broken by the thoughts it suggests to her. Such a cruel activity, like Mr. B.'s cruelty, is a breach of natural harmony.

Angling is a pastime indulged in by her namesake, the heroine of Sidney's *Arcadia*: 'There would they sitte downe, & pretie wagers be made betweene *Pamela* and *Philoclea*, which could soonest beguile the silly fishes; while *Zelmane* protested that the fitte pray for them was the hartes of Princes.'[2] Zelmane's protest presents the erotic meaning of the angling theme, popular in seventeenth-century poetry, in which the fish are glad to be caught by a beautiful woman, and the best 'bait' is her own allure, which takes her hapless lover. The best

---

[1] *Pamela*, pp. 174–5.
[2] Sir Philip Sidney, *The Countesse of Pembrokes Arcadia*, 1590, in *The Prose Works of Sir Philip Sidney*, ed. Albert Feuillerat, 1965, vol. i. lib. i, ch. 15, p. 96.

known use of this theme is Donne's 'The Bait'. Richardson plays with this traditional conceit, reversing it, presenting it from the woman's point of view, in which man is the cruel angler who catches and plays with her. Pamela, innocent and unsuspecting, has already been 'betray'd' and made to suffer, so her personal use of the metaphor is immediate and credible.

The phrase 'betrayed by false Baits' has an ominous overtone. The devil as an angler, taking souls by false baits, is an image frequently found in religious literature:

> He baiteth a hooke for vs, and by the going downe of the line, he knoweth we are sped . . . as he findeth vs qualified, so he fiteth himselfe for vs . . . Therefore, euerie baite that he layeth for vs being our bane, let vs not come within the length of his line, or within the libertie of his nettes.[1]

> The deuill I warrant you as hee is perfect in this angling occupation, so hee knoweth how to handle a fish that hee hath hooked, that hee may not breake from him . . . Hee playeth with his Fish, as the child playeth with his bird . . .[2]

> Whilst . . . we smile to see, how easily you beguile these silly fishes, that you catch so fast with this false Bait, possibly we are not much less vnwary ourselves . . . For . . . as the Apostles were Fishers of men in a good sense, so their and our grand adversary is a skilful Fisher of men in a bad sense: And too often in his attempts, to cheat fond Mortals, meets with a success as great and easie, as you now find yours.[3]

Such associations with the angling image imply that for Pamela it is not merely Mr. B. but the devil, acting through human agents, who is sporting with her, trying to bring her to 'Destruction' not only of her worldly reputation but of her soul. The emblem quietly emphasizes the spiritual, as well as the erotic, nature of Pamela's hazardous situation.

[1] Samuel Gardiner, *A Booke of Angling, or Fishing*. Wherein is shewed, by conference with Scriptures, the agreement between the Fishermen, Fishes, Fishing of both natures, Temporall and Spirituall, 1606, pp. 42–3.

[2] Ibid., pp. 92–3.

[3] Robert Boyle, *Occasional Reflections upon Several Subjects*, 2nd ed, 1669, section iv, 'Which treats of Angling Improv'd to Spiritual Uses', discourse iv, 'Upon Fishing with a counterfeit Fly', p. 212. Pamela's use of an ordinary 'occasion' for a striking meditation resembles, to some degree, the manner of Boyle, but her application is original.

Pamela's identification of her own situation with that of the fish resembles the meditation of the fisher in an old poem:

> As I the silly fish deceive,
>   So Fortune plays with me;
> Whose baits my heart of joys bereave,
>   And angles taketh me.
> I still do fish, yet am I caught,
> And, taken, am their taking taught.[1]

But Pamela sees more than 'Fortune' playing with her; she resents Mr. B.'s sporting (in a manner which seems to her diabolical) with her freedom, making her an object of pursuit and possession. 'Liberty' is all her cry—the word appears twice in the passage quoted above. Shortly before, she has attempted to argue her case to Mrs. Jewkes, who holds that Mr. B. has a right to do as he pleases with her; indeed, her 'jaileress' takes this for granted:

> To rob him of yourself would be the worst that could happen to him, in his Opinion.
> And pray, said I . . . how came I to be his Property? What Right has he in me, but such as a Thief may plead to stolen Goods?—Why, was ever the like heard! says she.—This is downright Rebellion, I protest![2]

Pamela is a downright rebel—although the freedom she seeks is not political, but primarily personal and spiritual. Any political or social connotations of her case arise from her native Protestantism. It is Pamela's steadfast demand for freedom, despite the disabilities involved in being female, poor, and of low station, that makes her such a revolutionary heroine—and aroused the suspicion and hostility of some members of the Establishment. Once she possesses liberty, then she can make a free decision—and the decision will be one in which she gives and hazards all she has, knowing if she returns to Mr. B. of her free will and he again deceives her, none will pity or understand. After the 'fishing scene' however, the reader can already hope that her symbolic action in releasing the carp prophesies a similar relenting on the part of her captor. This emblem,

[1] Robert Jones, *The Muses Gardin for Delights*, 1610, in *English Madrigal Verse*, ed. E. H. Fellowes, 1920, p. 599. For this and the preceding two references, I am indebted to Dr. Jonquil Bevan.
[2] *Pamela*, i. 167–8.

which comes at the mid point of the volume and at the mid point of Pamela's trials, is used to present her state of mind, to illustrate (like an inset picture) the situation of the action so far, and to prepare us for its outcome. It is in keeping with the pastoral theme, and traditionally associated with a love-situation; yet it appears with meanings that make it quite original. It connects Pamela, with some subtlety, with a tradition of rural meditation that gives her situation, and her own 'wit', an elegant moral significance. The charming if naïve engraving by Hayman and Gravelot (an illustration to the second edition) perfectly conveys this effect (Plate 1).

Up to the point where the free action of both Mr. B. and Pamela is rewarded by an equal and mutual love, conventional pastoral imagery is deliberately avoided. It is after their engagement that touches of the true romantic pastoral appear. Mr. Williams is reconciled with his patron in the meadow 'that has a pleasant Foot-way, by the side of a little Brook, and a double row of Limes on each Side'.[1] In the same meadow, with its 'shady Walk', Pamela, Williams, and Mr. B. meet and exchange compliments.[2] The harmonious natural surroundings emphasize the happy mood of reconciliation.

The language of the novel changes at its half-way mark. Richardson strives for a more 'poetic' rendering of love and fulfilment. He deliberately invokes poetry; Pamela in the Darnfords' drawing room plays upon the spinet, and sings 'a song my dear good Lady . . . brought with her from *Bath*'.[3] The song is appropriate, as it speaks of love, but its traditional hyperbole

> No more I'd wish for Phoebus' Rays
> To gild the Object of my Sight[4]

is remote from the direct observations of the servant-girl. This is a far cry from Pamela's bold, plain version of Psalm 137.[5] We may feel that the blunt little Protestant voice has become too soft and ladylike, but Richardson is concerned to show, not only that Pamela is equal to the life of the drawing-room, but also that the love between Mr. B. and Pamela is truly romantic. Mr. B. has now ceased to be the lustful predator and has taken his proper role as the woman's suitor.

---

[1] Ibid. ii. 54–5.   [2] Ibid., p. 87.   [3] Ibid., p. 64.
[4] Ibid., p. 65.   [5] Ibid. i. 188–90.

The assumption of right roles, the 'natural' relationship between wooer and wooed (or won), is for Richardson the *sine qua non* of romantic love. Once his hero and heroine are placed in the correct relationship, the traditional language of love is appropriate. The language is heard most clearly in the 'Garden Scene' almost at the end of the novel. Walking in the garden of Mr. B.'s Bedfordshire estate, the couple are over-taken by 'a little Shower',[1] and take refuge in the Summer-house which was the setting of B.'s first lustful attempt. Here the reformed Mr. B. gives Pamela new evidence of his care for her, and his tenderness cancels all the former scene. The two walk through the garden again:

Don't you with Pleasure, my Dear, said he, take in the delightful Fragrance, that this sweet Shower has given to these Banks of Flowers? Your *Presence* is so inlivening to me, that I could almost fansy, that what we owe to the *Shower*, is owing to that: And all Nature, methinks, blooms around me, when I have my Pamela by my Side. You are a Poetess, my Dear; and I will give you a few Lines, that I made myself . . . And then, in a sweet and easy Accent, with his Arms about me as we walk'd, he sung me the following Verses . . .

I

ALL Nature blooms when you appear;
The Fields their richest Liv'ries wear;
Oaks, Elms, and Pines, blest with your View,
Shoot out fresh Greens, and bud anew;
    The varying Seasons you supply;
    And when you're gone, they fade and die.

. . . . .

III

The purple Violet, damask Rose,
Each, to delight your Senses, blows.
The Lilies ope', as you appear;
And all the Beauties of the Year
    Diffuse their Odours at your Feet,
    Who give to ev'ry Flow'r its Sweet.[2]

It is difficult not to be reminded of the customary 'cue for a song' in modern musical comedy or in eighteenth-century

---

[1] *Pamela*, ii. 352.   [2] Ibid., pp. 355–7.

ballad-opera. This is a ballad-opera scene, something from a musical pastoral like Phillips's *The Chamber-Maid*. The author is pulling out all the stops. Having denied us lilies and roses in the world of the struggling serving-maid, having almost mischievously kept us among beans and sunflowers, he brings in the customary pastoral references at the end; marriage, not the conflict of passion, is idyllic. The glimpse of glorified rural life, with its implications of natural beauty, peace, and love, provides a fitting ending to the story of a rustic heroine and (despite his rank) a rustic hero. The mock-pastoral comedy, unusual, amusing, sometimes grotesque, now shades into the traditional pastoral comedy, whose object, like that of the romances of Sidney and Shakespeare, is to pass beyond the 'scornful tickling' of laughter and provide delight.

Richardson is never again to rely upon the pastoral motif. He uses nature as a symbol of harmony and reconciliation in *Grandison,* but everything in the last novel is larger, more civilized, more abstract. There is nothing like the immediacy of Pamela's beans in the mould, or the delicate 'Fragrance, that this sweet Shower has given'. The continuous use of the natural images in *Pamela* prevents anything like the overwhelming claustrophobic effect that is one of the basic means of arousing horror in *Clarissa*. Pamela, even in durance, is out-of-doors much of the time; the terrors of struggle in a confined space are introduced, but only briefly on each occasion. Her prison is never as strait as Clarissa's.

The rhythm of constriction–expansion, which is the basic rhythm of all Richardson's novels, is firmly set in *Pamela*. 'But, Oh! my Prison is become my Palace', says Pamela on her wedding day,[1] using a set of metaphors later to figure in a more important and complex manner in *Clarissa*. Like her sister heroines in the later novels, Pamela is 'enlarged' at the end of the novel: 'God! as thou hast inlarg'd my Opportunities, inlarge also my Will.'[2] The last part of *Pamela I,* like the whole of the sequel, foreshadows *Grandison* rather than *Clarissa*. Pamela is enlarged into happiness. Like Harriet, she arrives joyfully to what her husband calls 'your own House',[3] and there is much description of rooms, furniture, and happy servants. There is no hint of the ironies which later surround the 'house' theme in

[1] Ibid., p. 151.   [2] Ibid., p. 170.   [3] Ibid., p. 304.

Clarissa. Like the other Richardson heroines, Pamela finally makes an appearance in bridal array, in 'white, flower'd with Gold most richly',[1] but her bridal resembles Harriet's, not Clarissa's, in signifying a change to wordly happiness. The emphasis in *Pamela* is upon transformation, from servant-girl to gentleman's wife, from home spun to satin. Richardson loves ritual, and each of the novels moves towards a ceremonial moment. There are two major occasions in Pamela's case: the wedding, and the arrival home. Pamela's wedding is a poor affair from the point of pomp and circumstance, and keeps us waiting for her final bursting from the chrysalis, when she vanquishes Lady Davers and returns in triumph to Bedford-shire with Mr. B. This scene is the parallel to that in which she left the house, bidding good-bye and sorrowfully driving off, waving her handkerchief.[2] Now those who bad her farewell when she was, apparently, a doleful outcast welcome her back as their mistress. The triumphant reversal is in keeping with the folk-tale tradition, like Griselda's joyful reunion with the marquis in the castle from which she has been cast out, when she is stripped of her rude array and dressed in cloth of gold. The touches of folk-tale within the novel consistently prepare the reader for the ending: the choice of the three bundles for instance,[3] or the proleptic farewell 'Providence will find you out'.[4]

The pathos that surrounds the figure of old Andrews, the father sorrowfully seeking his daughter, has a ballad-like quality (in the tradition upon which Dickens also drew in creating old Mr. Peggotty seeking Em'ly). We see him, at daybreak, sitting mournfully outside Mr. B.'s gate, glad to be allowed even to enter the stable.[5] His position, like that of Griselda's father, is redeemed; after he arrives, tired and miser-able, at the Lincolnshire manor, he is welcomed in to rejoice with Pamela and make merry with the company.[6] There is here a hint of the religious as well as the secular parable; the stable signifies the Christian humility of the Andrews's lowly condition and at last the humble and meek are exalted. Figures used in this manner are in danger of becoming totally absurd if asked to do any more in a realistic narrative, and

---

[1] *Pamela*, ii. 321.   [2] Ibid. i. 130–3.   [3] Ibid., pp. 99–103.
[4] Ibid., p. 130.   [5] Ibid., p. 123.   [6] Ibid. ii. 68–70.

Richardson shows great discretion in pushing the Andrews back into the wings again, as soon as their artistic purpose is achieved. (Pamela also shows considerable worldly wisdom in desiring that her parents should not live with herself and her husband.)

Pamela has not achieved her complete fulfilment until she has won a place in society and found security in her relationship with her husband. These two achievements are signified in two episodes in the last part of the novel: Pamela's battle with Lady Davers and her adjustment to the history of Mr. B. and Sally Godfrey. These episodes embody a different kind of comedy from that of the major conflict, and they differ from each other. The tone of the novel is modulated as Pamela is shown fulfilling the demands of her new position—while still remaining her recognizable self. A new comedy of manners emerges which requires variety in development, and the author experiments with new narrative technique.

The scene with Lady Davers is one of the most vividly dramatic in the whole story (as Garrick evidently felt when he wrote himself into this scene in Dance's dramatized version of the tale). In the novel, the battle of tempers is presented as a staged scene, with careful indication of actions and business, and a counterpoint of dialogue in which feminine temper and sheer bitchery are marvellously called into play.[1] Pamela in this scene is still the pert girl whose description of Mrs. Jewkes was so memorably peevish:

She is a broad, squat, pursy *fat Thing*, quite ugly . . . Her Nose is flat and crooked, and her Brows grow down over her Eyes; a dead, spiteful, grey, goggling Eye, to be sure she has. And her Face is flat and broad; and as to Colour, looks like as if it had been pickled a Month in Saltpetre . . . She sends me a Message just now, that I shall have my Shoes again, if I will accept of her Company to walk with me in the Garden.—To *waddle* with me, rather, thought I.[2]

In such remarks Pamela in her former position has vented her feelings as a child does, in resentful muttered spite against an adult whom it cannot manage. With Lady Davers, Pamela is still somewhat childlike, but to some extent she has now grown up, and she is trying to be the grown-up lady, toying with her fan (which she bites in a most unladylike manner)[3] and veiling

[1] Ibid., pp. 195–220.   [2] Ibid. i. 151.   [3] Ibid. ii. 205.

her malice in a thin mock-courtesy which was not her habit with Mrs. Jewkes. As the bride of Mr. B., she can be assured of a position which Lady Davers cannot totally threaten, and there-fore can afford to struggle for self-control. Her sense of superior-ity is to some extent assisted by Lady Davers's bad behaviour; Lady Davers, despite her more mature years, has not grown up either, and gives way to childish bad temper, as when she calls Mrs. Jewkes 'Fat-face'.[1] (One feels that Pamela herself finds a certain satisfaction in this remark—like a good child watching an inimical naughty child insult an unpopular nursemaid.)

The battle with Lady Davers is primarily a conflict with the outer world, and can be treated dramatically. The next struggle is an inner one, and is told in a different way. Instead of the briskness of stage comedy, we have a slower process of emotional reflection as Pamela comes to terms with part of her husband's past and its present results. In the Sally Godfrey sequence, Richardson uses the flashback, which he is to use much more skilfully in *Grandison*, where again a past history is made known to the heroine, arousing anxious jealousy. The Sally Godfrey section is but clumsily done, resembling the inset story so common in novels of the time. Richardson, here experimenting with a new technique, makes sure that his only inset tale is very directly related to his main characters and to the total theme. Sally's history provides a kind of compressed thematic subplot to Pamela's own story; this is what happened in the case of a girl who did *not* preserve her virtue when attemp-ted by Mr. B. Her fate is not an easy one, but she is not treated unsympathetically. There is a gilding of romance about her tale, and in the description of her departure a pathos unusual both in this kind of brief inset tale and in a story of a fallen woman; Mr. B. recollects 'looking at her, as long as I could see her, and she at me, with her Handkerchief at her Eyes; and then I gaz'd at the Ship, *till* and after I had landed, as long as I could discern the least Appearance of it . . .'[2] It was Lady Davers's spite which gave Pamela the first hint of this affair. Her curiosity, which is natural and characteristic (she admits it is 'a Curiosity that is not quite so pretty in me')[3] stems from a real anxiety to be loved by Mr. B., and the reader realizes that she has a capacity for jealousy.

[1] *Pamela*, ii. 203.   [2] Ibid., p. 343.   [3] Ibid., p. 294.

Pamela is still spirited, and highly emotional, and does not herself know how she will behave under pressure. However, in this first major trial within her marriage she comes up trumps, not by complaisant yielding through prudence as the conduct books suggest, nor by calculation, but by spontaneous emotional reaction. When she meets 'Miss Goodwin', Mr. B.'s illegitimate daughter by Sally Godfrey, she finds her an engaging child while she thinks she is only Mr. B.'s niece; when she finds the girl is his child, her heart warms to her, and she plans to keep the 'pretty Dear' at home.[1] This seems neither unnatural nor hypocritical in Pamela; she is the kind of young woman who would be fond of children. The atmosphere of the neat 'Farm-house, noted for a fine Dairy',[2] where she meets the children, who have come to breakfast on 'delicate Cream, and Bread and Butter',[3] and look at the bee-hives in the garden, recalls the wholesome country environment of Pamela herself, and the healthy world of fresh air, growing things, and good food. Pamela's best impulses spring from her sound instincts. The child herself is the fruit of instinct unregulated, but still essentially good. There is not the to-do made about poor Sally and her child that one finds about similar situations in Victorian novels—Sally is not reduced to the misery of Little Em'ly, nor do the wretched mother and child have to die, as in Mrs. Gaskell's *Ruth*.

Mr. B. is attached to his own child, as he is attached to everything that is his. He has inherited a strong family feeling; to a simple person like himself, the basic blood ties would be extremely important. Pamela has a similar feeling for the sanctity of the family; they both enjoy belonging to a large coherent group. Here, as in *Grandison*, the greatest compliment that can be given to the outsider is a welcome into the unit, and the sign of the generous heart is its perfecting and widening of family ties. Pamela's previous loyalty to the B. family is rewarded by her being made mistress of the household, but the spirit of her membership is ever the same—duty, allegiance, affection. The emphasis upon the strength of family ties at the beginning and end of the novel cannot be ignored; it balances the spirit of rebellion against an unjust hierarchy which is present but can

[1] Ibid., pp. 332–4.   [2] Ibid., p. 329.
[3] Ibid., p. 331.

be over-stressed. In *Clarissa,* unlike the other two novels, the life of one type of family is shown to be hideous, and we are given a situation in which the familiar pieties cannot apply.

Pamela, who shares Mr. B.'s basic beliefs, is obviously a happy choice of wife. He admits, with disarming candour, that no woman from his own class would have suited him so well; a modern fine lady, badly brought up, cannot bear 'to be opposed in her Will'.[1] If Richardson is more prosaic, in allowing this to be said, than other authors who deal with the romance of misalliance, he is also more honest. The man who marries a woman of such a low rank must prefer a wife trained to obedience, and admiration of himself. Mr. B., to give him his due, does not think about Pamela's low station; he lives up to his great remark 'let us talk of nothing henceforth but Equality'.[2] It is her personality, both sprightly and docile, that attracts him. It is second nature to Pamela to try to please him—she truly admires him more than any other woman could do. Mr. B. can enjoy being generous to someone who tries to please, but finds it extremely difficult to make any first step at conciliation. Thus, his letter begging Pamela to return is, for him, a momentous step. At this point, he achieves a victory over his own temperamental pride and later, in asking Pamela to be his wife, conquers family and social pride (and his fear of being mocked). It should not be forgotten that Mr. B.'s eventual virtue is rewarded, as well as Pamela's consistent rectitude. He is never reformed into a total humility, which would be out of keeping with his character, and goes into his married life with a fair share of pride, arrogance, and quick temper. These qualities he admires, and, if he likes docility, he does not wish it exaggerated, even in a wife—submissiveness has to be spiced with a dash of the spirit that he admires in his own family, even in hot-tempered 'Captain Bab', his sister. Pamela provides the right mixture; Mr. B. is rewarded with a wife who suits him famously. The marriage is not presented as an impossible idyll, as its excellence is mingled with human frailty, and, while admiring, the reader may also smile at the comic aspects of the married lovers.

Part of the novel's artistry is its mixture of stability and turbulence. We go from stability (Pamela as servant in Lady

[1] *Pamela,* ii. 284.   [2] Ibid., p. 152.

B.'s household) through rebellion and struggle (Pamela fighting off Mr. B.) to a new-found and more complete state of harmony. Tranquility is the desideratum, but these rural lovers reach it through, not in spite of, their passions. The uncomplicated structure and 'artless' style of the country lass are suited to a story of relatively uncomplicated emotional drives. It is a story with a happy ending, and we are invited to laugh both with and at the characters. The comic pastoral has succeeded in commanding the reader's serious attention and involvement. The homely rusticity of style and setting focuses our attention on the sturdy little heroine, who is unrefined, earthy, and vitally important. Richardson refuses to bow to convention in a magic-wand revelation of the heroine's high birth, as his predecessors did and many of his successors were to do. Pamela is 'low', and her humble rank is as real as the kitchen-garden, or the dirt in which she plants the beans. In a play like *Silvia*, a minor figure, a clodhopping countryman, may be a humorous character. Richardson allows Pamela to be simultaneously a humorous character and a heroine.

The novel's strength lies in its comedy, because the reader cannot pretend that the heroine is other than she is, and yet must be involved in her destiny; it is proved on his pulses that her soul is as important as that of a princess. This comic pastoral is a vital statement of Christian equality. Reading the novel, one experiences the fact that lowliness—not aesthetically languorous or saintly humility but downright, practical, even comical lowliness—is worth regard. Richardson's pastoral comedy is not a convention, but a fusion of traditional elements in an unconventional manner; the result is a highly original artistic creation.

If the meaning of this comic pastoral is the dignity of the individual, it is also the dignity of the emotions and instincts. The uncomplicated emotional drives, when found in conjunction with goodwill, provide most of the joy of life. We remember the story as an account of a basic emotional moment —that of falling in love. The best-remembered and most often quoted passage from *Pamela* is justly that in which Pamela recognizes her own emotion:

O credulous, fluttering, throbbing Mischief! that art so ready to believe what thou wishest: And I charge thee to keep better Guard than thou hast lately done, and lead me not to follow too implicitly thy flattering and desirable Impulses. Thus foolishly dialogued I with my Heart; and yet, all the time, this Heart is *Pamela*.[1]

This heart is Pamela. She is governed by emotion and instinct, both in refusing to be Mr. B.'s property, and in acting upon her love for him. Both hero and heroine are their hearts, and fortunately for them, in each case the heart is right. They are both natural, in the good and not the pejorative sense. Nature in *Pamela* does not wear the ugly aspect we see in *Clarissa*. Love is part of a natural cycle which, in either its plainer forms (earth and sunflowers) or its prettier aspects (a garden after rain) is beautiful and beneficent—a recurrent vision of comedy. Pamela proclaims her allegiance to instinct in her honest admission to Mr. B.: 'I said, I had the less Merit in this my Return, because I was driven by an irresistible Impulse to it, and could not help it if I would.'[2]

It was Mr. B.'s instinct (as simple lust) that caused all the commotion, but his desire for Pamela as a mate was not amiss. Both arrive at happiness through force of instinct. Love is an 'irresistible Impulse'. It may need control, but basically its promptings are to be heeded. Pamela and Mr. B., in their pastoral comedy, are Richardson's simplest exponents of love as 'a natural Passion'.

[1] *Pamela*, ii. 12–13.   [2] Ibid., p. 39.

IV

Pamela Continued: Or, The Sequel that Failed

> Unhappy *Belvile*! What a Wife!: Protect her!
> No doubt he'd often have a Curtain-Lecture:
> Besides, a Girl, so ever-fond of Grace,
> . Might be devout in an improper Place;
> And pour forth Sermons from her fervent Mind,
> When the poor Man's quite otherwise inclin'd.[1]

THE immense popular success of *Pamela* is well known. The novel aroused great enthusiasm, but also excited almost equally great condemnation. The substance of adverse criticism of the novel has remained much the same over the centuries. The pious Charles Povey complained that the 'edifying' novel was really lubricious:

> These Scenes are Paradoxes to me, to be printed and called Virtue rewarded. Good God! Can amourous Embraces delineated in these Images, tend to inculcate Religion in the Minds of Youth, when the Blood is hot, and runs quick in every Vein? . . . Can a Man, expressing licentious Speeches in Converse with a Maid not yet deflower'd, reform the Age, or inspire Ideas in the Mind worthy of Example?[2]

The best adverse criticism emerged in parody, and the best parody remains a literary entertainment. Fielding's *Shamela*

---

[1] James Dance, *Pamela*. A Comedy, 1742, 'Epilogue', p. 2, ll. 12–17.

[2] Charles Povey, *The Virgin in Eden: or, The State of Innocency*, 1741, p. 69. Povey's own tale follows his maxim that 'sedate Reflections, secluded from every Temptation, direct the running Springs of unruly Youths' (p. 70). The allegorical fable bears no resemblance to a novel. Prince, scholar, and virgin journey to Abraham's House, where they are addressed by three tempters, 'The Duke of Worldly Honour', 'The Marquis of Masquerades', and 'The Countess of Sensual Pleasure', whom they easily defy. The medieval flavour and visionary touches make the book uncommon for its period.

(1742) is still often mentioned as if it were the last word on *Pamela*. Like the author of the now forgotten anonymous *Anti-Pamela: or, Feign'd Innocence Detected* (1742),[1] with its heroine Syrena Tricksy, Fielding shows that the behaviour of the 'virtuous' maiden is cunning policy. Fielding denounced *Pamela* as an affront to literature and to morality, and no doubt he was sincere in thinking this was what he found objectionable. Fielding's book is quick and witty. There are points at which he cleverly hits off aspects of *Pamela*: his heroine also is interested in food and drink, 'Mrs. Jewkes and I supped together upon a hot buttered apple-pie',[2] and writes to the moment, 'Well, he is in bed between us, we both shamming a sleep.'[3]

However, the book as a whole is not a true parody; it depends for effect not on exaggeration but on contradiction. Shamela is not a country girl, but a towny, daughter of an Irish female who is no better than she should be. She is not in the least in love with Mr. Booby, whom she holds in great contempt, and she is most definitely *not* a virgin. Fielding did not dare to make the seduction of an innocent girl, even if her innocence were only technical, the subject of satiric laughter. He takes seduction and rape seriously enough to want to avoid the issue—but that *is* the issue of *Pamela*. The parody would be more effectively directed against its target if Fielding had made Shamela an over-wise virgin, bent on marriage with her master, and drawing him in without his realizing her cleverness. Yet, if that were the case, Mr. B.'s attempts at force would still be repellent enough to make the reader sympathize with the heroine, which Fielding is anxious to avoid—and if the girl, however scheming, were admitted to be in love with her master, some degree of sympathy would certainly be evoked. Fielding is determined that the pretentious servant-girl should appear mean and vile. The low style can veil only a base heart.

It is certainly not just to see Fielding here opposing Pamela's prudery by championing sexual freedom. He uses Shamela's scheming and unabashed licentiousness to make her despicable, and to indicate how totally unsuited to a good marriage such

---

[1] Probably by Mrs. Haywood.

[2] Henry Fielding's *Joseph Andrews and Shamela*, ed. Martin C. Battestin, 1965, p. 323. References to Fielding's novels other than *Shamela* will be taken from the Shakespeare Head edition of his works.

[3] Ibid., p. 313.

a woman is. In a curious way, Fielding unconsciously upholds something of the *droit de seigneur*. In his novels, good-natured girls of the lowest classes (easily recognizable as such by their crude and common speech)[1] may, in the Maritornes tradition, offer kind relief to their superiors of the opposite sex (Betty the chambermaid in *Joseph Andrews*, Molly Segrim in *Tom Jones*). Such kindness is in them a natural and venial slip, as long as they ask little or nothing in return, and don't intrude where they don't belong. If they seem to make demands, they should be sent packing, which Mr. Booby was too foolish to understand. Girls of this rough, low type (to which Pamela, whose speech bewrayeth her at every turn, obviously belongs) should not insist too much on chastity; if they do, they cannot really mean it, as it is unnatural to their position in life—*argal*, a girl like Pamela is probably a hypocritical whore. Girls of the middle class (Nightingale's Nancy) should remain chaste, and virginity is a *sine qua non* for a marriageable girl of Sophia Western's rank. Eligible gentlemen may sow wild oats, but eligible young ladies certainly should not. Any low-class girl who insists upon similar consideration encroaches upon a prerogative of her superiors, and challenges the established dual (or triple) morality.

The most disturbing part of *Shamela* is the end, where Fielding explains quite clearly and seriously that *Pamela* is pernicious for the following reasons.

First, There are many lascivious images in it, very improper to be laid before the youth of either sex.

2dly, Young gentlemen are here taught, that to marry their mother's chambermaids, and to indulge the passion of lust, at the expense of reason and common sense, is an act of religion, virtue, and honour; and, indeed, the surest road to happiness.

3dly, All chambermaids are strictly enjoined to look out after their masters; they are taught to use little arts to that purpose; and lastly, are countenanced in impertinence to their superiors, and in betraying the secrets of families . . .

5thly, In Parson Williams, who is represented as a faultless character, we see a busy fellow, intermeddling with the private

---

[1] Fanny in *Joseph Andrews* may be considered an exception, but she is a symbolic figure rather than a character, speaks the most perfect English, and is really middle-class.

affairs of his patron, whom he is very ungratefully forward to expose and condemn on every occasion.[1]

Fielding here gives himself away—one realizes that the author belongs to the upper class, and Richardson's novel has aroused a fear of upstarts meddling with their betters. Even the ordained of the Church should know their place, as well as servant-girls. This is certainly not his own point of view in *Joseph Andrews*. In *Pamela*, the worldliness of some professed servants of God is pointed out. Mr. Peters, the clergyman, contemptuously refuses to assist Pamela, and his callous denial of Christian principles for the sake of his own place in the hierarchy provides one of the novel's more pointed social criticisms. Pamela realizes that she must fight alone, as almost all the powers not only of the state but of the Church are against her. Only the poor curate, Williams, offers his inadequate aid—and he is dismissed for his pains. As in *Joseph Andrews*, the poor help the poor, and the rich hold by their own. It is distressing to see Fielding, who is capable of such admirable satiric criticism of the same things, expressing so baldly in *Shamela* the views of the upper classes. Yet even in Fielding's great novels, the virtuous poor know their place, and require justice, not equality. He tends to treat the low and poorly educated (Partridge, Anderson) as figures of amiable fun. A girl like Molly must be comically lascivious, and her troubles cannot be treated very seriously.

What really bothered Fielding about *Pamela* was that it was subversive. It overthrew classical literary decorum in making a low, ungrammatical female its heroine; it overthrew social barriers in presenting a misalliance as not only possible but in given circumstances desirable. It even questioned the multiple standards of sexual morals. *Shamela* shows what a revolutionary book *Pamela* could seem. Richardson's novel affronted the old Etonian in Fielding, and he registered the reaction of the Establishment.

As well as providing material for criticism and parody, Richardson's story also inspired close imitation. Several writers eagerly cashed in on the popularity of the novel by opting the story of its characters for versions or continua- of their own. It is doubtful if the severest of his critics

---

[1] Fielding, *Shamela*, p. 338.

aroused Richardson's anger as much as such perverse flatterers. No novelist would view with equanimity the prospect of hacks bungling with the situation and characters he had created. Richardson bitterly and publicly complains of 'some Imitators, who supposing the story of PAMELA a Fiction, have murder'd that excellent Lady, and mistaken and misrepresented other (suppos'd imaginary) CHARACTERS'.[1]

These imitators, the authors of *Pamela's Conduct in High Life* (1741), *Pamela in High Life: or, Virtue Rewarded* (1741), and *The Life of Pamela* (1742), etc., did Richardson a double injury, in intentionally capitalizing on his popularity, and in un-intentionally forcing him to write his own continuation of *Pamela*. It is easy to see that he felt his own sequel was the only method of baulking the 'Imitators' and bringing the 'murder'd' Pamela back to her proper existence. Financially, too, there were excellent reasons for re-channelling the public's eager expenditure on *Pamela* tales back to Salisbury Court and away from Grub Street.

In many ways the best (and thus perhaps the most annoying) of Richardson's imitators was John Kelly, now identified as the author of *Pamela's Conduct in High Life*. Admirers of Richardson may find an unexpected charm in this book; it is of critical interest, as it shows what a contemporary felt to be the most saliently 'Richardsonian' characteristics. Kelly adopts Pamela's rambling style, and brisk down-to-earth expression, sometimes so well that a sentence could certainly pass for the original heroine's: '*Jackey* gaped with his Mouth open, just as I have seen a Country Fellow at a Puppet-shew.'[2] The central characters are pious, and discourse upon such topics as the sublime mode of the Psalms, and the ill behaviour of persons of fashion in church.

Kelly likes all the circumstances of 'High Life'. Part of the fun of his book is the tone of pleased excitement with which his characters enjoy their wealth—there is something about it which is reminiscent of *The Young Visiters*. Mr. B. [sic] provides two coaches for a party of four so that nobody has to sit backwards.[3] In nothing has Kelly followed his master more faithfully than in exhibiting his characters' lively interest in meat

---

[1] *Pamela*, iv. 'Advertisement', p. 457.
[2] [Kelly], *Pamela's Conduct in High Life*, pp. 213–14.　　　　[3] Ibid., p. 33.

and drink, as is seen in the description of a picnic breakfast for the coach-party:

Sir, answer'd *Abraham*, I have cold Chickens, cold Ham, and Neats Tongue, and I can promise your Honour a Glass of good Champaign and excellent Rhenish . . . I hope, Gentlemen and Ladies, I shall content you, and gain your good Word. Saying this, he brought a small Hamper out of the Boot of *Blunt*'s Coach, spread about a Dozen Sheets of Whited-Brown Paper, gave every one of us a sheet for a Napkin, with a Slice off a large Loaf for a Plate, *&c.* desired we would sit down, and he would set Breakfast on the Table . . . The Air had given us all Stomachs; we made a very good Meal, and were very merry.[1]

Kelly's imitation was a more formidable challenge to Richardson than he cared to admit. *Pamela's Conduct in High Life* is lively enough, with some passable conversation. It has not unsupported pretensions to being educative and edifying. The characters are, up to a point, recognizable as those we have met in Pamela. There is, however, one major defect—there is no plot. This defect is, unfortunately, shared by Richardson's own sequel.

Richardson's continuation of *Pamela* is the only one of his novels that he did not really wish to write. He had nothing especially new to say about Pamela; rather, there were things which he wanted to gainsay. Some impressions about *Pamela*'s immorality or 'levelling' tendencies must be erased or softened. However, as well as desiring to fend off criticism, he felt the necessity of not falsifying the point of the original work as his imitators and admirers were doing. It is striking how often, at that point and later, new versions of Pamela's story give the heroine an upper-class or aristocratic birth. As the obverse of Fielding's opinion that a girl of Pamela's style must be 'low' in every respect, those who held the heroine in esteem felt that a virtuous girl of such sensibility must have a high origin.

Kelly allows Pamela' high birth, as Richardson refused to do. She and her parents discover aristocratic relations in another Andrews family which came in with William the Conqueror. Her father's revelation of her true origin to his daughter is productive of unconscious humour: 'I fear'd the Knowledge of being deriv'd from two such ancient and unblemish'd Families

---

[1] [Kelly], *Pamela's Conduct in High Life*, p. 107.

as that of *Andrews*, and that of *Jinks*, might make her vain . . .'[1]
Kelly's instinct was the same as Goldoni's, when, in his *Pamela
Nubile* (1750), he makes Pamela's father a Scots nobleman and
former follower of the Pretender, who has sought safety in
obscurity and an incognitio. Goldoni, however, has to make
Andrews reveal all to Mr. B. before the marriage; as the
dramatist explains, the Italian nobility would never accept a
misalliance even in fiction, but in England a gentleman would
not lose all social position in marrying a servant.[2]

Even in England the idea did not win total acceptance, and
Richardson determined not to allow the public, misled by the
imitators, to mistake the point. He wanted to show that the
country flower could adorn the conservatory without being of
conservatory stock. The virtuous Christian soul is at home
anywhere, in high life or low life, and the only true gentilesse
is that which cometh from God alone.

Richardson had a case to prove, but no story. At the outset
he was driven by the necessity to negate, rather than a desire to
create. The lack of artistic excitement in *Pamela II* is painfully
evident to the reader from the first few pages. It disproves
Johnson's dictum that if you read Richardson for the story you
would hang yourself; we do read Richardson for the story, and
without one, without some well-conceived plot working through
conflict and suspense to resolution, he cannot write.

The lack of a story to tell is an almost insuperable barrier to
success, but Richardson was even more handicapped by his
new self-consciousness and uneasy awareness of the first novel's
critics. He also had the monumental difficulty of remodelling
characters already firmly moulded. If characters are to reappear
in a sequel, they should be originally designed as expandable,
which is not the case with the characters of *Pamela*. The first
story is closed, a complete unit. There is only one major and
complete character, and we know all about her. A character so
completely known could regain our close attention only by
precipitation into some new and interesting scene of conflict.
For a brief period, well on in the continuation, Richardson
provides a new suspense, but it occurs in an episode merely,
and cannot make taut the whole.

The technique of *Pamela I*, the one-line narration through

---

[1] Ibid., p. 121.　　[2] Carlo Goldoni, *Mémoires*, Paris, 2 vols. 1787, ii. 63–8.

letters describing the moment-by-moment feelings of a main character, also imposed severe limitations. The story and manner of the first novel were brilliantly in harmony, but the method allows the development of only one character. Richardson in *Pamela II* begins to experiment with methods of narration, using the flashback, and some variety in correspondents.

Richardson discovers the value of multiple narration only slowly; he begins to use it to some purpose in the Countess episode. However, one of the most noticeable differences between this novel and its predecessor is the number of characters with speaking parts (to use a dramatic analogy). The correspondents include not only the inevitable Pamela, Mr. B., the Andrews parents, and Lady Davers, but also Sir Simon Darnford, Polly Darnford, Jackey H., the Countess, and Sally Godfrey. The best of the new correspondents is the lively Polly Darnford, who saucily describes her life at home with her irascible father and peevish sister, and the progress of Mr. Murray's courtship first of herself and then of her sister. This is the first time that Richardson uses a true subplot (the story of Sally Godfrey in *Pamela I* is a past episode). Polly is Richardson's first portrait of the lively lady, the complement of a more sober heroine. The resemblance between Polly and Charlotte Grandison, the witty woman of a later novel, is most striking; indeed, they have the same married name: Lady *G.* The girl's relationship with her heavy father and spiteful sister, and the atmosphere of bourgeois life gone somewhat sour, anticipate the beginning of *Clarissa*, but Polly is more like Anna Howe than Clarissa.

The Darnfords are cruder than the Howes or the Harlowes. Sir Simon, like Mrs. Jewkes and Colbrand in the first novel, is a Richardsonian grotesque, with 'his dismounted Spectacles, his arch Mouth, and Gums of shining Jet'.[1] Although Sir Simon is intended principally as an *exemplum*, an awful warning of what Mr. B. might have become had he not mended his ways, he refuses to fulfil merely that doleful function, and becomes rather attractive. Richardson cannot help liking him. Sir Simon defines his own role:

I beseech you, Mr. *B*'s *Pamela*, stick me into some Posy among your finer Flowers—and if you won't put me into your Bosom, let

[1] *Pamela*, iii. 137.

me stand in some gay Flower-pot in your Chimney-Corner: I may
serve for Shew, if not for Smell. Or, let me be the Bass in your
Musick, or permit my humourous Humdrum to serve as a pardon-
able kind of Discord to set off your own Harmony.[1]

The occasional discord in the Darnford household may be
noisier than that at the Harlowes', but Polly and her father
achieve their own harmony. Even if he does fling Rabelais's
Pantagruel at his daughter's head, Sir Simon is a much more
manageable father than the respectable Mr. Harlowe. His
basically friendly relationship with his daughter is well suggested
in such light and naturalistic touches as her remark: 'My
Papa's Observation, that a Woman never takes a Journey, that
she don't forget something, is justify'd by me; for, with all my
Care, I have forgot my Diamond Buckle . . .'[2] The Darnford
scenes are somewhat crude, but they have their own energy
and humour. Unfortunately, Richardson was not at this point
capable of keeping all his characters wound up and going at the
same time; the end of Polly's story, her marriage, is rather
summarily dealt with, and Sir Simon sinks from view in the
last volume.

The Darnfords supply a refreshing vulgarity amid the awful
heavy gentility. Richardson, bedevilled by critics who saw
pernicious social views in *Pamela*, seems over-eager to placate
the higher classes and assert the *status quo*. Pamela, who radiates
a good influence on all around her is, despite her birth, as
'genteel' as anybody—which is not saying much, as Richardson's
notions of gentility were still largely guesswork. He is now
concerned to show that although virtue may be found in the
lowly cot, hearts just as pure and fair may beat in Hanover
Square. He had obviously begun to fear that the original Mr.
B. was too boisterous a gentlemen, and Pamela's husband
explains himself and his previous actions. In a long section in
which he recounts his own feelings during the attempted
seduction of Pamela, Mr. B. covers himself with moral white-
wash.[3] He says that even when he was concealed clad in his
dressing-gown, in Mrs. Jervis's closet, he had 'no such Intentions as they feared'.[4] Mr. B.'s narrative is not only long and
dull (one suspects the author has no new material, and is

---

[1] Ibid., p. 141.   [2] Ibid. iv. 55.
[3] Ibid. iii. 185–212.   [4] Ibid., p. 210.

reduced to retracing old ground) but also disagreeable. Who is this oily conscientious fellow? He is not our Mr. B.

Any other villainies among the higher classes are likewise palliated. Mr. Peters is rehabilitated. Pamela's former justified angry contempt for this atrocious cleric is now changed into a rather greasy sympathy: 'But when I came to know Mr. *Peters*, I had a high Opinion of his Worthiness; and as no one can be perfect in this Life, thus I thought to myself: How hard was then my Lot, to be a Cause of Stumbling to so worthy a Heart!'[1] She readily finds excuses for his former behaviour. Richardson, like Pamela, is determined to prove that he has 'Honour for the Clergy of all Degrees' and will not take it upon himself to censure the profession, which is 'too generally the Indication of an uncharitable, and perhaps a profligate Heart'.[2] This is all very well, but one feels the author is too bent on assuring the world and its powers and principalities that it is safe from any attack of his. Fresh from his first taste of criticism, and oversensitive, Richardson was too afraid of accusations of being a leveller—a timidity which he evidently conquered by the time he wrote *Clarissa*.

It is equally obvious that he was upset by the accusations (and implications drawn by parodists) that *Pamela* is lascivious. In the sequel he endeavours to avoid 'warm scenes', and this care hampers him, as he writes best on subjects of sexual tension. He manages the episode of Jackey's attentions to the servant Polly Barlow without the kind of detail one finds in *Pamela*, but the whole episode is slight and uninteresting, and the intentions (a contrast to Pamela's former conduct) too obtrusive. The group of inset stories in the penultimate letter of the novels provides material for about four novels.[3]

Despite such lapses into old-fashioned dull narration it should be remarked that in some ways Richardson has progressed in the art of narration since the first part of *Pamela*. In *Pamela II* he develops the manner of polite comedy in prose fiction. There are longer and more sustained conversations, which look forward to conversation scenes in *Grandison*. Pamela is not here, as in the first novel, always the central speaker. There is more variety in style of speech, and of tone (not

---

[1] *Pamela*, iii. 157.   [2] Ibid., p. 159.   [3] Ibid. iv. 402–36.

always perfectly controlled); contrast for example the edifying after-supper discussion among the gentle company[1] with the pert quarrel scene between Nancy and Polly Darnford,[2] or the quizzing at the masquerade.[3]

What Richardson is attempting—or seems to have discovered *en route* that he might attempt—is a picture of civilized life, which begins with the family, and radiates its influence outwards to society at large. In the best kind of family, and the best kind of society, both variety and harmony are possible, and different personalities can develop most fully by acting within the atmosphere of a refined and sensitive community. This was an aspect of Richardson's work which most strongly attracted Rousseau. In *Pamela II* the picture is but ill drawn, but the author was discovering, though slowly and ploddingly, new possibilities.

Marriage is the theme of *Grandison*, and in that novel there is a pattern of marriages, as there begins to be in *Pamela II*. The marriage pattern is not clear and coherent as it is in the later novel; one feels that Richardson found it happening rather than planned it from the beginning. This is typical of the novel as a whole—creative ideas are stumbled upon, and not completely dealt with. The author seems perturbed by the difference between 'nature' which establishes the basis of *Pamela*, where all is direct, and the idea of civilization. How far is refined but morally sound social life a function of nature and the passions? Richardson seems to be hovering on the brink of utterance about the relationship between nature and civilization, but does not utter fully. Whenever he appears to make a considered statement on the subject, his answer is on the side of nature. A promising image is used near the beginning of the sequel, when Pamela is spoken of as 'a fine Flower' which has been 'transplanted from the Field to the Garden'.[4] He seems to be trying to make Pamela and her perfect family group a picture of the art that nature makes, but it would be too much to say that this picture emerges with clarity. Yet it is suggested that 'high life', the 'Garden', is a reflection of nature no less than the 'Field'. Marriage, at its best the most civilized individual and social bond, arises from nature, and the best conduct

---

[1] Ibid. iii. 169–76.   [2] Ibid., pp. 336–40.
[3] Ibid. iv. 95–9.   [4] Ibid. iii. 167.

results from the passions, educated and rightly directed, but not condemned.

The education sections which conclude the novel fit in with this theme, but are not the stuff of which novels are made. If one is to debate in a novel such questions as whether a child should be struck in anger, the problem should be actively presented with a believable child misbehaving. After Rousseau, this sort of question is extensively treated in works of fiction, but it was Richardson who gave Rousseau the hint—that a novel could be used 'philosophically' to present the ideal life of nature, and to deal with theoretical topics such as education. Richardson provides an interesting mid point between Locke and Rousseau. He has a more optimistic view of the child than the old school which sees the child as a combination of vile passions, who must be forced by discipline towards righteousness. At times Richardson gives passion more allowance than Locke does. He is not purely a rationalist: 'May I, Sir, venture to say, That we should not insist upon it, that the Child should so nicely distinguish away its little *innate* Passions, as if we expected it to be born a Philosopher?'[1] Many natural elements in the child's make-up lend themselves to the formation of civilized values: affection, love of praise, curiosity, animal spirits. Each child is an individual, and the parent must observe 'their little Ways and Tempers, and how Nature delights to work in different Minds'.[2] Grace, both spiritual and secular, is built on the foundation of nature. Education works with the passions (that is, with nature) to an end which nature itself desires. The topic is not without possibilities, but Richardson's treatment is largely stodgy and unimaginative.[3]

Since Richardson felt that nature and the cultivated life are closely related, he could not resort to simple satire on the polite

[1] *Pamela*, iv. 308.
[2] Ibid., p. 300.
[3] The worst part of the educational sections is probably Pamela's description of the tales 'of good Boys, and of naughty Boys', with which she entertains her children (iv. 436–42). These are bald and unconvincing narratives, stark morality without any dress of delightful fiction. Probably no child since the beginning of the world has ever been truly edified by such priggish little tales, which appeal to the child's own self-conceit—although such stories have long had a nursery ambiance. The story of naughty children is particularly *mal à propos* as far as poetic justice goes. Why should a naughty girl, whose sin is sloth, die by breaking her arm? Is not this a fate which could overtake the industriously active?

world. He could not, for instance, take the course which Warburton and Pope thought he ought to have taken:

Mr. Pope and I, talking over your work when the two last volumes came out, agreed, that one excellent subject of Pamela's Letters in high life would have been, to have passed her judgment, on first stepping into it, on every thing she saw there, just as simple nature (and no one ever touched nature to the quick, as it were, more certainly and more surely than you) dictated. The effect would have been this, that it would have produced, by good management, a most excellent and useful satire on all the follies and extravagancies of high life; which, to one of Pamela's low station and good sense, would have appeared as absurd and unaccountable as European polite vices and customs to an Indian. You easily conceive the effect this must have added to the entertainment of the book; and for the use, that is incontestable. And what could be more natural than this in Pamela, going into a new world, where every thing sensibly strikes a stranger?[1]

There is some satiric intention in the novel. Richardson does deal with aspects of polite life which he sees as artificial, as opposed to the truly natural—the opera, for instance (a common object of attack) or the falsity and vice of masquerades. But he was not going to make Pamela into the likeness of a Persian or Indian visitor, asking *faux naïf* questions about dress, the Court, and hours of dinner. Her 'nature' includes a ready adaptation to the ways of polite life, and she is too shrewd about virtue and vice, wherever they manifest themselves, to make simplistic exclamations. The field flower has been transplanted to the garden, but not to some foreign planet. The garden is not in itself despicable. As he worked on the novel, Richardson seems to have discovered his own belief in the civilized life as the life of nature at its best. The satiric approach was not sympathetic to an author almost obsessed by seeing things from within, and not from the satirist's without. When there is a true moral conflict, his own heroine must be involved, and react with her passions, her heart, her own 'simple nature', not with detached observation.

Unfortunately, since he could not take the direct line of satire, Richardson lacks a basic frame of reference such as he

[1] *Literary Anecdotes of the Eighteenth Century*, ed. John Nichols, 9 vols., 1812–13, letter of Warburton to Richardson, 28 Dec. 1742, v. 582–3.

had had in the fable of *Pamela*. Unlike all his other novels, this
has no coherent image-pattern, no major motifs to sustain mood
and atmosphere. The metaphor of field and garden refers back
to the rustic heroine of the mould and sunflowers, and indicates
that this hardy and comparatively 'wild' nature will be shown
developing in a more graceful but no less 'natural' milieu. Had
the writer been more deeply sure of what he was saying,
the images would have suggested themselves more powerfully.
The floral–horticultural theme is not quite abandoned, but
this theme generally emerges in strained metaphors.[1] When
Richardson is completely sure of a theme, powerful images
present themselves as in *Pamela* and to an even greater extent
in *Clarissa*. Here he is only half certain, discovering what he
wants to say in saying it.

While searching for coherent themes and images, he makes
some useful discoveries. It is in this novel that he first uses the
device of reference to stage-dramas, a device to be brilliantly
employed in *Clarissa*. Pamela on her first visits to the theatre
sets down, at great length, her impression of a tragedy, Am-
brose Phillips's *The Distress'd Mother*, and a comedy, Steele's
The Tender Husband, after seeing them performed. The method
of dramatic reference is clumsy and uncertain; Pamela produces
two long and tedious essays which could be printed separately,
as, for instance, 'A Young Countrywoman's Considerations
upon Two Acting Plays'. There is more than a smack of the
Spectator about them. In *Clarissa* the author will be able to make
a brief dramatic reference as part of the texture of the novel, but
the remarks in *Pamela II* are too extended to be part of the novel
proper; they are decorative (at least in intent) and not purely
functional.

Yet the references to the plays have a functional significance
and a relation to the story as a whole. The discussion of *The
Tender Husband* seems primarily intended as a censure of the
immorality of even the best stage-comedy, but the play has
some relation to Pamela's forthcoming difficulties, as it deals
with marital discord and threatened divorce. Biddy Tipkin's
fantastic airs are a contrast to the good sense of the 'real' and
realistic young women like Pamela and Polly. The reference to
Phillips's version of Racine's *Andromache* ambitiously heralds

[1] e.g. *Pamela*, iv. 349–50.

the major complication of Richardson's novel. Pamela criticizes the treatment of the passion of love in most dramas: 'How
unnatural in some, how inflaming in others, are the Descriptions
of it!'[1] Yet she is begging the question—she cannot truly say
that exaggerated passion is unnatural, in the sense of being
unrealistic; she means that such passion is morally wrong, a
perversion of what love is in its ideal (which is its true) nature.
Pamela is here a kind of Neoplatonist, suggesting that the
artist should exhibit essential nature and not accidental
deviations, no matter how common.

> Then, Madam, the Love of *Hermione* for *Pyrrhus*, is not, I think of
> that delicate Sort which ought to be set before our Sex for an
> Example.—'Tis Rage, not Love, that of a Woman slighted; and,
> however just, supposing our Sex to have such revengeful Hearts,
> when slighted by the Man they love, is not so exemplary as one would
> wish . . .[2]

Pamela is not entirely out of sympathy with Hermione, and
quotes a passage (in which that heroine asks whether Pyrrhus,
about to marry Andromache, showed any remorse) with
approval, as 'charmingly natural'.[3] Mrs. Oldfield's Andromache
wins her sympathy, and she quotes at length the speech beginning

> But Heav'n forbid, that you should ever know
> A *Mother*'s Sorrow for an only Son,
> Her Joy! her Bliss! her last surviving Comfort!

describing it as 'sweetly moving, nobly pathetick'.[4]

Richardson's use of the dramatic reference is audacious, as he
intends the comparison between the play's scenes and his own
to be drawn. He will treat of passion in a more realistic manner,
and Pamela's wounded love, when she is a woman slighted,
becomes not rage, but exemplary generosity. Yet, ironically,
Pamela is to find the miseries of jealousy, and its temptations,
more real than she had considered in viewing the play. When
Mr. B. becomes entangled with the Countess, Pamela will feel
some of the jealous passion of Hermione, and, like Andromache,
is to become a 'Distress'd Mother' fighting to keep her only
son. The scene between Andromache and Hermione which so

---

[1] Ibid., p. 58.   [2] Ibid., p. 65.
[3] Ibid., p. 74.   [4] Ibid., p. 69.

moved Pamela will be reflected in the scene between Pamela and the Countess.[1] Andromache's speech about Astyanax,

> Let me go hide him in a desart Isle.
> You may rely upon my tender Care
> To keep him far from Perils of Ambition;
> All he can learn of me, will be to weep.[2]

will have its counterpart in Pamela's fears that her son may be taken from her:

> Tear not from me my dearest Baby, the Pledge, the beloved Pledge, of our happier Affections, and the dear Remembrance of what I once was! . . . let me watch over his Steps, and where-ever *he* goes, let *me* go; I shall value no Dangers nor Risques; the most distant Clime shall be native to me, where-ever my Billy is . . .[3]

In describing the affair with the Countess, Richardson is dealing with the subject that most interests him—the natural passion. The passions that motivate characters in high drama are real, but are presented in an artificial 'unnatural' manner. Richardson is laying claim to rival the dramatists in attention to 'Nature, Probability, and Morality'[4] as he presents the passions working themselves out in ordinary life. Yet, like the dramatists he is fascinated by the conflict of passions, and the individual's choice of conduct under stress.

The first part of the book seems to be a picture of the perfect marriage, resembling 'the Happiness of the First Pair before the Fall'.[5] This paradisial state, as so often happens, rapidly becomes boring to the reader. However, a serpent eventually enters this Eden. Pamela is faced with unexpected emotional events, both within and outside herself, and a free choice of conduct in a new, and painfully maturing, situation. Marriage does not put a stop to the development of the personality. Various well-meaning legislators had assumed that it could do so, especially for the partner most handicapped by assumed inferiority. Some of the general precepts regarding marriage are as inauthentic and artificial in their fashion as the acting plays are in another.

Part of Richardson's growing intention, even in the first part of the novel, seems to have been to examine the precepts

---

[1] *Pamela*, iv. 161–7.   [2] Ibid., p. 69.   [3] Ibid., pp. 176–7.
[4] Ibid., p. 86.   [5] Ibid. iii. 331.

regarding matrimony current in his time, and to debate them. The prevailing points of view on marriage could be called, by political analogy, 'Tory' and 'Whig'. One sees marriage as an absolute monarchy with the husband at the head; the other regards it as a balance of mutual responsibility, in which the monarch-husband rules only under law. The political analogy suggested itself to writers on matrimony, who employ such terms as 'Prerogative', 'Passive Obedience', and 'Liberty'. The Revd. John Sprint, a high-flyer in matters matrimonial, preached the wife's absolute obedience to her husband:

> *He shall rule over thee*: Wherein is implied, not only Subjection to him, in obeying his Commands, but it reacheth farther to the bringing under unto him the very Desires of the Heart to be regulated by him so far, that it should not be lawful for her to will or desire what she her self liked, but only what her Husband should approve and allow . . .[1]

Women who call their husbands by their Christian names and do not give them, literally, 'the Title of Lord and Master' are bent on usurping the male authority.[2] In this respect, Richardson, and Pamela, who never leaves off calling Mr. B. her master, are matrimonial royalists.

The answering pamphlet, 'By a Lady of Quality' (identified as Lady Mary Chudleigh), is something of a feminist squib. The author is a Whig on the subject of matrimony, and ingeniously compares Sprint's doctrine with that of 'Passive Obedience and Non-resistance'.[3] Her argument is for (near) equality:

> I own 'tis true that Woman was made for the Comfort and Benefit of Man: but I think it a much nobler Comfort to have a Companion, a Person in whom a Man can confide, to whom he can communicate his very Soul . . . than to have a Slave sitting at his Footstool, and trembling at every word that comes like Thunder and Lightning from the mouth of the domestic *Pharaoh*.[4]

The lady makes mincemeat of the divine's demand that the wife shall regulate 'the Desires of her Heart' to her husband's

[1] John Sprint, *The Bride-Womans Counsellor. Being a Sermon Preach'd at a Wedding, May the 11th*, 1699 at Sherbourn, *in* Dorsetshire, 1700 ed., p. 6.   [2] Ibid., p. 13.
[3] [Lady Mary Chudleigh], *The Female Advocate; or, a Plea for the just Liberty of the Tender Sex, and particularly of Married Women*. Being Reflections on a late Rude and Disengenuous Discourse, Delivered by Mr. John Sprint, 1700, p. 6.
[4] Ibid., p. 20.

will, so that she cannot even wish things were otherwise: 'This is a Tyranny, I think, that extends farther than the most absolute Monarchs in the World.'[1] One of her best thrusts is the reminder that the words of the marriage service, 'with my Body I thee worship' could never be applied to a slave,[2] and she ends with an assertion on behalf of womankind: 'There is indeed a very strong Inclination in us for the preservation of those things call'd Reason, and the Liberty of Rational Creatures . . .'[3]

The female characters in *Pamela* are much interested in discussion of the matrimonial relationship. Polly Darnford complains that husbands and fathers are alike dictatorial, and after marriage a girl is 'as much a Slave to an Husband, as she was a Vassal to her Father'.[4] Lady Davers comments that Pamela's husband will expect that she should 'never expostulate against his lordly Will, even when in the wrong, till thou hast obeyed it',[5] although she admits Mr. B. is not too bad as husbands go:

> Thou hast a sensible and a generous Heart to work upon; one who takes no Glory in the blind Submission of a Slave; but, like a true *British* Monarch, delights to reign in a free, rather than in an abject Mind. Yet is he jealous as a Tyrant of his Prerogative: But you have found the way to lay that watchful Dragon asleep . . .[6]

The dragon of Prerogative does awake from time to time, giving Pamela uneasy moments. She is distressed to find that 'Husbands have a Dispensing Power over their Wives, which Kings are not allowed over the Laws'[7] when Mr. B. refuses to allow her to perform what she feels a God-given duty and nurse her child.[8] Yet, unlike Sprint's ideal wife, she is allowed to engage in 'a smart Debate with Mr. B.',[9] and, when Pamela finally obeys her husband in this matter, the reader is meant to feel that this obedience is meritorious.

Richardson also feels that women are capable of education, and that it is 'Policy more than Justice' which keeps them

---

[1] [Chudleigh], *The Female Advocate*, p. 28.
[2] Ibid., p. 36.   [3] Ibid., pp. 48–9.   [4] *Pamela*, iii. 78.
[5] Ibid., p. 100.   [6] Ibid., p. 103.   [7] Ibid., p. 390.
[8] This duty had been stressed by Jeremy Taylor; see *The Great Exemplar*, 1649, Discourse 1, 'Of nursing Children in imitation of the Blessed Virgin-Mother', pp. 33–9.   [9] *Pamela*, iii. 390.

uninstructed; men may have no advantages in 'Nature or Genius'.[1] Mr. B. tutors Pamela in languages and general reading, just as Swift's young new-married lady is supposed to undertake a brisk course of instruction to make up for the intellectual laxity of her girlhood. Both Swift and Richardson's heroine speak glowingly of the educational opportunity afforded to a woman by the conversation of a polite and learned gentleman.[2] Although Richardson and Swift are alike in believing that a married woman should cultivate the 'durable Qualities' of mind, Pamela cites Swift's *Letter to a Young Lady* as an example of that '*unmanly* Contempt, with which a certain celebrated Genius treats our Sex in general'.[3] Certainly, Swift's tone is that of one addressing an inferior, and perhaps more important, he leaves contemptuously out of account the emotional basis of marriage. Richardson and Swift may both see marriage as a potential feast of reason, but the latter stops well short of the flow of soul. Swift condemns Love, 'that ridiculous Passion which hath no Being, but in Play-Books and Romances'.[4] For Richardson, love is the essential passion, and to treat it as ridiculous and negligible, or to deal with marriage as if it were solely a question of certain quasi-political arrangements, is to deny nature more dangerously than the 'Play-Books and Romances'. There is a kind of boldness in any professed moralist of his period setting forth the view that the best marriage is based on this 'ridiculous' passion. He endeavours to combine the elements of dry good sense (as seen in the conduct books for women, of which Swift's is one) and the traditional stuff of romance.

This combination is more difficult than it seems, especially as the author is dealing with life in the married state, not a courtship which fades off into the 'happy-ever-after'. If love is truly the basis of marriage, some of the generally accepted precepts become unsatisfactory. Neither will it be sufficient merely to debate about 'Prerogative' and 'Liberty' when a tense emotional situation arises.

---

[1] Ibid. iv. 365.
[2] Compare *Pamela*, iv. 364 with Jonathan Swift, *A Letter to a Young Lady on her Marriage*, 1727, in *The Prose Works of Jonathan Swift*, ed. Herbert Davis, ix. 91.
[3] *Pamela*, iv. 367.
[4] Swift, *A Letter to a Young Lady on Her Marriage*, p. 89.

The complexity of the marriage theme may have struck Richardson himself only gradually. It is doubtful if he had planned Mr. B.'s relationship with the Countess from the beginning of the book. It seems more likely that he had started out with the idea that Pamela would be harassed by the attentions of an unwanted admirer—hence the incident of the verses which Pamela discovers under her pew at church.[1] This incident seems to promise further developments which never take place; the author apparently abandoned the episode as unpromising. The virtuous married Pamela could give no encouragement to a rake, and for Mr. B. to become jealous over an impossibility would make him a monster. To introduce a marital complication, Richardson seems to have decided to put the shoe on the other foot—to let us see Pamela's jealousy of Mr. B.'s suspected entanglement with another lady. The advantages of this over the previous scheme are numerous: it allows the use of suspense as to the relationship (a kind of suspense which could not have existed had Pamela been the object of a male flirt), it has a shock effect in letting us see a virtuous woman suddenly feeling alienated from her husband, and it takes Mr. B.'s reputation as a rake out of mothballs. The situation also allows the author to deal in an original manner with one of the commonest subjects of conduct books.

Once he has a theme of sexual tension, Richardson is in a fair way to prosper. The scenes in this section (the only part of the novel one could conscientiously recommend to the general reader) are more spirited, more dramatic. Both descriptions of the masquerade scene have a good deal of wit, even if of a clumsy variety, and we are allowed to see the scene from both angles: first from Pamela's uneasy, unverified suspicion, and later from Mr. B.'s half-guilty, half-proud knowledge of how far he is letting himself go. Mr. B. emerges again as a credible, if not very creditable, character, as he indulges in heavy flirtation, partly restrained by honour and prudence, but unwilling to let the bait slip:

> But I fansy thy Wife is either a *Widow*, or a *Quaker*?
> Neither, reply'd I, taking, by Equivocation, her question literally.

---

[1] *Pamela*, iii. 230.

And art thou not a marry'd Wretch? Answer me quickly!—
We are observ'd.

No—said I.

Swear to me, thou art not—

By St. *Ignatius* then: For, my Dear, I was no *Wretch*, you know.[1]

Although she is but slightly sketched, the Countess is not an incredible picture of the woman who, not bad but bored, enjoys playing with fire. There is a certain solidity in the settings in which she appears which helps to make her believable, as when, after Mr. B. has embraced her, she rings for her maid: 'And it is plain, she was not so angry as she pretended; for her Woman coming, she was calmer: *Nelthorpe*, said she, fetch my Snuff-box, with the Lavender in it.'[2] So much of the *Pamela* sequel, in contrast to the first book, lacks anything concrete in objects or setting that the snuff-box seems a welcome, even vivid, stroke of realism.

The atmosphere surrounding Mr. B. and the Countess is touched with elegant ennui; Richardson has not done badly in suggesting a life in which flirtation is a diversion, entered into *pour passer le temps*. The scene in which Mr. B., the connoisseur, compares the beauties of Pamela and the Countess for the latter's benefit has a particularly good setting:

She and I were alone in the Bow-window of her Library, which commands a fine View over *Windsor* Forest, but which view we could not enjoy; for it rain'd, and blew a Hurricane almost, which detain'd us within, altho' we were ready dress'd to go abroad.

I began a Subject, which never fails to make the worst of Weather agreeable to a fine Lady; that of praising her Beauty . . .[3]

Such scenes may serve the purpose prescribed by Warburton and Pope, of depicting the 'follies and extravagancies of high life', but that is not their primary intent. The danger is not mere folly, but the perilous reality of natural temptation which artifice encourages. Mr. B.'s primary temptation is his egotism. His persistent callousness to both ladies during the flirtation is heartless, and his complacency at getting out of a corner and reinstating himself with his wife is repellent. To Pamela, nothing of the situation is 'absurd and unaccountable'; it seems

---

[1] Ibid. iv. 209.   [2] Ibid., p. 214.   [3] Ibid., p. 222.

all too likely that Mr. B. is attracted to a handsome young woman. Pamela is not detached, and it is her feelings which count.

Because of the conflict with her own feelings, and because of the dual perspective on the situation (Mr. B.'s and Pamela's), this is one of the few points where the novel's texture becomes satisfactorily thickened. We know that Pamela, during her uneasiness, tries to keep her feelings from her husband: 'I did not think I could, especially in this Point, this most *affecting* Point, be such an Hypocrite. It has cost me—Your Ladyship knows not what it has cost me! to be able to assume that Character!'[1] Yet according to her husband's later account, her melancholy at this time was getting on his nerves, and effecting the reverse of what she wished:

> For myself, what can I say? Only that you gave me great Disgusts (without Cause, as I thought) by your unwonted Reception of me: Ever in Tears and Grief; the Countess ever chearful and lively: And apprehending, that your Temper was intirely changing, I believ'd I had no bad Excuse to endeavour to make myself easy and chearful abroad, since my Home became more irksome to me, than ever I believ'd it could be.[2]

This glimpse of emotional cross-purposes commands the reader's interest, and leads the way to the brilliant use of varying points of view in *Clarissa.*

Pamela valiantly does her best to follow the rules of right conduct for wives in such a case, by being patient and kind, not mentioning to her husband the cause of her distress, and being discreet about it to others, 'drawing a kind Veil over his Faults, and extenuating those I could not hide'.[3] Such behaviour accords with received maxims regarding the best course for the wife on suspecting her husband's adultery:

> Remember, That next to the danger of *committing* the Fault your self, the greatest is that of *seeing* it in your *Husband* . . . To expostulate in these Cases, looketh like declaring War, and preparing for Reprisals . . . Be assur'd that in these Cases your *Discretion* and *Silence* will be the most *prevailing Reproof;* and an *affected Ignorance,* which is seldom a *Vertue,* is a great one here: and when your *Husband*

---

[1] *Pamela,* iv. 144.   [2] Ibid., p. 231.   [3] Ibid., p. 147.

seeth how unwilling you are to be uneasie, there is no stronger
Argument to perswade him not to be unjust to you.[1]

Pamela endeavours to exercise obedience and compliance;
she has to see her husband go off on parties of pleasure which
include the other woman without seeming anxious, and she is
forced to entertain the countess in her own home. The scene
in which the Countess and her sister come to call is well done,
with effective contrast between superficial politeness and under-
lying uneasiness and jealousy on both sides. Pamela's unspoken
thoughts reveal some of her old malicious, even vulgar, self:
'You have a charming little Master, I am told Madam; but
no Wonder, from such a Pair! O dear Heart, thought I, i'n't
it so!'[2] Pamela's pride in her own innocence does not seem
priggish here; rather it seems an attempt to reassure herself
before a formidable antagonist to whom, she fears, all is already
lost. Her feelings about her baby are natural, as is her impulse
to use him as a psychological weapon, to show the Countess
that Mr. B. is tied to his wife: '*Polly*, bid Nurse bring *my Billy*
down—*My*, said I, with an Emphasis.'[3]

Her love for the child and her maternal pride in her womanly
achievement, become fused with her jealousy. Her unhappiness,
as she watches the Countess fondle the child, is too believable
for us to criticize harshly the feelings she so candidly sets before
us: 'I wonder'd the dear Baby was so quiet; tho', indeed, he is
generally so: But *he* might surely, if but by Sympathy, have
complained for his poor Mama, tho' she durst not for herself.'[4]
The more she fears her husband is lost to her, the more she sees
the baby as an extension of herself, and her excessive devotion
to the child continues to alienate her husband. The path of
apparent obedience is leading into danger.

Obedience has its limits. When she hears that her husband
and the Countess are to set up house together, Pamela is ready,
after one last try, to throw in her hand. She cannot acquiesce
beyond a point. Both piety and nature rebel. She has been
truly married, to the man she regarded as her best friend; after
the reality she has known, she cannot put up with a sham. The
hollow form of her married status has no appeal—even separation

---

[1] George Savile, Lord Halifax, *The Lady's New-years Gift: or, Advice to a Daughter*,
3rd ed., 1685, pp. 35–7.
[2] *Pamela*, iv. 162.   [3] Ibid.   [4] Ibid., p. 164.

would be preferable. When she fears that the 'polygamy' scheme is to be carried out, she abandons her policy of silence in a burst of grief-stricken candour. She is by this time in a nervous state, as can be seen in the feverish care with which she prepares for her 'Trial'.

> Here is the Bar, at which I am to take my Trial, pointing to the Backs of Three Chairs, which I had placed in a join'd Row, leaving just Room to go by on each Side—You must give me, Sir, all my own Way; this is the first, and perhaps the last Time, that I shall desire it.[1]

Mr. B., unaware of the suppressed emotion his cruelty has caused, fears that her wits are disordered. The disorder (which as Pamela insists pertains to the heart, not the head) has been there all the while; in following the policy of prudent silence, she has contradicted her own nature. The activity of communication is a relief, and her little stage-set represents a hold on reality—an appeal to the abstract idea of justice through the foolish semblance created by the backs of chairs. She is also trying to establish a formal mode of communication; acting the roles assigned in the trial will paradoxically enable them both to be honest.

The trial is an image which refers us back to *Pamela I* where Pamela in captivity felt herself to be on trial before an unjust judge. There as here the word is used in its double sense: prosecution for an offence, and testing or putting to proof. Pamela now puts herself on trial; really, as they both know, it is Mr. B. who has committed the major offence, but it is the testing of them both. At this moment of truth, Pamela comes out well; there is real generosity in her offer to go quietly away, leaving the Countess in full possession, because, if all is as she fears and Mr. B. is tired of her, she has lost everything. Like all of Richardson's heroines, Pamela is at her best when defying the world. All the maxims of prudence are against her; according to them, and to general opinion, she ought to keep tight hold on her new-found status, and her marital position, preserving her good name and worldly advantage by treating her husband with aloof courtesy whenever he condescended to leave his mistress and visit her, and clutching her allowance,

---

[1] *Pamela*, iv. 184.

her carriage, and her diamonds. If she left Mr. B. she would create a scandal of which she would be the victim. A divorced woman, or one separated from her husband, was (unless of supremely high rank, or a member of what has been called 'Café Society') a social outcast. Mr. B. would still be accepted; his wife would have lost all claim to notice, and would be blamed, not pitied. Pamela possesses courage.

Pamela's courage stems from the fact that she prefers freedom —with whatever painful consequences—to mere convention, and nothing less than the truth can make her free. In this sequence she is consistent with her character as heroine in *Pamela I*, the girl who makes the daring rather than the safe decision when she is free to make a choice. Richardson acknowledges prudence as a virtue, and all his heroines possess it, but for each of them something else matters more than mere worldly prudence. The laws of God and of conscience are not necessarily congruent with the maxims of society. Pamela's Protestantism is here shown in her refusal to shelter behind safe custom. Her disregard for safety is highly moral, but it is not orthodox.

The ending of the episode is a happy one for Pamela, but it is only when she forsakes her policy of silence and speaks from the heart that her victory is possible. Victory comes through contravening the laws of conduct books, and acting from passion and nature. Even the best of the conduct books have a cool and bloodless tone in dealing with such a marital situation; the authors drily weigh up disadvantages and advantages. They suppose a relationship in which detachment is possible. Halifax suggests that the husband's guilt can be turned to the wife's material advantage: 'Besides, it will naturally make him more *yielding* in other things: and whether it be to *cover* or *redeem* his offence, you may have the good Effect of it whilst it lasteth . . .'[1] Such advice seems designed for the arranged marriage, or match of convenience, rather than for the union based on love. It reduces the husband to an erring fool, a manageable source of money, jewels, concessions, and the wife to a calculating hypocrite who sees in an emotional situation an opportunity for practical gain. Even the more pious Allestree, counselling unlimited patience on the part of

[1] Halifax, *Advice to a Daughter*, p. 37.

the wife, 'a patient Submission being the one Catholicon in all distresses',[1] and advising that 'A Wise Dissimulation, or very calm notice is sure the likeliest means of reclaming [*sic*],'[2] assumes a distance between the pair that makes pretence feasible, and ignores the harmful effect dissembling might have on the wife.

Richardson is more 'romantic' in insisting that the relationship is one of love, and can be maintained only by real communication. Practical calculation, even well-intentioned dissimulation, can kill both friendship and love in marriage. It is typical of Richardson that as soon as he examines a situation closely he begins to query abstract theoretical statement. The individual soul and the individual situation carry their own authority. No particular situation allows moral licence, but the individual works out his moral salvation according to religious principle which can transcend custom, or general rules of self-interest. The conduct books deal with situations in a generalized way, whereas particular situations have their own nature, and actions and reactions are rarely as straightforward as the books imply. Mr. B.'s infidelity is partly a device to attract his wife's attention; when she pretends to notice nothing, she is thwarting his subconscious desire. It is appropriate that he starts to stray at the time of the birth of his first child, when Pamela's attention is absorbed first in her pregnancy, then in the new joys of the nursery. Subsequently, her concealed misery and hostility make her a poor companion, and drive him to other company. Her husband is almost as relieved as Pamela when the situation is aired, and most happy at realizing afresh how much she does love him. His ego requires constant bolstering, which is one of the reasons for his flirtation with the attractive Countess. Mr. B. wants his wife to express her feeling, not to act as a pattern of rigidly 'correct' conduct. The jealous shrew is detestable, but the icily complaisant wife is almost equally repellent.

Richardson has to some extent taken the feminist side in showing, not explicitly but dramatically, a husband who is inferior to the wife. In treating marriage as friendship, not as a mere matter of contract and custom, he has spoken for the equality of personality, and declared himself a Whig in matters

[1] Allestree, *The Ladies Calling*, p. 183.   [2] Ibid., p. 184.

of matrimony. Rather, indeed, he transcends such a defined position in pointing out that marriage cannot be treated merely in terms of bargaining, or of matrimonial politics.

The novel seems, especially at the beginning, a bland sop to the Establishment; yet when Richardson comes to circumstances of emotional stress, and his creative interest is aroused, he treats the situation in an unorthodox manner. His main attack is not upon the superficial follies of society—the 'vile masquerades'—but upon artificial standards of behaviour, however they manifest themselves, when they threaten the reality of 'nature'. The trivial and false appearances of the masquerade are dangerous, but so is the mask of prudent hypocrisy that Pamela tries to assume. Her conventionally 'good' but false reaction helps to encourage all three—herself, her husband, the Countess—to become false selves. The playbooks are wrong, or misleading, in encouraging a superficial allegiance to an exaggerated idea of passion, but the dramatists are also right in dealing with passion's intensity. The decorous conduct books are right in principle, but not in application; they tend to deny passion altogether. Pamela's response is 'simple nature', but not as Warburton meant; the artifice she vanquishes is not only that of frivolity, but that of empty formality. It is not her saintly silent martyrdom that reclaims Mr. B., but her passion.

The life of elegant society is not necessarily bad, nor the enemy of nature; at its highest, it is an art, the flowering of nature, in contradistinction to artificiality which ignores or debases what is natural, and the danger of artifice issues from sources other than those we customarily suspect. In *Grandison*, Richardson celebrates the beauty of civilized life as the highest achievement of human nature. There too, artificiality is vanquished; Harriet and Clementina achieve freedom and happiness through admitting love, not through submitting to conventional modest concealment. After writing the *Pamela* sequel, and having experienced a conviction as to the value of the civilized ideal, Richardson was imaginatively prepared to write *Grandison.* He had learned a great deal about possible themes, and about the manner of using epistolary narration; he had begun to develop his characters' contradictory points of view, in a manner he was to use extensively in *Clarissa.*

Pamela II lacks any of the depth of either the tragic novel, or of the last comedy. The sound is forced, the notes are few; although *Pamela II* moves into a new field in dealing with domestic and social life, the title of the first great novel of domestic comedy is reserved for *Grandison*. But no admirer of *Grandison*, or of Jane Austen's novels, should be sorry that the second *Pamela* was written.

V

Tyrannic Love and Virgin Martyr: Tragic Theme and Dramatic Reference in *Clarissa*

RICHARDSON's next and greatest novel is a development from *Pamela I*, but a development in a different direction. The author evidently saw that the themes of the first novel—captivity, sexual conflict, the stress on the individual personality forced to deal with a hostile environment—could carry more serious implications than they do in *Pamela*. The nature of passion becomes something different in *Clarissa*. In both of the Pamela novels, passion functions on a practical level. Pamela's fierce Protestantism, her spiritual development through searching her own conscience, make her a strong individualist, but her individuality seeks and finds recognition in society. Both her problem and its solution are secular. Both she and Mr. B. possess desires which the world is capable of satisfying in a manner conducive to happiness. But the war between male and female, tyrant and victim, need not be resolved into harmony. Given the characters, and the basic fable from which the story is drawn, the happy ending is essential to the first novel, but with other characters, and a similar but more disturbing situation, the story has a tragic dimension. What happens when the irresistible force meets the immovable object? While Richardson first recognized the possibilities of the love conflict as a theme in writing *Pamela*, *Clarissa* is not the same kind of novel. Richardson's own references to it indicate that he was conscious of creating something new in his prose tragedy, and it is evident that he was keenly alive to its implications.

Clarissa and Lovelace are both overpowering grand characters. True, they are realized in every detail, as is Pamela, although the kind of detail differs; we see them against the background of ordinary life, where dress and furniture, tea-caddy and elbow chair are recognizable and familiar, and, as in *Pamela*, the inward detail, the subtle half-conscious modes of thought, are fully rendered. Yet here this minuteness all creates and enforces the full being of characters of great passion and dynamic will. Each—Clarissa as well as Lovelace—is born to love totally, in his own way, and each rejects all terms of compromise. Immoderate people in a world which counsels a debased moderation, they find themselves solitary in a society which has little to say to them. The reader rejects the world of Lord M. and the Harlowes, even of Belford and Anna who supply an ostensible norm. The moralist (even Richardson) must have more dramatic sympathy with Lovelace than with the world from which he springs. He is interesting not because he is rakish up to the limit of social acceptability (like Peregrine Pickle for instance) but because he goes far beyond that; he is committed with startling intensity to an obsession with desire and will which finds its only worthy object in Clarissa. He is incessantly eager for power, which is both his object and his function. Any exertion of his authority gives him an almost sensual pleasure:

> I have changed his name by virtue of my own single authority. Knowest thou not, that I am a great Name-father? . . . Quality too I create. And by a still more valuable prerogative, I degrade by virtue of my own imperial will, without any other act of forfeiture than for my own convenience. What a poor thing is a monarch to me![1]

By appearing to burlesque his attitude, Lovelace is able to express it. His wit allows him to enjoy an ironical understanding of his own conceit, but the conceit is quite real. He is half in jest and wholly in earnest when he says airily 'The Law was not made for such a man as me.'[2] He cannot be happy unless his own desires can make his own law: 'What signifies power, if we do not exert it?'[3] His love of Clarissa offers a sufficient reason for himself, the assurance of a motive and object, which will allow him to give his ingenuity and will their full bent. 'What

---

[1] *Clarissa*, iv. 44.   [2] Ibid., p. 45.   [3] Ibid., p. 135.

stupid creatures are there in the world! . . . Thou, Jack, wilt never know one half of my contrivances . . . What a capacity for glorious mischief has thy friend!'[1] His love is demonic because it is the expression of a ruthless self-love, almost as uncomfortable for the possessor as for his victims because it is so unremittingly active. In watching Lovelace we are seeing a self-consciousness working at full strength and speed. Unlike the 'stupid creatures' (and unlike Mr. B., for instance) Lovelace finds it impossible to sacrifice power for the sake of comfort. The living self within, the living will, must be constantly proved against the dead world of matter without—the dead world including all other human beings. The price of his freedom is eternal hostile vigilance.

If Lovelace's ceaseless psychic energy is fascinating, so, and equally, is the dynamic power discovered in Clarissa. Richardson is not merely presenting in Clarissa a more talented, educated, and articulate Pamela. At the very beginning of the story, Anna Howe praises Clarissa's superiority over other young ladies, but we are at the outset misled in thinking this is a difference of degree, not of kind. We may think that Clarissa is just another supremely virtuous, beautiful, and accomplished heroine, of the kind who usually achieve felicity by the end of the last volume. We are gradually undeceived, as the implications of her situation, and the nature of Clarissa herself, become clear to us, and to her. She is a person whose spiritual perception is abnormally developed in proportion to her other capacities, excellent as these are. This makes her, for all her attempts at prudence, sometimes lacking in the more efficient kind of common sense—she has sense, but not of the common variety—and makes her intractable, just when her antagonists expect her to give way.

In Clarissa, Richardson created a personality possessing spiritual genius, a rare quality and one likely to lead its possessor into serious difficulty. Through all the horror of her suffering she never becomes a figure of mere pathos. The reader's sympathy is evoked, and not because she is a conventional nice young lady with proper ideas, or a Beauty forced into the embraces of a Beast. The reader is held because she demands the same kind of attention as Milton's Satan; she manifests

---

[1] Ibid. iii. 113.

a strength of will and desire which resists all obstacles and humiliations, and, fiercely asserting her integrity, refuses to be a mere victim.

Unlike Lovelace, Clarissa is not shown as fully aware of her own nature and capacities from the beginning of the novel. She is vaguely conscious that she is not like other members of her family, but she sees their differences as accidental, not fundamental. She tries to see herself as part of her family and in its own terms, even while the reader recognizes that she is expressing a virtue drawn from her own inner vision, and not from any example given in her own world. Clarissa is, even more than Dorothea Brooke, a Saint Theresa of her time. The Harlowes have the negative and conventional notion of 'virtue' for which Richardson, one of its sharpest critics, has been attacked ever since *Shamela*; they think that Solmes is a 'good man' only because he has wisely refrained from the expensive sins of lust and open debauchery, and it is Clarissa who corrects them.[1]

A basic difference in moral attitude, different in kind rather than in degree, is expressed in the subtle contrast between Clarissa and her mother. Mrs. Harlowe, who emerges very vividly from her relatively brief appearances in the novel, is a likeable character of good but weak intentions. Her sphere of activity has narrowed to a constant attempt to keep the peace and placate her husband. Like a domestic, less sinful Gertrude of Denmark, she is happiest in the orbit of the strong, upset and confused when two strong members of her family become antagonistic and make contradictory demands upon her. She is naturally bound to side ultimately with the apparently stronger claimant, in the muddled belief that this will be for the good of all. The good, to Mrs. Harlowe, means the serene. She attempts to help and appease Clarissa with small and covert efforts at assistance (such as conniving at the correspondence with Lovelace) which are morally rather pointless as she cannot help betraying her daughter when the struggle becomes more difficult. The stress of family warfare and of her

---

[1] *Clarissa*, i. 109–10; ii. 229–30. She horrifies her family by publicly rebuking Solmes, who for his own purposes greasily attempts to discuss the badness of Lovelace's reputation; understanding Solmes's motives, she pointedly remarks, 'The text about *casting the first stone* affords an excellent lesson' (ii. 229).

own efforts to do well by all takes its toll in nervousness and (psychologically well observed) in afflictions of the digestive system. Poor Mrs. Harlowe, who has no real will of her own, illustrates the fact that submission of the will to the will of others does not lead to harmony, external or internal. She is the picture of the virtuous woman, the obedient wife, according to the same code as that which advised a woman in Pamela's marital situation to be blind to her husband's infidelity, and in his portrait of her Richardson illustrates the defectiveness of the code of female docility. At the very beginning of the novel, while Clarissa is being tempted to be the obedient child, to be mindless and will-less for the rewards of parental approval and empty serenity (a kind of parody of the Christian childlike soul), we are shown in the portrait of Mrs. Harlowe that negative obedience, an abrogation of spiritual perception, is not the answer to moral and spiritual challenge. We already realize that such conventional weakness as her mother's could not be Clarissa's response to life. She cannot prostitute herself in the conventional marriage, she cannot enslave her will to others; in the light of the Christian knowledge of the soul's integrity and responsibility she rebels. To her family, the rebellion seems bad and unfeminine. Her own world remains hostile to her virtue, and refuses to accord it the name of goodness. Yet it is her family who rendered her consciousness active; by the time she goes off with Lovelace she has, as the reader knows, developed a will and strength which equal his. The supposed object is definitely a conscious subject.

Because Clarissa is, like Lovelace, a strong and subtle personality capable of exercising will, she can resist all his attempts upon her. He endeavours to reduce her to abject submissiveness; his fantasies continually play with her as a submissive erotic object: 'the haughty Beauty will not refuse me, when her pride of being corporally inviolate is brought down; when she can tell no tales, but when (be her resistance what it will) even her own Sex will suspect a Yielding in Resistance . . .'[1] When her resistance is stronger than he anticipated, he finally resorts to the expedient he had originally thought inadmissible, and takes her by force. The rape has a symbolic significance to himself; sexual penetration of an unconscious woman gives

[1] Ibid. v. 305–6.

him little if any erotic pleasure (his simple lust is not as perverse as his personality) but he thinks that the act of possession, an act of sexual insult, revenge, and triumph, will give him perfect mastery and secure possession. He is astounded when Clarissa, instead of being transformed into a toy by his magic act, asserts her freedom: 'My soul is above thee, man! . . . Urge me not to tell thee, how sincerely I think my soul above thee!—Thou hast in mine, a proud, a too proud heart, to contend with!'[1]

Circumstances can no longer be created and disposed of as Lovelace wishes. Clarissa scornfully rejects what he confidently offers: 'What amends hast *thou* to propose!—What amends can such a one as Thou make . . . for the evils thou hast so inhumanly made me suffer?'[2] Clarissa's assertion of her own freedom is also an effective attack upon his power. After the rape she has more power over him than he has over her. He feels this more acutely than she realizes, as with one part of his divided nature he also sought love, and has continually and now finally made love impossible. Clarissa's own capacity for love is not deranged by her lively will, whereas Lovelace's will and his capacity for love are at odds. Clarissa's passion, the love of God, allows her to grow in harmony, to achieve a greater identity which does not demand the satisfaction of power over others to realize itself as free. Lovelace's sustaining principle does not allow him to achieve any harmony—the principle of continual warfare works only in terms of victory or defeat. Thwarted, and abandoned by Clarissa, he counts himself defeated, and whenever he lets himself recognize this defeat he suffers diminishment, and disintegration.

Both Clarissa and Lovelace might be said to live in the imagination. There is something more real for each than the 'reality' which the world sees. Clarissa's love of God (which her conventional 'Christian' society takes no more seriously as a motive than does the Georgian England encountered by Parson Adams) is an active force which continues to create her knowledge of herself. She emerges from a placid life, in which this genius—or madness—would not ordinarily make itself known, into the heat of combat, but the struggle, first with the Harlowes and then with Lovelace, evokes the essential Clarissa. To the world around her, her principle is incomprehensible. Friends

---

[1] *Clarissa.* iv. 215–16.   [2] Ibid. v. 351.

and advisers are always looking for a way to patch things up, long after the world in which things can be so mended has ceased to be of primary importance to her. She is, without knowing it, a martyr for her faith, and the eighteenth century, hardly less than the twentieth, finds martyrdom displeasing. To live and die in faith—the substance of things hoped for, the evidence of things not seen—seems crazed to the respectable. The word 'martyrdom' in common speech bears negative connotations of passive suffering, but it means, of course, 'witnessing'. Clarissa is a 'martyr' in that original sense; the novel shows us Clarissa's continual assertion of her freedom as a witness to a principle without which life becomes stagnant and individuality meaningless.

Lovelace also lives on the evidence of the unseen. His allegiance is to the invisible power of his own will, which is the way in which he has chosen to recognize his consciousness. The choice of free identity as supreme value means that he and Clarissa are more like each other than like anybody else around them. Unlike Mr. B., the witty and articulate Lovelace is not instinctive. If his fault were too much sexual instinct, his case would be relatively simple, but he has very little absolute lust. Like Clarissa, he has sublimated his instincts, but they are not subordinated to spiritual vision, but to his ego. Rather, it should be said that Lovelace's kind of egotism is a sort of spiritual vision to which everything else has become subordinate. His egotism inspires and is sustained by his imagination, through which most of his thoughts, feelings, and actions are presented, to himself as well as to others. His imagination connects his will and his actions. The audacity of imagination, an intensity of vision rendering all his fantasies very powerful, which manifests itself in his plots against Clarissa, prevents them from seeming comic in the way that Mr. B. with his bungling stratagems is comic. Lovelace is committed to his own imagination, and continually acts under its command, which makes him one of the first Romantic heroes.   •

Indeed, both Clarissa and Lovelace could be described as Romantic characters. They appealed immensely to readers of the Romantic period, an era when this novel was widely read and exerted great influence on other writers. Clarissa and Lovelace both seek what cannot be found in the ordinary world.

Clarissa is an extremely odd novel, noticeably different from the dominant fiction of Richardson's own day. The concept of irreconcilable opposites is almost alien to the social-minded fiction of the mid eighteenth century. There is tragic vision in eighteenth-century literature—who can doubt it who reads *The Dunciad* or *Gulliver's Travels*—but it is expressed in social terms. The struggle of individual wills against each other is not what primarily interested authors of this period. Most of the works of this period which examine individual human nature in an interesting way are works of comic, not tragic vision; they show individuals in the process of accommodating themselves to society, not tearing each other apart.[1] Villains (such as Blifil) appear in order to be mocked and overcome, or, like the heroes of sentimental comedies (and like Mr. B), to be corrected and reformed. The heroes of Defoe, Fielding, and Smollett have strong egos, but their extrovert egotism does not try to create a world, but to find a place in it. Success, not absolute power, is their primary aim. There is much sexual activity, but not much sexuality. For the heroes of Fielding and Smollett, sex is an activity and a pastime, like fighting, a sequence of incidents and not, any more than their religion, a governing principle of life. Richardson is the first major English novelist to present sexuality as a constant vital principle of human life, both conscious and subconscious. At the same time he is also one of the first (and few) novelists to treat spiritual life seriously. The importance he gives to both has been attacked, and apologized for, during the last two centuries.

Richardson's hero and heroine are grand characters, rebels against the social law and the rules of moderation. Richardson shows the grandeur of their passions, the magnificence of their obsessions. The inner dialectic of will and desire, both in outward actions and deep folded within the layers of the mind, is known and experienced by the reader in sharing their lives. Coming upon Richardson's tragic novel in the midst of all the social-minded fiction of the 1740s, the student may well feel startled, as if he had stumbled into a dark labyrinth beneath a cheerful Georgian square. One wonders how the author was able to conceive of such characters, such a kind of action.

[1] I except Defoe's *Roxana*, an interesting if imperfect tragedy. The kind of tragedy showing the degeneration of a character is different from Richardson's.

The modern reader may tend to see the characters and action in the light of later psychological novels, such as Rousseau's *La Nouvelle Héloïse*, Laclos's *Les Liaisons dangereuses*, or even the works of George Eliot and Henry James. All of these are indebted directly or indirectly to Richardson's influence, but Richardson could not be indebted to novels like that. There were no other novels quite 'like that'. For his primary inspiration, Richardson was indebted to the drama.

Discussing Clarissa, Richardson told Aaron Hill 'I intend more than a Novel or Romance by this Piece . . . it is of the Tragic Kind.'[1] The material of his tragedy is drawn from Restoration dramatic tragedy. That Richardson is fully aware of what he is doing is made abundantly clear by his use of quotation from and allusion to certain Restoration plays. Richardson makes the implications of Restoration heroic tragedy a part of the drama of Clarissa and Lovelace.

Within the novel, it is Lovelace himself who most frequently alludes to and quotes from the tragic plays. He is sophisticated and intelligent, delighting in the range of literary reference he has at the command of his ready wit. McKillop says 'Lovelace's attitudes lead him to use a style which blends a half-playful use of the rhetoric of tragedy and heroic play with the colloquialisms of the fine gentleman of comedy',[2] and he thinks the quotations Lovelace uses serve him as 'a rhetorical commentary on his own moods'.[3] They do this, but they do more, as they are related not only to what he is superficially thinking, but also to what he unconsciously realizes about his and Clarissa's situation. He insists upon adopting the role which suits his desires at the moment, and he is always in earnest when he identifies himself with a character or a speech. He adopts self-pleasing disguises to himself, which he feels free to throw off at any moment. The irony of his situation is that he has identified himself too thoroughly, diagnosed the disease and prognosticated his own fate all too accurately. Once we notice what Lovelace's quotation simply, at their various levels of meaning, we realize that Clarissa is also fulfilling the role of a heroic type found in the tragedies.

---

[1] Richardson to Hills 7 Nov. 1748, *Selected Letters*, p. 99.
[2] A. D. McKillop, *The Early Masters of English Fiction*, 1956, p. 71.
[3] Idem, *Samuel Richardson: Printer and Novelist*, p. 149.

The mode of heroic tragedy is so alien to us that we can easily miss the meaning of these dramas. Anthologies of Restoration plays, and university courses, tend to concentrate on the comedy of the Restoration period, and produce for a tragic work Dryden's *All for Love*, which is not a typical example of Restoration tragedy in general, nor a characteristic work of Dryden the dramatist. The student of English literature, often unfamiliar with the works of Corneille and Racine, finds the themes and language of heroic plays so remote that he tends to dismiss them as antique curios. Stage history, however, assures us that Restoration heroic tragedy had real dramatic effect and received popular acclaim. In their time—that is, for two or three generations—playgoers and play-readers responded not only to their spectacle, but to their psychological verisimilitude. It is worth while recovering an ear for this language to discover its import. The import is startling enough—even violent.

The central characters of these dramas are wrapped in a dream of power. The desire for political power is felt like a physical lust—and sexual lust is known in terms of power. The grandeur and havoc of incessant desire are expressed with nightmarish fervour. Because we, on the other side of Romanticism which has offered other images for similar conditions, do not readily comprehend the mode, the gestures seem at first artificial, over-elaborate. Once the spirit of the works is comprehended, one can see that these gestures are images of psychological forces. Gestures and statements are electric with the energies of an inner spirit eager to consume the world. Almost every character is haunted and impelled by some supreme emotional idea. The recurrent major type in such plays, the tyrant-hero, is completely obsessive, taken over by a sense of psychological force which is impatient to possess or destroy that which is not itself. The ruler is intoxicated by the delusive notion of his absolute will. The limitations of the arbitrary exercise of the will are seen most convincingly in the ironies of the relationship between the sexes, a relationship which shows most clearly a fundamental truth of human life: love is not to be achieved by an effort of will or an exercise of power. The Emperor in *Aureng-Zebe*, Maximin in *Tyrannick Love*, Muley Moluch in *Don Sebastian* (all by Dryden), the hero of Lee's *Mithridates* or of Rochester's *Valentinian*[1] are only a few among the many characters in drama who attempt (or threaten to attempt) to possess a woman against her will. In these plays, which might be called 'variations on the theme of Lucrece', forced conquest leads only to disaster, and the hero-villain is forced to discover that he cannot, even by violation, conquer the will of the woman he loves. The hero is defeated, remorse comes too late, and the woman is, in the strength not merely of innocence but also and primarily of opposing will, the victor even in death.

Because of its difference from other novels of the time, *Clarissa* is often treated *in vacuo*, as if it were largely unrelated to anything else in literature, or to any ideas about human existence other than the novelist's fantasies, which emerge, so modern critics would have us believe, in perverted sexuality or in morbidly escapist religion. Or, the novel is seen in social terms as a manifesto of the middle class, to which Clarissa's religion and death give 'a supernatural sanction . . . making it the embodiment of the order of the universe'.[2] Yet Richardson is here consciously moving away from the view that the social is the only important relationship. His tale of 'tyrannic love' is drawn from the heroic plays which have so often been seen as the last defiant statements of a dying aristocratic order and which can scarcely be viewed as manifestoes of the middle class on the march. Since Restoration authors and audiences were evidently interested by the theme of rape as a convincing and appropriate expression of psychological conflict, they too must be considered 'perverted' if Richardson is so labelled—but such a wide condemnation seems of little value.

At the centre of every important tragedy of this kind, expressed in imagery as well as in characterization, is a fascinated presentation of the close relationship of love to hate. Dryden and Lee understand this as well as does Laclos, although they express it differently. It is evident that Richardson understood and appreciated the dramatists' presentation of the egotistical heroes in whom love and hatred are obsessively allied.

Lovelace's nature is clearly established in his first full appearance in the novel. In his first letter to Belford, when he is describing his love for Clarissa, his mind moves from love to

---

[1] Adapted almost wholesale from Beaumont and Fletcher's *Valentinian*.
[2] Dorothy Van Ghent, *The English Novel: form and function*, 1953, pp. 56–7.

revenge, and he recalls Placidus's famous speech on the love of Maximin for Catharine:

I check myself, and leaving the three first Lines of the following of Dryden to the family of the whiners, find the workings of the passion in my stormy soul better expressed by the three last:

> *Love various minds does variously inspire;*
> *He stirs in gentle natures gentle fire;*
> *Like that of incense on the altar laid.*
> *But raging flames tempestuous souls invade:*
> *A fire, which ev'ry windy passion blows;*
> *With Pride it mounts, and with Revenge it glows.*

And with REVENGE it *shall* glow![1]

A critic of Dryden has commented on this particular passage: 'The tempest, fire and wind imagery is revealing. Through it, Dryden suggests the interrelation between extravagant emotional states and the evils of pride, revenge and lust. Maximin's passions are a form of emotional disorder and have their origins in the nature of his personality and beliefs.' He points out that 'Dryden's wit is a form of psychological analysis. The imagery defines the emotional distempers that lie behind a dramatic character's ranting and bombastic speeches.'[2] The view that Dryden's heroes, victims of their own passions and fantasies, are treated ironically by the author, presented as both absurd and perversely grand, seems justified and can also serve as a view of Lovelace whose egotism is also ironically treated, shown to be not only sinister but also absurd. Lovelace's overblown pride is expressed in his view of himself as a 'tempestuous soul', although he is too witty not to assume a semi-facetious tone in adopting this description. Dryden's dramatic verse becomes part of Richardson's own fictional language, contributing imagery and content, used ironically by the character and ironically about the character.

The role Lovelace most often adopts is that of the tragic tyrant-lover. Essentially his arrogance is akin to that of the tyrant-hero:

> I must, and what I must be sure I will.
> What's Royalty, but pow'r to please myself?[3]

[1] *Clarissa*, i. 215. See Dryden, *Tyrannick Love, or the Royal Martyr*, 1670, II. i, p. 19.
[2] Bruce King, *Dryden's Major Plays*, 1966, pp. 40–1.
[3] Dryden, *Don Sebastian, King of Portugal*, 1690, II. i, p. 21.

In moments of confidence Lovelace most naturally thinks in terms of the heroic lovers and their beautiful victims; there is, for example, the excited letter after Clarissa has come away with him, when in exultant mood he describes her in lines pertaining to Dryden's Almeyda (from a description which in the play arouses the Emperor's lust)[1] and also speaks of her as 'my GLORIANA',[2] remembering the beautiful victim of Augustus in Lee's *Gloriana* and forgetting that Gloriana was ultimately the victor in the sexual battle. He alternates between cruelty and besotted sensual love, using the one to inflame the other quite in the manner of the tyrant-heroes; he sometimes borrows their very words to heighten his own sensations, as when he quotes Lee's *Borgia*.[3]

Lovelace enjoys all the various sensations of love and rage indulged by the tyrant-hero. He recognizes the possibility of resistance on the part of the woman, and welcomes it; opposition will be a stimulus to his will. He meets the arguments of Belford, who urges Indamora's plea (slightly misquoted)

> *Sweet are the joys that come with willingness.*[4]

with Boabdelin's reply:

> *It is* Resistance *that inflames desire,*
> *Sharpens the darts of Love, and blows its fire.*
> *Love is disarm'd that meets with too much ease;*
> *He languishes and does not care to please.*

The women know this as well as the men. They love to be addressed with Spirit:

> *And therefore 'tis their golden fruit they guard*
> *With so much care, to make possession hard.*[5]

He is making the same mistake as Dryden's Emperor, who erred notably in supposing Indamora would enjoy being conquered against her will. Such contemptuous generalizations about women are always shown in the heroic plays to be erroneous.

---

[1] *Clarissa*, iii. 361; see Dryden, *Don Sebastian*, ii. i, p. 32.
[2] *Clarissa*, iii. 361.
[3] Ibid. v. 29; see Nathaniel Lee, *Caesar Borgia*, 1680, ii. i, p. 24.
[4] *Clarissa*, iv. 10.
[5] Ibid., p. 134; see Dryden, *Aureng-Zebe*, 1676, ii. i, pp. 19–20.

Lovelace exults in the woman's resistance, when it is of the kind he expects, because it seems to provide an excuse and motive for vengeance. Love felt as revenge is more satisfactory to the will than the love or lust which merely asks for and expects a return. He arouses in himself the emotions which he can enjoy: 'Love and Rage kept then my heart in motion . . . Even the affronted God of Love approved then of my threatened vengeance against the fair promiser . . .'[1] These are the sentiments and the language of a Muley Moluch[2] or an Augustus.[3]

Like the tyrant-heroes of the stage, Lovelace seizes upon the 'Vengeance', the 'Rage', which gives him the right to conquer and humiliate the woman, even, if necessary, by sheer force. His threats about Clarissa's fate, his belief that after the act of sexual possession she will lose all personal will and identity in humiliated subjection, are totally in keeping with the actions and attitudes of tyrannic lovers:

> As haughty Vertue's sharpest punishment,
> Thou shalt live still, but not live innocent.
>
> .   .   .   .   .
>
> Thy Virgin-pride shall vanish into air.[4]

Lovelace believes that he can adopt these attitudes, enact these egotistical barbarities in defiance of all the tragedies to which he refers, and escape scot-free. He thinks himself preserved by his wit, and by his own sense of comedy.

The tragic plays to which he refers might have taught him otherwise. There is in the tragedies a type of villain other than the tyrant-lover, a type which is closely related to the comic rakes and to Lovelace. The Machiavellian schemers of Restoration tragedy are witty (as the tyrant-lovers are not) and cunning in achieving an object of sexual or political desire. They enjoy using witty contrivances against others, delighting in them as if they were monstrous 'practical jokes'. Dryden's Zulema is one of the best examples of this type. He is mockingly contemptuous of virtue, and delights in using others as his unwitting tools. He

---

[1] *Clarissa*, iv. 379.

[2] e.g. Muley Moluch to Almeyda: 'Thou hast restor'd me to my native Rage;/ And I will seize my happiness by force.' (Dryden, *Don Sebastian*, II. i, p. 35.)

[3] See Lee, *Gloriana, or the Court of Augustus Caesar*, 1676, III. ii, pp. 26–8.

[4] Ibid. III. ii, pp. 27–8; cf. *Clarissa*, v. 305–6.

flippantly dismisses the possibility of love as a personal relationship:

> Dream on; enjoy her Soul; and set that free;
> I'm pleas'd her person should be left for me.[1]

In the tragedies such characters, who represent in another
aspect the power mania and self-deception seen in the tyrant-
heroes, are also proved wrong and come to no good end.

Corrupt egotism and the lust for power displayed in the sex
relationship are dealt with in two distinct and antithetical ways
in Restoration drama. In the comedies, the rake is treated with
approval. His assumption of the power to subjugate women is
seen as admirable, and his cynicism is attractively witty. The
two kinds of hero are kept sharply distinct by the context in
which they appear. Restoration audiences could approve of
Etherege's Dorimant, and disapprove of Dryden's Morat, or
Lee's Augustus. What is seen as *hubris* in the tyrant-hero or
scheming villain of tragedy is seen as sexual genius in the rake
of comedy. Each type had been kept insulated from the other.
Nicholas Rowe had eventually queried (if rather feebly) the
convention that separated the two types and had pointed out
the resemblance in his play *The Fair Penitent* (1703). The character and actions of the rake Lothario are introduced in the context of tragedy.[2] Richardson much more effectively combines
the two conventions that had once existed apart.

These dissimilar conventions are united in the creation of
Lovelace, a character who himself is highly conscious of these
literary conventions. He is more sophisticated than the characters in the dramas to which he refers, because these dramas
themselves are included in the scenery of his mind; he can
maintain the shifting perspectives of reader, audience, actor,

---

[1] Dryden, *The Conquest of Granada by the Spaniards*, part i, 1672, III. i, p. 33.

[2] Belford compares Clarissa's story to that of *The Fair Penitent*, largely attacking
Rowe's play and its heroine (*Clarissa*, vii. 132–5). Belford's remarks are introduced
mainly in order to enable Richardson to insist, within the novel itself, that the
differences between the two works are more interesting than any resemblances,
thus forestalling the inevitable critical comparison. In a footnote which Richardson
himself appends to Belford's letter, he cites examples of good tragedies (as opposed
to Rowe's play).

Richardson lists Otway's *The Orphan* and *Venice Preserved*, Lee's *Theodosius*, and
Shakespeare's *King Lear*, *Othello*, and *Hamlet*, as examples of good tragedy. In his
earlier life, Richardson had attended the theatre; see his letters to Lady Bradshaigh, 15 Dec. 1748, *Selected Letters*, pp. 104–6, and 8 Dec. 1753, ibid., p. 250.

director, and character in his versatile reactions to drama and to life. It is quite noticeable that Lovelace thinks in dramatic terms. He is constantly boastful about his own ability to act and assume roles, and not only admires plays but humorously thinks also of writing them.[1] The seduction process itself seems to him like a play,[2] he imagines himself and Clarissa as characters in a play,[3] and he is often reminded of plays; for example, he reminds himself of Horner in *The Country Wife*,[4] and Morden reminds him of Chamont in Otway's *The Orphan*.[5]

One of the interesting implications of Lovelace's aesthetic delight in drama, and in dramatic situations in 'real life', is that, as we are invited to see, he thinks of tragedy and comedy as two equal and open alternatives, between which he is continually free to choose. He believes that he can cull the pleasures of heroic moments in life as freely as he does in his florilegium of personally apposite quotations, while at the same time deciding to maintain himself as the hero of comedy.

Lovelace's dramatic allusions express the effect, and also surely to some extent a cause, of his delusion of perfect freedom. He is not only audience and actor, but also the great erratic dramatist of the story of Robert Lovelace and Clarissa Harlowe, the author who can choose the mode of his drama as freely at the end as at the beginning of the play, who by deciding the attitude of his principal character (Robert Lovelace) has indeed really settled to the satisfaction of the most intelligent portion of his audience (that same gentleman) the genre of his audacious piece from the outset. His aesthetic response manifests his power and his irresponsibility. No action is seen by him as begetting real consequences that interfere with the dramatic harmony of the work as he has designed it. He has only to will that the whole shall be comedy, and since that is his choice, comedy—that is, the admirable victory of the powerful male— it will be. The heroic colouring will serve to heighten the full comic effect: 'How universally engaging it is to put a woman of sense, to whom a man is not married, in a passion, let the reception given to every ranting scene in our plays testify.'[6] He refuses to see the relation of tragedy to life because he does not

---

[1] *Clarissa*, iii. 162.   [2] Ibid. iv. 56.
[3] Ibid., p. 50.   [4] Ibid. vii. 19.
[5] Ibid., p. 287.   [6] Ibid. iii. 94.

greatly care for plays in which the male does not come off best:

> I believe, generally speaking, that all men of our cast are of my mind—They love not any Tragedies but those in which they themselves act the parts of tyrants and executioners; and, afraid to trust themselves with serious and solemn reflections, run to Comedies, in order to laugh away compunction on the distresses they have occasioned, and to find examples of men as immoral as themselves . . .

> Sally answered for Polly . . . and . . . Mrs. Sinclair . . . for all her acquaintance . . . in preferring the comic to the tragic scenes.—And I believe they are right; for the devil's in it, if a confided-in Rake does not give a girl enough of Tragedy in his Comedy.[1]

Lovelace has concluded that tragedy is feminine (and therefore inferior), comedy masculine (and therefore superior). Unconsciously he deeply believes that since the male must always be the superior force, the tragic in life need never take precedence over the comic unless a weak male permits the usurpation. Lovelace, the 'confided-in Rake' assumes that 'her Tragedy' is always subordinate to 'his Comedy'. He does not consider the possibility of his comedy becoming subordinate to her tragedy, a possibility which becomes more probable with his every action.

In their context, Lovelace's generalizations about the two kinds of dramatic appeal arise out of an apparently innocent theatrical excursion which he is using for his own ends. At a time when Clarissa is fairly hopeful and Lovelace still has opportunity to change his plans, he takes Clarissa to see *Venice Preserved*. The allusion to Otway's play is made much more quickly and deftly than the allusion to *The Distress'd Mother* in *Pamela II*. There is no tedious recounting of the plot; Richardson assumes that his readers will remember the play and see the point. This play acts in the novel as a kind of touchstone for tragedy. It reflects the situation of the novel's protagonists, although not in too jarringly obvious a manner. Belvidera, like Clarissa, suffers under a father's curse. Lovelace, like Jaffeir, is in love; like Renault he is willing to break his faith to the woman committed to his charge, betraying honour to gratify lust. Lovelace is using the opportunity of Clarissa's absence from

---

[1] Ibid. iv. 152.

the house to have her correspondence examined—a mean action, which is also an act of betrayal, although he is quite willing to watch the sufferings of the victims of treachery presented on the stage, and to indulge in aesthetic sympathy with them. It is ironic that Lovelace thinks the woes of Belvidera will 'unlock and open my Charmer's heart . . . But it were worth while to carry her to the Play of *Venice preserved*, were it but to show her, that there have been, and may be, much deeper distresses than she can possibly know.'[1] The distresses of Belvidera become those of Clarissa; the play foreshadows what is to come: madness, abandonment, death. Clarissa, in her incoherent communications during her temporary derangement after the rape, recalls snatches of the play she has seen a few weeks ago.[2] Her security then, Lovelace's apparent solicitude, her hopes—these were the illusions, and what was seen only as pertaining to dramatic illusion has become reality.

At the time when they see the play, Clarissa notes that Lovelace is moved by it; he is moved, however, merely as a connoisseur. He is primarily concerned with the major drama which he is creating. Ready as he is to enjoy any emotional thrill the theatre can offer him, he is the more thrilled with enjoyment of the exciting comedy which he has projected from the theatre of his mind on to life itself. He is sensitive to every exquisite turn of emotion, fascinated by every unfolding of the action as he sees it. A faithful imaginist, he refuses to entertain any action or meaning not produced by his thick-crowding fancy. He does not see that he dismisses comedy precisely at the most dangerous point for himself. Comic action, even in the most licentious Restoration comedies, is controlled by a social law. The hero may go to the farthest boundaries of permitted action, in seducing all the willing females who foolishly make themselves accessories to his plan. Yet he does not overstep a certain social pale, although he reaches the frontier. Steady and intelligent resistance from a wilful personality meets with his respect, and to some extent even the rake-hero capitulates. The heroine (such as Etherege's Harriet or Congreve's Millamant) makes demands to which the hero accedes. One of the reasons why Lovelace is so grand and so terrible is that he cannot really recognize the limitation of any social law. The social balance

---

[1] *Clarissa*, iv. 156.   [2] Ibid. v. 333.

and order, even (if remote) a kind of domesticity intimated by the comedies, are alien to him. Although his conscious allegiance is to the comic, he is more truly at home with the tyrant-lovers in their moments of absolute will and heroic glory. More truly a Hobbist than any of the heroes of the comedies, he will be satisfied with nothing less than absolute power, uncontrolled will. When his will to conquer is aroused by Clarissa's unexpected steady resistance he forsakes the role of the comic hero without letting himself recognize that this is what he is doing. At the major turning-point, Clarissa's flight to Hampstead, when he can no longer pretend that she will yield to seduction, he decides to take her by force. He allows himself, in his pursuit of her, all the trappings of the comic hero, and enjoys the fun of his disguises and inventions.[1] His motives and attitudes have, however, become entirely those of the heroic monarch, absolute in love. Ever labouring under the delusion that he is comic hero and comic dramatist, Lovelace merges the role of the comic rake more and more into the role of the tragic tyrant, a larger role because it allows the free action of the uninhibited will. He is destroying himself, but in a sense he has by now no choice. All his previous choices have made him the tragic hero; the comic role has never been large enough for him. He is unconscious that he has truly taken up the tragic alternative, and that once assumed it cannot be cast aside.

Lovelace's illusion, that all responds to the play of his imagination, that he is the creator of the whole drama, is a striking

---

[1] Lovelace is one of the company of the rakes of comedy in his delight in assuming a disguise and setting up a situation based on pretence. Many of his dishonest devices are adopted from comedy. For instance, the device of testing a woman's love by feigning illness, which is used by Lovelace to such effect (*Clarissa*, iv. 291–5), is employed by Fowler in James Shirley's *The Wittie Faire One* (1633, III. i) and by Valentine Legend in William Congreve's *Love for Love* (1695, IV. i).

The device of pretending the house is dangerously on fire in order to gain access to a trembling Clarissa in the middle of the night (*Clarissa*, iv. 385–99) could have been suggested by Howard's *The Vestal Virgin*—a play which could be either tragedy or comedy, with alternative endings provided. Mutius suggests to Sulpitius that he frighten his beloved out of coyness by setting fire to her house:

> . . . the coyest then
> Will leap into the next mans arms:
> I have been thank'd for saving them
> Out of the very Fire that I kindled.

(Sir Robert Howard, *Four New Plays*, 1665, *The Vestal Virgin: Or, The Roman Ladies*, II. i, p. 195.)

refinement of the illusion of absolute power seen in the tyrant figures of the heroic plays. The consistent illusion, which could arise only from a sophisticated intellect, and from an imagination of warped poetic power, contributes to the deepest irony of his situation.

The illusion of magnificent power destroys the possibility of love—as Lovelace should have learned through the tragedies. As in the dramas, the heroine sets up a counteraction through an opposing will, which teaches the hero too late that he does not possess such arbitrary power as he had assumed, that that kind of power does not exist. Lovelace, in assuming the role of a Maximin, has himself chosen to cast Clarissa in the role of the virgin martyr, of the woman whose resistance is not a basically submissive device for inflaming desire but a defiant assertion of freedom.

Clarissa herself does not see the relationship with Lovelace in the terms of art. Although she has written a book on the 'principal acting plays'[1] her actions are not dominated by dramatic images. She is denied the assurance Lovelace has, that of seeing everything in terms of an aesthetic master plan. Her will is tested at each point, in every circumstance, her reactions are always in terms of principle—and principle not as dry conduct-book rule, but living moral desire. Lovelace, for whom such principles do not exist off the theatre stage, cannot understand that her principles are real, that her moral desires might be as strong as his own deep wishes.

Clarissa's resemblance to the tragic heroines is pointed out from the beginning by Lovelace's allusions to the tyrant-heroes. The reader is increasingly warned of the position Clarissa will be forced to assume in her fight for spiritual and moral existence. Clarissa herself does not quote from the plays of Dryden and Lee; there are no equivalent assumptions of suitable roles to be found in any allusions she makes. She is not 'play-acting' with life, and does not choose a role artificially. The role of the victim is thrust upon her when Lovelace, without her knowledge, chooses the part of tyrant-lover. For the reader, as distinct from the characters, Lovelace's use of the dramatic rhetoric highlights Clarissa's heroic situation.

---

[1] *Clarissa*, iv. 201. (This 'book' would be a young lady's essays written for her own instruction and the amusement of a few friends, not intended for publication.)

Richardson was openly adopting situations and language from the drama for his novel; it seems that he expected his readers would see that the situations in which Clarissa is involved do, in the centre of the novel, resemble more and more closely the situations of the dramas.

Like so many of the tragic heroines, Clarissa is reduced to pleading with her lover to spare her violation. The scene before the rape, in which Clarissa sinks down on her knees, imploring Lovelace's pity, is Richardson's version of a scene often enacted upon the stage. Her desire for death rather than dishonour is typical of all the victim-heroines.[1] Like the heroines, she scorns her ravisher, and her speeches to Lovelace after the rape echo the words of other victims who, like herself, are still superior to the men who think they have conquered.

My Father's dreadful curse has already operated upon me in the very letter of it, as to This life; and it seems to me too evident, that it will not be your fault, that it is not entirely completed in the loss of my Soul, as well as of my Honour . . . Hear me out, guilty wretch!— abandoned man!—*Man*, did I say? . . . since the mortal worryings of the fiercest beast would have been more natural, and infinitely more welcome, than what you have acted by me . . . And well may'st thou quake; well may'st thou tremble, and falter, and hesitate, as thou dost, when thou reflectest what I have suffered for thy sake, and upon the returns thou hast made me![2]

'Twill be a mercy, said she, the highest act of mercy you can do, to kill me outright upon this spot . . . Or help *me* to the means, and I will myself put out of the way so miserable a wretch! And bless thee for those means![3]

Her reproaches, for which Richardson uses a markedly rhetorical style, resemble those of Lucina to Valentinian:

> Wilt thou not kill me Monster, Ravisher?
> Thou bitter Bane o' th' Empire, look upon me,
> And if thy guilty eyes dare see the Ruines
> Thy wild Lust hath laid level with Dishonour,
> The sacrilegious razing of that Temple,
> The Tempter to thy black sins would have blusht at,
> Behold, and curse thy self . . .

---

[1] See for example Dryden, *Don Sebastian*, II. i, p. 34; also Lee, *Gloriana*, III. ii, p. 26.

[2] *Clarissa*, v. 347–8.   [3] Ibid., pp. 375–6.

> What restitution canst thou make to save me
>
> Fly from me,
> Or for thy safeties sake and wisdom kill me;[1]

or of Semandra to Mithridates:

> 'Tis sure, thou hast undone this helpless Creature,
> And turn'd to mortal paleness all her Beauties;
> Thou hast made her hate the Day which once adorn'd
> Her op'ning Sweets: how wretched hast thou made me!
>
> Dost thou repent? or are they but feign'd tears?
>
> Then hadst thou thus dissolv'd, I shou'd have blest thee:
> But now, thy black Repentance comes too late.
> What, Ah! what satisfaction canst thou make?[2]

to take but two illustrations from a number offered by the dramas. Like these and other tragic heroines, Clarissa refuses the tyrant-persecutor her love after the act which he thought would ensure submissive love for ever. Lovelace's defeat is manifest even to himself when she clearly chooses to die rather than to be what he would have her. Clarissa's victory is signalized in the 'pen-knife scene', after which she is 'the triumphant subduer'.[3] Despite his unceasing efforts and ever wilder flights of fancy, Lovelace is after this juncture always on the decline, and Clarissa in the ascendant.

Lovelace's fate is that of the tyrant-hero. He, the man of action, is baulked, unable to act, and his decisions are irrelevant, meaningless (like Lovelace's 'decisions' to marry Clarissa, to forget her, to possess (literally) her heart). He has allowed his unbridled will to create a situation in which he is what he always claimed not to be, the slave of circumstance. Clarissa's death is a fact which his imagination is powerless to alter, although he has been its cause.[4] His conscience begins to

---

[1] Rochester, *Valentinian*, 1685, IV. iii, pp. 48–9.

[2] Lee, *Mithridates, King of Pontus*, 1678, IV. i, pp. 52–3.

[3] *Clarissa*, vi. 65–71. Similar scenes are traditional in stage drama; see for example the scene between the Duke and Amidea in James Shirley's *The Traytor*, 1635, III, F2ᵛ–F4ʳ. Such scenes were already being adapted in prose tales of Richardson's period.

[4] Compare Lovelace's refusal to believe that Clarissa is dying, and his horror at her death, with Valentinian's angry grief:

trouble him; like Lee's Mithridates he is tormented by a dream of death showing his fate in the next world, separated from the woman he has injured.[1] Like Lee's Borgia, he wishes to have embalmed the body of the woman he has once taken against her will, and whose death he has caused, a grim parallel to the possession of the body but not the person in the act of rape.[2] He has brought about his own ruin through his moral insanity, as every such tyrannic lover has done. The woman has destroyed him, although this has not been her design. In the tragedies, as in Richardson's novel, the heroine is the hero's 'Nemesis'.[3]

At the end of the novel, after all Lovelace's assertions about his power to choose not only an action but the action's meaning as well, the power to choose is seen in terms of spiritual choice. Lovelace's inability to change means that his suffering is un-directed and purposeless; his psyche is imprisoned, his choice made before he knew it. Clarissa is able to choose the meaning and spirit of her action, to interpret and hence to change her suffering. Even in imprisonment, even at the point of death, her suffering is purposive, a means of growth, not a passive con-dition. The virtue she finally presents is greater than that offered by the standards of the heroic plays, although it com-prehends these standards. The inward Christian life which enabled her to combat her own family and gave her an under-standing of freedom continues to grow. She can will self-fulfil-ment in a more complete and spiritual sense than that found in the heroines' retaliatory self-destruction. She has been grand in her vivid defiance, but it is a mistake to think that Richard-son is merely nodding at conventional piety in not allowing Clarissa to die by committing suicide. Had she stopped at the pagan level, the principles for which she stands and by which she acts would have been incompletely realized. Christianity allows to the female as well as to the male a knowledge of spiritual existence which makes for a different end from the

> And was there but one,
> But one of all the World that could content me,
> And snatcht away in shewing?
>
> (Rochester, *Valentinian*, v. i, p. 62.)

[1] *Clarissa*, vii. 158–60; cf. Lee, *Mithridates*, iv. i, pp. 48–9.
[2] *Clarissa*, viii. 47–8; cf. Lee, *Caesar Borgia*, v. i, p. 59.
[3] *Clarissa*, iv. 379.

harsh negative act of vindication and triumph. Suffering is also action. After all her experience of pain—violation, insanity, imprisonment, poverty, and sickness—Clarissa knows unity and joy. Her kind of joy is foreign to the heroines of the tragic dramas. At last her personality no longer has to operate on the old lines of battle, defeat, and victory. The will to be has been given a meaning which is not to be expressed in aggressive terms.

Yet the militancy was necessary. If Clarissa had let go, if she had allowed herself at any stage to give in, to be object and not subject, the possibility of reaching this religious illumination would have been lost. Christian freedom of spirit cannot be given to a soul which has willed its enslavement. Like the Restoration tragedians, Richardson felt the necessity of defending individual spiritual freedom, of showing the individual resisting all the pressures of enticement or oppression which would urge the free spirit to give in. Saint Catharine proudly says to Maximin

> To my respect thou hast no longer right:
> Such pow'r in bonds true piety can have.
> That I command, and thou art but a Slave.[1]

As Clarissa tells Lovelace 'My soul is above thee, man! . . . Thou hast in mine a proud, a too proud heart, to contend with!'[2] Once we recognize Richardson's debt to the drama in the character of Clarissa as well as of Lovelace, it becomes impossible to assert that Lovelace is 'the representative of the Cavalier attitude to sex, in conflict with the Puritan one represented by Clarissa'.[3] Attitudes to sex are not neatly divided according to political or religious tenets. In terms of literary history, Clarissa could well be called 'a Cavalier heroine' exhibiting an unconquerable regal will. Her declaration, 'Tho' a slave, a prisoner, in circumstance, I am no slave in my will!'[4] is in the Cavalier heroic mode.

The tragic theme which Richardson takes up from tragic drama develops an ethic of freedom, examines what freedom can and cannot be. Assumption of 'imperious will' over others is a fallacy. In a masculine world of power, the masculine temptation is to think that a depraved lust for power is the only

---

[1] Dryden, *Tyrannick Love*, I. i, p. 22.   [2] *Clarissa*, iv. 215–16.
[3] Ian Watt, *The Rise of the Novel*, 1957, p. 227.   [4] *Clarissa*, vi. 27.

creditable conscious activity. In opposition woman assumes
the right of freedom and of choice, rights usually thought of as
the male prerogative. The love relationship, so entangled with
fantasies and emotional needs, aggression and submission,
half-conscious notions of submission and conquest, inferior and
superior, is one of the great arenas of the struggle of wills, an
arena in which the reality of identity, usually so slowly recognized, can be strikingly shown. In *Clarissa* as in the heroic
tragedies the sexual battle is a spiritual combat, and the terms
'soul' and 'will' are constantly invoked.

Such a combat would not be necessary if social, moral, and
sexual life had not degenerated, because of the depravity of
human nature, into a struggle for power. Clarissa's world, which
has long given up Christianity without knowing it, is the world
as described by Hobbes, a world in which survival means
conquest, and the governing motive is the appetite for power.
The Harlowes's mode of life, apparently governed by the
reasonableness of Lockean social values, is Hobbist at its core.
The family we see here is not a model of harmonious society,
but a divided kingdom, with the father an absolutist asserting
prerogative over rebellious and encroaching children, and the
menace of faction constantly threatening this microcosm of the
great world. It is a group not unlike the families and kingdoms
portrayed by Dryden in *The Conquest of Granada* and *Aureng-
Zebe*. The spirit of Locke and of post-Revolutionary England is
reflected in the consuming interest in property, but property is
a symbol of power. The vicious are protected by a society based
on property and can, like the Harlowes and Solmes, carry on
their game of power under the pretence of fair play, with the
forces of respectability to assist them. Property is both a weapon
and a trophy. There are no rational socially agreed bonds about
property which cannot be evaded or misused. The will of
Clarissa's grandfather bequeathing her all that property—the
story begins with the association of 'will', 'death', and 'property'
—is an example of a legal and social contract, easily definable
in Locke's language about the nature of property, but absurdly
frail in the world of active wills engaged in the struggle for
power. 'Your Father's *living* Will shall controul your Grandfather's *dead* one';[1] Bella's sneering pun is highly significant.

[1] Ibid. i. 337.

The Harlowes regard what they feel to be Clarissa's access to power with great hostility; they do their best to wrest property from her—even the 'property' of her person and self—and to prove to her that she cannot be a power in her own right. As far as property goes they are entirely successful; Clarissa owns nothing. There is for instance all that 'old family plate' which her grandfather, with pitiable arrogance, had decreed should be 'kept *to the end of time*'; it remains locked 'in a large iron chest', and is destined, unused and unenjoyed, to trundle its way from one legal testament to another, an image of the absurdity of mere possession.[1]

In a society in which life is waged rather than lived, Lovelace is justified in living openly a life of Hobbist domination. He dares to be what others (Mr. Harlowe, James Harlowe, Solmes) would like to be if they dared. The personal imperial principle manifested in Lovelace's will, and Clarissa's Christian morality are curiously parallel. Both acknowledge, in quite different ways, the freedom of the will, the sovereignty of the self. The person who practises either may be dangerous to society— a Clarissa nearly as dangerous as a Lovelace—but he will also be a proclamation that the human spirit need not be small. A world is hardly great enough to satisfy the infinite desires of the soul. The rewards of mere conformity, the security that comes from making over the vital faculty of the will to others, give satisfaction to neither Clarissa nor Lovelace. The Hobbist tyrant-hero and the Christian heroine both prove the falsehood of many of the gifts their society pretends to offer. In them are revealed the natural passions which society tries to smother, or rather, the instincts and desires which others in their own passion for power endeavour to corrupt and use for their own purposes. Lovelace's natural sexual vitality is felt to be in many ways preferable to the Harlowe family's, and Solmes's, abuse and betrayal of sex. The desire for freedom which is the basis of Lovelace's mania is a natural and rightful desire. Unfortunately in him it has become a passion for utter dominance, perverting his sexuality to an extent which he can never really recognize. He makes the deeply tragic error (the temptation of some men at all times) of mistaking arrogant violence for freedom; he really does feel that rejection of society constitutes, in itself,

---

[1] *Clarissa*, i. 317; viii. 111.

superiority to it, that the energy of assault is eternal delight, that cruelty and love are the same thing. He attempts to deprive Clarissa of her freedom to be, to destroy the vitality from which her own sexuality springs. Her passion for freedom is aroused, and she fights back unremittingly and fiercely. Part of her tragedy is of course that she is a woman capable of love who is placed in a situation which entails, whatever choice she makes, the denial of the kind of love she has to give. The loss of a real marriage based on fully human love is a real loss to Clarissa, not the less so because it was never offered to her. Her defence of her full humanity is a defence of love against the claims which would destroy it; her strength surprises Lovelace who makes the facile assumption that views different from his own are the weak offspring of ignorance or hypocrisy. In her struggle against Lovelace, with all its attendant sufferings, Clarissa realizes more and more fully that the Christian spirit, by the power of God's love, is always free, and that this true freedom transcends the life of power and conquest, relinquishes the concepts and motives of dominance and subjection. The spiritual life of Clarissa becomes more and more evidently not the decorous niceness of a good girl but her natural passion, and a ground of being.

The themes of the heroic dramas supply the grand design of 'The History (or rather Dramatic Narrative) of Clarissa'.[1] Richardson transformed the stuff of heroic tragedy for his own work. The dramas deal with outward action, and have to convey psychological states through action and through long emphatic speeches which strain dramatic credibility. It is, incidentally, very difficult to present on the stage a character in an extreme state of emotion, since this emotion must be developed through speech (more particularly self-descriptive or self-analytical speech) in order to become sufficiently known. Dramatists who attempt this are in danger of being accused of hyperbole and rant—even Shakespeare has not always been held guiltless. (Racine, the master of this art, has never been really popular in Britain, and it seems highly unlikely that the British or American public will rediscover Dryden's drama.) The Restoration dramatists were faced with real artistic problems in endeavouring to present states of mind both extreme

---

[1] Richardson, Postscript to *Clarissa*, viii. 309.

and complex. To show what these states of mind mean, they had to simplify the character so that the meaning of his emotions would emerge. The character is then held in one state too long, like the frame of a moving picture held in a still. The result is that the characters seem like large abstractions rather than individuals. The method of presentation makes the personages in the play seem more rigid than the persons we recognize in life, although their emotions are violent and fluctuating. Richardson is able to adopt whatever conventions of drama suited him without being subject to the dramatist's limitations. While we are always aware of the dominant mental states, attitudes, and principles of the characters in *Clarissa*, their emotions are seen in complex fluctuation from moment to moment, and the suspense is heightened because the reader is aware of conflicts within and between the characters of which they cannot themselves be quite aware.

Richardson recognized that the story of the tyrant-lover and the proud, violated woman is, however violent some of the action, essentially a story of inward states, of psychological tension. In his novel the material of the drama is transmuted to the activity of the inner life—the very narrative form which Richardson himself had discovered means that *all* is inner life. Theme and development are entirely harmonious; it is doubtful that the author ever consciously thought first of one as a literary end and then hit on the other as literary means. (The critic must recognize that words such as 'recognized', 'discovered', 'based upon', and so forth, are metaphors pertaining to the vocabulary of criticism, and not the language of creation itself.)

As we shall see, Richardson drew upon other literary sources (to return to the language of criticism), or rather, accepted suggestions offered by other literary kinds—from the developing feminine novel to religious and devotional literature—which provided the means of reflecting the inward action of *Clarissa*, ways of expressing the flow of personal consciousness in its greatest torrents and smallest eddies. These too he transforms, for all the action of the novel happens in a world—or worlds—created by the perceivers. The imagery of the novel takes the reader into a world which is recognizable and surprising, as solid as a prison wall and as shifting and phantasmal as a dream. The reader does not merely watch the imaginative libidinous obsession of Lovelace, the ordeal of Clarissa; he experiences these for himself. Richardson's ability to create a world for his novel and to draw the reader into it is perhaps the greatest manifestation of his genius; an examination of what he achieves in this way in *Clarissa* provides a most rewarding study of this novel, and an attempt to carry out such an examination will, in the present work, occupy the major chapters on *Clarissa*. But an author's creative power to fashion such a world, to convey such an experience, can work only in co-operation with the ability to create and understand the dynamic force of his characters. Richardson's world in *Clarissa* exists because of the characters who inhabit and perceive it. The author keeps his eye steadily on Clarissa and Lovelace; he knows, from the first word of the novel to the last, why they are important.

VI

Clarissa and Earlier Novels of Love and Seduction

> He said, that men had generally too many advantages
> from the weakness, credulity, and inexperience of the
> fair Sex: That their early Learning, which chiefly con-
> sisted in inflaming Novels, and idle and improbable
> Romances, contributed to enervate and weaken their
> minds . . .[1]

COLONEL Morden's opinions, as quoted by Lovelace, express
Richardson's own attitude to most of the popular novels of the
early eighteenth century. Richardson drew extensively on a
tradition of dramatic tragedy in his novel, and was at pains to
introduce references and quotations within the work to make
his intention evident. His novel, consciously written in the
grand manner, was seen by the author as the latest work in an
ancient and most noble literary tradition.

Yet *Clarissa* is a novel, not a play, and the form, although it
incorporates many aspects of dramatic tragedy, is not, and
could not be, a stage drama, By the mid eighteenth century
English prose fiction had already developed manners and conventions of its own, and such fiction must be considered as part
of the background of *Clarissa*. Richardson's *Pamela* had been
accused of being 'inflaming', as the author was fully aware.
The type of suspense used in *Pamela* owed a good deal to the
tradition of the rape story, but *Clarissa* resembles the earlier
tales of love and seduction much more closely, as well as being
directly related to the conventions of the bourgeois novel of
courtship in a way that *Pamela* is not. In *Clarissa*, Richardson
was adapting the conventions of the 'inflaming Novels' and
'idle Romances' which he condemns.

[1] *Clarissa*, vii. 283.

As we have seen, the epistolary method of narration which he uses with such success was derived from techniques which had been developed by minor English novelists (largely female) earlier in the century. In *Pamela*, Richardson had developed the device of writing 'to the moment' much further than his predecessors, but his first novel is closer to theirs than to *Clarissa* in the simplicity of the narrative device. The narration is in a straight line; there is one main narrator, one set of letters. A few answering letters are included, but these are unimportant; only one person's emotions are under close scrutiny. In *Clarissa*, Richardson took an unprecedented step in including a large number of correspondents, all of whose letters affect the action, and achieved a dramatic irony of which his predecessors were incapable in the use of the four main correspondents whose letters, for most of the novel, run parallel to each other. Certain conventions, already established, required only development along lines already set, but the ironic conception of the tragedy demanded some innovation in the epistolary technique.

For instance, the position of the heroine's female confidante had already been established in novels, both those told in letters and those narrated in the first person. In most epistolary amatory novels, however, in which writing to the moment is of importance, the correspondence is between the hero and heroine. In *Clarissa*, both heroine and hero write letters, but one of the surprising things about the novel is that the number of letters between Clarissa and Lovelace is almost negligible. A letter is a symbol of communication, as well as a narrative device, and one of the ironies of the novel is that the heroine and hero are never really communicating with each other, because they do not understand each other, and their modes of thinking and feeling are in marked contrast. The ironies of the contrast are brought out by the use of parallel letters, in which the same scenes are described by hero and heroine in different terms; this device is one of the most notable creations of Richardson's genius.

Yet, at times, when Lovelace is writing to or of Clarissa, the style resembles the tones of passion in which the lover of the novel writes to his beloved. Compare, for example, Lovelace's letter, as summarized by Clarissa, in which he begs for an interview,[1] with Lysander's to Cleomira, written to the same

[1] Ibid. ii. 108–9.

purpose.¹ Lovelace's fervent tone in speaking of Clarissa (e.g. 'I burn more than ever with impatience to be once more permitted to kneel at the feet of this adorable woman')² has much the same flavour as the perfervid utterances of Lysander and his kind in their letters.³

For the manner of the rake addressing a male confidant, for which the novels in letters did not provide a convention, Richardson could draw upon the published letters of the Restoration rakes and wits, such as Rochester and Etherege, and the tone of the letters suggests that he did so. The manner of rakish freemasonry, which Richardson has caught quite well, is the manner of Rochester writing to Henry Saville:

> *To be from you, and forgotten by you at once*, is a Misfortune I never was *criminal enough to merit*, since to *the Black and Fair Countess*, I *villanously betray'd* the daily Addresses of your divided Heart: You forgave that upon *the first Bottle*, and upon *the second*, on my Conscience, wou'd have renounc'd *them and the whole Sex* . . .⁴

Lovelace's letters have the quality of flippant arrogance found in some of Rochester's phrases ('as ever thou dost hope to *out-do* MACHIAVEL, or *equal* ME')⁵ and the outrageous gaiety which Lovelace adopts is similar to the Earl's:

> *You*, who have known me *these Ten Years* the *Grievance of all prudent Persons*, the *By-word of Statesmen*, the *Scorn of ugly Ladies*, which are very near All, and *the Irreconcilable Aversion of fine Gentlemen*, who are the Ornamental Part of a Nation, and yet found me seldom *sad* . . .⁶

The amused tone in which Lovelace relates his past amours, and describes the folly and vanity of the fair sex,⁷ is like that of

---

¹ Haywood, *The British Recluse: or, the Secret History of Cleomira, Suppos'd Dead*, 2nd ed., 1722, pp. 26–7, also pp. 37–8. (I can find no earlier edition of this novel than what is called the second.)

² *Clarissa*, vii. 168.

³ The fervent utterances are not necessarily totally unrelated to life; some lovers may have written in this manner. Otway's love-letters have the same floridity, but he and the novelists were writing in an accepted high style. See *Love-Letters* by Mr. Thomas Otway, in *Familiar Letters: Written by the Right Honourable John late Earl of Rochester, and several other Persons of Honour and Quality*, 1697, pp. 77–92.

⁴ Rochester, *Familiar Letters*, 1697, p. 26.

⁵ Ibid., p. 2.   ⁶ Ibid., p. 37.

⁷ For Lovelace's account of some of his escapades, which also reveal a low opinion of women, see the stories of the sensuous bride (*Clarissa*, iv. 348–9), the French Marquise (ibid., pp. 283–5), and the Parisian devotee (ibid. vi. 392–3).

Etherege describing the consolation of the German widow.[1]
The manner of the worldly-wise rake describing events in witty
and detached style, and recounting with amusement his own
words and actions, was not traditionally a feature of the love-
novel in letters. Richardson adapts the conversational epistle of
the witty rake into the conventions of the epistolary amatory
novel. The use of the rakish tone in narration guards against
the dangers of an over-passionate and florid style; Richardson
uses the methods of sentimental analysis with more caution
than his predecessors, and with much more variety.

Another advantage of the epistolary form which Richardson
perceived, and his predecessors had not, is that it allows a great
many tricks to be played with time within an ostensibly straight
progressive narrative. Each letter fixes a scene, and a mood,
making the fluid and transient into something concrete and
lasting. No moment can be recaptured, but the letter which
describes it can be quoted, or re-read, or referred to much later
when circumstances shed upon that past moment a new light.
The past is always being made a new part of the present.
Richardson is also most careful to fix the time in which each
letter is written, and one of the effects of this precision is that in the
arrangement of the letters there are subtle variations in tempo.
For instance, after Clarissa's escape from Sinclair's to Covent
Garden, there is an interchange of letters between herself and
Anna Howe, beginning with the letter dated 5 July from Anna,
who is cruel because she has been misled into believing that
Clarissa must have complied with Lovelace's wishes.[2] Clarissa
in reply explains in great detail the visit of Lovelace's pretended
relations to Hampstead, and all the circumstances and stratagems surrounding the rape—which the reader has not known in
full before; her letter of 6–8 July[3] is a long-awaited complement
to Lovelace's account of 12 and 13 June.[4] Anna Howe responds
with sympathy and self-reproach,[5] and Clarissa replies describing her present situation, including her certainty that she
is to die, and her religious state of mind.[6] The last letter of
this exchange is Clarissa's, dated 13 July. The next letter is

---

[1] See a letter to the Duke from Sir George Etherege in *Miscellaneous Works
Written by His Grace, George, Late Duke of Buckingham*, 1704, pp. 131–40.
[2] *Clarissa*, vi. 153–9.　　[3] Ibid., pp. 159–95.　　[4] Ibid. v. 301–14.
[5] Ibid. vi. 195–204.　　　　　　　　　　　　　　　　[6] Ibid., pp. 204–14.

Lovelace's to Belford, dated 7 July, in which he wishes Clarissa could be found, and amusingly describes his family's treatment of him.[1] The date of the letter indicates that it was written at the time when Clarissa was describing his villainy. The two main characters are not seen simultaneously; the reader has gone forward with Clarissa, and then dropped back in time to meet Lovelace again. The two characters are being moved at different speeds, and here Clarissa is, in every sense, ahead of Lovelace in her understanding of the situation.

Richardson's age was ready for a complex novel in letters; it had been accustomed to the letter form, either as substance or ornament, in stories dealing with love. The public was also prepared to read tales dealing with the problems of conduct encountered in courtship because of family opposition. The conflict between duty and inclination in the matter of marriage, which is the basis of the plot of *Clarissa*, and is dealt with for about a quarter of the whole novel, was already a staple of domestic fiction.

In the period before Richardson's work appeared, Mrs. Mary Davys had skilfully introduced the theme of filial obedience in conflict with the heart's inclination into a dramatically realized situation in a novel. *The Lady's Tale* has a more developed and believable heroine than is usually the case in such prose fiction, and the setting is recognizably middle-class—there is a solidity about Abaliza's home and family that we often search for in vain in the novels of Mrs. Davys's contemporaries. The basis of the story, and the arguments presented, bear a strong resemblance to those in the first part of *Clarissa*. The usually untroubled relationship between Abaliza and her parents is established at the beginning of the story, with their affectionate reunion on her return home. When they tell her a marriage is being arranged for her, she is a trifle appalled at the prospect of matrimony. As she tells her mother: 'I think it is a State that requires more Sedateness and Gravity than is usually found in Eighteen . . . I do assure you Madam . . . it wou'd have been more agreeable to my temper, had you injoin'd me to Celibacy for Life . . .'[2] When she meets her proposed suitor, Adrastus, she finds him stupid and disgusting, and is unwilling to give her

---

[1] *Clarissa*, vi. 214–18.
[2] Davys, *Works*, vol. ii, *The Lady's Tale*, p. 126.

hand where she cannot give her heart.[1] She pleads with her father not to make her marry:

Can that Parent love a Child, that would sacrifice its worldly Happiness to its own Caprice? Beside, what can be more solemn than the Charge given us in the Marriage Ceremony, where we are commanded in the Presence of Heaven to declare we have no Impediment, and can there be a greater, than to give my self to a Man I hate?[2]

Her father says she should learn prudence and consult her own good. She endeavours to reassure him, promising 'I will never dispose of myself while you live, without your Approbation and Consent; for I can with much more pleasure deny the Man I love, than take the Man I loath.'[3] In this novel, it is moving to find Abaliza pleading with her father in such a manner, because the relationship between them has been shown to be affectionate, and their conversation is usually a pleasant exchange of raillery. The reader is reminded, as is Abaliza, that her father does possess a serious authority over her, which he could exercise to make her life miserable.

Abaliza's pleas are the same as those Clarissa desperately makes to her parents:

I presume not, I say, to argue with my Papa; I only beg his mercy and indulgence in this *one* point, on which depends my present and perhaps my *future* happiness; and beseech him not to reprobate his child for an aversion which it is not in her power to conquer . . . In every-thing but this *one* point, I promise implicit duty and resignation to his will. I repeat my offers of a Single Life; and appeal to him, whether I have ever given him cause to doubt my word.[4]

Clarissa repeatedly promises her parents that she will not marry any one of whom they disapprove. As she explains to Anna Howe:

Let me but be permitted to avoid the man I *hate*; and I will give up with chearfulness, the man I *could prefer* . . . *This* is a sacrifice which a child owes to parents and friends, if they insist upon its being made. But the other, to marry a man one *cannot endure*, is not

---

[1] Ibid., p. 140.   [2] Ibid., pp. 141–2.
[3] Ibid., p. 142.   [4] *Clarissa*, i. 175.

only a dishonest thing, as to the man; but it is enough to make a creature who wishes to be a *good Wife*, a bad or indifferent one . . .¹

Both heroines are right, by the standards of their time, in asking to be allowed a negative voice in the choice of a husband; the right of refusal, if not of choice, should be left to the young lady. This is the precept set down in the conduct books in discussions of a daughter's rights and duties.² In Defoe's *Religious Courtship*, the wise aunt counsels the impatient father not to command his daughter to marry a person to whom she has an abhorrence: 'the very Laws of Matrimony forbid it; . . . and to promise what she knew at the same Time would be impossible for her to perform, would be to perjure herself . . .'³ Clarissa sees that a marriage to Solmes would be a life contrary to promises solemnly made: 'Every day, it is likely, rising to witness to some new breach of an altar-vowed duty!'⁴

It is worth remarking that both Mrs. Davys's Abaliza and Mrs. Haywood's Anadea express, like Clarissa, a desire to live single rather than marry. By the time Richardson wrote his novels, it would appear that the preference for the single life had become a convention, particularly in descriptions of a heroine faced with unwelcome suitors. (Harriet, in *Sir Charles Grandison*, has the same attitude when she is pressed by other suitors before she meets Sir Charles.) Some modern critics have seen in Clarissa's wish indications of frigidity, or worse; the vulgarized psychology of this type of criticism shows a disregard for the conventions from which *Clarissa* is derived, as well as for the intent and structure of the novel. The heroine's wish to live single is an expression of her innocence, modesty, and chastity— qualities which the eighteenth century thought excellent things in a woman. The desire for the single life can also be an expression of youthful ignorance of the power of love, a power which the heroine is shortly to experience, as Harriet does. More than that, the wish is an expression of the heroine's independence. In the novels of female writers such as Mrs. Davys, the character of the heroine is beginning to be established as that of an individual in her own right, who does not desire to live merely

¹ *Clarissa*, ii. 100.
² On this point, see Katherine Hornbeak, op. cit., pp. 18–21.
³ Daniel Defoe, *Religious Courtship*, 1722, p. 99.
⁴ *Clarissa*, ii. 71.

as the adjunct of a man, at least not of any man. It is this right which Richardson championed so strongly in the delineation of his female characters.

In Mrs. Davys's *The Lady's Tale* Abaliza's distress is realistically and dramatically presented. When she pleads against an enforced betrothal, she is not in love with anybody else; her protestation that she cannot marry a man whom she dislikes is, like Clarissa's, completely genuine. It is not an excuse made because she loves another man, as is usually the case with stage heroines, from Juliet onwards. Complications do arise when Abaliza falls in love with the young Alcipius, but Mrs. Davys refuses to allow her heroine to abandon the sacred duty of filial obedience. Since her father is a kind and understanding parent, Abaliza's situation resolves itself happily.

In this novel, Mrs. Davys endeavours to create a system of relationships in which both filial duty and the force of love are allowed their full weight. The sprightly style of the narrative allows no moral pontification, but the characters are shown to be virtuous and responsible in social duties. In traditional stage comedy, rules of conduct and of social duty can be flouted with impunity. A father's choice can be brushed aside: 'Fathers seldom chuse well', remarks Hipollita in *The Gentleman Dancing-Master*.[1] In some of the sentimental plays, such as Steele's *The Conscious Lovers* (1722), family duty is presented with exaggerated seriousness, but it is more usual for the father to be presented as comically or repellently short-sighted, and for young love to triumph by somewhat disingenuous means, as in Steele's *The Tender Husband* (1705), or Mrs. Centlivre's *The Busybody* (1708). The novelists were more realistic in presenting the problems of behaviour within the family in a manner neither exaggeratedly sentimental nor comic. The codes of behaviour, and the family, were there to be recognized in ordinary life. In the eighteenth century, the father possessed enormous power to dispose of his daughter's hand in marriage as he saw fit.

That Richardson did not exaggerate the pressure put upon Clarissa, and the misery of the prospect confronting her, can be seen in the true stories of two women of the period, Mrs. Delany (*née* Mary Granville) and Lady Mary Wortley Montagu. At the age of seventeen, Mary Granville was compelled to marry

---

[1] William Wycherley, *The Gentleman Dancing-Master*, 1673, I. i, p. 2.

Alexander Pendarves, a boorish, sickly, and debauched gentleman of nearly sixty years of age. She felt 'an invincible aversion towards him',[1] but her attempts to make that aversion
clear to her suitor only made him, like Solmes, the more eager.
Her uncle, Lord Landsdowne, acted a tyrannical part in the
spirit of Mr. Harlowe: 'I was not entreated, but commanded.'[2]
While at her uncle's house the girl was rushed through her
'courtship' and into marriage and misery: 'Never was woe
drest out in gayer colours, and when I was led to the altar, I
wished from my soul I had been led, as Iphigenia was, to be
sacrificed. I was sacrificed. I lost, not life indeed, but I lost all
that makes life desirable . . .'[3]

Lady Louisa Stuart describes Lady Mary Wortley's difficult
position when her father commanded her to marry a suitor
whom she disliked.[4] Lady Mary, whose life so often reads like a
novel, eloped with Mr. Wortley, but the result was not entirely
happy, and her father never quite forgave her. Even when she
had thus defied paternal authority, that authority had something sacred about it. Lady Bute recalled her mother's behaviour, even as a married woman, when her father entered:
'Lady Mary instantly starting up from the toilet table,
dishevelled as she was, fell on her knees to ask his blessing.'[5]
A father's blessing or a father's curse were solemn things. If
obedience is recognized as important in ordinary life, then
comic disregard of parents' wishes cannot be maintained.[6]

---

[1] *The Autobiography and Correspondence of Mary Granville, Mrs. Delany*, ed. the Right
Honourable Lady Llanover, 3 vols., 1861, i. 24.

[2] Ibid., p. 26. The marriage turned out as badly as might have been feared;
Mr. Pendarves was irritable and jealous, and was also given to bouts of squalid
debauchery. The wretched union was ended after seven years by Pendarves's
death, which his manner of living had hastened. Mrs. Pendarves got nothing of the
estate which the Granvilles had so coveted, as her husband had not altered his
previous will. She remained a widow with slender means for twenty years, until
she found a deserved happiness as the wife of Dr. Patrick Delany. Mrs. Delany's
'autobiography' describing this part of her life is contained in a series of letters,
begun in 1740, written to the Duchess of Portland, and not published until
1861.   [3] Ibid., pp. 29–30.

[4] *The Letters and Works of Lady Mary Montagu*, ed. W. Moy Thomas, 2 vols., 1893.
'Introductory Anecdotes' by Lady Louisa Stuart, i. 62–3.   [5] Ibid., p. 79.

[6] Such a dramatic situation can be used in a non-comic manner, and there is
evidence that Richardson had *Romeo and Juliet* in mind when he wrote his novel.
(See his letter to Lady Bradshaigh, 15 Dec. 1748, *Selected Letters*, p. 104.) If an
impasse is reached, the conflict has tragic possibilities. Once the social duties are
recognized, the situation is certainly much more serious.

Mrs. Davys poses an ideal according to which all her characters eventually act. Richardson in *Clarissa* poses the same ideal, and shows his characters (except the heroine) straying widely from it. Clarissa's father is *not* reasonable; such a situation has in it the seeds of tragedy. Richardson develops the domestic situation in which filial duty is in conflict with inclination, not as the whole of the action, but as the background on which he superimposes the story of attempted seduction and successful rape. This type of seduction story was another traditional novel theme, but is not usually found so closely interwoven with the tale of the dictatorial parent's choice, and not in a novel emphasizing the domestic duties. In general, it can be said of the earlier novels that the more emphasis is placed on filial obedience, the less emphasis there is on the seduction theme. Once the precepts of social duty enter the book itself, they are the standards by which the heroine is to be judged, and, if she associates with a rake, her conduct is too reprehensible to be sympathetic. This was the difficulty that faced Richardson at the outset of his novel; it was a daring stroke to combine the domestic setting and social moral standards of the more realistic novel of courtship with the plot of the seduction tale. Clarissa leaves her father's house, and the middle section of the novel consists entirely of the seduction/rape story. Clarissa must be shown therefore to leave unwillingly, almost unwittingly; she must be presented throughout as a virtuous girl, not as an amorous wench, or a fool. Yet she must not be overpowered, nor abducted unconscious from her father's house; the novel depends on her departure being a conscious act, and, to some extent, a choice, although a choice made by Clarissa in a moment of great agitation, and deceived by the illusion which Lovelace consistently and plausibly makes her exchange for reality. The scene of the actual elopement, with the dialogue at the garden door, is one of the best in the novel, and must have been one of the most difficult for Richardson to manage.[1] It is at this point that the domestic courtship story merges with the seduction tale.

The structure and suspense of *Clarissa* depend upon the seduction process. Of the minor novelists of the eighteenth century, nobody understood the importance and interest of this

[1] *Clarissa*, ii. 343–59.

process as a theme for prose fiction better than did Mrs. Haywood. She prided herself upon her understanding of 'Nature' and 'Love', and moved her audience, although we may feel that they were too easily pleased. No less a person than Richard Savage, in a poem printed in front of the second part of *Love in Excess: or, The Fatal Enquiry* (1719), complimented her in terms which Richardson's readers, over twenty years later, would have applied to him:

> When thy COUNT pleads, what Fair his Suit can flye?
> Or when thy Nymph laments, what Eyes are dry?
> E'en Nature's self in Sympathy appears,
> Yields Sigh for Sigh, and melts in equal Tears;
> For such Descriptions thus at once can prove
> The force of Language, and the sweets of Love.[1]

During the twenties and thirties she reigned supreme as untiring chronicler of love, passion, and the vagaries of the heart.[2] It is interesting to compare her *novelle* with Richardson's great seduction story.

Her world is a limited one, governed according to a philosophy of love as intense as that of the romances, but more mundane and more cynical. Although basically sympathetic to passion, she sees how the sexes mistrust and abuse each other. She intended five of her novels to be published under the inclusive cautionary title 'The Danger of giving Way to Passion'. Examples of the various ways in which men deceive women, or they deceive themselves, are found in her books, as in *Clarissa*, in which Richardson set out 'To warn the Inconsiderate and Thoughtless of the one Sex, against the base arts and designs of specious Contrivers of the other'.[3] For example, women are often beguiled by the pretence of Platonic love, and can deceive themselves with the notion that their friendship with a

---

[1] Richard Savage, in Haywood's *Love in Excess: or, The Fatal Enquiry*, 1719, part ii, pp. iii–iv.

[2] It is not impossible that Richardson may have met Mrs. Haywood. His friend Aaron Hill was a friend and admirer of the female author (he contributed the epilogue to her first play, *The Fair Captive*, in 1721). Richardson printed her comedy *A Wife to be Lett* (1735). (See Sale, *Samuel Richardson: Master Printer*, pp. 173–4). It is not possible to judge to what extent, if at all, he knew her works; his reference to her as an author is not very complimentary. (See *Selected Letters*, p. 173 n.) The interesting thing is that he is freely drawing upon the same conventions, and style and phrasing are in places remarkably similar to hers.

[3] Richardson, Preface to *Clarissa*, i. xv.

rake can reform him: 'I fancied I could make a Prosylite of him . . . The love of Souls, I aimed to inspire, that so we might enjoy a Noble, Disinterested, and *Platonick* Friendship.'[1] The speaker here, Anzania, is deceived, and her intended proselyte, Lorenzo, rapidly uses the friendship to make a conquest of her.

Richardson is equally cynical about this type of friendship. Lovelace remarks:

My passion for my Beloved . . . I boasted of. It was, in short, I said, of the *true Platonic kind;* or I had no notion of what Platonic Love was.

So it is, Jack; and must end as Platonic Love generally does end.[2]

He censures Clarissa's error in hoping 'to have the merit of reclaiming him'[3] and Clarissa eventually criticizes herself, calling her earlier desire to reform the rake 'presumptuous'.[4]

Mrs. Haywood's novels, like Richardson's, are a compendium of maxims about love. This device can be found in the seventeenth-century *romances* and in English Restoration drama, both comic and tragic; Mrs. Haywood has adapted the technique and is able to make it work as part of the texture of a more modern prose narrative. The *sententiae*, which are not mere embellishments, are closely connected with the main theme, and invite the reader to test their validity. The taste for general statement, typical of the age, is found here in statements dealing with lust and love. Richardson shares a desire to unite particular and general, and his *sententiae* are often strikingly similar to those of Mrs. Haywood, as some of the following examples illustrate.

On the nature of love:

Love is ever credulous, and inspires so good an Opinion of the darling Object, that it is not without great Difficulty the Heart which harbours it, can be brought to believe any thing to the prejudice of what it wishes . . .

(Haywood)[5]

CREDULITY is the God of Love's *prime minister* . . .

(Richardson)[6]

---

[1] Haywood, *The Fruitless Enquiry*, 1727, p. 29.
[2] *Clarissa*, iv. 151.   [3] Ibid. vi. 108.
[4] Ibid., p. 137.
[5] Haywood, *Lasselia; or the Self-Abandon'd*, 1724, p. 42.
[6] *Clarissa*, iii. 129.

Love (ingenious in Invention,) . . .

(Haywood)[1]

Love, my dearest Life, is ingenious . . .

(Richardson)[2]

[Anadea] knew so little of the encroaching Nature of the Passion she had entertained . . .

(Haywood)[3]

For Love is an encroacher. Love never goes backward. Love is always aspiring.

(Richardson)[4]

On the nature of women:

Women are Taught by custom to deny what most they Covet, and to seem angry when they are best pleas'd; believe me . . . the most rigid Virtue of 'em all, never yet hated a Man for those faults which Love occasions.

(Haywood)[5]

Nor are women ever angry at bottom for being disobeyed thro' excess of Love. They like an uncontrollable passion.

(Richardson)[6]

Both of the last two quotations are dramatic utterances; the first is among the few instances where Eliza Haywood uses the speech of a character ironically. The Baron in *Love in Excess* is meant to seem coarse, and is proved wrong, like the Emperor in *Aureng-Zebe* when he tells Indamora that force is 'the best excuse of Womankind' and that resistance is assumed to in-flame desire. Mrs. Haywood was beginning to explore the effectiveness of the 'false maxim' in presenting character and situation, something which Richardson does more consistently and cleverly, as in Lovelace's statement quoted above. Both authors use the maxims about love to explore the subject as well as to define it, suggesting various shadings within the emotion.

The heroes of Mrs. Haywood's tales are handsome rakes, who are usually villains as well. The charm of the rake-hero is emphasized, and his cruelty emerges during the course of the action. Like Lovelace, he is spirited, handsome, witty. Euph-

[1] Haywood, *Love in Excess*, part i, p. 3.   [2] *Clarissa*, iii. 109.
[3] Haywood, *Secret Histories*, vol. i, *The Fatal Secret*, pp. 213–14.
[4] *Clarissa*, iv. 352.
[5] Haywood, *Love in Excess*, part ii, p. 43.   [6] *Clarissa*, iii. 340.

emia in *The Surprize* describes Bellamant's attractiveness, 'the manly Majesty which sparkled in his Eyes',[1] as Anna Howe describes Lovelace's appearance, 'so elegant and rich . . . yet no affectation . . . but all manly . . .'[2] Mrs. Haywood's heroes also have a command of florid hyperbole, with which they soften the hearts of their fair ones. D'Elmont evades Amena's remonstrances with the lover's rhetoric: 'Oh! thou inhuman and Tyrannick Charmer . . . (seizing her Hand, and eagerly kissing it) . . .'[3] The perfidious 'Courtal' woos Belinda, who first treats his protestations of love as raillery:

He wou'd not suffer me to proceed, but falling on his Knees before me, and looking up in my Face with a Tenderness unutterable, O hold (cry'd he) lovely Insulter! give not to the most Almighty Truth, a breaking—bleeding Heart, e'er yet sent forth, so injurious an Epithet.—By Heaven! . . . you are dearer to my Soul than Health, than Grandeur, Knowledge, Light, Life, or my eternal Peace . . .[4]

Lovelace commands this kind of language:

He threw himself upon his knees at my feet—Who can bear, said he [with an ardour that could not be feigned, his own eyes glistening] Who can bear, to behold such sweet emotion?—O charmer of my heart [and, respectfully still kneeling, he took my hand with both his, pressing it to his lips] command me *with* you, command me *from* you; in every way I am all implicit obedience—[5]

In the passages from Mrs. Haywood, it can be seen that she has developed the description of the love situation by using direct speech, and, as it were, stage directions ('seizing her hand', 'falling on his Knees before me')—the same technique which Richardson uses, with the same purpose, that of capturing the situation in its immediacy within the prose narrative.

A dialect of sexual passion is common to both authors, in the constant use of the words 'Liberty', 'Freedom', 'Encroacher'. Cleomira could not resist Lysander's 'proceeding from one Freedom to another';[6] Belinda weakly struggles against 'the encroaching Liberty' of her lover's hands.[7] As Lovelace, the student of the seduction process, comments, 'Love, when

[1] Haywood, *The Surprize; or, Constancy Rewarded*, 1724, p. 9.
[2] *Clarissa*, vi. 452.   [3] Haywood, *Love in Excess*, part i, p. 27.
[4] Idem, *The British Recluse*, p. 104.   [5] *Clarissa*, ii. 354–5.
[6] Haywood, *The British Recluse*, p. 47.   [7] Ibid., p. 113.

acknowledged, authorizes freedom; and freedom begets freedom; and I shall then see how far I can go.'[1] Richardson,
however, explores the language more fully. There are ironic
overtones to the use of such words as 'liberty' and 'freedom'
which have meanings other than these sexual ones, and in
ironic contrast to them; Clarissa is a prisoner who desires to be
free.

That the language of Mrs. Haywood tends to seem trite is not
perhaps so much owing to the quality of that language in itself
as to the inanity of the personages involved—they have little
character, and so one cannot be very interested in their emotions
except as they reflect situations and states of mind interesting
to, or recognized by, the reader. That her descriptions do
succeed, to a limited extent, in doing that, is a quality of her
language. If the emphasis of the language were on the physical
relationship only, she could be labelled 'pornographic', but the
stress is on the emotional reaction of the heroine, and the inner
turmoil to which love and sexual desire give rise.

Richardson's language differs in many ways from that of
contemporary major novelists, not least in that he has developed,
by drawing upon the drama and the minor novels, a language
of love, not just a language about love. Love relationships in
Fielding and Smollett are rather static, and the state of mind
involved in being in love is not elaborated upon. Sexual desire
is treated briefly:

> The capuchin came to me, and asked if I was insensible to love,
> and so hard-hearted as to refuse a share of my bed to a pretty maid,
> who had a *tendresse* for me.—I must own, to my shame, that I
> suffered myself to be overcome by my passion, and with great
> eagerness seized the occasion, when I understood that the amiable
> Nanette was to be my bed fellow.—In vain did my reason suggest
> the respect that I owed to my dear mistress Narcissa; the idea of that
> lovely charmer, rather increased than allayed the ferment of my
> spirits; and the young Paisanne had no reason to complain of my
> remembrance.—Early in the morning, the kind creatures left us to
> our repose . . .[2]

or with comic distancing: 'Here ensued a parley . . . at the

---

[1] *Clarissa*, iv. 281.

[2] Tobias Smollett, *The Adventures of Roderick Random*, 2 vols., 1748, vol. ii, ch.
xlii, p. 54.

conclusion of which they retired into the thickest part of the grove.'[1] The hero's love for the heroine is generalized, part of the novel's given data, not a process in which the novelist is interested. A description indicating the grace and beauty of the heroine is almost sufficient to indicate that the hero is in love with her and deserves her as a prize. It must be added that the erotic emotional language is occasionally used by a novelist such as Smollett, but it is in context very flat, not necessarily only because it is stilted in itself, but because this is not the way that this novelist's imagination operates, nor has it much to do with the emotional life of the hero (the extrovert Roderick is motivated chiefly by a desire for success and a strong determination that others shall not get the better of him). The reunion with Narcissa is presented in the language of the love novelist:

How was my soul transported when she broke in upon my view, in all the bloom of ripened beauty! . . . You, whose souls are susceptible of the most delicate impressions . . . who have suffered an absence of eighteen long months from the dear object of your hope, and found at your return the melting fair, as kind and constant as your heart could wish . . . conceive what unutterable rapture possessed us both, while we flew into one another's arms! . . . When I thus encircled all that my soul held dear,—while I hung over her beauties,—beheld her eyes sparkle, and every feature flush with virtuous fondness,—when I saw her enchanting bosom heave with undissembled rapture . . . Heavens! what was my situation![2]

The language is descriptive, not analytical, and rather perfunctory. We are not invited to see any connection between this Roderick, rewarded with a virtuous bride, and the Roderick who felt compelled to take revenge upon Melinda for refusing him by subjecting her to public humiliation.[3] Roderick's emotions don't have that kind of internal existence, and the reader knows that the love passage quoted above really stands for something else, for the pot of gold at the foot of the rainbow, or the reward of the successful combatant in life.

Richardson's use of the language of love is designed (like Mrs. Haywood's in her lesser degree) to convey the erotic as

---

[1] Fielding, *The History of Tom Jones a Foundling*, Shakespeare Head edition, Oxford, 1926, 4 vols., vol. i, book v, ch. x, p. 261.
[2] Smollett, *Roderick Random*, vol. ii, ch. lxvii, pp. 347–8.
[3] Ibid., ch. l, pp. 143–57.

constantly significant. Using the style and vocabulary available to him, he is able to convey desire, warmth, tenderness, admiration, hostility. Like all attempts to convey such feelings the language is conventional to a certain degree, but it has its own force, not least because Richardson is aware of the ironies involved in the love-situation, and the possibility of self-contra-diction. (Mrs. Haywood is not blind to these ironies: Courtal, in the passage quoted above, is not going to be faithful, whereas D'Elmont courts Amena only to amuse himself: ' 'till by making a shew of Tenderness he began to fancy himself really touch'd with a passion he only design'd to represent'.)[1]

Like Lovelace, and like the heroes of comedy, Mrs. Haywood's heroes are adept at disguises and intrigue, and capable of using deception to win possession of their fair ones. 'Lysander' in *The British Recluse* walks by Cleomira's house in disguise, and also assumes a disguise to court Belinda. In *Lasselia*, the courtly lover is disguised as a rustic when he follows the heroine into the country, revealing himself suddenly, when much to her surprise 'He threw off his upper Garment, and a black Peruke which had served him as a Disguise . . .'[2] This kind of 'un-masking' scene is not unlike that in *Clarissa*, when Lovelace at Hampstead unbuttons his cape, throws off his slouched hat, and reveals himself.[3] Lovelace delights in secrets and disguises. Once, he hints, he obtained access to a woman's bedroom by being disguised as a parson.[4] The *fabliau* element in such a story relates it not so much to the stage tradition as to the old tradition of amorous and bawdy tales (of which Boccaccio's are best known) which Eliza Haywood was drawing upon, particularly in the collection of stories in *The Fruitless Enquiry*. In her better-constructed *novelle*, it is evident that she is trying to work such tales into the substance of more modern fiction, in which the interest depends more on the emotion aroused by an incident than on the event itself. Some of the incidents used by Richardson seem to go back to the same kind of source, such as the story of the French *marquise*, a bawdy little tale from Lovelace's past experience, and related by him in the novel,

---

[1] Haywood, *Love in Excess*, part i, p. 13.
[2] Idem, *Lasselia*, pp. 23–4.
[3] *Clarissa*, v. 88.
[4] Ibid. vii. 6.

where it serves to vary the seriousness of the main narration with the effect of an inset *fabliau*.[1]

A tale like that of the French *marquise* is of a type dear to Mrs. Haywood, who enjoys permutations of amatory situations, and touches of the slightly bizarre. Richardson occasionally uses such touches, usually as freaks of Lovelace's sexually stimulated imagination rather than as actual events within the novel. One of Lovelace's oddest whims might have been based on one of Mrs. Haywood's novels. In *The British Recluse*, the heroines Cleomira and Belinda find, after each has related her sad tale, that they have a seducer in common—Cleomira's 'Lysander' is the same man as Belinda's 'Courtal'. On the basis of this mutual experience, they strike up a firm friendship: 'These fair Companions in Affliction past some time in bewailing their several Misfortunes, sometimes exclaiming against the *Vices*, sometimes praising the *Beauties*, of their common Betrayer . . .'[2] They have a constant topic of conversation: 'Their common Misfortunes was a Theme not to be exhausted, and they still found something for which to condole each other.'[3] They retire to the country, taking a house together 'where they still live . . . happy in the real Friendship of each other . . . and free from all the *Hurries* and *Disquiets* which attend the Gaieties of the Town'.[4]

One of Lovelace's sadistic fantasies is the creation of a situation in which the future bond of friendship between Clarissa and Anna Howe shall be similar to that between Cleomira and Belinda:

How sweetly pretty to see the two lovely friends, when humbled and tame, both sitting in the darkest corner of a room, arm in arm, weeping and sobbing for each other![5]

And when I have executed That my vengeance, how charmingly satisfied may they both go down into the country, and keep house together, and have a much better reason than their Pride could give them, for living the Single Life they have both seemed so fond of![6]

It is as if Lovelace, who often speaks and thinks in a Haywoodian manner, had read *The British Recluse* with an ironic

---

[1] Ibid. iv. 283–5.   [2] Haywood, *The British Recluse*, p. 136.
[3] Ibid., p. 137.   [4] Ibid., p. 138.
[5] *Clarissa*, iv. 195.   [6] Ibid. v. 49.

perception of 'sour grapes' in the feminist ending, and imagined such a situation of feminine defeat from the ego-satisfying view of the rake in the case.

Mrs. Haywood's novels are all, in their way, fantasies, with little relation to known reality; they are often cheap enough, but they have a kind of power. The seduction and rape tale can have a good deal of suspense. Relentless passion stalks the heroine, who becomes increasingly powerless, in a hot-house world of seduction where there is no escape. The hero has unlimited time and money at his command; even the friends surrounding the heroine can be bought or won over by the hero, as Lysander bribes Cleomira's guardians, the Marvirs, to assist him. Don Ferdinand, in *Idalia*, has a house and servants at his command, as Lovelace has Sinclair's. It is interesting to compare the two novels, as at some points they are similar.

Idalia is induced to come to an evil house; the irony with which it is mentioned is like that of Clarissa's descriptions of 'Mrs. Sinclair's': '''Twas easy for her to find the House, the *good Woman* of it waited at the door for her approach . . .'[1] When Idalia finds only Ferdinand, instead of the friend she expected, she tries to leave, but is prevented by Don Ferdinand's ardent advances. Like Richardson's heroines, Idalia, when forced to endure her lover's 'eager graspings', saves herself by fainting, as her lover (like Richardson's heroes upon occasion) is not unmoved by such a display of horror.[2] When Idalia regains her senses, she falls on her knees and pleads with Ferdinand, but he is not to be dissuaded; however, he finds her more resolute than he anticipated. She snatches a dagger, and threatens first him, and then herself:

> It would have been easy for him to have wrested it from her afterwards; but she perceiving his Intent, turn'd the Point to her own Breast, and invoking all the Saints and Angels to be witnesses of her Vow, swore she would strike it thro' her Heart the moment he attempted to disarm her. 'No, barbarous Man (*pursu'd she*) . . . thou now shalt find there's one among us who dares meet Death to fly Dishonour— . . . behold and tremble at my *Virtue*'s Bravery!'[3]

This scene is a Haywoodian version of scenes in stage drama, as is Richardson's 'penknife scene' in *Clarissa*;[4] Mrs. Haywood

---

[1] Haywood, *Idalia, or the Unfortunate Mistress*, 1723, p. 11.
[2] Ibid., pp. 14–15.   [3] Ibid., pp. 16–17.   [4] *Clarissa*, vi. 67–9.

anticipated Richardson in weaving this type of dramatic scene
into a prose narrative dealing with a rake-hero, and a successful
rape. In Mrs. Haywood's story, the heroine's display of heroic
valour occurs before the rape, and is not a victory, as she is
outwitted by the hero. Ferdinand counterfeits extreme contrition, and is forgiven. Since it is too late for Idalia to go home,
he persuades her to remain in the house, saying that he is
leaving. He reassures her about the people of the house, and
gives her the key to the door, so she is lulled into a false sense of
security.

She had not been an hour in Bed, before she felt the Clothes
thrown off, and something catch fast hold of her: The Voice and
Actions of the Person told her it was no other than *Don Ferdinand*, as
did his own Behaviour and Confession afterward, that the Story of
his Repentance was but forg'd . . . and the Delivery of the Key only
an Artifice to engage her Trust; there being a Back-Door to the
House, by which he immediately entered, and came into the
Chamber thro' a Closet, which had a Passage into another Room.

WHAT was now the Distraction of this unhappy Lady, wak'd
from her dream of Vanity to certain Ruin! Unavoidable Destruction! She rav'd, she tore, did all that Woman could, but all in vain—
In the midst of Shrieks and Tremblings, Cries, Curses, Swoonings,
the impatient *Ferdinand* perpetrated his Intent, and finished her
Undoing.[1]

In Mrs. Haywood's novels, the heroes are successful enough
in midnight attempts to justify Lovelace's confidence in '*nightly
surprizes*'.[2] Her novels are full of lush amorous scenes; almost
every one has a set piece in which the beautiful heroine is discovered at night at a moment when she is most vulnerable to
the hero's attempt. The treacherous D'Elmont obtains access
to Melliora's room by means of a back stairs, and a secretly
made key to her door, and coming uninvited into 'the Happy
Chamber' gloats over the beauty of his beloved, asleep and
half-exposed,[3] as earlier he had enjoyed seeing her in 'Charming
Dissabillee' with 'Hair unbraided' and in loosely flowing garments which 'discover'd a Thousand Beauties, which Modish
Formalities conceal'.[4] The discovery of the heroine in negligent

---

[1] Haywood, *Idalia*, pp. 21–2. Compare the style of the last sentence with that of
Lovelace describing the climax of his 'dream' (*Clarissa*, vi. 12).

[2] Ibid. iv. 217.

[3] Haywood, *Love in Excess*, part ii, pp. 46–7.   [4] Ibid., p. 35.

attire is one of the high points in the Haywoodian seduction or
rape novel. Such warm descriptions resemble some passages in
Clarissa, notably those in the 'fire scene' when Lovelace by
stratagem gains access to Clarissa's room at midnight:

> But, O the sweet discomposure!—Her bared shoulders and arms,
> so inimitably fair and lovely: Her spread hands crossed over her
> charming neck; yet not half concealing its glossy beauties: The
> scanty coat, as she rose from me, giving the whole of her admirable
> shape, and fine-turn'd limbs . . .[1]

Melliora, surprised, like Clarissa, by the sudden irruption of
her lover, puts up a defence of cries to heaven, appeals to his
honour and his avowed love, and protests 'I do Conjure you,
even by that Love you plead, before my Honour, I'll resign my
Life!'[2] Mrs. Haywood's Melliora is, however, although sincere
in defending her honour, extremely susceptible to D'Elmont's
advances, as was his previous victim, Amena. The hearts of
Mrs. Haywood's heroines are usually of the lover's party, and
their reactions are such as to justify Lovelace's confidence that
'Love was ever a traitor to its harbourer'[3] and that 'pure
Nature, taking advantage of Nature' can be relied upon.[4]

Once a Haywood heroine has fallen victim to the wiles of a
seducer, even if the final favour has not yet been forced or
granted, she pours forth complaints in scenes of recrimination
which recall the 'grand style' of the ravished victims of the
stage plays: 'Why ye Monsters of barbarity, said she, do you
delight in beholding the ruins you have made? Is not the
knowledge of my Miseries, my everlasting miseries, sufficient to
content you?'[5] *Clarissa* has similar scenes of recrimination, but
Clarissa is not guilty of complicity in her own undoing, as are
most of the Haywood heroines. Occasionally, however, Mrs.
Haywood dabbles at the edge of the Richardsonian situation.
Idalia is guilty in that she is foolish, and too trusting, but she
harbours no secret desire for the hero. In this story, which like
Clarissa is a tale of rape, not of ordinary seduction, the heroine
does not forgive the hero. Ferdinand thinks that 'Time and
Assiduity may work upon her',[6] but he is proved wrong, and
Idalia is resolute in refusing him: 'Hell, Hell is not so dreadful

---

[1] *Clarissa,* iv. 392.   [2] Haywood, *Love in Excess,* part ii, p. 49.
[3] *Clarissa,* iii. 95.   [4] Ibid. iv. 375.
[5] Haywood, *Love in Excess,* part i, p. 28.   [6] Idem, *Idalia,* p. 42.

as the Thoughts of seeing him again!'[1] Ferdinand, still separated from Idalia, is killed in a duel. This part of the novel is a kind of *Clarissa* in little, and maintains its interest, although it falls off sadly after the Ferdinand section.

As far as her reading public, if not the literary one, was concerned, Mrs. Haywood established the seduction novel as a minor genre in English fiction, and it is to this genre that Richardson's work ultimately belongs, although before Richardson it was not from a literary point of view a respectable form of fiction. The novel in letters was already established, although it took Richardson to realize its full potential. The use of letters as a form of narration, either partial or complete, was already connected with the novel of love. If Mrs. Haywood, an experimenter with the letter form, had realized that the epistolary novel could well be combined with the seduction plot, she might have produced a very minor *Clarissa*—but she was not a Richardson, and did not.

Richardson combines the world of the bourgeois novel of courtship with the fantastic world of the novel of rape and seduction. *Clarissa* combines the tones of both; it has the humour, realism, and conversational speech of the one with the high-pitched and florid style of the other. The thoughtful heroine of the bourgeois novel has been pitched into the tense situation and dream-like atmosphere of the seduction story. Mrs. Haywood has preceded Richardson in introducing the language and incidents of some of the stage plays, both tragic and sentimental, into the prose tale of love and seduction. In doing so, she developed the possibilities of prose narration in this kind of story, with elements from the old romances and traditional tales of love and intrigue. Her novels may be inferior, but they are inferior as novels, not bad plays. In her victimized heroines and handsome villainous heroes she does make us feel the fascination of the rabbit by the snake, and creates an atmosphere of pent-up passion, an atmosphere which is not the result of the action alone, but also of the emotions of characters involved. The lubric scenes which are her great set pieces are carefully built up. She suggests an environment in which even the resisting heroine is helpless because she is imprisoned in a world of sexual passion. All-conquering passion triumphs when

[1] Ibid., p. 35.

F

the heroes emerge through back door and secret entrances, breaking in upon the heroines' false security.

The locked doors, passages, back stairs, walls, and keys which Richardson uses so effectively were already a traditional part of the amatory tale. Richardson transforms the hackneyed devices of the rape novel, increasing their suggestive power. Doors, walls, entrances are important images in *Clarissa*. In this novel, more effectively than in the earlier tales of rape and seduction, passion bursts through the security of normality, and passion imprisons all. Richardson combines these images with the religious theme, which in his novel becomes another source of intense emotion.

Richardson saw the deeper, more universal application of the main conflict in the rape tale. He uses the same situation as that in many of the early novels to create real instead of pasteboard tragedy. He harked back to the tradition of great tragedy on the same theme, and had no desire that his work should be associated with the flimsy and disreputable novels. Yet he uses the same techniques, the same devices, the same language as are found in those, and was fortunate in having predecessors who had already developed the domestic English novel. What Coleridge calls 'the close, hot, day-dreamy continuity'[1] is a development from the novelists earlier in his century who had dealt with themes of passion, and had endeavoured to examine the characters through the stream of their emotions, to show the mechanism of the clock, not just the face.

[1] Samuel Taylor Coleridge, in *The Literary Remains of Samuel Taylor Coleridge*, ed. Henry Nelson Coleridge, 2 vols., 1836, ii. 376.

VII

Holy and Unholy Dying: The Death-bed Theme in *Clarissa*

IF Richardson took hints from novelists like Mrs. Haywood in expressing the tension of inner emotional life, *Clarissa* is none the less a novel about interior emotion on a far wider scale, expressing a different artistic and moral purpose. If Mrs. Haywood's novels state: 'In love, intensity of inner emotion is what matters', Richardson's novel says: 'Interior life, the life of consciousness, is what matters above all.' The theme of the love novels is given a wider implication. The love conflict can be effectively presented (even in light sensational literature) in terms of imprisonment of the intense consciousness which finds no safety within or without. But this can be seen as an aspect of the truth of life itself, that it is a matter of the intense consciousness imprisoned by fate and outer circumstances, ardently hoping and fearing and knowing no security. The strange intense dream-like continuum which is consciousness comprehends death too. The thinking reed knows that which destroys him; the manner of his knowledge and the action of his will in light of this knowledge create and complete the manifestation of his true identity.

Richardson's tragedy follows the pattern of dramatic tragedy, but his is a tragedy in which event is translated into the language of the inner world. In heroic tragedy, death is an action of the will—a particular elaborate gesture in murder or suicide. It is the end embraced by almost superhuman persons, who have been involved in the conflict of crowns and states, and have spurned all else in clinging to one idea, whether ambition, honour, or love. But death is not a peculiar option—all men die, and it is the nature of consciousness to accommodate that fact by avoiding or acknowledging it in various ways.

There is a whole body of literature dealing with the awareness of death, of facing death, upon which Richardson drew. The devotional literature of the seventeenth and eighteenth centuries deals with the death of the average human being, good or bad, reprobate or saved soul, and it views all from a specifically Christian standpoint. The drama of death, even when played out in a world of bed-curtains and cordials, friends and physicians, bears some relationship to the statements of heroic tragedy. In both heroic plays and devotional literature the soul and the world are at odds. The world is too small for the spirit; the glorious soul reaches upwards towards the heavens. In the Christian devotional literature, the meanest individual has the stature accorded in drama only to the great and noble; he has heroic potential, is part of a supra-mundane world, is hero or villain, citizen of heaven or hell.

It is a mistake to think that Richardson added the deathbed scenes to *Clarissa* for the sake of extra pathos or morbid effect. Even when the details are a trifle too insistent (which is true only in Belton's case) such scenes serve as a defined expression of the importance of individual life, conscience, and consciousness. Without Richardson's belief in the superlative importance of the individual psychic life, from the minutest nuance of perception to the most demanding exercise of the will, there would be no *Clarissa*. The activity of transforming matter into spirit is the incessant essential action of the self; the narration in letters is in this novel an image of the material world transformed into consciousness, and the characters present themselves and all that concerns them as consciousness engaged in activity. (If *Clarissa* were narrated in, for instance, third-person and past tense—if one could imagine such a thing—the novel could not have the same meaning.) Not only the world around them, but also some aspect of each of the individual characters offers the temptation to devalue this life of the spirit. The impotence or tragic absurdity of trying to believe that the material world is primary, and individual life accidental, is conveyed from the beginning by the narrative form. How can the Harlowes make such a fuss about estates, and money, and plate, and silks, when these can be known only through the mind, as we see through their presentation in Clarissa's letters, in which everything exists in perception and judgement? For Richardson, consciousness and spirit are the same, and from the beginning he has passed the judgement that the spirit has a larger destiny than it realizes, even wishes to realize.

It could be argued that this emphasis upon personal consciousness makes Richardson one of the first Romantic writers (the Romantics themselves seem to have thought so in their enthusiasm for him). Such a suggestion might even be true, but it seems more important to understand Richardson as a Christian artist, his emphasis upon spiritual life a Christian theme. For Richardson, the love of God is a natural passion. As he dared to include in his tragic novel the theme of the soul facing death, the end and test of its inevitable conflict in life, he drew with some confidence upon devotional literature which, since the early seventeenth century, had laid increasing emphasis upon the state of mind of the dying person, and had lent itself to a degree of psychological investigation. (It may be that Richardson felt justified in using the techniques of self-revelation and psychological analysis to the extent he does in *Clarissa* (an extent which encompasses Lovelace's libidinous fantasies) because psychological analysis had been employed in the religious literature.) In his particular references the author makes explicit for us influences which had shaped his own imaginative ideas of human nature, and amplifies both irony and tragedy in the novel. To understand these influences, and their meaning and effect within the novel, it would seem advisable to undertake a fairly detailed examination of Richardson's use of religious works and deathbed scenes in *Clarissa*.

Richardson was quite aware that he was adapting traditional devotional material, and wished his readers to notice the fact. A number of religious and devotional works which deal with the art of dying are explicitly mentioned in *Clarissa* and thus brought to our attention, just as the references to the tragedies provide a constant background to the novel. Among the books to be found in Clarissa's apartment at Mrs. Sinclair's are several religious works, including the sermons of South and Tillotson.[1] Clarissa has other devotional works at her disposal; when she asks her family to send her her books as well as her clothes and money, her brother sends her only a select library of books dealing with death:

They were brought me on Thursday; but neither my few guineas

[1] *Clarissa*, iii. 318.

with them, nor any of my books, except a *Drexelius on Eternity*, the good old *Practice of Piety*, and a *Francis Spira*. My Brother's wit, I suppose. He thinks he does well to point out death and despair to me.[1]

The three books mentioned are of varied authorship. Drexelius was a famous Jesuit preacher of the late sixteenth century, whose works were translated into English in the middle of the seventeenth century.[2] Lewis Bayly, author of the popular *Practice of Piety*, was a sixteenth-century Anglican, with a strong Puritan bias. The themes of both works are the same—the necessity of considering our end, the danger of damnation, the joys of salvation, the briefness of time—and are delivered with the same intensity. There is an irony in James Harlowe's sending them to his sister, as Clarissa is going to die in the manner approved by Drexelius and Bayly. If taken in another way, these books are messages of hope, because they point a way to salvation. Only the *Francis Spira* is a message of despair; this interesting little book describes the death of an apostate who met his end deprived of grace and hope.[3] James Harlowe sent the book to his sister as a direct insult, indicating that her case was desperate. It is not, but the deaths of Belton and Mrs. Sinclair furnish illustrations of the death of despair. James and the rest of the family ought to be contemplating the message of death, as they have been blind to all but the things of this world. There is perhaps also a concealed implication that the Harlowes in rejecting Clarissa are in a sense apostates, like Spira, and have thrust grace from them, as he did.

---

[1] *Clarissa*, iv. 28.

[2] *The Considerations of Drexelius upon Eternitie*, by Hieremias Drexelius, translated by Ralph Winterton, printed in Cambridge, 1636, and appearing in subsequent editions, is an emblem book, an interesting fact in the light of the emblematic elements in Richardson's imagery. Drexelius, a Roman Catholic writer, is as austere in his contemplation of the world as any 'Puritan' writer could be. The word 'Puritan' has become rather meaningless. 'Puritanism's spiritual inwardness and its fear of the flesh' (Ian Watt, *The Rise of the Novel*, p. 243) is unsatisfying as an explanation of *Clarissa*. There is 'spiritual inwardness' in Loyola, and 'fear of the flesh' in Drexelius. The ascetic attitude to the world and the flesh has been a continuous element in Western thought.

[3] The story of a sixteenth-century Italian who apostatized from Protestantism and repented too late was adapted into an English play, *The Conflict of Conscience*, by Nathaniel Woodes, printed in 1581. A Continental prose narrative was later translated by Nathaniel Bacon as *A Relation of the Fearful Estate of Francis Spira*, and went through several editions in the mid seventeenth century. The edition referred to in this chapter is that of 1653.

Jeremy Taylor's great classic, *Holy Living and Dying*, is also mentioned in an ironic context. Before the rape, when Lovelace brings his pretended relatives to Hampstead in order to decoy Clarissa back to the brothel, he stands aside at one end of the room, feigning lack of interest in the conversation which the 'ladies' have with Miss Harlowe. Clarissa later remembers the incident, and sees that his choice of a book at that time was an anomaly, and should have warned her that he was only pretending to read, and was still directing a scene of his own devising.

The grand deluder was at the farther end of the room, another way; probably to give me an opportunity to hear these preconcerted praises—looking into a book, which, had there not been a preconcert, would not have taken his attention for one moment. It was *Taylor's Holy Living and Dying*.

When the pretended Ladies joined me, he approached me with it in his hand—A smart book, This, my dear!—This old divine affects, I see, a mighty flowery style upon a very solemn subject. But it puts me in mind of an ordinary Country Funeral, where the young women, in honour of a defunct companion, especially if she were a virgin, or *passed for such*, make a flower-bed of her coffin.[1]

Lovelace's elaborate conceit shows that he can think of death only in terms of his ruling passion. His remarks have a sinister implication; Clarissa is to be a virgin no longer, even if she will 'pass for such'. His remarks are flippant, but, as he does not realize, they foreshadow Clarissa's own funeral, which is indeed like that of a virgin, and at which young girls strew flowers on her corpse. Lovelace is incapable of thinking of death except as a subject which can be treated aesthetically. Clarissa will exemplify 'Holy Dying', and Lovelace its grim opposite. If he had taken Taylor seriously he could have read his own fate there. His plans and actions at that moment are directly opposed to everything that Taylor enjoins, and his own conceit has echoes of a grim Taylorian contrast—flowers decking a corpse. His lighting upon Taylor before the rape could be looked upon as a warning given him by Providence before he commits an act which severs him from grace, and makes his death fearful to contemplate. It is a mark of Richardson's literary tact that this is not stated, even by Clarissa, who sees

[1] *Clarissa*, vi. 171-2.

only that Lovelace's reading Taylor was a falsehood she should have detected.

Anna and Clarissa are familiar with the religious works of another author, the poems of John Norris of Bemerton. Anna sends Clarissa fifty guineas enclosed in Norris's *Miscellanies*,[1] which Clarissa returns. References to this interchange puzzle Lovelace when he reads some of their letters: 'Now, what the devil can this mean! ... The devil take me, if I am *out-Norris'd*!'[2] If Lovelace had been well read in religious poetry, he might have known the work of this Anglican Neoplatonist, many of whose poems celebrate friendship, and the union of virtuous souls in Heaven.[3] His most notable poems deal with the mysterious parting of the soul from the body at the moment of death, and speculate on the joys of eternity.[4] Lovelace is 'out-Norris'd' by Clarissa's joyful acceptance of death. Even Belford is acquainted with the works of this author; in endeavouring to console the dying Belton, he quotes from Norris's 'The Meditation', another poem dealing with the mystery of death.[5]

Belford also quotes a passage from John Pomfret's *A Prospect of Death*.[6] This allusion, which would have been immediately recognized by most of Richardson's contemporary readers, illuminates for us the tradition on which he drew in creating the deathbed scenes in the novel.[7] In the devotional literature

---

[1] *Clarissa*, iii. 288.   [2] Ibid. iv. 188.

[3] e.g. 'The Parting' in John Norris's *A Collection of Miscellanies*, 1687, pp. 17–19. Compare the tone of lament for a friend's death with Anna Howe's lament for the loss of Clarissa (*Clarissa*, viii. 86–9).

[4] See Norris, 'The Prospect', *Miscellanies*, pp. 120–1.

[5] *Clarissa*, vii. 180. See Norris, 'The Meditation', *Miscellanies*, pp. 30–1.

[6] *Clarissa*, vii. 181. This poem, by John Pomfret, rector of Malden, was first issued as *A Prospect of Death: A Pindarique Essay*. Written by the Right Honourable the late Earl of Roscommon, in 1704, and was reprinted in subsequent collections of Roscommon's works. In the first edition of *Clarissa*, Richardson ascribes the poem to Roscommon; in the third edition, he corrects the error, substituting the name of 'Mr. Pomfret' for that of the Earl, but the phrase 'the noble poet' remains on an ensuing page (vii. 184), an anomaly explained by Richardson's original mistake. I have used the 1704 edition, as Richardson may well have done so, and the poem is better printed and set out there than in some later editions.

Perhaps Pomfret should be better known to us; this poem is of some importance in the development of the Pindaric elegy in English poetry. He was popular in the eighteenth century. Johnson, who insisted that Pomfret be included among the *English Poets*, praises him with restraint: 'He pleases many, and he who pleases many must have merit.' (See *The Lives of the most Eminent English Poets*, 4 vols., 1781, i. 432.)

[7] J. W. Draper discusses Pomfret's poem as an example of a compromise between

dealing with the deathbed, and in the early eighteenth-century poetry deriving from this tradition such as Young's *Night Thoughts* (1742–5) and Blair's *The Grave* (1743), the psychological state of a dying person is examined in theological terms: what does it feel like to be dying? what is the state of mind of the dying sinner? or the dying saint? The pattern followed by Pomfret is the same as that of the later Uvedale, whose poem *The Death-Bed Display'd* professes to be 'grounded on a Passage in Doctor Taylor's *Holy Dying*', and could equally claim to be 'a sort of POETICAL Sermon'.[1] Like Taylor, Pomfret first describes the pains of dying, dwelling in detail on the feebleness of the senses.[2] Pomfret also continues to describe and contrast the state of the wicked at point of death with that of the righteous. When the wicked die,

> If any Sense at that sad Time remains,
>   They feel amazing Terrors, mighty Pains,
>   The Earnest of the vast stupendious Woe,
>   Which they to all Eternity must undergo;[3]

but the pure soul

> Looks thro' the Darkness of the glooming Night,
>   And sees the Dawning of a glorious Day.

The good man has his own virtues for advocates, and is comforted by visions of angels: 'All is calm within, and all without is Fair.'[4]

In Richardson's novel, Clarissa's death is set between those of Belton and Mrs. Sinclair, just as in traditional religious literature the end of the wicked and that of the righteous are set side by side. Belton's deathbed is an *exemplum*, showing the state of the sinner who has put off repentance until his last days.

Puritan and classical traditions in funereal poetry. (See Draper, *The Funeral Elegy and the Rise of English Romanticism*, 1929, pp. 205–6.) He thinks such compromise developed into meditative poems on death, such as those of Young and Blair, and was the background to the romantic melancholy of Gray and others. Draper examines only the poetic tradition, neglecting the influence of devout prose writers who deal with similar themes.

[1] Thomas Uvedale, *The Death-Bed Display'd: with the State of the Dead*. A sacred Poem, 1727, p. iv.

[2] Pomfret, *A Prospect of Death*, 1704, pp. 2–3. Compare Jeremy Taylor, *The Rule and Exercises of Holy Dying*, 1651, ch. 2, sect. 4, pp. 72–3.

[3] Pomfret, *A Prospect of Death*, p. 6. Compare *Holy Dying*, ch. 2, sect. 4, pp. 73–4.

[4] Pomfret, *A Prospect of Death*, p. 7. Compare *Holy Dying*, ch. 2, sect. 4, pp. 74–6.

The episode is a fictional presentation of a favourite theme of the divines: the evils of a late repentance.[1]

Belton has all the classic symptoms of the dying sinner as represented in devout literature. The physical approach of death is described with the same details which we find in Taylor:

> When the sentence of death is decreed, and begins to be put in execution, it is sorrow enough to see or feel respectively the sad accidents of the agony, and last contentions of the soul, and the reluctancies and unwillingnesses of the body. The forehead wash'd with a new and stranger baptisme, besmeared with a cold sweat, tenacious and clammy, apt to make it cleave to the roof of his coffin; the nose cold and undiscerning . . . the eyes dim as a sullied mirror . . . the feet cold, the hands stiffe, the Physitians despairing, our friends weeping . . . the nobler part . . . assaulted by exteriour rudenesses . . . at last, faint and weary, with short and frequent breathings, interrupted with the longer accents of sighes . . . it retires to its last fort . . .[2]

When Belford arrives, Belton is so weak he cannot rise;[3] later he faints.[4] His lips become 'clammy, half-cold';[5] he begins to lose the power of speech.[6] The terrible change in his appearance, indicating, as Taylor says, 'the violences which the soul and spirit suffer',[7] is minutely depicted: 'His eyes look like breath-stained glass! They roll ghastly no more; are quite set: His face distorted, and drawn out, by his sinking jaws, and erected staring eyebrows . . . to double its usual length, as it seems.'[8]

The real horror of a deathbed, however, lies not in physical suffering, but in the emotional and spiritual state of a sinner. Belton, like the dying sinner described by the divines, is violently afraid of death. Tillotson, in his sermon 'The wisdome of religion justified, in the different ends of good and bad Men', impressively describes the troubles that afflict the dying sinner.

> But especially at the approach of death, what a sad preparation for that is an impious and wicked life? How does his conscience then fly in his face, and how bitter is the remembrance of those sins which he committed with so much pleasure and greediness? What a terror is the almighty to him, and the apprehension of that ven-

---

[1] See Taylor, *Holy Dying*, ch. 4, sect. 5, and Tillotson, *Sermons on Several Subjects and Occasions, By the most Reverend Dr. John Tillotson*, 12 vols., 1742, vol. i, Sermon x.
[2] Taylor, *Holy Dying*, ch. 2, sect. 4, pp. 72–3.   [3] *Clarissa*, vii. 171.
[4] Ibid., p. 173.   [5] Ibid., p. 183.   [6] Ibid.
[7] Taylor, *Holy Dying*, ch. 2, sect. 4, pp. 72–3.   [8] *Clarissa*, vii. 208.

geance that threatens him . . . ? And in the midst of all this anguish and horror, which naturally spring from an evil conscience . . . he is destitute of all comfort and hope . . . his whole life hath been a continued affront of the divine majesty, and an insolent defiance of his justice; and what hopes can he now reasonably have of his mercy?[1]

Belton revolves his own mental anguish, and considers what Lovelace's suffering will be in the same case.[2] Despite his suffering, Belton fears that his repentance is ineffectual, that he has only 'kept his vices until they left him'.[3] He could be echoing Taylor: 'Religion is no religion . . . if we part with our money when we cannot keep it, with our lust when we cannot act it, with our desires when they have left us . . .'[4] Belton repeats his fears that the time for repentance is past:

> I, who have despised all warnings . . . but left all to the last stake; hoping for recovery against hope, and driving off Repentance, till that grace is denied me; for, oh! my dear Belford! I can now neither repent, nor pray, as I ought; my heart is hardened, and I can do nothing but despair!—[5]

The idea that the power to repent is lessened during the course of a sinful life is common in religious literature. The sense of gracelessness at death is powerfully expressed in a Calvinistic picture of a reprobate's death in *A Relation of the fearful Estate of Francis Spira,* and in its seventeenth-century Anglican imitation, *The Second Spira.*[6] In the latter, the sinner, addressing the clergyman and friends gathered about his deathbed, speaks with dramatic force about his wretched state: '*If Christ dy'd for Sinners,* 'tis for such as Repent and Believe; but

---

[1] Tillotson, *Sermons,* vol. x, Sermon clxxxvii, pp. 4324–5. (N.B. pagination is continuous from vol. v to vol. xii of this edition.)

[2] *Clarissa,* vii. 176–7.   [3] Ibid., p. 175.

[4] Taylor, *Holy Dying,* ch. 4, sect. 5, p. 193.

[5] *Clarissa,* vii. 178.

[6] *The Second Spira: Being a fearful Example of an Atheist who had Apostatized from the Christian Religion, and died in Despair* at Westminster, Decemb. *8. 1692.* By J. S. a Minister of the *Church of England,* a frequent Visitor of him during his whole Sickness. 3rd ed., 1693. This pamphlet, attributed to John Sault, claims to be an authentic record of an actual event, by one who witnessed the death of a reprobate, but in arrangement and tone it owes much to the original *Francis Spira.* The two works would often have been bound together for gentlemen's libraries (e.g. copies in Bodley, Wood 879). It is not impossible that Richardson has both in mind when he mentions *Francis Spira.*

tho' I would, I can do neither, I have outstood my Day of Grace, and am hardned, and turned Reprobate . . . his Justice will vindicate itself upon such obstinate perverse Sinners as I . . .'[1]

In Richardson's novel, Mowbray and Belton represent the two phases of the sinner's attitude to death, as traditionally conceived by the divines. In days of health the atheist may think he has nothing to do at death but 'to act this last part as decently as he can, being secured by his own principles against all future misery and danger, because death makes an utter end of him'.[2] This confidence will, however, fail the sinner when he comes to die:

> But when these men fall into any great calamity, or death makes towards them in good earnest, then is the trial of these principles . . . and we commonly see that they do not only fail those who trust in them, but they vanish and disappear like dreams and mere illusions . . . and the man . . . can now feel no substance and reality in them . . . but GOD, and the other world, begin to be as great realities to him, as if they were present to his bodily eye.[3]

Mowbray, 'the hardened fellow',[4] represents the sinner in the flush of callous health. He is a worse infidel than his friends, and is sure that Belton's state of mind is the result of low spirits: 'Our poor friend is already a peg too low; and here thou art letting him down lower and lower still.'[5] Like the deathbed attendants of whom Taylor speaks, who would prefer a dying man to act 'with a contenance like an Orator, or grave like a Dramatick person',[6] Mowbray is annoyed by his friend's lack of restraint: 'I have seen many a man, said the rough creature, going up Holborn-hill, that has behaved more like a man than either of you.'[7] He yawns at Belton's sufferings, and tries to comfort him with a passage from Dryden and Lee's *Œdipus*; this passage, which indicates that in fearing death we are frightened only by imagination, supports his view that Belton's sufferings are the result of low-spirited fancies.[8]

The interposition of the atheist's counsel, to be contrasted

[1] *The Second Spira*, p. 18.
[2] Tillotson, *Sermons*, vol. x, Sermon clxxxvii, p. 4309.
[3] Ibid., p. 4310.   [4] *Clarissa*, vii. 173.
[5] Ibid., p. 172.   [6] Taylor, *Holy Dying*, ch. 3, sect. 2, p. 82.
[7] *Clarissa*, vii. 173.
[8] Ibid., p. 179; See Dryden and Lee, *Œdipus*, 1679, iv. i, p. 50.

with its refutation in experience, was already a device employed in dramatically narrated deathbed scenes. In *The Second Spira* the dying man's atheist friend sends him a long letter, mocking the fear of death, and advising him how to meet his end:

> A common Evil that every Body bears, ceases to be an Evil . . . But perhaps your Melancholy suggests unto you, that 'tis a dismal thing to Launch out into an unknown Abyss, to be you know not where, nor what. I answer, I dream sometimes of frightful things . . . but when I awake all vanishes. Thus, if we will examine Death, and its supposed Consequences, by the Prejudices of a Melancholy and Distracted Brain, we may be miserable, proportionable to the height of our Folly; but if by our Reason we take a View of these Formidable Monsters, they grow tame and familiar to us . . . Death it self is nothing; and after Death there's nothing; and why should I be afraid of nothing? Take Courage, Man, and either Die like your self, Master of your Fate and Happiness, so long as it is to be kept; or Recover, and Live Worthy the Character of a Person that knows how either to Live, or Die.[1]

The reply of 'the Second Spira' shows that he is unconvinced: 'I am sure those Monsters will be less tame and familiar the more you think of them, for since no Reason discovers what an unexperienc'd death is, or the unknown change consequent thereupon, how can we judg [*sic*] of things that we know not?'[2] And he explains:

> That there's a God I know . . . That there's a Hell, I am as certain, having received the earnest of my Inheritance there, in my Breast . . . That there's a natural Conscience, which is not the effect of a prejudiced Education, I now feel with Horror and Amazement, being continually upbraided by it with the Registry of my Impieties, and a bringing of all my Sins fresh into my remembrance . . .[3]

This response is, in essence, the same as Belton's reply to Mowbray's quotation:

> But Belton turning his head from him, Ah, Dick! (said he) these are not the reflections of a dying man!—What thou wilt one day feel, if it be what I now feel, will convince thee that the evils *before* thee, and *with* thee, are more than the effects of imagination.[4]

Because of his apprehension as to his eternal fate, Belton is the reverse of stoical in facing death. In miserable panic, he

---

[1] *The Second Spira*, pp. 28–9.   [2] Ibid., p. 33.
[3] Ibid., p. 36.   [4] *Clarissa*, viii. 179–80.

anxiously begs the doctor for life.[1] As Belford comments, Belton is 'vexed at the doctor, but more at death',[2] and 'would have worshipped the doctor . . . could he have given him hopes of recovery'.[3] It is a commonplace of the devout books that the dying man, in desire for reprieve, turns anxiously to the doctor.[4] Taylor counsels the sick person to treat his physician with courtesy, and to follow his advice, but not to demand impossibilities.[5] When Belford says that Belton 'continued impatient'[6] after the interview with the doctor, the word 'impatient' has a technical meaning likely to escape us. The sin of impatience is a rebellion against Providence, and the enemy of submission and humility. In theological terms, Belton's peevish reproaches to the doctor are a sign of this sin, which is traditionally worst in those who have brought their evil upon themselves.[7]

Because of his fear and guilt, Belton is unwilling to send for a clergyman: 'The poor man could not, he said, bear the thoughts of one; for that he should certainly die in an hour or two after.'[8]

It is a very great evil both in the matter of prudence and piety, that they fear the Priest as they fear the Embalmer; or the Sextons spade; and love not to converse with him . . . and think of his office so much to relate to the other world, that he is not to be treated with, while we hope to live in this . . .[9]

Belton's fear of the clergyman is another sign of the sin of impatience, and a symptom of spiritual weakness and ignorance.

His tormented conscience revenges itself upon him, in dreams and hallucinations which are signs of uncleansed guilt:

Did you not see him? turning his head this way and that; horror in his countenance; Did you not see him?

See whom, see what, my dear Belton!

O lay me upon the bed again, cried he!—Let me not die upon the floor!—Lay me down gently; and stand by me!—Leave me not!—All will soon be over!

You are already, my dear Belton, upon the bed. You have not

[1] *Clarissa*, viii, pp. 202–3.   [2] Ibid., p. 204.   [3] Ibid., p. 205.
[4] e.g. Drexelius, *Considerations*, The ninth Consideration, pp. 297–8.
[5] Taylor, *Holy Dying*, ch. 4, sect. 1, pp. 164–5.
[6] *Clarissa*, vii. 205.
[7] See Taylor, *Holy Dying*, ch. 3, sect. 9, *passim*.
[8] *Clarissa*, vii. 205–6.
[9] Taylor, *Holy Dying*, ch. 5, sect. 2, pp. 245–6.

been upon the floor. This is a strong delirium; you are faint for want of refreshment . . . Let me persuade you to take some of this cordial julap. I will leave you, if you will not oblige me.

He then readily took it; but said he could have sworn that Tom Metcalfe had been in the room, and had drawn him out of bed by the throat, upbraiding him with the injuries he had first done his Sister, and then Him, in the duel to which he owed that Fever which cost him his life.

Thou knowest the Story, Lovelace, too well . . . But, mercy on us, if in these terrible moments all the evils we do, rise to our affrighted imaginations! —If so, what shocking scenes have I, but still what more shocking ones hast thou, to go through, if, as the noble poet says,

If, any sense at that sad time remains![1]

Belford's quotation from Pomfret reminds us of Pomfret's ultimate source, the powerful passage in *Holy Dying* in which Taylor describes the fears that haunt the imagination of the dying reprobate:

He that hath lived a wicked life . . . if he have but sense of what he is going to suffer, or what he may expect to be his portion, then we may imagine the terrour of their abused fancies, how they see affrighting shapes, and because they fear them, they feel the gripes of Devils . . . calling to the grave, and hasting to judgement, exhibiting great bills of uncancelled crimes, awaking and amazing the conscience, breaking all their hope in pieces, and making faith uselesse and terrible, because the malice was great and the charity was none at all.[2]

Richardson has created a dramatic scene from the traditional descriptions of deathbed remorse and terror. In Belton he tries to create a real character through which to realize the general-ized idea of the dying sinner. He endeavours to make Belton's torment real by including homely detail, by describing every look and motion so as to make the scene strongly visual, and by using direct speech, even the utterances of terrified delirium. It is interesting that even a century earlier, in Taylor, the older and simpler concept of the Devil or devils haunting the death-bed is no longer quite acceptable. The devils that haunt men's last moments become the creations of guilty conscience working on 'abused fancies'. Richardson develops this idea, avoiding

---

[1] *Clarissa*, vii. 184.   [2] Taylor, *Holy Dying*, ch. 2, sect. 4, pp. 73–4.

carefully any suggestion that Belton is actually tormented by the angels of Satan (the word 'devil' is not even mentioned in this passage). Awakened conscience revenges itself upon a particular sinner in the form of a subjectively created hallucination which is relevant to a particular guilty episode in his life. That the apparitions which terrify the sinner owe their being to psychological disturbance does not lessen their horror—or their theological import. For Taylor, and even more for Richardson, the denizens of hell—or of heaven—find their natural habitat in men's subconscious minds.

Belton is so terrified that he dies wishing for annihilation: 'To hear the poor man wish he had never been born! To hear him pray to be nothing after death! Good God! how shocking!'[1] As an indication of dying despair this wish recurs in devout literature. Theologically, such a wish is an indication of an extreme degree of impatience, almost of blasphemy; it is also to be considered as an absurdity, an impossible demand. Such a prayer indicates the sufferer's state of despair, as it does, equally dramatically, in *The Second Spira*: 'Oh that thou wouldst let go thy Hand, for ever forget me, and let me fall into my first nothingness again; as my Righteousness could have profited thee nothing, so my Impieties have done thee no hurt, therefore Annihilate me, and let me Perish to nothing . . .'[2] In the context of *Clarissa*, in which the nature and processes of being, and the sacredness of identity, are celebrated both in fable and in artistic form from the first word to the last, the wish not to be, the sin against consciousness, is felt to be a blasphemy.

The account of Mrs. Sinclair's end is likewise a picture of death in despair, 'the most dismal condition that can be imagin'd on this side of hell, and very like to it',[3] but her condition is worse, and the novelist's treatment of it is different. Belton's death arouses sympathy in Belford, and is meant to arouse a similar response in the reader, as Belford's is the controlling point of view in that part of the novel. Mrs. Sinclair's suffering is treated unsympathetically, evoking nothing but disgust. Her life has made her diabolical; in pursuing her trade she has battened on the souls and bodies of others. In tormenting Clarissa, and helping Lovelace to ruin her, she has been moved

[1] *Clarissa*, vii. 207.   [2] *The Second Spira*, p. 24.
[3] Tillotson, *Sermons*, vol. x, Sermon clxxxvii, p. 4325.

by a delight in sin for its own sake; her pleasure in seeing Clarissa debased is sensual in its intensity, without the excuse of a natural desire, and she is more cruel to Clarissa than even Lovelace. A love of sin for its own sake is, in the teaching of the divines, 'an exemplification of the malice of the devil';[1] the habit of sinning produces in the soul

new, unnatural, and absurd desires; desires, that have no real object . . . but, like the sickness and distemper of the soul, feeding only upon filth and corruption . . . and giving a man the devil's nature, and the devil's delight; who has no other joy or happiness, but to dishonour his Maker, and to destroy his fellow-creature; to corrupt him here, and to torment him hereafter.[2]

Among examples of such viciousness, South instances such as Mrs. Sinclair. 'And to shew the true love and faithful allegiance that the old servants and subjects of vice ever after bear to it, nothing is more usual . . . than to hear, that such as have been strumpets in their youth, turn procurers in their age.'[3] The scene of Mrs. Sinclair's death is a picture of hell. Her deathbed attendants are her 'cursed daughters',[4] in all their midnight squalor:

with faces . . . that had run, the paint lying in streaky seams not half blowz'd off, discovering coarse wrinkled skins: The hair of some of them of divers colours, obliged to the blacklead comb where black was affected; the artificial jet, however, yielding apace to the natural brindle: That of others plastered with oil and powder; the oil predominating: But every one's hanging about her ears and neck in broken curls, or ragged ends . . . And half of them (un-padded, shoulder-bent, pallid-lipt, limber-jointed wretches) ap-pearing, from a blooming Nineteen or Twenty perhaps overnight, haggard well-worn strumpets of Thirty-eight or Forty.[5]

The prostitutes themselves are images of death and judge-ment. Their arts to make themselves beautiful and youthful are now powerless: 'Thinking to deceive the world men cosen themselves, and by representing themselves youthfull, they certainly continue their vanity, till *Proserpina* pull the perruke from their heads.'[6] The harlots are diseased and decaying;

[1] Robert South, *Sermons Preached upon Several Occasions*, 5 vols., 4th ed., 1737, vol. ii, Sermon v, p. 193.

[2] Ibid., pp. 195–6.   [3] Ibid., p. 183.   [4] *Clarissa*, viii. 55.

[5] Ibid., pp. 55–6.   [6] Taylor, *Holy Dying*, ch. 3, sect. 7, p. 126.

Belford feels 'half poisoned by the effluvia arising from so many contaminated carcases'.[1] Sin is, as the divines say, 'a sick and diseased condition',[2] and is here made to appear so. The midnight atmosphere suggests the Judgement Day, and the crowd of wretches who flock around, 'eyes half-opened, winking and pinking, mispatched, yawning, stretching',[3] appear like a multitude of awakened dead on the last day.

The dying Mrs. Sinclair is an image of a damned soul already in hell:

> Her misfortune has not at all sunk, but rather . . . increased her flesh; rage and violence perhaps swelling her muscular features. Behold her then, spreading the whole tumbled bed with her huge quaggy carcase: Her mill-post arms held up; her broad hands clenched with violence; her big eyes, goggling and flaming-red as we may suppose those of a salamander; her matted griesly hair, made irreverend by her wickedness . . . spread about her fat ears and brawny neck; her livid lips parched, and working violently; her broad chin in convulsive motion; her wide mouth, by reason of the contraction of her forehead . . . splitting her face, as it were, into two parts; and her huge tongue hideously rolling in it; heaving, puffing, as if for breath; her bellows-shaped and various-coloured breasts ascending by turns to her chin, and descending out of sight, with the violence of her gaspings.[4]

When Belford first heard of Mrs. Sinclair's fever, he compared it to the fire hereafter which he thinks awaits the 'cursed crew'.[5] Here we see her, as it were, already in flames and torment, just as the reprobate Francis Spira was smitten by fever and suffered agonies of conscience 'in a burning heat'.[6] Mrs. Sinclair's 'flaming-red' eyes are compared to those of a salamander, a creature used as an emblem for the damned soul, always burning and never fully consumed.[7] The physical ravages wrought by the approach of death, described in Belton's case with the detail of the traditional deathbed scene, are increased and made more nightmarish in the picture of Mrs. Sinclair, and the details, which go beyond the bounds of realism, are intensified by emblematic significance. The manner in which she acquires her fatal illness—breaking her leg in drunkenly

---

[1] *Clarissa*, viii. 61.　　　　　[2] Tillotson, *Sermons*, vol. 1, Sermon xii, p. 289.
[3] *Clarissa*, viii. 56.　　　　　　　　　　　　[4] Ibid., p. 57.
[5] Ibid., p. 36.　　　　　　　　　[6] *Francis Spira*, p. 26.
[7] Drexelius, *Considerations*, The second Consideration, pp. 29–30.

falling down stairs[1]—has a submerged symbolic import. Her
sin is an abuse of reason, a drunkenness of the soul; falling is an
image of damnation, like the fall of Lovelace in his dream. Even
the commonplace detail of the stairs could have been suggested
by an image in a religious emblem book.[2]

Like Belton, she is guilty of bringing sickness upon herself,
but she is more wicked than he, and her impatience, in the
theological as well as the ordinary sense, is worse. Her rage and
violence in confronting pain and death are sufficient to speak
ill of her spiritual state,[3] and her persistence in her old sins of
anger and cursing shows that she is in a state of reprobation.[4]

She is conscious of her guilt, but is incapable of repentance.
When Belford tells her, in the midst of her wild screams, that
if she is patient, she might yet 'get into a frame more proper for
her present circumstances',[5] she retorts: 'Who, I? . . . *I* get into
a better frame! *I*, who can neither cry, nor pray! Yet already
feel the torments of the damn'd! What mercy can I expect?
What hope is left for me?'[6]

That she cannot pray is a sign of reprobation; it shows that
her heart is hardened through repeated sin. Such is the state of
Francis Spira: 'It's wonderful, I earnestly desire to pray to God
with my heart, yet I cannot . . . such are the punishments of the
damned . . . they repent of their loss of heaven . . . yet their
repentance doth them no good, for they cannot mend their
waies.'[7] The regret for sins committed which arises out of the
fear of hell is not to be confused with repentance, because
obedience and love of God play no part in the emotions of
fear.[8] Panic at death is simply the result of a wicked life, and not
a change to a virtuous state.

But now they finde *they have done amisse and dealt wickedly*, they
have no bank of good works, but a huge treasure of wrath, and they
are going to a strange place, and what shall be their lot is uncertain;
(so they say, when they would comfort and flatter themselves) but in
truth of religion their portion is sad and intollerable . . .[9]

---

[1] *Clarissa*, viii. 36.
[2] Drexelius, *Considerations*, The second Consideration, p. 35.
[3] See Taylor, *Holy Dying*, ch. 3, sect. 6, pp. 124–5.
[4] Ibid., sect. 9, pp. 154–5.   [5] *Clarissa*, viii. 58.
[6] Ibid., pp. 58–9.   [7] *Francis Spira*, p. 45.
[8] See Taylor, *Holy Dying*, ch. 4, sect. 6, p. 203.
[9] Ibid., ch. 2, sect. 2, p. 65.

When Mrs. Sinclair cries 'who can tell *where* I shall be?'[1] she is flattering herself; her destination is all too certain. She dies as the wicked are supposed to do, 'timorously, and uncomfortably, as if they were forced out of their lives by the violencies of an executioner'.[2] Her fear and impatience are even worse than Belton's, and her clinging to life is more desperate. She wishes to be deluded by her doctors into thinking she may recover, and the doctors, unlike the physician who attends Belton, are vain, greedy, and callous; all the circumstances of her death, as well as her spiritual state, are similar to Belton's, but worse. Like Belton, she has superstitious fears of seeing a clergyman: 'Send for a Parson!—Then you indeed think I shall die! . . . Who sends for a Parson, while there is any hope left?— The Sight of a Parson would be death immediate to me!'[3] She tries to buy God off with useless promises,[4] and refuses to attempt to cure her soul. Not only does she refuse to see a clergyman, but also (unlike Belton) she rejects any attempts at religious converse on the part of Belford. Belton's future case is precarious, but Mrs. Sinclair's is certain. With even more vehemence than he, she prays for annihilation:

> *Die*, did you say, Sir?—*Die*!—I *will not*, I *cannot* die!—I know not *how* to die!—*Die*, Sir!—And *must* I then die?—Leave this world?— I cannot bear it! . . . I cannot, I will not leave this world. Let others die, who wish for another! who expect a better!—I have had my plagues in This: but would compound for all future hopes, so as I may be nothing after this![5]

Belford has hoped and prayed for Belton, but even he gives up Mrs. Sinclair. She is already in hell, and she and her crew have now come into their inheritance of 'the infernal mansions'.[6] Her case is that of complete despair; as Francis Spira, another reprobate who wished for annihilation, says, '*verily desperation is hell it self*'.[7]

The death of Clarissa, set between the deaths of Belton and Mrs. Sinclair, is an illustration of a theme dear to the divines: 'The difference between good and bad men is never so remarkable in this world, as when they are upon their death-bed.'[8]

---

[1] *Clarissa*, viii. 58.   [2] Taylor, *Holy Dying*, ch. 2, sect. 2, p. 64.
[3] *Clarissa*, viii. 65.   [4] Ibid., p. 64.   [5] Ibid., p. 59.
[6] Ibid., p. 60.   [7] *Francis Spira*, p. 41.
[8] Tillotson, *Sermons*, vol. ix, Sermon clxvi, p. 3932.

For every detail concerning the condition of Belton and of Mrs. Sinclair under the pangs of death, there is a corresponding detail relevant to Clarissa's behaviour and circumstances, and pointing the contrast. The particulars are closely related to the traditional descriptions of the deaths of good and bad men in the pious works of the seventeenth century, descriptions upon which moralizing poets of a later date (such as Pomfret) had also drawn for their material.

Clarissa is an example of holy dying, not only in her last moments, but in the long process of true repentance which she undergoes, which the divines made an essential preliminary to a holy death. The word 'repentance', which today bears only a vague and general meaning, had a definite, almost technical significance in the works of the divines. Repentance involves not only being sorry for thought, word, or deed, but truly loathing the sin itself, not merely its consequences. It involves amendment and reparation, and, finally 'contrition', or sorrow for sin because of the love of God. When the religious connotations of 'repentance' as so often expounded by the divines are considered, a touch of daring which eludes the modern reader becomes apparent in such simple and seductive lines as Dryden's

> Let not Youth fly away without Contenting;
> Age will come time enough, for your Repenting.[1]

Lovelace, like a seventeenth-century wit, uses the word in various senses. Before his designs are completed, he treats it in the comic manner. 'We must all of us do something to repent of',[2] he says, mockingly pretending to excuse his conduct by inverting the logic of a devout truism. Shortly before the rape, he pretends to justify himself to playing, with savage jocularity, upon Clarissa's repentance: 'Nor, let me tell thee, will her own scheme of penitence, in this case, be half so perfect, if she do *not* fall, as if she *does*: For what a foolish penitent will she make, who has nothing to repent of?'[3] Lovelace knows that his reverse logic, by which he pretends sin must be justifiable if its result, repentance, is an acknowledged good, is not the accepted truth; earlier, however, when he hypocritically acted the part

[1] Dryden, *King Arthur, or, The British Worthy*, 1691, II. i, p. 16.
[2] *Clarissa*, iv. 343. [3] Ibid. v. 285–6.

of a penitent for Clarissa's benefit, his 'Rakish notion' that 'he should have near as much merit in his repentance, as if he had never erred' struck her unfavourably.[1] It is only after he has lost Clarissa that his mind runs more seriously upon repentance, and he then realizes it is more difficult than he had previously believed. The regret that comes 'By fits and starts'[2] cannot properly be called repentance.

Even when he reveals that he is aware of some of the theological language about repentance, when he complains that Clarissa is hindering his spiritual regeneration and repentance by not letting him 'repair',[3] Lovelace can think only in terms of obtaining what he wants and avoiding unpleasant consequences. Clarissa's repentance is complete; she takes responsibility for her own actions, and accepts the consequences. She has to a superlative degree the virtue of patience. Belton and Mrs. Sinclair are guilty of impatience, a complex sin which finds its issue in repining under affliction, and in anger against God. Clarissa, at the beginning of her illness, when she has been a prisoner and is suffering the severest trials from her family, accepts tribulation, using the traditional phrase 'the School of Affliction'.[4] She resists the temptation to impatience by having recourse to the traditional recollection: 'Better people, she says, have been more afflicted than she, grievous as she sometimes thinks her afflictions: And shall she not bear what less faulty persons have borne?'[5] This is the temper advocated by Taylor: 'Consider how many excellent personages in all Ages have suffered as great or greater calamities then this which now tempts thee to impatience.'[6]

Clarissa generously blames herself, her own 'rashness', for the sins of her lover and her family.[7] She forgives her family, endeavouring 'to find reason to justify them at her own expence', and 'as much a stranger to Revenge as Despair, is able to forgive the author of her ruin'.[8] She is a complete contrast to Mrs. Sinclair, who curses everyone she can consider responsible for her condition. Forgiveness of others is a part of repentance, as is reparation. Clarissa's petition for her family's forgiveness and

---

[1] *Clarissa*, iii. 162.   [2] Ibid. vi. 344.   [3] Ibid. vii. 139.
[4] Ibid. vi. 420.   [5] Ibid. vii. 135–6.
[6] Taylor, *The Rule and Exercise of Holy Living*, 1650, ch. 2, sect. 6, p. 150.
[7] *Clarissa*, vii. 78.   [8] Ibid., p. 135.

blessing is an act of reparation; she wishes to heal the breach of which she was a cause, for their sake as well as hers. Even if her unforgiving family will not relent, divine forgiveness is assured to true repentance: 'God will forgive her, tho' no one on earth will.'[1]

Repentance and resignation are not, in the terminology of the divines, passive states; they are active efforts of the human personality in seeking a relationship to God. Remorse occasioned only by fear is a static state, allowing little development, and is not much help in facing death. Clarissa repents, not from fear of hell, but from desire of heaven. Belton and Mrs. Sinclair cling to the world, whereas Clarissa wishes freedom from it; as Mrs. Norton says, 'worldly joy claims no kindred with the joys we are bid to aspire after'.[2] All her life has been, as the divines advocated, spent in 'careful preparation for death and a better life',[3] and her last weeks exhibit the approved preparation for the great change. Belton and Mrs. Sinclair shrink from knowing the extent of their illness; Clarissa accepts hers with joy. Richardson, however, carefully attempts to repudiate any suggestion that she is responsible for shortening her own life. Lovelace, always learned in doctrine when it is convenient to be so, admonishes Belford that Clarissa ought to remember that helping to cause one's own death is a sin.[4] Clarissa knows this, and explicitly asks the doctor to clear her of 'any imputations of curtailing, thro' wilfulness or impatiency . . . a life that might otherwise be prolonged'.[5]

Clarissa's illness (probably galloping consumption) is certainly a trifle mysterious, though no more so than that of Milly Theale in *The Wings of the Dove,* a much more modern novel which is equally haunted by death. In this novel too the author examines (although not in a religious context) the effect of death's approach upon the beautiful martyr-heroine and upon those around her. James—more sophisticated than Richardson in his exact consciousness of what he is doing—takes it for granted that a mortal illness can be a datum for which specific causes and medical details need not be supplied. In both instances, the heroines are, to put it simply, too good for the

[1] Ibid. [2] Ibid., p. 119.
[3] Tillotson, *Sermons,* vol. ii, Sermon xxxiv, p. 444.
[4] *Clarissa,* vii. 13–14. [5] Ibid. viii. 277.

world in which they find themselves. Excellence is in itself a kind of mortal illness, as it is not native to the world, nor can it flourish there. Both Milly and Clarissa are ill, have symptoms and the attentions of doctors—enough to satisfy the reader if he takes the author on his own terms. In each case, it is the reaction to the knowledge that she is dying that lets the character reveal herself more fully.

Although, in contrast to Belton and Mrs. Sinclair, Clarissa is innocent of causing or hastening her end, she is eager to know when her release will come: 'Tell me how long you think I may hold it? And believe me, gentlemen, the shorter you tell me my time is likely to be, the more comfort you will give me.'[1] This is a dramatized version of the reactions of the ideal sufferer postulated by the divines: 'He that looks upon death only as a passage to glory, may welcome the messengers of it as bringing him the best and most joyful news that ever came to him in his whole life . . .'[2]

Clarissa meditates upon death, as her letters show, in the manner and with the results approved by Taylor: 'the frequent use of this meditation . . . will make death safe and friendly . . . and that we shall sit down in the grave as we compose our selves to sleep, and do the duties of nature and choice'.[3] Lovelace complains of this very composure in Clarissa: 'She'll persuade herself, at this rate, that she has nothing to do, when all is ready, but to lie down, and go to sleep.'[4]

Clarissa prepares for death both practically and symbolically when she sells her clothes to buy a coffin. In selling her 'rich dressed suits'[5] in order to defray the expenses of her last illness and funeral, she is enacting, outwardly and visibly, the spiritual process traditionally known as dressing the soul for death.

In sicknesse, the soul begins to dresse her self for immortality; and first she unties the strings of vanity that made her upper garment cleave to the world and sit uneasily . . .[6]

As the soul is still undressing, she takes off the roughnesse of her great and little angers, and animosities . . .[7]

The image of dress is frequently used in *Clarissa*. It is a sign

[1] *Clarissa*, vii. 222.   [2] Tillotson, *Sermons*, vol. i, Sermon viii, p. 215.
[3] Taylor, *Holy Dying*, ch. 1, sect. 1, p. 50.   [4] *Clarissa*, vii. 343.
[5] Ibid. vi. 334.   [6] Taylor, *Holy Dying*, ch. 3, sect. 6, p. 105.
[7] Ibid., p. 108.

of riches and vanity; the Harlowes think they can smother the heroine's protesting spirit by thrusting 'patterns of the richest silks' upon her.[1] Lovelace constantly takes pride in his own dress and appearance, and also enjoys describing Clarissa's appearance in her primrose gown with 'diamond snaps in her ears'.[2] Dress is also a means of disguise. Lovelace changes his apparel to enact the part of an old man;[3] the prostitutes, by assuming gold tissue and lace, can appear as fine ladies.[4] Dress is the symbol of the outward semblances by which the world makes its judgements; Clarissa in selling her clothes is renouncing the world and the flesh. Pious writers constantly employed the image of dress in this manner:

> *Things to be meditated vpon, as thou art putting off thy clothes.*
> 1. That the day is comming when thou must bee as barely *vnstript* of *all* that thou hast in the *world*, as thou art now of thy *clothes* . . .[5]

Wedding clothes are frequently mentioned in *Clarissa*, naturally enough since the novel deals with several projected marriages. Clarissa is importuned with choice clothes by her family; Bella suggests mockingly that she should be married to Solmes in black velvet[6]—a striking image which, early in the novel, suggests a marriage to death.[7] Lovelace in search of Clarissa goes to Smith's attired 'in a never-worn suit, which I had intended for one of my wedding-suits'[8] and hopes that his bridegroom-like appearance will have its effect on Clarissa. Anna Howe makes wedding preparations, and Clarissa, thinking of these, transfers the image to a description of her own state:

> Let my dearest Miss Howe purchase her wedding garments—And may all temporal blessings attend the charming preparation! . . . As for me, never Bride was so ready as I am. My wedding garments are bought—And tho' not fine or gawdy to the sight, tho' not adorned with jewels, and set off with gold and silver (for I have

---

[1] *Clarissa*, i. 304.   [2] Ibid. iii. 28.
[3] Ibid. v. 74-7.   [4] Ibid., pp. 298-9.
[5] Lewis Bayly, *The Practise of Pietie*, 11th ed., 'Profitably amplified by the Author', 1619, p. 335.   [6] *Clarissa*, i. 345-6.
[7] The image of a black wedding, expressing the horror of a hated sexual union as fearful to the heroine as death itself, is a rather Jacobean touch. See *Comedies and Tragedies Written by Beaumont and Fletcher Gentlemen*, 1647, *The Custome of the Countrey*, I. i, p. 4.   [8] *Clarissa*, vii. 141.

no beholders eyes to wish to glitter in); yet will they be the easiest, the *happiest* suit, that ever bridal maiden wore—for they are such as carry with them a security against all those anxieties, pains, and perturbations, which sometimes succeed to the most promising outsettings.[1]

The wedding garments so frequently mentioned at the beginning of the novel have now become the burial dress and the coffin which Clarissa has bought by selling the clothes of her worldly prosperity. But the phrase 'wedding garment' also has Biblical echoes.[2] The soul must be fitly dressed for its union with the heavenly Bridegroom (to whom Lovelace, pursuing Clarissa dressed in his gay 'wedding-suit', is a kind of Satanic anti-type) and for the marriage supper of heaven. The word 'preparation', used at the beginning of the novel in its ordinary sense in descriptions of wedding preparations, has been changed to 'preparation' in its theological sense.

Belford admired the 'serenity with which she can talk of death, and prepare for it, as if it were an occurrence as familiar to her as dressing and undressing'.[3] Clarissa follows literally the injunction of Jeremy Taylor: 'first dresse thy soul, and then dresse thy hearse'.[4] She orders her coffin, to the dismay of her household (Plate 2). She keeps it in her room: 'It is placed near the window, like a harpsichord, tho' covered over to the ground: And when she is so ill, that she cannot well go to her closet, she writes and reads upon it, as others would upon a desk or table.'[5] This 'shocking and solemn whimsy',[6] as the apothecary calls it, stands out as one of the most bizarre and surprising things in the novel—particularly surprising to find in a work written as late as 1748. It reminds us abruptly of the seventeenth-century use of the *memento mori*, of John Donne wearing his winding sheet. Death for Clarissa is not just the serene, rational, and pious death of an Addison who can call his scapegrace stepson to his death-bed to see how a Christian can die.[7] It is the great adventure,

---

[1] *Clarissa*, vii. pp. 405–6.   [2] Matthew 22: 11–13.
[3] *Clarissa*, vii. 276.   [4] Taylor, *Holy Dying*, ch. 3, sect. 8, p. 140.
[5] *Clarissa*, vii. 359–60.   [6] Ibid., p. 359.
[7] The anecdote about Addison's death is related by Edward Young in a work on which he and Richardson collaborated. (See Young, *Conjectures on Original Composition*, 1759, pp. 99–109.) Richardson, who was fond of the story, asked Young not to labour the point, as it might discourage those whose friends had not been granted an easy death. (See his letter to Young, 29 May 1759, *Correspondence*, ii. 54–6.)

which fascinates her imagination. She acts out the injunctions (taken more seriously and less metaphorically in the previous century than in her own) to contemplate all aspects, physical and spiritual, of her death. Her action is a literal expression of the spirit of Taylor's *The Golden Grove* (1655) and its emblematic frontispiece (Plate 2). Taylor and Donne would have understood her working upon her coffin; it is difficult to imagine such an idea occuring to Addison.

Louis L. Martz, in The *Poetry of Meditation*, discusses the influence of religious works of the Counter-Reformation upon English poetry, and stresses the importance of the *ars moriendi* tradition to the Roman Catholic writers, who found meditation upon death an instrument for increasing self-knowledge and the love of God.[1] The consideration of the deathbed, with the 'composition of place' and 'application of the senses' advocated by Loyola, made the meditation upon death more personal and dramatic. One's own death should be imagined and practised with the aid of the senses, 'for the blow that can be struck but once should be well-rehearsed'.[2] Martz analyses the influence of these writers on English poets such as Donne and Herbert, not only in their works, but in their lives. The same tradition and mood can be found in Taylor, and *Clarissa* is probably the last major example in English literature of this kind of contemplation of death. Clarissa considers death not only with her intellect but also with her senses and imagination. The actual burial dress and coffin must be designed, handled, and made familiar. The manner of dying, in *this* place, with these people, under these particular circumstances, must be contemplated. Clarissa tells the doctor she does not want to move to the country to die; she imagines and rehearses her death with complete 'composition of place':

> But if I were to be at the trouble of removing into new lodgings (a trouble which I think now would be too much for me) and this only to *die* in the country, I had rather the Scene were to be shut up here. For here have I meditated the spot, and the manner, and every-thing, as well of the minutest as of the highest consequence, that can attend the solemn moments.[3]

[1] Louis L. Martz, *The Poetry of Meditation*, 1954, ch. 3, pp. 118–52.
[2] *The Spiritual Combat* (anonymous), quoted by Martz, *The Poetry of Meditation*, p. 137.
[3] *Clarissa*, vii. 277.

Clarissa defends her possession of the coffin, and desires her friends to look at it with her: 'Don't you lead back, said she, a starting Steed to the object he is apt to start at, in order to familiarize him to it, and cure his starting? The same reason will hold in this case.'[1] Her imagery is the same as Taylor's, when he advises overcoming fear and discontent by examination and familiarity: 'For then we shall perceive that like Colts and unmanag'd Horses, we start at dead bones and livelesse blocks, things that are unactive as they are innocent.'[2]

Clarissa's condition is in emphatic contrast to that of Belton and Mrs. Sinclair, in terms of 'patience', 'repentance', 'preparation', and 'hope'. Every detail of her circumstances points the contrast. They refuse to see a clergyman; the minister comes early to attend upon Clarissa, and she, of all the characters who die, is the only one to take the Sacrament.[3] They rail upon their physicians, and the doctors are, especially in Mrs. Sinclair's case, money-grubbing and callous; Clarissa makes friends with her physician and apothecary, and they are generous and kind.[4] Except for Belford, the attendants upon the deathbeds of Belton and Mrs. Sinclair are hard-hearted and uninterested. Clarissa makes new friends, even a new family, of the Smiths and the widow Lovick, Mr. Goddard, and the doctor, 'finding out something *paternal* and *maternal* in every one'.[5] This is one of Richardson's best touches in this part of the novel, as it reminds us of the cruelty of Clarissa's parents, the origin of her misfortune, and does not allow us to lose the girl in the suffering woman and dying saint.

Her last moments, in great contrast to those of the dying sinners, are calm and tranquil. She does not die without suffering the physical symptoms of dissolution; she takes part in the common lot. But she is also a saint, whose death is a union with God, and as such is fitted to be marked by an easy death. The idea that an easy death can be a mark of God's favour to one he loves can be seen in Taylor's description of the Countess of Carbery:

But God that knew her fears, and her jealousie concerning her self, fitted her with a death so easie, so harmlesse, so painlesse, that it did not put her patience to a severe triall. It was not (in all appear-

---

[1] *Clarissa*, vii. 336.   [2] Taylor, *Holy Living*, ch. 2, sect. 6, p. 148.
[3] *Clarissa*, vii. 214.   [4] Ibid. vi. 333.   [5] Ibid.

ance) of so much trouble, as two fits of a common ague; so carefull was God to remonstrate to all that stood in that sad attendance, that this soule was dear to him: and that since she had done so much of her duty towards it, he that began, would also finish her redemption, by an act of a rare providence, and a singular mercy.[1]

Clarissa's death is likewise a singular mercy. She is supported by Christian hope, which has comforted her early in her illness, when she was most unhappy and friendless:

She said, That tho' this was so heavy a day with her, she was at other times, within these few days past especially, blessed with bright hours; and particularly, that she had now-and-then such joyful assurances (which she hoped were not presumptuous ones) that God would receive her to his mercy, that she . . . was ready to think herself above this earth while she was in it . . .[2]

In her last scene, her state is the direct opposite of the despair in which Belton and Mrs. Sinclair are plunged. She tells her friends 'I am all blessed hope—Hope itself',[3] and adds that they cannot know 'what *foretastes*—what *assurances*'[4] she has received.

For the devout of the seventeenth century, and their successors in the eighteenth century, what Tillotson calls the 'ravishing sight of the glories of another world, that stedfast assurance of a future blessedness',[5] was not an illusion, but as real and recognizable as the physical fact of death. Taylor describes comfort mercifully granted the Lady Frances, and adds that

a little glimps [*sic*] of heaven, a minutes conversing with an Angel, any ray of God, any communication extraordinary from the Spirit of comfort which God gives to his servants in strange and unknown manners, are infinitely far from illusions; and they shall then be understood by us . . . when our new and strange needs shall be refreshed by such unusuall visitations.[6]

Clarissa has visions of hope, as Belton has visions of despair, although Richardson is not as explicit in Clarissa's case, and wisely refrains from enlarging upon her 'foretastes' and 'assurances'. It would be vulgarizing her hopes and debasing the tone of the novel to expatiate upon angelic apparitions. But the

---

[1] Taylor, *A Funerall Sermon, Preached At the Obsequies of the Right Hon and most vertuous Lady, The Lady Frances, Countess of Carbery*, 1650, p. 33. The sermon is sometimes listed as *A Funerall Sermon on 2 Samuel xix. 14.*
[2] *Clarissa*, vii. 268–9.   [3] Ibid. viii. 3.   [4] Ibid.
[5] Tillotson, *Sermons*, vol. iii, Sermon xl, p. 150.
[6] Taylor, *A Funerall Sermon*, p. 34.

description of the states of both exactly tallies with the contrast in Taylor between the dying sinner who sees 'affrighting shapes',[1] and the dying saint who goes forth 'full of hope, sometimes with evidence, but always with certainty',[2] and is received into the angelic throng.

Clarissa in her religious sensibility, as in most other aspects of her personality, is an odd character to meet in the literature of the mid eighteenth century. When measured by standards of ordinary prudence and the reasonable ethics of the world, which apply, for example, to the creations of Fielding and Smollett, Clarissa scarcely seems respectable. She is too uncompromising, too fervent. She is a failure in controlling the world around her. She loses too much to make it entirely comfortable for the reader to identify himself with her, and she persists in remaining triumphant even in longing for death. Modern critics have found her longing for death the reaction of a child enacting an ego-satisfying fantasy,[3] or an expression of badly sublimated sexuality.[4] Dorothy Van Ghent is particularly repelled by the religious tone, and exceptionally severe on the heroine. She sees in the novel what she calls 'the Puritan myth' and the 'myth of family life' with the two coinciding at the death of Clarissa, in which Clarissa's return to God is 'a supernatural equivalent of the necessary "return" of all daughters to the parental authority'. She adds that 'The values that are given final sanction here are the typical values of the right-thinking bourgeois family: the father's authority is supreme . . . there must . . . be no love, except in so far as love can serve the family economy.'[5] She sees the deathbed scene and all the allusions to it as 'capping a code of Puritanism in morals, paternal authoritarianism in the family, and the cash nexus as the only binding tie for society at large'.[6] The modern attitude is a perversion of the meaning of Richardson's novel. Clarissa escapes paternal authoritarianism, and that authoritarianism is shown to be wrong. The domestic atmosphere of the Harlowe family is evil, and Richardson knows it is. The incapacity of this money-grubbing family to love is pointed out explicitly

[1] Taylor, *Holy Dying*, ch. 2, sect. 4, p. 74.
[2] Ibid., p. 75.
[3] See Morris Golden, *Richardson's Characters*, 1963, p. 67.
[4] See Alan Wendt, 'Clarissa's Coffin', *PQ*, xxxix (Oct. 1960), 481–95.
[5] Van Ghent, *The English Novel*, p. 60.   [6] Ibid., p. 61.

when Colonel Morden says, in response to Belford's praise of Mrs. Lovick who is as careful of Clarissa as a mother, that she had better be '*more* careful . . . or she is not careful at all'.[1] Even when her family have (too late) accepted their daughter again, Clarissa does not belong with or to them. Anna Howe, viewing her friend's body lying in state in the Harlowes's house, bursts out 'But why, Sir, why, Mr. Morden, was she sent *hither*? . . . She has no Father, no Mother, no Relations; no, not *one*!'[2] Clarissa never returns to her family. She has forsaken any adherence to the 'cash nexus'; Lovelace is more attached to it than she, in his confidence that money, combined with ingenious scheming, can accomplish everything. Clarissa's dying words, when she laments the denial of her family's blessing, and then adds 'BUT GOD ALMIGHTY WOULD NOT LET ME DEPEND FOR COMFORT UPON ANY BUT HIMSELF',[3] are a manifesto, a declaration of independence from society, especially the bourgeois kind of society which Miss Van Ghent sees her as representing. Her meditations upon death and her desire for it are 'Puritan' only in the vaguest and most popular sense, as such meditation and desire were inculcated by a long Catholic tradition, which appears in the devout literature of the seventeenth century. In order to read *Clarissa* correctly, it is necessary to understand what Christianity meant to the heroine and her author; however much we repudiate the religion itself, or this form of it, we should realize that it does not represent what is usually called the 'Protestant ethic'. It is an ascetic, other-worldly religion; we shall continue to find Clarissa unreasonable until we understand that for her, as for Taylor and Tillotson, there is a meaning of 'reason' which makes it reasonable to meditate upon and desire death.

The last, and most interesting, deathbed scene in the novel is that of Lovelace. By describing at length the death of the unrighteous, in the scenes involving Belton and Mrs. Sinclair, Richardson has freed himself of any necessity for dwelling on the death of Lovelace. It comes in a brief description, in which the narrative viewpoint is not that of an old friend or Christian moralist, but that of a detached observer:

Contrary to all expectation, he lived over the night: But *suffered*

[1] *Clarissa*, vii. 447.   [2] Ibid. viii. 87.
[3] Ibid. vii. 459.

much, as well from his *impatience* and *disappointment*, as from his wounds; for he seemed *very unwilling to die*.

He was delirious, at times, in the two last hours; and then several times cried out, as if he had seen some frightful Spectre, Take her away! Take her away! but named nobody. And sometimes praised some Lady (that Clarissa, I suppose, whom he had invoked when he received his death's wound) calling her, Sweet Excellence! Divine Creature! Fair Sufferer!—And once he said, Look down, blessed Spirit, look down! —And there stopt;—his lips however moving.

At nine in the morning, he was seized with convulsions, and fainted away; and it was a quarter of an hour before he came out of them.

His few last words I must not omit, as they shew an ultimate composure; which may administer some consolation to his honourable friends.

Blessed—said he, addressing himself no doubt to Heaven; for his dying eyes were lifted up—A strong convulsion prevented him for a few moments saying more—But recovering, he again with great fervour (lifting up his eyes, and his spread hands) pronounced the word *Blessed*:—Then, in a seeming ejaculation, he spoke inwardly so as not to be understood; At last, he distinctly pronounced these three words,

LET THIS EXPIATE!

And then, his head sinking on his pillow, he expired; at about half an hour after ten.[1]

Lovelace's end, the climax towards which the novel has been moving, is conveyed by a description which is extremely compressed by comparison with the other dying scenes. The detached observer, Lovelace's foreign valet, de la Tour, puts little interpretation upon the scene, but reports only the facts. The hints he drops about Lovelace's true spiritual condition are given unawares. He speaks of Lovelace as 'impatient', and the reader recognizes the similarity to Belton and Mrs. Sinclair. He has no time to repent, and the implications of this have been emphasized before. Like Belton, he is haunted in delirium by one whom he has injured. He does not pray—at least, he mentions the name of God neither in fear nor supplication.

Yet, although the conventional elements of the sinner's deathbed are all there, and the reader knows to the full,

---

[1] *Clarissa*, viii. 276–7.

because of the previous scenes, what they imply, the salient point of this scene is not in its deathbed conventionalities. By now, the reader can take these and their meaning for granted, and Richardson's imagination is given freer play. Here Richardson moves farthest from the traditional deathbed scene in showing the dying sinner, not cowering in fear of hell, or lamenting his inability to repent, but calling upon the spirit of the one whom he has most loved and most injured to intercede for him. Unlike the apparition which Belton sees, the spirit of Clarissa is not a fiend from hell come to snatch the wicked soul; she is the last reproach, but also the last saving grace. The vision which Lovelace fears is also the saint whom he invokes. His last prayer is a mystery; it may be, as de la Tour thinks, that he addresses 'Heaven' in the usual sense of prayer, but it is more evident that it is a last cry to Clarissa. Lovelace's ruling passion in death is his love for Clarissa; he can see heaven only through her.

The cry to the beloved woman, which is like the last speech of a dying hero in a tragic drama, is here seen in a Christian context, as a prayer. The effectiveness of it, as a prayer, is intentionally a mystery. De la Tour's interpretation, that Lovelace's last words show 'an ultimate composure', and may 'administer some consolation to his honourable friends' is ironic. With all the previous emphasis upon the hazard of deathbed repentance, the graceless state of the hardened sinner's soul, the signs of sin manifest in impatience, the deathbed of Lovelace is shadowed with threatening darkness which there is no need for Richardson to stress.[1] Yet suffering offers the possibility of expiation. Belford prays that Belton's 'tortures' may 'expiate' his offences.[2] The amount Lovelace suffers is left intentionally imprecise. There is no detailed examination of his psychological state; we are offered only a few clues. We do

---

[1] Dying horror, remorse, and prospects of eternal retribution are not absent from heroic tragedies. See the dying speech of Mithridates:

> My Soul is on the Beach, and streight must lanch
> Into th' Abyss of the black Sea of Death,
> Where Furies stand upon the smoaky Rocks,
> Prepar'd to meet one greater than themselves.
>
> (Lee, *Mithridates*, v. ii, p. 66).

See also the last scenes of *Cæsar Borgia* and *Nero*.

[2] *Clarissa*, vii. 209.

not know whether his prayer for expiation was such that it could be granted, and we are not meant to know. The obvious answer is that it is not. However, it is Clarissa upon whom he calls, and Clarissa is a saint, the one person in Lovelace's world who has redeemed nature from the general curse. Her prayer has been—and still would be—that he should be saved. If he is damned, her prayer is unanswered. It is a riddle without an end.

Because Richardson has, in Belton's case, made clear the torments that can prey upon the dying sinner, the agonies of remorse, half-repentance, and despair, he can leave Lovelace's death as an enigma, without any description of his inner state beyond the brief hints conveyed by a dispassionate stranger. It is essential for Richardson's purpose that we consider Lovelace in relation to his eternal fate; if Clarissa is to be seen *sub specie æternitatis* so must he. Yet to deal directly with Lovelace's state of mind, to analyse his conscience too minutely, to evaluate his repentance or despair would be to diminish him as a character. To gloat over his final damnation would destroy the tone of the book, and, by making its religious outlook cheap, pervert everything Clarissa symbolizes.[1]

The morality of *Pamela* has been found offensive because it seems finally to contradict itself, and to gainsay what the characters have represented. The religious tone of *Clarissa*, most evident in the deathbed scenes, presents a different kind of morality, and does not destroy the integrity of the novel. It is suited to the novel because the theme of the noble-minded and injured heroine, as it came from the tragic drama, led naturally to the victory and justification of the heroine-martyr before heaven. In *Clarissa*, a Christian heroine is the central figure, and the heroic reward is the Christian reward; the assertion of glory merges into the Christian scheme of trial and spiritual glory.

The use of the deathbed scene in a novel poses great problems for the novelist. Such scenes can be stereotyped, or mawkish; characters can be lost in undifferentiated *exempla*.

[1] It would be wrong to suppose that Richardson himself delighted excessively in the doctrine of hell and damnation. On the contrary, he expressed sympathy for Hartley's theories, expressed in *Heaven Open to All Men* (1743), and added 'I could hope that the Doctrine [i.e. Hartley's] is true'. (See letter to Lady Bradshaigh, 30 May 1754, *Selected Letters*, p. 308.)

Richardson involves his artistic skill in endeavouring to over-come these problems. The deathbed scenes do not exist as isolated parts of the novel; they are involved in the complete delineation of a character. The tone and style of each deathbed description is different. The description of the dying Mrs. Sinclair, with all its techniques of caricature and exaggeration, balances the scenes about Belton and Clarissa, in which a softer tone is dominant. Each of the three scenes is united with the others in being seen from the same point of view, that of Belford. Richardson endeavours to preserve the structure of the novel (which has hitherto depended so much on the develop-ment of the main characters' feelings and perceptions) by developing the character of Belford through his participation in each of these scenes.

Clarissa's death does not, of course, consist in a few scenes; it dominates the last quarter of the novel. What interests us about her during this part of the book is not merely that she dies, or dies triumphant, but what happens to her, how she develops while facing death. The growing of her friendship for Belford is important: it indicates a personality that is not rendered static by the approach of death. Belton and Mrs. Sinclair remain more or less fixed in one state, too weak to change. Clarissa is still capable of exploring life. Her independence and talent for friendship are evinced in her impulsive greeting to Belford: 'I am glad to see you, Mr. Belford . . . I *must* say so—let mis-reporters say what they will.'[1] That Belford should respect and like her is admirable enough, but to be expected. He is the ordinary sensual man who still owes allegiance to the good. When Clarissa and Lovelace have drawn apart, Belford, whose character is at a midway point between the good of the one and the evil of the other, can understand and interpret both. He moves like an awkward ambassador between the courts of virtue and vice. That Clarissa should like him is less conven-tional. She has been destroyed by a rake who has pretended honour, but she refuses to give up her friendship for the man who is honourable, even though her association with him is damaging her chances of a reconciliation with her family. Her change from distrust of him to growing confidence and affection shows the health of her judgement, and this example of her

[1] *Clarissa*, vii. 218.

ability to continue exploring life and experience makes her exploration of death seem the more valid.

In *Clarissa*, the importance of death and of the imagery surrounding death increases Richardson's power to play tricks with time. The devotional literature is full of a sense of the value of time in its incessant passage towards eternity. 'The glasse is always running, and the clock never stands still: The houre passeth away by flying minutes.'[1] A sense of the urgency of time, the importance of each irrecoverable minute is part of the atmosphere of the novel. The characters seem intent upon capturing the fleeting moment by arresting it on paper. Richardson is extremely careful about noting times: the precise hour at which a letter is begun or continued is stated, so that the reader notes developments in events and emotions from hour to hour.

In dealing with Clarissa's death, Richardson wishes to give us two senses of time. The reader must feel that Clarissa's time is extremely short. She is being cut off in youth; her nineteenth birthday ushers in her death. Lovelace's reaction emphasizes the shock of such a young death: '*Nineteen* cannot so soon die . . .'[2] Clarissa herself is eager to find out precisely how short a time she may be given to prepare for death: 'Ten days?— A week?'[3] Richardson also wishes us to feel that the short time Clarissa has left is a long one, measured by another scale. As she says, 'Hours now are days, nay years.'[4] This last is the method of measuring time advocated by the devout writers. A short life is long enough to prepare for heaven if we but follow the spiritual rule.

If we were thus minute and curious in the spending our time, it is impossible but our life would seem very long. For so have I seen an amorous person tell the minutes of his absence from his fancied joy, and while he told the sands of his hour-glasse, or the throbs and little beatings of his watch, by dividing an hour into so many members, he spun out its length by number, and so translated a day into the tediousnesse of a moneth. And if we tell our dayes by Canonical hours of prayer, our weeks by a constant revolution of fasting dayes, or dayes of special devotion, and over all these draw a black Cypresse,

---

[1] Drexelius, *Considerations upon Eternitie*, The sixth Consideration, p. 180.
[2] *Clarissa*, vii. 344.   [3] Ibid., p. 222.
[4] Ibid., p. 406.

a veil of penitential sorrow, and severe mortification, we shall soon answer the calumny and objection of a short life.[1]

Measured by this standard, Clarissa's last days make her much older than the old wretch Sinclair, or the aged foolish Lord M. 'A fortnight or three weeks' gives her, as she says, 'full time'.[2] Richardson gives us the impression of a normal length of time by making full use of Belford as main narrator. Clarissa's own letters express her thoughts and feelings, her inner rather than her outer life. In her spiritual development, time and events are of decreasing importance. At the very end, time almost stands still for her: 'Is it Wednesday still, said she: Bless me! I know not how the time goes: But very tediously, 'tis plain.'[3]

In this section of the novel, almost every character who has played a part earlier is brought in again. There is even a new correspondent (though not a new character), the clergyman Brand, whose verbose and pharasaical misjudgements sustain the Harlowes' reluctance to be reconciled to their daughter.[4]

It is ironic to reflect that Clarissa, despoiled and outcast, has now fulfilled the Ladies Calling. In answering her vocation to reject the world and its offerings, to shun secular glory and ambition, this daughter of the Harlowes has almost turned her world upside down. Her life, her vision, and her fate were not envisaged by the friends who gave pious conduct books to young girls in the hope of training dutiful daughters and wives. Aspiring after a heavenly crown may be a dangerous occupation for a young lady, or for anyone who really means it, and the world is uncomfortably tested by the saints.

Amid all the confused response of the lamentably consistent Harlowes, we are conscious of Clarissa, alone and independent, hastening towards the grave, until her time comes to a full stop: 'She departed exactly at 40 minutes after Six o'clock, as by her watch on the table.'[5] The realistic watch, pointing to the hour and minute of her death, is a variation upon the inexorable hour-glasses and clocks of traditional religious imagery.

Time was—time ends. Clarissa's time is now eternity. The conventional images of death, which figured in Belford's unhappy

[1] Taylor, *Holy Dying*, ch. 1, sect. 3, p. 29.
[2] *Clarissa*, vii. 222.
[3] Ibid., p. 452.
[4] For Brand's letters see *Clarissa*, vii. 309-15, 414-34.
[5] Ibid. viii. 6.

dream, have a real meaning for Clarissa, as she makes clear in the devices she has designed to ornament her coffin.[1] Among the symbols she has chosen, which include the winged hour-glass of time, is a striking traditional image:

The principal device, neatly etched on a plate of white metal, is a crowned Serpent, with its tail in its mouth, forming a ring, the emblem of Eternity: And in the circle made by it is this inscription:

CLARISSA HARLOWE
April x
[Then the year]
ÆTAT xix.[2]

Eternity encompasses the child of time, as is beautifully illus-trated in one of Wither's emblems, which succinctly includes a deathbed scene in the background on the right (Plate 2). Time, with all its offspring, is 'a Fading-flowre'; Clarissa, the beautiful girl who bloomed only to die (ætat. xix) is not merely a fading flower, but an heir of eternity. She has escaped the prison of time, in which all the characters of the novel have been captive, and (because of the pressure of time felt through the narrative form itself) have been seen to be captive. Time cannot be conquered by possessing, by making more prisons. Dictating, as her grandfather attempted to do, that material objects should be 'kept *to the end of time*'[3] is an ironic futility. (The family plate is to the Harlowes a valuable like Clarissa, whom they also want to keep locked up; they succeed only too well, as she too is deposited in a safe labelled chest.) Yet it is within time, surrounded by eternity, that the soul works out its salvation.

In religious works such as Taylor's the daily struggle between good and evil in the active conscience is recognized and analysed, and there is a powerful consciousness of the shortness of human life, of 'the skull beneath the skin', which we are so willing to admire in the 'Metaphysical' poets. In Richardson's novel there is the same tension, and the same consciousness of

---

[1] *Clarissa*, vii. 337. The devices upon Clarissa's coffin, and those which Belford dreams, 'flying Hour-glasses, Death-heads, Spades, Mattocks, and Eternity', are traditional motifs. See the borders decorating broadside elegies in the collection of facsimiles in John. W. Draper's *A Century of Broadside Elegies*, 1928. Most of these images figure in George Wither's *A Collection of Emblemes, Ancient and Moderne*, 1635.

[2] *Clarissa*, vii. 338.   [3] Ibid. viii. 111.

death. The novel's imagery expresses the sense of mortality. In seventeenth-century religious literature, the inner conscious-ness is emphasized in connection with the consciousness of death, so that mundane reality is seen in relation to inner life and eternal destiny. One of the devices of the religious writers is to use commonplace objects or events and to develop them as images related to death. The extent to which Richardson, in the deathbed scenes, used many of these images in the same way—the startled horse, the watch, dressing and undressing— has been seen; Richardson uses the technique even more extensively throughout the whole novel, and this technique, adapted from religious literature, enabled him both to be realistic and to transcend 'realism'. Clarissa's world is distorted, constantly seen in new perspectives where the real and the symbolic melt into each other, sometimes in a frightening manner. Even the more 'realistic' scenes have other signifi-cances. The next two chapters will discuss Richardson's use of imagery in *Clarissa*, and its effect upon the novel as a whole.

VIII

A Fine and Private Place

RICHARDSON's use of imagery in *Clarissa* is very skilful. His technique is to use an image consistently but in several different ways, so that meanings multiply; the effect is that of a play upon ideas, like the play on words in a pun. One of the most notable images in *Clarissa* is that of the 'house', with the related ideas and words 'mansion', 'estate', 'lodgings', and so on. The parts of a house—rooms, doors, walls, windows, locks—are used to suggest confinement, partition, imprisonment. His use of imagery throughout the novel is a striking combination of elements from the amatory novels and from religious literature to achieve effects particularly suited to his tragic theme.

The use of the house imagery is not exactly pictorial—but rather, as it were, cinematic. Physical objects are seen in relation to the motion, physical or mental, of a character. We know where rooms stand in relation to each other in the various dwellings and how the characters move to and fro in each of the houses described (Harlowe Place, Mrs. Sinclair's, Mrs. Moore's, Smith's) even though we hardly know what the rooms actually look like. Rooms, walls, and doors reflect psychological states—the frustration of an effort to communicate, the endeavour to remain separated from another person, the attempt to erect or break down psychological barriers between personalities.

Space, or the lack of it, is important in suggesting the emotional condition of a character. Throughout the novel, Richardson develops the idea of increasing compression, of walls closing in, in an effect of claustrophobic horror. We move from the large estate to the coffin and grave, the final house, the ultimate enclosure.

At the beginning of the novel, Clarissa is in nominal possession of a house and estate of her own, through her grandfather's will. This inheritance causes her family's jealousy; not only does it give her material advantages which they resent, but it seems to give her a social claim to independence. They are afraid they will lose control over her, and for the sake of family aggrandizement, and to assert their authority, they press her marriage to Solmes. Her estate becomes a trap for her, not a means to freedom. The word 'estate' is repeated over and over in the first part of the novel, as the Harlowe family greedily calculate the prospects of her estate being joined to that of Solmes and then reverting to their possession. Clarissa, nominally the owner of an estate, becomes a prisoner in her parents' house.

At first, she has freedom to move, to visit Anna Howe, to receive visitors in the parlour. Then, when she endeavours to avoid Solmes and retreats to her chamber after his visit, she is ordered not to come down until she has expressed willingness to comply with her parents' command.[1] Her motions are continually cut short. When she goes down to her sister's parlour, Mr. Solmes enters, and she tries to hurry away, but is commanded not to stir.[2] She retreats to her own parlour and then attempts a flight: 'My feet moved (of *themselves*, I think) farther from the parlour where he was, and towards the stairs; and there I stopped and paused.'[3]

This kind of involuntary dream-like motion is repeated throughout the novel. Clarissa's refuge in her chamber becomes a confinement in which she is cut off, physically and morally, from the rest of the family. They hold conferences from which she is shut out. She must listen for voices of those she cannot see, and the Harlowe house becomes a maze in which she wanders, treading an intricate path through house and grounds to avoid those who wish to avoid her, according to her parents' command.[4]

Her privacy is invaded by constant emissaries, who come to cajole and threaten. Her energy is not abated as she tries to struggle out of an imprisoning situation; she is restless and paces to and fro like a caged animal: 'I walked backward and forward. I threw down with disdain the patterns. Now to my closet retired I; then quitting it, threw myself upon the Settee;

---

[1] *Clarissa*, i. 99–112. [2] Ibid., p. 153.
[3] Ibid., p. 157. [4] Ibid., p. 167.

then upon this chair; then upon that; then into one window, then into another—I knew not what to do!'[1] She is reduced to a half-life of loneliness, when the outside world is made up of disembodied voices and echoing sounds. She listens from the stairs-head to her parents' angry converse in the study;[2] later, she hears but does not see the members of the family arriving at Harlowe Place for their conclave: 'And oh! how my heart fluttered on hearing the chariot of the one, and then of the other, rattle thro' the courtyard, and the hollow-sounding footstep giving notice of each person's stepping out . . .'[3]

Two short scenes emphasize her separation from her family. In the first Clarissa, in the poultry yard, hears the mean laughter of her brother and sister and Solmes, all exulting over their treatment of her. 'The high Yew Hedge between us, which divides the Yard from the Garden, hindered them from seeing me.'[4] Clarissa listens to their cruel remarks until their voices die away. Later, when she is contemplating an escape with Lovelace's aid, she walks in the garden and is warned that she must hide, as her father does not wish to see her.

I struck into an oblique path, and got behind the yew-hedge, seeing my Sister appear; and there concealed myself till they were gone past me . . .

You cannot imagine what my emotions were behind the yew-hedge, on seeing my Father so near me. I was glad to look at him thro' the hedge, as he passed by . . .[5]

These two garden scenes create the effect of a maze, in which Clarissa walks, invisible and separate. The yew-hedge is a reflection of the dark mental maze through which she moves, trying to find the right way out when there is no right way.[6]

Clarissa's envious sister, Arabella, particularly enjoys tormenting her, teasing her with the idea of freedom while enjoying closing her in. When Clarissa declares she will go to her parents (as her sister has pretended to suggest), Bella 'got between me and the door, and shut it'.[7] (This action is exactly like Lovelace's later.) Bella pursues her sister with taunts:

Why don't you go, Miss?—following me to my closet, whither I

---

[1] *Clarissa*, i. p. 308.   [2] Ibid.   [3] Ibid., p. 327.
[4] Ibid. ii. 40.   [5] Ibid., p. 252.
[6] The 'yew-hedge' is emblematic as well as realistic, as yew is an emblem of death. Yew is part of the hideous bouquet in the prison scene.   [7] Ibid., p. 48.

retired, with my heart full, and pulled the sash-door after me; and could no longer hold in my tears.

Nor would I answer one word to her repeated aggravations, nor to her demands upon me to open my door (for the key was on the inside); nor so much as turn my head towards her, as she looked thro' the glass at me. And at last, which vexed her to the heart, I drew the silk curtain, that she should not see me, and down she went muttering all the way.[1]

If her family can impose partitions, so can she. Clarissa guards her privacy jealously. The Harlowe family is not unlike Lovelace in trying to despoil her of her privacy, both physical and mental. In Lovelace's case the invasion is a threatened sexual invasion, but it is partly so in the Harlowes's endeavours to imprison Clarissa and then to force her to Solmes.

The moral barriers between Clarissa and the rest of her family are indicated by the physical barriers between them. In imprisoning Clarissa, the Harlowes are trying to crush her will into so small a compass that she cannot act. In a sense they are trying to kill their youngest child, in trying to smother her will and independence, just as Lovelace (using some of the same tactics) tries to destroy the Clarissa who is and make her into the weeping submissive object of delight he would have her be. Marriage to Solmes would be, as the rape is, physical and moral outrage. To sanction it by her will, even in a weak assent wrung out of her by fatigue, would be a complicity in evil comparable to the consent which Lovelace expects to win from her. To Clarissa, a consent to marriage with Solmes seems like psychological suicide. Her obstinate will struggles valiantly as her family closes her in, trying to render her a passive captive. Her sense of physical and emotional claustrophobia bursts out when she says 'I had rather be buried alive, indeed I had, than have that man!'[2] She repeats, before Solmes himself, 'I will undergo the cruellest death—I will even consent to enter into the awful vault of my ancestors, and to have that bricked up upon me, rather than consent to be miserable for life.'[3] In a sense, Clarissa is already bricked up in a family tomb. Her mind runs upon burial alive. This is entirely credible as the stifling quality of her imprisonment has been made evident in the doors that have shut her in, the walls that have

---

[1] Ibid.   [2] Ibid. i. 127.   [3] Ibid. ii. 207.

surrounded her. Hence Richardson is able to use the device of
the significant dream without straining the realism of the narrative. Clarissa dreams that Lovelace

> carried me into a church-yard; and there, notwithstanding all my
> prayers and tears, and protestations of innocence, stabbed me to
> the heart, and then tumbled me into a deep grave ready dug,
> among two or three half-dissolved carcases; throwing in the dirt and
> earth upon me with his hands, and trampling it down with his feet.[1]

The terrifying, stifling quality of Clarissa's imprisonment
by her family is most powerfully brought out in the long
scene in which Clarissa has the dreaded interview with Solmes,
an interview which the family are determined will end with
her acceptance of the hated man as a husband. Their cruelty,
like that of Lovelace, is aroused by resistance, and their
sadistic humour is given full play. The imagery of walls and
doors in this scene contributes immensely to the total effect.

Clarissa receives Solmes in her parlour. As usual in Richardson's novels, the rooms in which the characters move are
described in relation to each other. We are given an impression,
not of shapes and colours, but of motion in space and of the
boundaries set to that space.

> There are two doors to *my* parlour, as I used to call it. As I
> entered at one, my friends hurried out at the other. I saw just the
> gown of my Sister, the last who slid away. My Uncle Antony went
> out with them . . . And they all remained in the next parlour, a
> wainscot partition only parting the two.[2]

Through one of the two doors Clarissa tries to withdraw, but
is prevented; through the other, she tries to plead with her
family, but the door is shut against her. At last she begs per-
mission to retire 'for a few minutes into the air'.[3] She is soon
brought back again to the parlour, 'as a person devoted'[4]
(the idea that she is a captive sacrifice is repeated later in the
novel, at her return to Sinclair's). After she has been tormented by her brother, her uncle and Solmes, she hears

---

[1] *Clarissa*, ii. 283. The relevance of the dream to Clarissa's sexual fears is
obvious. The macabre effect is not unlike that of a dream described in a Jacobean
play, e.g. the dream which Vittoria relates to Flamineo, in John Webster's *The
White Devil, or, The Tragedy of Paulo Giordano Ursini, Duke of Brachiano, With the Life
and Death of Vittoria Corombona the famous Venetian Courtizan*, 1612, I. i, p. CI^r.

[2] *Clarissa*, ii. 202.   [3] Ibid., p. 213.   [4] Ibid., p. 216.

through the door her father's threat against her. 'Yet, not knowing what I did, or said, I flew to the door, and would have opened it: But my Brother pulled it to, and held it close by the key . . .'[1] She pleads with her father through the closed door: 'O let it be the door of mercy! and open it to me, honoured Sir, I beseech you!—But this once, this once! altho' you were afterwards to shut it against me for ever!'[2] The door is opened to her, but in cruelty, not mercy:

> The door was endeavoured to be opened on the inside, which made my Brother let go the key on a sudden; and I pressing against it (all the time remaining on my knees) fell flat on my face into the other parlour; however, without hurting myself. But every-body was gone . . .[3]

There is a nightmarish quality in this incident. The bursting of one barrier leads only to further imprisonment, and a greater hopelessness, just as, later in the novel, Clarissa's attempts to escape from Lovelace either are thwarted immediately or bring her to another prison and a greater desolation.

Throughout the scene, the partitions are emphasized. The objects of which we are conscious are the wainscot partition and the doors. The rooms are described economically, in terms of space; the important thing about the next parlour is its emptiness. There is never any detail to distract us from the main effect, which is to present movement in space. The major impression here is one of enclosure—Clarissa is caught, like a bird in a cage, just as she is later at Sinclair's.

From the beginning, the separation between Lovelace and Clarissa is emphasized by the physical barriers between them. Lovelace prowls around her father's walls, like Milton's Satan around Paradise. The letters between them are placed in a wall. At one point when Clarissa returns to retrieve a letter she has just left for him, and finds it gone, she realizes 'In all probability, there was but a brick wall, of a few inches thick, between Mr. Lovelace and me, at the very time I put the Letter under the brick!'[4] Anna Howe later comments 'But a *few inches of brick-wall* between you so lately; and now such *mountains*!'[5]

The brick wall between Clarissa and Lovelace signifies their

---

[1] Ibid., p. 221.   [2] Ibid.   [3] Ibid., p. 222.
[4] Ibid., p. 114.   [5] Ibid., p. 148.

spiritual separation. Neither is able to see the other; at the moments when they are apparently most united they are still divided by insurmountable barriers. When Lovelace seems to be trying to break into her prison at Harlowe Place to help free her from it—as when he obtains the key to the garden door and enters, surprising Clarissa in the wood-house[1]—he is only offering her the way to another prison.

Such walls and garden doors are the stuff of the amatory novel. For instance, Cleomira in *The British Recluse* immured in her mother's house watches her lover going down the road,[2] and sees his servant 'peeping over the wall'.[3] The key to a garden door plays an important part in the meetings of D'Elmont and Amena in *Love in Excess*.[4] In *Clarissa*, these novelettish elements sustain the general theme of attack and imprisonment, and acquire new significance as sexual symbols.

The symbol of Clarissa's abduction by Lovelace is the garden door. When she unbolts the already unlocked door, she is taking a step on a fatal course. Lovelace pleads with her to fly, and tries to draw her further from the door; she retreats, repeating 'Let me go back.'[5] He reassures her by telling her that she is free to retreat; 'The key lies down at the door',[6] and she is reassured as to her safety. But the key is really Lovelace's instrument of power. He uses it to terrify her, as he threatens to unlock the door and walk into the house with her, if she flies from him. He gives her the key, still threatening to enter with her, and she is about to open the door to return when Lovelace startles her: '*They are at the door, my beloved creature*! And taking the key from me, he fluttered with it, as if he would double-lock it. And instantly a voice from within cried out, bursting against the door, as if to break it open . . .'[7] In terror, Clarissa is persuaded to run with Lovelace; she looks back and sees 'a man, who must have come out of the door, keeping us in his eye, running now towards us, then back to the garden; beckoning and calling to others, whom I supposed *he* saw, altho' the turning of the wall hindered *me* from seeing them . . .'[8]

---

[1] *Clarissa*, i. 255–70.
[2] Haywood, *The British Recluse*, pp. 29–31.
[3] Ibid., p. 33.
[4] Idem, *Love in Excess*, part i, pp. 19–30.
[5] *Clarissa*, ii. 352.
[6] Ibid.
[7] Ibid., p. 358.
[8] Ibid., p. 359.

The wall hides the truth from her; her family has not been aroused, and the whole scene is a result of Lovelace's stratagem. The Harlowe wall now shuts her out, not in, and she is a prisoner in Lovelace's power. She is caught in a world in which people are separated from one another by barriers, and reality is hidden. The open door, and the key which Lovelace brandishes, are symbols of his rape of her. In a way, the rape has already been committed—it is implicit in Lovelace's key. He has acquired power over her, and has pierced through one of the protecting walls of the fortress.

When the Harlowe family's design is thwarted, their cruel desire to confine and kill still pursues their victim, expressed in Arabella's malicious letter to Clarissa: 'Your drawings and your pieces are all taken down; as is also your own whole-length picture, in the Vandyke taste, from your late parlour: They are taken down, and thrown into your closet, which will be nailed up, as if it were not a part of the house; there to perish together . . .'[1] When they cannot torment Clarissa in person, they do so in effigy and symbolically kill and bury her. In Bella's spite there is all the malevolence of black magic, the mutilation of an image. Clarissa's portrait, nailed up in her closet to 'perish' foreshadows her body's death and her burial in the Harlowe tomb. As far as Harlowe Place is concerned, the walls have closed in upon their daughter as far as possible.

When Clarissa has been tricked into flight, one of her primary concerns is to find some place to stay. She and Lovelace move restlessly from the inn to Sorlings' to London, as Clarissa searches hopefully for a place of security, not realizing that whatever place she finds will be a cage; to Lovelace she is already 'a captive'.[2] She hopes to find respectable lodgings in London, and decides that the city is 'the most private place to be in'.[3] Lovelace refers ironically to the prospect of private lodgings in London: 'There are extraordinary convenient lodgings in my eye in London, where we could be private, and all mischief avoided.'[4] The words 'private' and 'convenient' assume several meanings, and the idea of lodgings in London becomes fraught with sexual suggestion. The suggestion is most evident in the description of possible lodgings in London,

[1] Ibid. iii. 283.   [2] Ibid., p. 79.
[3] Ibid., p. 169.   [4] Ibid., p. 254.

the businesslike list really prepared by Lovelace. Five lodgings are listed; there is an especially detailed account of the 'good accommodations in Dover-street',[1] a description which seems as practical as a house-agent's advertisement. When the reader considers what the lodgings really may be, the description of the house and its owner is seen to contain some disturbing suggestions.

> She rents two good houses, distant from each other, only joined by a *large handsome passage*. The *inner-house* is the genteelest, and is very elegantly furnished . . .
> A little garden belongs to the inner-house, in which the old gentlewoman has displayed a true female fancy, having crammed it with vases, flower-pots, and figures, without number.
> . . . The apartments she has to lett are in the inner-house: They are a dining-room, two neat parlours, a withdrawing-room, two or three handsome bed-chambers; one with a pretty light closet in it, which looks into the little garden; all furnished in taste.
> . . . She bragged, that this was the way of all the Lodgers she ever had, who staid with her *four times as long as they at first intended.*[2]

The house is a brothel, and the 'widow', the 'relict of an officer', is a procuress. Clarissa, innocently deciding to take the lodgings in the inner house, is imprisoning herself in the heart of the brothel, separated from the actual place of business by very little space, and completely cut off from the world of good reputation and sexual innocence. The very phrases 'inner-house', 'large handsome passage', 'garden' and 'figures' have the overtones of sexual metaphors. The garden, furnished in 'true female fancy' suggests the daily business of the brothel, as in Lovelace's metaphor: 'These women . . . used always to oblige me with the flower and first fruits of their garden!'[3] The other 'lodgers', the seduced women who remain there to ply their trade, do indeed stay much longer than they intended.

Clarissa thinks she has chosen the lodgings, but she has been beguiled into a new prison, and lodges in a kind of hell. Lovelace exults in her captivity, comparing a captured woman to a bird in a 'well-secured cage'. He vividly describes the behaviour of the captured bird which 'beats and bruises again its pretty head and sides, bites the wires, and pecks at the fingers

---

[1] *Clarissa*, iii. 194.   [2] Ibid., pp. 194–5.   [3] Ibid., p. 312.

of its delighted tamer'.[1] Clarissa's struggles to escape her cage, her clinging to freedom, excite Lovelace, while he confidently expects that she, like the 'ensnared Volatile', will at last become tame and submissive.

Once Lovelace has, contrary to Clarissa's plans, taken up residence under the same roof, he is sure she cannot escape him. He pretends to share her disapproval of the arrangements, and feigns a search for a new house, which will be set up as she directs, and to which, he indicates, they will go as man and wife. He successfully amuses her for a while with the highly circumstantial account of the widow Fretchville's house.[2] A house of her own represents independence and security to Clarissa, as Lovelace knows when he skilfully plays upon her expectations by the pretended arrangements. He tells her that 'the intention I had to fix her dear self in the house before the happy knot was tied, would have set her in that independence in *appearance*, as well as *fact*, which was necessary to shew to all the world, that her choice was free . . .'[3] The pretence becomes cumbersome, and Lovelace rids himself of Mrs. Fretchville and her house by visiting smallpox upon the imaginary widow,[4] but the ruse has been useful in keeping Clarissa ignorant of her true captivity.

Although Lovelace has been successful in imprisoning Clarissa, he has not taken into account her capacity to lock him out, physically and spiritually. She retreats behind barriers of reserve and 'punctilio' which are signified by the closed door. Upon her arrival she insists that her chamber must be her retirement, and examines the doors and windows, and their fastenings.[5] She constantly retreats to her own room as a refuge, as she does when Lovelace takes a letter from her and she snatches it back and retires: 'out she shot to her own apartment (Thank my stars she could fly no further!); and as soon as she entered it, in a passion still, she double-locked and double-bolted herself in'.[6]

The scenes in Mrs. Sinclair's house are full of locked doors, and rapid movements in a small space. The barriers are now put up by Clarissa, and the suggestion of breaking through barriers becomes more violent than at Harlowe Place. Clarissa

---

[1] Ibid. iv. 13.   [2] Ibid. iii. 343.   [3] Ibid. iv. 248–9.
[4] Ibid., pp. 242–3.   [5] Ibid. iii. 325.   [6] Ibid. iv. 53.

entreats not to be 'broken in upon',[1] and the phrase carries
suggestions of physical and mental assault; it is connected with
Lovelace's metaphor of the walled city besieged.[2] Her chamber
door becomes the object of Lovelace's assault and conquest.[3]

There is one interlude in this section of the novel which is a
relief from the confinement among close chambers and locked
doors. There is a brief description of an airing taken by Clarissa
and Lovelace 'to Hamstead, to Highgate, to Muswell-hill;
back to Hamstead to the Upper-Flask . . . Then home early
by Kentish Town.'[4] Richardson is not interested in extensive
descriptions of natural scenery, but the background he sketches
in has its effect: 'Delightfully easy she: And so respectful and
obligeing I, all the way, and as we walked out upon the Heath,
to view the variegated prospects which that agreeable elevation
affords, that she promised to take now and-then a little excursion with me.'[5]

The impression of space, freedom, and fresh air is a welcome
change, and this is one of the more poignant moments in the
book as during the walk on the Heath, Clarissa and Lovelace
are almost at unity—as nearly so as they ever become. Lovelace
is still free to change his mind. If he could let himself love her
truly, as part of him desires, they could both escape the hellish
house of Mrs. Sinclair and the evil to come. However, the peace-
ful interlude has been carefully planned by him, as a preliminary
to the test of his mock illness. Soon we are back in the confined
and artificial atmosphere of Mrs. Sinclair's house, the hurried
'running up stairs and down', and loud whispers at Clarissa's
door.[6] The success of his 'illness' in proving Clarissa's love for
him encourages Lovelace in attempting the surprise attack on
the night of the fire.

The fire scene is described very vividly in Lovelace's mock-
serious manner; he mentions the medley of voices about the
house, the trampling, the screams, and running up and down
stairs.[7] As at the Harlowes', Clarissa has to rely on the overheard and unseen—now she is doubly a victim, since what she
is meant to overhear is a delusion. The cries alarm her, and
Lovelace eagerly hears her door 'unbar, unbolt, unlock, and

---

[1] *Clarissa*, iii. 74.   [2] Ibid. iv. 250, 362.   [3] Ibid., pp. 56–7.
[4] Ibid., p. 285.   [5] Ibid., pp. 285–6.
[6] Ibid., p. 292.   [7] Ibid., pp. 388–9.

open'.[1] He seizes his opportunity, and enters Clarissa's chamber. To his own surprise he is softened by her real terror and resistance to his attempts upon her, and withdraws. He soon returns to the attack; then 'I thought I heard her coming to open the door, and my heart leapt in that hope; but it was only to draw another bolt, to make it still the faster . . .'[2]

The next day she will not see him, and he can only attempt to converse with her through the door, and catch a glimpse of her through the keyhole. His attempt has betrayed him, and resulted in his frustration. The barriers between himself and Clarissa increase as she shuts herself away from him. Clarissa's knowledge is her power. She has been a willing prisoner because she has been deluded; now she suspects both Lovelace and the house, and flies from her captivity.

Both *Pamela* and *Clarissa* possess many elements of the setting of the seduction novel—the imprisonment in false security, the locked doors through which surprise entrances can be effected. In *Pamela* (which is in many ways artistically a preliminary exercise before *Clarissa*) Richardson uses these devices with more skill than such writers as Mrs. Haywood were capable of maintaining, but they are still simple, without the kind of cumulative importance they have in *Clarissa*. Pamela knows her true situation from the time of her abduction to Mr. B.'s estate; the struggle is a simple conflict of wills between the two characters. Clarissa is not aware for a long time of the forces she has to combat. Pamela's escape from Mr. B. is often prevented, but when she is finally set free, she is free, and once coercion has been removed, she can, like an Ibsenite heroine, give her love of her own volition. Clarissa thinks she has escaped from the brothel, but she flies into a world which is bent on her imprisonment—for her, freedom cannot exist.

Clarissa innocently supposes that she is able to choose freedom, even in loneliness and grief, even when she feels almost lost in an extent of unknown space, as she seems to when she stops on the road to Hendon and looks down over the valley and London, not knowing where to turn.[3] She retraces some of the steps of her earlier, pleasanter journey with Lovelace, going to Hampstead and stopping at the Upper-Flask.[4] Perhaps

[1] Ibid., p. 389.   [2] Ibid., p. 297.   [3] Ibid. v. 70.
[4] Ibid., pp. 68–9. Richardson is most exact in his use of London geography in

Hampstead has come to represent happiness, or at least freedom, to Clarissa, even though the freedom it offers is delusive.

When Lovelace discovers Clarissa's escape, he rages against her and the Sinclair house, 'this worse than infernal habitation',[1] and wanders about the house in aimless hurry.[2] As soon as he discovers where she is gone, he is elated at the delightful prospect of recapture: 'Had she but known how much difficulty enhances the value of any-thing with me, and had she the least notion of obliging me by it, she would never have stopt short at *Hamstead*, surely.'[3] Clarissa, in what she fondly supposes is a farewell letter to Lovelace, reproachfully says that 'She is *thrown upon the wide World*.'[4] He remarks ironically upon this: 'Now I own, that Hamstead-Heath affords very pretty, and very *extensive* prospects; but 'tis not the *wide world* neither: And suppose *that* to be her grievance, I hope soon to restore her to a *narrower*.'[5] Clarissa is not to have 'extensive prospects' either in the sense of space in which to move and breathe, nor in the sense of freedom of mind to choose her own life. The reference to a 'narrower' world is dramatically ironic; Lovelace succeeds in bringing Clarissa to the coffin and grave.

Lovelace, disguised as an old man, pursues Clarissa to her new lodgings at Mrs. Moore's house. His movement through the house to the climax of his penetration of Clarissa's sanctuary and the doffing of his disguise expresses the excitement of sexual conquest. The scene in which he moves slowly up stairs, hobbles through the room, and, coming to the closet, induces Clarissa to open the door and, then suddenly manifests himself[6] is, like the scene at the garden door of Harlowe Place, a symbol of the rape.

Clarissa, horrified at discovery by him, thinks desperately of escape:

Let me look out—[I heard the Sash lifted up] Whither does that path lead? Is there no possibility of getting a coach? . . . Cannot I steal to some neighbouring house, where I may be concealed till I

Clarissa. It is amusing to note that he may have added to the popularity of the Upper Flask Tavern for parties who visited Hampstead Heath by mentioning it in *Clarissa*. See John Thomas Smith, *Nollekens and his Times*, 2nd ed., 2 vols., 1829, i. 68.

[1] *Clarissa*, v. 17–18.	[2] Ibid., p. 26.	[3] Ibid., p. 58.
[4] Ibid., p. 64.	[5] Ibid.	[6] Ibid., pp. 79–88.

can get quite away? . . . A barn, an outhouse, a garret, will be a palace to me, if it will but afford me refuge from *this man*![1]

Her refuge has become another prison. Mrs. Moore's house is not, like Mrs. Sinclair's, a house of evil, but it is a place of moral mediocrity. The women, Mrs. Moore, Miss Rawlins, and the widow Bevis, are easily flattered and deluded, and their vanity, avarice, officiousness, and sexual curiosity make them easy prey to Lovelace, whom they believe in preference to Clarissa. When Clarissa attempts to leave the apartment and the house, Lovelace shuts the door against her,[2] just as the door in the parlour at Harlowe Place was shut when she attempted to escape from Solmes. When Clarissa furiously reminds him that he has no right over her, he replies that he will follow her 'were it to the world's end'.[3]

Still swayed by some belief in Lovelace and by the great hope, carefully fostered by Lovelace, of eventual reconciliation with her family, Clarissa consents to put herself under the protection of his relatives. Lovelace, now the prisoner of his own actions, must act quickly; he feels the only way to make sure of her is to take her by force. Her last defences would then be destroyed, and, he thinks, she could put no more barriers between them; the walls will be destroyed, the city subjugated.

To carry out this final act in privacy and security, it is necessary to lure Clarissa back to the brothel. Clarissa returns, with the well-dressed harlots who masquerade as Lovelace's relatives, to Mrs. Sinclair's house, and is persuaded to enter for a few moments. The return to the house is described by Clarissa:

But think, my dear, what a dreadful turn all had upon me, when, through several streets and ways I knew nothing of, the coach slackening its pace, came within sight of the dreadful house of the dreadfullest woman in the world; as she proved to me.

Lord be good unto me! cry'd the poor fool, looking out of the coach . . .

. . . Won't the man drive on? . . . *Man*, drive on, putting my head out of the coach—*Man*, drive on! —tho' my voice was too low to be heard.

The coach stopped at the door. How I trembled! . . .

Immediately came the old creature to the door. A thousand

[1] Ibid. v. 127–8. [2] Ibid., p. 135. [3] Ibid.

pardons, dear Madam, stepping to the coach-side, if we have any-way offended you—Be pleased, Ladies [to the other two] to alight.
. . .

I was afraid I should have fallen into fits: But still refused to go out—Man!—Man!—Man! cried I, gaspingly, my head out of the coach and in, by turns, half a dozen times running, drive on!—Let us go!

My heart misgave me beyond the power of my own accounting for it; for still I did not suspect these women. But the antipathy I had taken to the vile house, and to find myself so near it, when I expected no such matter, with the sight of the old creature, all together, made me behave like a distracted person . . .

Come, my dear, said the pretended Lady: Give me your hand; holding out hers. Oblige me this once.

I will bless your footsteps, said the old creature, if once more you honour my house with your presence.

A croud by this time was gathered about us; but I was too much affected to mind that.

Again the pretended Miss Montague urged me; standing up as ready to go out if I would give her room. Lord, my dear, said she, who can bear this croud?—What will people think?

The pretended Lady again pressed me, with both her hands held out—Only, my dear, to give orders about your things.

And thus pressed, and gazed at (for then I looked about me) the women so richly dressed, people whispering; in an evil moment, out stepped I, trembling, forced to lean with both my hands (frighted too much for ceremony) on the pretended Lady Betty's arm—O that I had dropped down dead upon the guilty threshold!
. . .

Hasten, then.—Come, my dear, to me, as she led me through the passage to the fatal inner house—Lean upon me—How you tremble!—how you falter in your steps!—Dearest Niece Lovelace [the old wretch being in hearing] why these hurries upon your spirits?—We'll begone in a minute.

And thus she led the poor Sacrifice into the old wretch's too-well known parlour.[1]

This description of Clarissa's return to Mrs. Sinclair's house is excellent in its rhythmic movement. The effect is a dream-like horror; Clarissa is shut in the coach which remains obstinately motionless despite her frantic desire to drive on, and her efforts to scream are scarcely audible. Slowly she is induced to move

---

[1] *Clarissa*, vi. 180–5.

and is drawn towards the yawning open door, and down the long passage. Her walk into the house, amid the hushed gazing crowd, is, like the compulsive motion of a nightmare, slow and irresistible. The scene is related to the funeral scene at the end of the book, with its slow motion and heavy ceremony that leads to the open tomb. The door of the harlot's house is the door of the pit. Once she is within the brothel, in the fatal inner house which is an image of hell, the women reveal themselves as the devils which Lovelace himself says they are, and Lovelace is able to carry out the triumphant act which is a kind of murder.

The difference between *Pamela* and *Clarissa* is most evident in such a scene as this. Mr. B.'s Lincolnshire estate and the house, the 'handsome, large, old, and lonely Mansion . . . with all its brown nodding Horrors of lofty Elms and Pines about it'[1] look sinister enough to Pamela, and the house is her prison for a while, but she is soon to be eagerly hastening back to it, once she can do so of her own free will, and is eventually to be the mistress of the estate. Even during her imprisonment, the estate as she describes it is full of wholesome natural life. Pamela, as the reader sympathetically realizes, exaggerates the horrors of the general aspect of things, because she hates her own situation; the estate is, after all, only a country residence with its grounds about it. Clarissa, shut up in the brothel, is innocent of her truly evil situation, until she is made passive and helpless as Pamela is never helpless. Unlike Mr. B.'s estate, the brothel is truly evil in itself—more evil than Clarissa knows until it is too late—and nothing natural or good can grow or breathe there. There is nothing in *Pamela* to equal the claustrophobic horror of the scene of Clarissa's return to the brothel, in which her enervated reason, fed on delusion, mistakenly controls her powerless instinctive fear of the deadly trap.[2]

Lovelace's invasion of Clarissa's body is itself only a final symbol of his invasion of her whole person by breaking through all defences. Clarissa, in the wanderings of her temporary insanity, describes the rape in metaphors of doors broken open:

[1] *Pamela*, i. 143.

[2] It is not perhaps irrelevant to note that Richardson suffered from a nervous condition related to what we now call claustrophobia. He could not bear being in a crowded and confined place; this neurosis prevented him from going to plays, or to church, in his later middle age. See his letter to Lady Bradshaigh, 1749, *Selected Letters*, p. 134.

'But when all my doors are fast, and nothing but the key-hole open, and the key of late put into that, to be where you are, in a manner without opening any of them—O wretched, wretched Clarissa Harlowe!'[1]

Without realizing it, Lovelace has destroyed his own defence as well. Hitherto Clarissa has lived in a confused world of disguise and illusion, her vision half-obscured by barriers, condemned to hear voices muffled behind partitions, to be surprised by what lurks behind separating walls. Now her innocence and theory have become experience (to use the contrast so dear to Lovelace), and the barriers of ignorance are destroyed. For the first time since she has been in Lovelace's power, Clarissa is aware that she is in prison. Her sense of being imprisoned, stifled, buried alive is evident in her plea to Lovelace to shut her in a private madhouse,[2] or to bury her: 'Dig a hole deep enough to cram in and conceal this unhappy body . . .'[3] Her imprisonment is conveyed in claustrophobic images, in her attempts to escape:

Insolent Villain! said the furious Lady. And, rising, ran to the window, and threw up the Sash [She knew not, I suppose, that there were iron rails before the windows] . . .

I clasped her in my arms, people beginning to gather about the window: And then she cried out, Murder! Help! Help!—And carried her up to the Dining-room, in spite of her little plotting heart (as I may now call it) altho' she violently struggled, catching hold of the banisters here and there, as she could.[4]

In each description of her attempts at escape, our attention is drawn to the physical barriers to her freedom as they express the power of Lovelace's will. Clarissa's violent motion is seen within a closely and heavily confined space; her struggles are those of life against death, spirit against matter. The brothel is a house of death. Richardson stresses its tomb-like qualities, its cramped confinement, its silence to the world outside. When Lovelace makes his last attempt upon Clarissa, everything is locked and shut, and the house is as completely shut away from the world outside as a coffin: 'The Street-doors also doubly secured, and every shutter to the windows round the house fastened that no noise or screaming should be heard . . .'[5]

[1] *Clarissa*, v. 335.   [2] Ibid., p. 337.   [3] Ibid., p. 371.
[4] Ibid., p. 360.   [5] Ibid. vi. 65.

This last attempt, which culminates in the 'penknife scene', depends like the attempt in the 'fire scene' on a device to make Clarissa open her door. Again, the open door is to Lovelace a symbol of sexual triumph; the words are an echo of those in the earlier scene as he exultingly hears her *'unbolt, unlock, unbar,* the door . . .'[1] Clarissa, with her new knowledge, is not however now so vulnerable. She keeps the key to her door, and returning, locks herself in again.[2] Her possession of the key is a symbol of her power over Lovelace; she can still separate herself from him. He had not realized that although the human will may be confined to a small space, it still possesses the power to shut others out. Lovelace is shut forever away from Clarissa's love.

When Lovelace is absent, and Clarissa has intimidated the brothel-keeper into leaving the key in the street door, Clarissa escapes in disguise, in a journey that is a reversal of Lovelace's invasion in disguise of the lodgings at Moore's. Again Clarissa escapes into another prison; she finds refuge in the Smith's shop, but is soon arrested on the action of the brothel's inmates. The scene of the arrest is like that of the return to Sinclair's, in the long description and slow rhythm. Again Clarissa, standing in a commonplace street, seems free, and is actually powerless. She is arrested at the door of Covent Garden church, and forced to get into the officers' chair.

Looking about her, and seeing the three passages, to wit, that leading to Henrietta-street, that to King-street, and the fore-right one, to Bedford-street, crouded, she started—Any-where—Any-where, said she, but to the Woman's! And stepping into the chair, threw herself on the seat, in the utmost distress and confusion—Carry me, carry me out of sight—Cover me—Cover me up—for ever—were her words.

Thy villain drew the curtains: She had not power: And they went away with her through a vast croud of people.[3]

As when the coach stops at Sinclair's house, Clarissa is surrounded by a crowd of onlookers who do not understand her situation or help her. Indeed, they cut off any routes of escape; the world conspires to trap her. She is drawn into the enclosed space and shut off from sight, in a dream-like helplessness. This scene, in which the crowd follows the chair with its

[1] Ibid.   [2] Ibid., p. 71   [3] Ibid., pp. 273–4.

drawn curtains to the officer's house, also prefigures the journey of Clarissa in her coffin.

The scenes in the spunging-house are among the most powerful in the whole novel. The prison room in officer Rowland's, with its barred windows and heavy locks, is openly and avowedly what Clarissa's other residences have been covertly. Harlowe Place, Mrs. Moore's lodgings, and Mrs. Sinclair's house have all been so many gaols in disguise. Now the veil of appearance has been stripped off, and reality appears in the naked ugliness of forced constraint. The endeavour of one human being to deny the freedom of another is ugly and sordid. Harlowe Place and Sinclair's are full of fine show; material prosperity covers them in the eyes of the world. Harlowe Place is built on wealth and the love of gain; spacious as it may appear, with its fine rooms and extensive gardens, its narrowness of mind and heart make it into a place of confinement, as Clarissa found when imprisoned in it. Mrs. Sinclair has all the attributes of a bourgeois householder. She has many fine apartments to offer; she is '*aforehand* in the world'.[1] She and the Harlowes have much in common; both are willing to build their prosperity on the exploitation of human beings. Both houses trade in human flesh.

The prison is at least free from the pretence of respectability. It is quite nakedly a place of misery. Belford, in his horrified letter to Lovelace, describes the prison room at length. The room is described in more detail than any other in the novel. Richardson indulges in this wealth of detail because everything points the contrast between this place and the other houses, and yet suggests the ironic similarity between them. Everything in the room is old, broken, cheap, worn, and decaying:

A horrid hole of a house, in an Alley they call a Court; stairs wretchedly narrow, even to the first-floor rooms: And into a den they led me, with broken walls, which had been papered, as I saw by a multitude of tacks, and some torn bits held on by the rusty heads. . . . The windows dark and double-barred, the tops boarded up to save mending; and only a little four-paned eyelet-hole of a casement to let in air; more, however, coming in at broken panes, than could come in at That. . . . An old, tottering, worm-eaten table, that had more nails bestowed in mending it to make it stand, than the table cost fifty years ago, when new.

[1] *Clarissa*, iii. 195.

On the mantel-piece was an iron shove-up candle-stick, with a lighted candle in it, twinkle, twinkle, twinkle, four of them, I suppose, for a penny.

Near that, on the same shelf, was an old looking-glass, cracked thro' the middle, breaking out into a thousand points; the crack given it, perhaps, in a rage, by some poor creature, to whom it gave the representation of his heart's woes in his face.[1]

The wretched room with its broken walls and decrepit furniture expresses Clarissa's state. She is in abject poverty, having lost everything that the world values: money, friends, family, reputation—even, for a while, her sanity. She has lost that saleable commodity, her virginity. Everything she has had —her estate, her good name, the admiration of friends, her health and beauty—has become valueless to her, as useless and decayed as her prison furniture. Her body is 'broken' (as in Mowbray's cheap pun 'Where will she mend herself?'),[2] and the cracked walls and crumbling furniture are emblems of this breaking, and of the crumbling of her body as she draws to death and dissolution. Her hopes and her love are broken wrecks, a mockery of themselves. The cracked mirror, like the walls, expresses what Lovelace later calls 'an incurable fracture in her heart'.[3] It is also related to the mirror image which recurs in the novel. Earlier when Clarissa is living in a false world, the glass sometimes shows the truth, as when Clarissa surprises Lovelace's ugly expression in the pier glass.[4] Now, when the world appears as it really is, the mirror represents the false, and is destroyed.

The crazy, worn-out worthless objects which furnish the room point ironically at the futility of material possessions. The property which people attempt to accumulate is as subject to decay as reputation, beauty, or health. The conveniences and appurtenances which successful Harlowes or harlots are able to purchase offer nothing to the life of the spirit—they are a mockery. The Harlowe hopes of family aggrandizement, the proud Harlowe estate, are as ugly and fragile as anything here. Clarissa, deprived of everything they value, is 'the thing itself', opposed to the rotten creations of vanity, pride, and greed. The Harlowe family and inhabitants of the brothel have imprisoned

[1] Ibid. vi. 296–7. [2] Ibid., p. 95.
[3] Ibid. vii. 348. [4] Ibid. iv. 112.

themselves in a world which is as ugly as this prison room. Clarissa, who holds to her essential freedom, is more free in prison than she was as the possessor of an estate.

The prostitutes Sally and Polly come to her, to offer her 'liberty' and 'handsome apartments' at Mrs. Sinclair's. The futility of their efforts, and the fact that they are living in a different world from hers are evident in the long conversation between them, with the short, riddling sentences, like stichomythic dialogue in an Elizabethan play:

> But we two will bail you, *Miss*, if you will go back with us to Mrs. Sinclair's.
> Not for the world!
> Hers are very handsome apartments.
> The fitter for those who own them!
> These are very sad ones.
> The fitter for *me*!
> You may be very happy yet, *Miss*, if you will.
> I hope I shall. . . .
> Why, you don't think of tarrying *here* always?
> I shall not *live* always.[1]

The inhabitants of Harlowe Place and the brothel fail to admit that they will not live always. They imprison themselves in the false security of their estates, or 'handsome apartments'. Clarissa has discovered that the world has no house, no lodgings, no home to offer her. The habitations which the world offers her are built out of corruption and the corruptible; they are as dark and decrepit inwardly as this house is outwardly. Clarissa, suffering from 'the *worst of Orphanage*',[2] is offered a home in a brothel, and a position as one of the 'daughters' of the 'mother' Mrs. Sinclair—a travesty of what she truly desires. Clarissa rejects this offer, and makes no effort to find a home for herself; she accepts the prison: 'These are my lodgings now; are they not?'[3]

Clarissa, through Belford's agency, is returned to her lodgings at Smith's. The shop is the only home she has, and, ironically, the only house in which she is not to be bought and sold. But she is again a captive, imprisoned by illness and death. The progress of her illness is traced by her growing incapacity to move, until she is almost totally confined: 'Next, I was

[1] *Clarissa*, vi. 280–1.   [2] Ibid. vii. 273.   [3] Ibid. vi. 279.

unable to go to *Church*; then to go *up* or *down stairs*: Now hardly can move from one *room* to *another*; and a *less room* will soon hold me.'[1]

The section of the novel between Clarissa's arrest and her death is not intended to be merely a series of pathetic scenes. What we are meant to see is the development of a mind which has passed from innocence to experience. Disguises and partitions have been removed—Clarissa no longer moves in a world of half-heard conversations, and ingenious illusions. Freed of the tragic absurdity which has hitherto characterized her actions, she is no longer to be deceived into making inappropriate responses to reality. She has desired security and love, and now realizes that the world can have little of either to offer, and can give neither perfectly. The word 'house', acquires new meanings. At first, Clarissa laments the loss of past happiness: 'O! that I were as in months past! as in the days when God preserved me! . . . As I was in the days of my *childhood*—when the Almighty was yet with me; when *I was in my Father's house* . . .'[2] Clarissa may have been innocent and happy in the house of her father Harlowe, but that house was not in itself innocent or happy. It is no more a fit habitation for her than the brothel; she is dead to it and can return only in death. The Harlowes do not seem to be her relations;[3] the home she belongs to is not Harlowe Place. In her riddling letter to Lovelace, she both deceives him and tells him no more than the truth: 'I am setting out with all diligence for my Father's House.'[4] Her 'Father's House', her true home, is something very different from Harlowe Place.

Since the idea of 'home' now means something not to be found on earth, the idea of an earthly house acquires a new meaning. Clarissa, who has been so long in search of safe lodgings, finally buys the only permanent and secure lodgings that the world affords. When she says she wishes to 'purchase a house', she buys a coffin.[5] This, unlike the house inherited from her grandfather, is the only house she is able to call hers. It is hers to care for; she designs the devices and chooses the inscriptions upon it. She calls it her '*palace*' and speaks of its being sent '*when furnished*' to the Harlowe family tomb.[6] The macabre

[1] Ibid. vii. 400.   [2] Ibid. vi. 405.   [3] Ibid. vii. 110.
[4] Ibid., p. 189.   [5] Ibid., p. 223. See Plate 2.   [6] Ibid., p. 339.

metaphor 'furnished' echoes Clarissa's earlier searches for lodgings, and the description of Mrs. Sinclair's apartments as 'elegantly furnished'. Clarissa, with her last house, is self-sufficient. It is as if she had done what she said she would not—taken possession of her house and estate; she is at last independent.

In this last part of the novel, the former positions of Lovelace and Clarissa are reversed. Lovelace is now the prisoner of a situation. He lives through some of Clarissa's former experiences—the sense of helplessness, even temporary madness, are visited upon him. In a memorable comic scene he invades Smith's shop and house looking for Clarissa.[1] This scene is closely related to his search for her at Moore's; again he goes from room to room of a strange house, searching for the door that will open to show him his beloved. Here, however, his actions are comic and ineffectual. Wounded by frustration and unexpected failure, he has that night his frightening dream,[2] which is a parallel to Clarissa's earlier one. The barriers between them have become a great gulf. Lord M.'s black cloak smothers and encloses him, separating him from her, as she dreamed that she was to be smothered in the grave.

Lovelace's fear of separation from Clarissa leads him to outburts of impotent rage. He is angry even at Belford for being able to see her 'while *I* . . . am forced to keep aloof, and hardly dare to enter the *city* where she is!'[3] The image of the barred door, the door which he thought he could force open once for all, recurs to him: 'Thou hast, I doubt, made her bar up the door of her heart, as she used to do her chamber-door, against me.'[4] His state is shown in his movements which, like Clarissa's in her various prisons, are jerky and violent, but circumscribed. He describes his constant pointless riding towards London and back, longing but forbidden to see her, as he rides 'backwards and forwards in so short a compass!'[5] When he is driven insane by Clarissa's death, his actions in his frenzy are closely akin to those of Clarissa trying to escape from the brothel. Mowbray unsympathetically describes Lovelace 'running up and down the room, and throwing up the sash, and pulling it down . . .'[6]

---

[1] *Clarissa*, vii. 142–54.   [2] Ibid., pp. 158–60.   [3] Ibid., p. 407.
[4] Ibid., p. 141.   [5] Ibid., p. 396.   [6] Ibid., p. 466.

In contrast to Lovelace's frenzied motion there is the slow ceremonious journey of Clarissa's hearse to Harlowe Place. Throughout the novel, her life has been a series of journeys from one prison to another. The effect of these abrupt and violent journeys is resolved in the slow funeral procession to which all these have tended, and of which they have been types.

The Harlowes, shut in by their pride, have refused a reconciliation with their daughter, even when she was dying. 'The Honour of the house . . . is all the cry!'[1] They have been prisoners of their house and its dubious 'honour'. Now they are 'struck with a remorse that shall burst open the double-barred doors of their hearts',[2] but they open these doors, like those of their house, only to death. In the beginning, they endeavoured to make of Clarissa a will-less, life-less creature, and thus she returns to them; they shut her in her room, locked away her portrait, and she returns to them in a coffin.[3]

[1] Ibid., p. 352.   [2] Ibid., p. 391.
[3] Like *Pamela*, *Clarissa* has its elements of ballad and folk-tale. The insistence upon funeral detail and the reaction of each member of the family can be found in a ballad like 'The Gay Goshawk', although there the scene is ironic, as the girl feigns death to be united to her true love. Many obvious folk-themes can be seen in the novel: the ugly elder sister, the father's and brother's curse, the flight of the maiden to escape unwanted marriage, the handsome treacherous lover. The maiden's acceptance of imprisonment rather than changing her love or agreeing to an imposed match is a stock motif. In a French ballad, 'Le Roi Loys', the king, after imprisoning his daughter for seven years visits her in her tower to ask how she fares. She replies

> J'ai les pieds pourris dans la terre
> Et les côtés mangés des vers.

(Claude Roy, *Trésor de la poésie populaire française*, 1954, p. 110.)

The interwoven motifs of love, death, return to father's house can be found in a rather strange French ballad with religious overtones, 'Le rosier blanc'.

> Dessous le rosier blanc
> La belle s'y promène
> Blanche comme la neige
> Belle comme le jour;

the princess is abducted by the youngest of three captains who are all in love with her and taken to an inn in Paris. To escape rape, 'pour mon honneur garder', she feigns death and the three captains bury her in her father's garden, 'Dessous la fleur de lis'. At the end of three days she speaks to her father from the grave, asking him to free her. (Ibid., pp. 108–9.)

The violent end of Lovelace at the hands of one of Clarissa's family is a link with the unfortunate lovers of many ballads and tales in which love brings about destruction;

Like Lovelace, the Harlowe family imitates the sufferings they had imposed on Clarissa. Gathered within the house, they listen anxiously to the sounds that betoken their dead daughter's arrival, the 'lumbering heavy noise up the paved inner Court-yard',[1] as Clarissa had listened to the family carriages arriving for the important conclave. The coffin is laid on a table in Clarissa's parlour—the room in which her family and Solmes tormented her. Even Clarissa's body is shut away by a partition—the lid of the coffin, which her parents cannot bear to put aside.[2] They withdraw into the next parlour without being able to look upon her, thus repeating the movements of Clarissa when she sought her father in the next parlour and found it empty.

From Harlowe Place, Clarissa goes to the last mansion of the Harlowes, the family vault, in a short journey which summarizes the action of the whole novel. The tomb is implicit in the Harlowes' house. They have driven her from her home to the grave. There is one certain triumph in Clarissa's will; she said that she would rather be bricked up in the family vault than marry Solmes, and she has her wish. She has her will in little else from beginning to end; a 'Will' in the legal sense brings on a conflict of 'wills' in the moral sense, in which none achieve what they desire. Lovelace has his will of Clarissa in the carnal sense, but in no other way. Clarissa's 'Will' in the legal sense is the subject of dispute even when she is newly dead; the Harlowe family cannot resist the temptations to avarice, and the story goes full circle, with that family quarrelling about a 'Will' at the beginning and at the end. Clarissa's earnest desire that none of her family should take it upon themselves to revenge her goes unheeded; Colonel Morden, her kindest relative, contravenes her will in killing Lovelace. The human will, as far as it desires to arrange this world to its own satisfaction, is seen in the novel as almost futile. Clarissa, whose will is strong and uncorrupt, is laid away lifeless in the family vault. The walls have closed in upon her for the last time: 'In that little space . . . is included all human excellence!'[3]

in another mode, such a story would have ended with the rose and briar springing from their graves.

[1] *Clarissa*, viii. 75.   [2] Ibid., p. 91.   [3] Ibid., p. 97.

PLATE 1

a. Frontispiece to Richard
Allestree's *The Ladies Calling*

b. Frontispiece to Richard
Allestree's *The Gentleman's Calling*

c. Pamela Fishing: illustration
from *Pamela*, 2nd edition

PLATE 2

a. Clarissa's House: illustration from *Clarissa*, 7th edition, frontispiece to Vol. vii

b. Frontispiece to Jeremy Taylor's *The Golden Grove*, 17th edition

c. George Wither, *Emblemes*, Book II

d. Francis Quarles's *Emblemes*, Book V

PLATE 3

a. 'The Figure looking up to its Corn-cutter': Dame Elizabeth Carteret's monument in Westminster Abbey, from illustration in Ackermann's *Westminster Abbey*

b. Map of Tendernesse (*Carte du Tendre*) from Mlle de Scudéry's *Clélie*, in *Clelia*, translation by J. Davies and G. Havers, 1678 edition

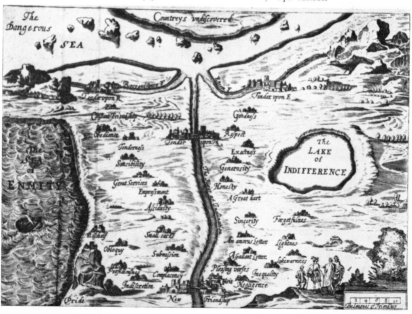

PLATE 4

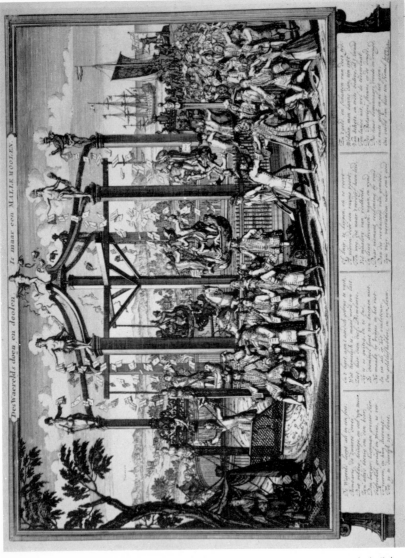

'The One-go-up the Other-
go-down picture-of-the-
world vehicle': illustration
from *Het groote Tafereel der
Dwaasheid*

In the course of the novel, Richardson has invested the word 'house' with ambiguous meanings. 'House' means a dwelling place, and also family pride or pride in an establishment (both the Harlowes and Mrs. Sinclair are taken with the 'honour' of their separate 'houses'). The Harlowe house, both as physical estate and as family pride, becomes a prison to Clarissa, and the Harlowes and Lovelace drive her from one prison to another. 'House' in the context of Mrs. Sinclair's establishment comes to mean 'brothel'. It then becomes 'prison', then 'coffin' and the 'solemn mansion'[1] of the grave.

This thematic image is drawn from religious literature. Material from the devotional literature is no mere interpolation, brought in abruptly to provide a series of deathbed *exempla* in the latter part of the book; it provides part of the texture of the novel from beginning to end. Throughout the book, houses are prisons and coffins, places of implicit mortality. Clarissa's world is a hospital in which to die. The imagery found in its elementary form in the novels of rape and seduction —the doors, gardens, walls, passages, and enclosed rooms— is developed by Richardson who brings out its sexual implications far more cleverly than the light novelists, at the same time combining such imagery with the motif of imprisonment. In the early novels, rape and seduction are sometimes suggested by the atmosphere in which they take place; the victim is imprisoned behind walls from which she can find no egress, but through which the assaulter can irrupt (e.g. the rape scene in Mrs. Haywood's *Idalia*). Richardson develops the theme of imprisonment, suggesting the partitions between individuals at variance with one another. The body itself is a house which may be broken, a lodging from which the inhabitants can flee. Clarissa forsakes her body, as she escaped from Mrs. Sinclair's house. The devotional writers contrast the permanence of the eternal mansions of peace not only with the insecurity of the 'vanishing glory . . . made but of clay'[2] of worldly possession, but also with 'our tabernacles, and ruinous houses'[3] of flesh, the 'rotten cottage'[4] of the body itself. The

---

[1] Ibid., p. 99.
[2] Drexelius, *Considerations*, The third Consideration, pp. 59–60.
[3] Ibid., The first Consideration, p. 24.
[4] Idem, *The School of Patience*, translated by R. S., 1640, p. 73.

body is a decaying house, and a prison: we are 'confined to a Prison, and . . . look through a Grate all our lives . . .'[1] The image of Clarissa as a bird, the 'ensnared Volatile' in Lovelace's cage,[2] has a wider significance: a traditional emblem of the soul is the bird in a cage, awaiting its release (Plate 2).[3]

From the time she leaves Harlowe Place until she rests in her last 'house', Clarissa is a homeless wanderer, moving from lodging to lodging. Her earthly pilgrimage is developed from an image popular in seventeenth-century devotional literature: 'we are here but as Travellers in an Inn, it is not our Home and Country, it is not our Portion and Inheritance . . .'[4] Her earthly home (Harlowe Place) and her earthly inheritance (her grandfather's estate) are contrasted throughout with her heavenly inheritance, and her home in heaven.

The symbolic significance of much of Richardson's imagery is fused with his realism so exceedingly well that we may not be conscious of the effect he is creating, but from beginning to end he employs powerful suggestions to make us assent imaginatively to the final effects and the more overt statements which emerge with Clarissa's death and funeral. The Harlowe house *is* the brothel, *is* the prison, *is* the tomb. In creating the effect of walls closing in more and more oppressively around the victim, he forces the reader to participate in the sense of nightmarish claustrophobia which his heroine endures.

The characters who act as gaolers are themselves prisoners— of the body, of time and chance, of their own wills. Those who attempt to imprison another are creating a world of walls and locked doors in which they too are trapped, cut off from their victim. The lonely fact of individual identity is proved in death, and the last partition between the hunter and the hunted is that between the living and the dead, a partition which is symbolized by the ceiling of the vault 'which now (while they mourn only for her, whom they jointly persecuted) they press with their feet'.[5]

---

[1] William Sherlock, *A Practical Discourse Concerning Death*, 1689, p. 43. Richardson evidently knew this popular devotional work; it is mentioned in *Sir Charles Grandison*, v. 46.   [2] *Clarissa*, iv. 13; see above, pp. 196–7.

[3] Francis Quarles, *Emblemes*, 1635, book v. The accompanying verse is an extended conceit comparing the soul to a caged bird (pp. 280–1). Another emblem depicts the soul mournfully looking out of the bony grating of a great skeleton in which it is imprisoned (ibid., p. 272).

[4] Sherlock, *A Practical Discourse Concerning Death*, p. 9.

[5] *Clarissa*, viii. 99–100.

Clarissa's persecutors—the Harlowes, Mrs. Sinclair, Lovelace —are the uncreators, assuming the role of Death—who, as Lovelace realizes, is like the Harlowes the possessor of great estates.[1] The glories of blood and state will fall at last to his possession. In the pervasive imagery of the novel Richardson proves on our pulses what pious or contemplative writers were content to leave as abstract reflections: 'Rooms of State, and sumptuous Furniture, are resigned, for no other Ornament than the *Shroud*, for no other Apartment than the gloomy *Niche*.'[2] In using this pattern of imagery so consistently, often in the understated manner of apparent realism, Richardson has shown himself to be a consummate novelist, and has achieved a kind of effect not available to the dramatists upon whom he drew for some aspects of his plot and characters. He has forced the reader to participate in his heroine's situation, making him enter her terrifying enclosed ever-narrowing world. The movement of the novel from frustration to calm is conveyed not only through the dramatic moments of dialogue and action but in the atmosphere and setting of each scene. The frenetic and confined activity which pulsates through most of the novel is resolved into calm in the ritual to which everything has moved —Clarissa's funeral, which signifies the last imprisonment to which life tends, and the final release of the triumphant martyr-heroine.

[1] Ibid. vi. 370–1.
[2] James Hervey, *Meditations among the Tombs*, 1746, p. 51. Richardson printed this book; see Sale, *Samuel Richardson: Master Printer*, pp. 174–5.

IX

The Visual Image in *Clarissa*

IN *Clarissa*, as we have seen, some of the main images are concerned with the definition of space, and with movement in space. The reader feels confined, released, frustrated, or freed, without being impressed by much visual detail. Richardson balances these effects by creating the occasional set pictorial scene. The characters stay still long enough in a specific setting for the reader to imagine them in terms of largely visual impressions. The 'realistic' picture is also dramatic; characters are described in terms of posture and attitude. Shapes and groupings are more important in Richardson's pictures than colours. The set scene also summarizes the relationships of the characters to each other and the tensions between them, and is sometimes more overtly symbolic in the special significance it gives to the central personage in the scene. The symbolism in Richardson's 'pictures', as well as the vivid dramatic gestures and the emphasis upon the grotesque or incongruous elements in recognizable and ordinary surroundings, make the oft-expressed comparisons with Hogarth seem inevitable, although these comparisons concentrate only upon the grotesque elements in both. In *Pamela*, there is the occasional description of a grotesque personage, like Mrs. Jewkes or Colbrand. There are also set scenes, of the type that Highmore drew upon for his illustrations; one remembers particularly Pamela's marriage. In *Pamela II*, both grotesque caricature and dramatic scenes are rare, but the scene in which Pamela confronts her husband across the row of chairs is pictorially vivid. As we have seen, the emblematic device is used only twice in *Pamela*—the sunflower, the angling for the carp. Both images are effective, and add a depth of suggestion without detracting from the realism, but compared to the images used in *Clarissa*, they are static. *Clarissa* has much more to offer the visual imagination than

Pamela: not only are there a greater number of grotesque characters, and more vivid dramatic groupings within a scene, but there is also an astonishing continuous play of images that appeal to the eye. The appeal of these images is bizarre, disturbing; they impress us with the fact that Clarissa is living in a distorted world. Frederic Antal, in his book on Hogarth, has commented upon the surrealistic elements in the painter's work, and his non-realistic use of emblems.[1] Richardson, in his method of playing upon images, and his use of the emblematic and symbolic, is much more closely related to this aspect of Hogarth's work than is Fielding.

The function of a Richardsonian set scene is to summarize the previous action at some crucial point in the narrative, and it may also suggest what is to follow. There is, for example, the group at tea in Harlowe Place, grouped like a conversation piece, with the ugly Solmes pressing against the shrinking Clarissa, who is faced by her angry parents.[2] In the Penknife Scene, Clarissa stands at one end of the room in dramatic pose, like a figure in a stage *tableau*, or in the central background of a canvas, dominating the group of harlots and the astonished Lovelace at the other end of the room. The two protagonists' posture is symbolic, and the space between them is tense with the possibility of sudden motion.[3]

In the 'Prison Scene' the appearance of the room, with its decrepit furniture and broken walls, is described in remarkable detail. Its broken appearance has a symbolic function, like the decaying rooms and cracked walls in some of Hogarth's pictures.[4] In one corner Clarissa kneels, in white radiance, a figure of redemption amid universal disorder and death. A couple of the images are so explicitly significant as to be almost entirely emblematic, like the pictures which appear on the walls of Hogarth's rooms.[5] The broken mirror signifies her lost virginity, and the fragmented relation of appearance and reality. A more surprising decoration is the 'large stone-bottle without a neck, filled with baleful Yew, as an Ever-green, withered

[1] Frederick Antal, *Hogarth and His Place in European Art*, 1962. See especially chapters vi and vii, pp. 97–138.
[2] *Clarissa*, i. 100.
[3] Ibid. vi. 65–71.
[4] e.g. the cracked walls in Plate V of *A Harlot's Progress*.
[5] e.g. the symbolic pictures on the walls in scenes in *Marriage à la Mode*.

Southernwood, dead Sweet-briar, and sprigs of Rue in flower'.[1]
This detail is entirely unrealistic; no officer's wife is likely to
take the trouble to supply a prisoner with such a lugubriously
tasteful bouquet. It is a mark of Richardson's success in imposing his own reality upon us that this incongruity has not been
widely noticed and derided. The flowers are all emblematic:
the yew signifies death; southernwood (or wormwood), bitterness; dead sweet-briar, dead love; rue, remorse and regret. The
rue is reminiscent of Ophelia, and she seems to have been one
of the Shakespearian characters Richardson had in mind when
creating Clarissa.[2] The bouquet is also similar to the list of
emblematic plants for funeral garlands mentioned by the forsaken Amidea in Shirley's *The Traytor*.[3] Clarissa's is a funeral
bouquet, in unspoken contrast to the bridal flowers she once
might have had. The yew reminds us of the yew hedge which
separated Clarissa from her family in the Harlowes' garden.[4]
Detail formerly naturalistic is now given full significance.

There is a more subtle symbolism in the vividly drawn scene
of Lovelace in Smith's shop. He sits behind the counter in the
shopkeeper's carved chair, amusing himself in the role of the
tradesman, serving a pretty girl while the shopkeeper, his wife,
and assistants stand about in suspicious surprise.[5] Lovelace's
action seems natural, as he delights in assuming a new role, but
it also suggests the mercenary world in which most of the characters have acted. Their world is full of buying and selling; the
Harlowes try to sell Clarissa, the harlots endeavour to induce
her to sell herself for their profit. Lovelace, although he prides
himself on his aristocratic birth, has tried to buy Clarissa, and
has spoken of her in terms of 'goods' and 'property'.[6] The metaphors of value, cost, purchase, price, which run through the
novel are related to the characters' possession of money on the
most realistic level. The scene in the shop, its concrete picture
of trade, also provides a symbolic picture of the buying and
selling in which Lovelace has been engaged.

The scene at Mrs. Sinclair's deathbed[7] has often been admired

[1] *Clarissa*, vi. 298.
[2] Ibid. v. 333. Clarisssa when deranged has already quoted one of Ophelia's
speeches.
[3] Shirley, *The Traytor*, 1635, IV. i, p. H4ᵛ.
[4] *Clarissa*, ii. 252.   [5] Ibid. vii. 142–54.
[6] Ibid. iv. 294; v. 17.   [7] Ibid. viii. 54–6.

for its pictorial quality. It combines elements of Hogarth's *Death of the Harlot* and *The Harlot's Funeral*. The two doctors who stand disputing with each other, ambitious to display their knowledge and uninterested in their patient, are extremely like the two doctors who appear in *The Death of the Harlot*. The affected French physician in Richardson's scene seems yet another variant of the popular caricature based on Dr. Misaubin, who is recognizable as the more excited of the two unhelpful doctors in Hogarth's picture.[1] In Richardson's scene, the group of harlots, touzled, dirty and ugly, stand about the bedside of Mrs. Sinclair, as the group of prostitutes, with appearances appropriate to their profession, stand about the coffin in *The Harlot's Funeral*. This deathbed scene is in grouping and detail an intentional contrast to the deathbed of Clarissa: Clarissa, pale and fragile (as unlike the fat flushed bawd as possible) lies in bed surrounded by a carefully defined group of figures. The attitudes and posture of each person in the *tableau* are exactly described; the whole is a combination of various attitudes and visages expressing grief, like dolorous figures on a monument.[2] The grouping is orderly, in contrast to the irregular grouping of figures around Sinclair's deathbed; postures and gestures express grief and piety in the one scene, and fear and confusion in the other.

As well as these set scenes which are also part of the action of the novel, there is also a constant play of visual images related to the main theme and drawn from certain kinds of artistic representation. Richardson's knowledge of art was probably very limited, but a consideration of some of the images used in *Clarissa* would indicate that what experience he had of the visual arts made a deep impression upon him. The images drawn from such arts are almost entirely emblematic in function. Most of them are subjective: i.e. they are seen in the mind's eye of one of the characters, either recalled, imagined, or dreamed. The

[1] Dr. Misaubin, a French doctor, settled in London and became a licentiate of the College of Physicians in 1719. He was popularly described as a quack, and caricatured, probably because of his foreign origin, his physical peculiarities, and his arrogance. Watteau drew a caricature of him, copied in an engraving by Pond, and well known; Hogarth's caricature (see Plate V of *A Harlot's Progress*) is a variation on Watteau's. Misaubin is also ridiculed in Fielding's *The Mock Doctor* (1732). Misaubin died in 1734, but the comic type of the dubious and affected French doctor had been established.

[2] *Clarissa*, viii. 1–2.

association of ideas in a character's mind often plays upon some work of art or type of work of art which is already known to the character (and to his creator). Because the novel is written in terms of the characters' minds, the author is able to use images in a surrealistic manner without destroying the realism of the narrative. Too many such emblems as the prison bouquet could not be supported by the realistic structure; emblems and images which appear in the mind can create their effect without straining naturalism.

There are two objective artistic representations referred to in the novel: Clarissa's portrait 'in the Vandyke taste' at Harlowe Place, and the engraving of Saint Cecilia over the door of her room at Mrs. Moore's. Both of these are present at the time of the action. Other images drawn from the arts are subjective: they are imagined (like Lovelace's description of the Fair),[1] recalled (like his description of the funeral monuments),[2] imagined and recalled (like his description of Death the Wooer),[3] or dreamed (like his dream of the ascent of Clarissa).[4] Richardson makes most of his interesting and complex visual images the products of Lovelace's mind. Lovelace has an image-making facility; his mind, like Hamlet's, generates one image after another. Clarissa is a character about whom symbols cluster, but she herself tends to *think* in matter-of-fact terms, or conventional abstractions. She describes her own emotions very powerfully, but she rarely searches for similitudes. Much of what imagery she does use is traditional, as in her use of fables, or her references to devotional literature. Unlike Lovelace, she is not obsessed with the desire to be original. Only when under great mental and emotional pressure does she indulge in a conceit, as when she describes the resemblance between Solmes and the handle of his stick,[5] or thinks that the sun coming through her prison bars mocks her.[6] When she does use imagery, she means what she says: we are persuaded that Solmes does look like the carved head of hazel, and that she does think of her burial clothes as a wedding-suit.[7] The emblems on her coffin, designed by herself, are her last creations as an

[1] *Clarissa*, vi. 109–10.   [2] Ibid., p. 108; also vii. 331–2.
[3] Ibid. vi. 370–1.   [4] Ibid. vii. 158–60.
[5] Ibid. i. 155.   [6] Ibid. vi. 287.
[7] Ibid. vii. 406.

artist, and her most starkly symbolic work, but they express exactly what she means. We know that Clarissa has been an artist; she both drew and painted, but (unlike Mrs. Anne Killigrew, or a later artistic heroine, Jane Eyre) she was entirely realistic. In describing her dear friend, Anna Howe praises her talent: 'In this, as in every-thing else, *Nature* was her *Art*, her *Art* was *Nature*.'[1] Clarissa, she says, 'observed *when but a child*, that the Sun, Moon, and Stars, never appeared at once; and were therefore never to be in one piece: That bears, tygers, lions, were not natives of an English climate, and should not therefore have place in an English landscape . . .'[2]

Clarissa searches for the truthful, even the literally truthful. Lovelace is a romantic maker; his mind dwells in the fascinating borderland of truth and fiction, and delights in what is bizarre and startling. He plays with the workings of his own mind, and enjoys seizing upon a traditional emblem or symbol and perverting its usual meaning. His imagination is strongly pictorial, and the story is enhanced by a number of mental pictures which make Lovelace's character and narrative vivid, and strengthen the symbolic structure of the whole novel. Richardson is not inhibited by the artistic strictures of Clarissa's creed; anything may inhabit his hero's mental landscape.

Lovelace's visual imagination often resembles that of the cartoonist. He moves from abstract idea to emblem, and from emblem to complete picture. When he is irritated by Belford's solemn accounts of Belton's death and Clarissa's failing health, he turns upon him with ridicule:

None but a fellow, who is fit for a drummer in death's forlorn-hope, could take so much delight, as thou dost, in beating a dead march with thy goose-quills.

Whereas, didst thou but know thine own talents, thou art formed to give mirth by thy very appearance; and wouldst make a better figure by half, leading up thy brother-bears at Hockley in the Hole, to the music of a Scots bagpipe. Methinks I see thy clumsy sides shaking (and shaking the sides of all beholders) in these attitudes; thy fat head archly beating time on thy porterly shoulders, right and left by turns, as I once beheld thee practising to the hornpipe at Preston.[3]

In the first paragraph, the abstract idea of a man's being a

Ibid. viii. 232.   [2] Ibid., pp. 232–3.   [3] Ibid. vii. 140.

harbinger of death is made visual and emblematic in the picture of death's drummer, and the emblem elaborated. Death's army is a 'forlorn-hope'; Belford, the writer of gloomy news, is drumming with goose-quills, a transformation of the metaphor 'drumming on'. The image makes the bearer of such news himself grotesque; Belford's absurdity is further amplified in the next paragraph, where he is depicted as a figure, not of horror, but of fun. Lovelace, like a cartoonist, enjoys denigrating. Belford's appearance is combined with a ludicrous occupation which, as in a cartoonist's motif, is connected with him by visual similarity. Belford, who looks like a bear and a bear-leader, is suddenly seen as the fat and solemn head of a ridiculous procession. As is the case with the butt of a cartoonist, Belford's real attributes—his shape, his awkwardness, his solemnity, his endeavours to conform to his company and to perform what is demanded of him—coincide with the attributes of the caricature. The incongruity is momentarily appropriate. Some elements of this description may have been drawn from political cartoons of Richardson's time. The picture differs from Lovelace's egotistical fantasies, such as that in which he imagines Hickman thrown off a boat and swimming for life.[1] There is a slight touch of possibility about the Hickman fantasy, with its long sequence of planned action and its slender root in fact, but the transformation of Belford into bear-leader needs no probability; like the cartoonist's picture, it is free of any logical sequence in fact and action. It exists solely for itself, as a grotesque image with a content of pictorial surprise, and has an odd appropriateness which evokes assent.

A more elaborate picture, also with elements of the cartoon, is the description of the Fair, which is an image made by Lovelace in an attempt to justify himself:

And, after all, what have I done more than prosecute the maxims, by which thou and I, and every Rake, are governed, and which, before I knew this Lady, we have pursued from pretty girl to pretty girl, as fast as we had set one down, taking another up;—just as the fellows do with their flying coaches and flying horses at a Country-fair—With a *Who rides next! Who rides next!*

But here, in the present case, to carry on the volant metaphor (for

[1] *Clarissa*, iv. 272.

I must either be merry, or mad) is a pretty little Miss just come out
of her hanging-sleeve coat, brought to buy a pretty little Fairing;
for the world, Jack, is but a great Fair, thou knowest; and, to give
thee serious reflection for serious, all its Joys but tinselled hobby-
horses, gilt gingerbread, squeaking trumpets, painted drums, and so
forth.

Now behold this pretty little Miss skimming from booth to booth,
in a very pretty manner. One pretty little fellow called Wyerley perhaps; another jiggeting rascal called Biron, a third simpering varlet of
the name of Symmes, and a more hideous villain than any of the rest,
with a long bag under his arm, and parchment Settlements tagged
to his heels, ycleped Solmes; pursue her from Raree-show to Raree-
show, shouldering upon one another at every turning, stopping
when she stops, and set a spinning again when she moves. And thus
dangled after, but still in the eye of her watchful guardians, tra-
verses the pretty little Miss thro' the whole Fair, equally delighted
and delighting: Till at last, taken with the invitation of the *laced-hat
orator*, and seeing several pretty little bib-wearers stuck together in
the flying-coaches, cutting safely the yielding air, in the One-go-up
the Other-go-down picture-of-the-world vehicle, and all with as
little fear as wit, is tempted to ride next.

In then suppose she slily pops, when *none of her friends are near her*:
And if, after two or three ups and downs, her pretty head turns
giddy, and she throws herself out of the coach when at its elevation,
and so dashes out her pretty little brains, who can help it?—And
would you hang the poor fellow, whose *professed trade* it was to set the
pretty little creature a flying?[1]

Here, Lovelace's mind moves from a simple simile to a
complex picture. The rake's occupation, taking one girl up
after setting another down, reminds him of the rides offered at
a fair, and a fair has literary and emblematic associations.
Clarissa is seen as a childlike and ignorant girl—the verbal
devices throughout, particularly the repetition of 'pretty little'
serve to diminish Clarissa and the world around her—in the
midst of Vanity Fair, and the Bunyanesque idea is developed
in detail. The fair is full of booths, selling trashy ware, and of
commonplace shows—worldly goods and honour such as the
Harlowes covet. The 'pretty little miss' is surrounded by
grotesque and stupid figures; Solmes, with his long bag and the
'Settlements tagged to his heels' is a caricature laden with the
kind of explicitly significant *impedimenta* which early cartoonists

---

[1] Ibid. vi. 108-10.

frequently used. At the end of the fair (as it were to one side of
the picture) is the inviting figure in the laced hat beside the
flying coaches. The fairground ride had been used in pictorial
art as an emblem; its relation to the traditional idea of the
Wheel of Fortune is obvious. It is interesting to compare
Lovelace's sketch of the fair with Hogarth's *An Emblematical
Print on the South Sea Scheme.* Antal comments on Hogarth's
print:

His treatment was close to the emblematic, popular Dutch
caricatures with printed keys to individual motifs, whilst the traditional symbolism took on a more bourgeois form—Self-interest,
Trade, Speculation, with traces of the mentality of the popular
prints in which everyone tries to cheat everyone else. The focus of
interest is a merry-go-round on which speculators are riding,
operated by directors of the South Sea Company in a street close to
Wren's Monument . . . The comic group of South Sea Company
speculators poised in mid-air on wooden horses is reminiscent of a
similar motif in an anonymous Dutch engraving on the Law scandal,
dated a year earlier and well known in this country . . .[1]

The Dutch print to which Antal refers, *The Actions and Designs
of the World go round as if in a Mill,* shows the speculators, encouraged by the showmen, crowding to ride in the boats of a
horse-drawn roundabout, taking their dizzy journey; one is seen
falling off (Plate 4). It is an emblem such as this that Lovelace
recollects and transforms into his large animated picture.
Richardson, through Lovelace, adapts an emblem of greedy
folly and instability for an image of sexual conquest, and the
transformation for such a purpose is typical of Lovelace's
imagination at work. The girls in Lovelace's flying coaches are,
like the cartoonist's speculators, tempted by this apparent
enjoyment because of blind self-interest. Their apparent motion
is actually meaningless, a futile and dangerous occupation
which may well end in a fall. Their complacency serves only to
emphasize their stupidity. Clarissa is pictured as falling from
the coach at its elevation, a dizzying image here connected
with the sexual fall, as well as with the destruction that awaits
pride and confidence. Such a fall, Lovelace wishes to intimate,
is the just reward of those who insist upon undertaking a
venture to which they are unsuited; the rake, like the callous

[1] Antal, *Hogarth and His Place in European Art*, pp. 80-1.

'*laced-hat orator*', cannot be blamed. His wit is involved in throwing the blame upon Clarissa, even accusing her of selfishness and stupidity in wanting him to love her.

The tawdry fairground, associated with a fall, can be seen in Hogarth's *Southwark Fair* (1733). This picture mocks the false shows in a carnival of cheap dramatic illusion; *The Actions of the World go round* satirizes self-interest, money-grubbing, and sham. Elements of both are combined in Lovelace's picture. The emblem is adapted to convey a sexual meaning, but it is still associated with the original satire on commercial interest. The picture of a world of cheap commerce is a satire on the economic spirit of the Harlowes, but Lovelace implicitly associates himself with them, presenting himself as a tinselled swindler. If they have their place in a garish and sordid world, so has he; the '*laced-hat orator*' is a false show, enticing girls with his offers of a futile experience. The whole emblematic picture sums up the plot of the novel and is a caricature of it. Lovelace creates this emblematic cartoon because, at this moment, he wants to denigrate Clarissa, and he does so by denigrating not only Clarissa, but her family, her lovers, her (and his) whole world, and himself. He sardonically accepts his place in the tawdry show; if he does not question his predestined role, why should she? Momentarily, he sees both of them as types in a ludicrous world. Lovelace's satire has a different point and purpose from that in the cartoons on the South Sea Bubble. Their purpose is to point out human vice and folly, so that humanity may mend its ways. Lovelace mockingly twists the usual purpose by accepting the cartoon world for the real, and demanding that the actions of the real world should conform to the satiric norm of vice and stupidity. The ridiculous, he intimates, and the real, are customarily one and the same; anyone who, like Clarissa, questions the pattern or wishes to deviate from it must be wrong.

Lovelace draws upon an older emblem in his conversation with Hickman, whom he tells that Clarissa is encouraging the attentions of another lover. Hickman protests that, in her situation, this is shocking, and cannot be true. Lovelace insists that she is, and elaborates upon it:

'Tis true, very true, Mr. Hickman! True as I am here to tell you so!—And he is an ugly fellow too; uglier to look at than me.

Than *you*, Sir! Why, to be sure, you are one of the handsomest men in England.

Well, but the wretch she so spitefully prefers to me is a mis-shapen, meager varlet; more like a skeleton than a man! Then he dresses—you never saw a devil so bedizened! Hardly a coat to his back, nor a shoe to his foot: A bald-pated villain, yet grudges to buy a peruke to hide his baldness: For he is as covetous as hell, never satisfied, yet plaguy rich.

Why, Sir, there is some joke in this, surely . . . But, Sir, if there be any truth in the Story, what is he? Some Jew, or miserly Citizen, I suppose . . .

Why, the rascal has estates in every county *in* England, and *out of* England too.

Some East-India Governor, I suppose . . . But, I fansy, all this time you are in jest, Sir. If not, we must surely have heard of him—

Heard of him! Ay, Sir, we have all heard of him—But none of us care to be intimate with him—except this Lady—and that, as I told you, in spite to me—His name, in short, is DEATH!—DEATH, Sir, stamping, and speaking loud, and full in his ear; which made him jump half a yard high.[1]

The scene between the two men is comic and grotesque; Lovelace supplies vividly pictured detail to emphasize Hickman's stupidity and fear at the communication: 'He looked as if the frightful Skeleton was before him, and he had not his accounts ready. When a little recovered, he fribbled with his waistcoat buttons, as if he had been telling his beads.'[2] The conversation has a mounting suspense, and the contrast between Lovelace's jerky riddling phrases and Hickman's puzzled slow tones is marked. We are forced to share some of Hickman's ridiculous obtuseness as Lovelace makes his macabre jest. Lovelace rids himself of pent-up emotion, as he so often does, by mockery. When his own emotions are wrought upon, he turns to elaborate images as a means of escape. His image here is Death the Wooer, a figure in the grim Dance of Death so often pictured in the Middle Ages, still to be seen in Lovelace's time in church windows, and in the emblem books.[3] Love-

[1] *Clarissa*, vi. 370–1.
[2] Ibid., p. 371.
[3] The image of Death the Wooer appears in literature. It is most effectively used by Shirley in *The Traytor*; the heroine Amidea (who has figured in a scene of chaste

lace's words conjure up the figure of death, the grinning skeleton, making his bow to the lady. To deceive Hickman, and to amuse himself, he describes this 'wooer' in terms applicable to the ordinary contemporary suitor, touching on his bad taste in dress, his lack of peruke, his estates. There is an implied comparison between this wooer and Solmes, Clarissa's persistent suitor; he too was ugly, covetous, mean, as well as the owner of important estates. Looking back, we can see that Solmes was at the beginning the figure of Death coming to Clarissa; his wooing was the first cause of her accepting this new 'suitor'. The vivid and horrible image, animated as Lovelace's emblems usually are, provides a complement to Clarissa's description of her preparations for death as preparations for a wedding-day. Both of Clarissa's projected marriages—to Solmes and to Lovelace—have led to this third marriage. This simple emblematic image, given new vitality by its unexpected context, provides a pictorial representation summarizing the action of the whole novel. Wooing has meant death for Clarissa, and from the beginning Death has stalked the Lady.

Lovelace draws on his memory of familiar forms of artistic representation, recreating and reinterpreting them in ironic terms. Two of his more striking images are of funeral monuments, in descriptions which prepare the reader (but not

---

heroic virtue very like the penknife scene in *Clarissa*) is forsaken by her former suitor, Pisano. She says to her faithless love, on his way to his wedding

	Let me beseech you then, to be so kinde
	After your owne solemnities are done,
	To grace my wedding, I shall be married shortly.
Pisa[no]	To whom?
Am[idea]	To one whom you haue all heard talke of,
	Your fathers knew him well: one, who will never
	Give cause I should suspect him to forsake mee,
	A constant lover, one whose lips though cold
	Distill chast kisses . . .
	. . . death my lord
	I hope shall be my husband . . .
	(*The Traytor*, 1635, IV. i, p. H4 .)

The conceit also figures in funeral elegies of the seventeenth century. See the epitaph (*c.* 1648) for 'Mistris *Abigail Sherard*' in Draper's *A Century of Broadside Elegies*, p. 49.

Richardson was almost certainly thinking of *Romeo and Juliet*, and old Capulet's speech: 'Death is my son-in-law, Death is my heir', *Romeo and Juliet*, IV. v. l. 38.

Lovelace) for Clarissa's death and funeral. The first to be described is an Elizabethan or Jacobean memorial:

> She had formed pretty notions how charming it would look to have a penitent of her own making dangling at her side to church, thro' an applauding neighbourhood: And, as their family increased, marching with her thither, at the head of their boys and girls, processionally as it were, boasting of the fruits of their *honest desires*, as my good Lord Bishop has it in his Licence. And then, what a comely sight, all kneeling down together in one pew, according to eldership, as we have seen in effigie, a whole family upon some old monument, where the honest chevalier in armour is presented kneeling, with uplift hands, and half a dozen jolter-headed crop-eared boys behind him, ranged *gradatim* or step-fashion according to age and size, all in the same posture—Facing his pious dame, with a ruff about her neck, and as many whey-faced girls all kneeling behind *her*: An Altar between them, and an opened book upon it: Over their heads semi-lunary rays darting from gilded clouds, surrounding an atchievement—motto, IN COELO SALUS—or QUIES—perhaps, if they have happend to live the usual married life of brawl and contradiction.[1]

The monument is vividly described; the arrangement of figures and devices, and the details such as the short hair and the ruff, furnish our memory with all that is needed to recreate the image. Richardson, through Lovelace, is recalling and describing a type of monument not uncommon in Anglican churches. Lovelace caricatures the conventional monument by denigrating it, and offering an alternative meaning to the one intended. What he chooses to see in the memorial is not sweet domestic piety but an image for the rigidity and hypocrisy of marriage and family life. The thought of Clarissa's death makes his mind run uneasily on funeral effigies, while his irritation with her, at the idea of her marrying him to reduce him to respectability, makes him think of images which represent marriage as a snare and delusion. Complex and involved ideas and emotions are represented in Lovelace's image of the family 'in effigie'. Lovelace mocks marriage, and the family as an institution, by choosing to see it this way, as affectedly stiff and formal, stilted, and ridiculous. The formal piety expressed in the

---

[1] *Clarissa*, vi. 108.

monument is, he indicates, probably belied by fact and experience.

The stilted grouping on the monument is a parody of the set groups within the novel, of the mourners around Clarissa's bedside, or the Harlowe family around her coffin. The mocking irony of Lovelace's interpretation of respectable family life reflects directly upon the Harlowes. This family rigidly conform to formal patterns and codes, at least outwardly. In their world, family piety is a hypocrisy; duties and submissions are demanded of the individual member who must conform, and their whole family life is riddled with 'brawl and contradiction'. Their rigidity is as absurd and exasperating as the stiffness of the monumental figures is to Lovelace.

The other description of a funeral monument refers to a particular piece (not now extant) in Westminster Abbey (Plate 3).[1] Again, Lovelace's mind moves from an abstract idea to an emblem which can represent it, and again he chooses an image which lends itself to mockery. He jealously makes fun of Belford, who has spoken of Clarissa's good influence upon him:

When I came to that passage, where thou sayst, that thou considerest her as one sent from Heaven, to draw thee after her—for the heart of me, I could not for an hour put thee out of my head, in the attitude of Dame Elizabeth Carteret, on her monument in Westminster-Abbey. If thou never observedst it, go thither on purpose; and there wilt thou see this Dame in effigie, with uplifted head and hand, the latter taken hold of by a Cupid every inch of stone, one clumsy foot lifted up also, aiming, as the Sculptor designed it, to ascend; but so executed, as would rather make one imagine, that the Figure (without shoe or stocken, as it is, tho' the rest of the body is robed) was looking up to its Corn-cutter: The other riveted to its native earth, bemired, like thee (*immersed* thou callest it) beyond the possibility of unsticking itself. Both Figures, thou wilt find, seem to be in a contention, the bigger, whether it should pull down the lesser about its ears—the lesser (a chubby fat little varlet, of a fourth part of the other's bigness, with wings not

[1] Engraving by T. Sutherland from drawing by G. Shepherd, found in William Combe's *The History of the Abbey Church of St. Peter's, Westminster, its Antiquities and Monuments*, published by Rudolph Ackermann, 2 vols., 1812, vol. ii. Combe gives no information about the date of the monument's erection, or about its sculptor, he contents himself with calling it 'a singular monument'. Dame Elizabeth, relict of Sir Philip Carteret, died in 1717 at the age of fifty-two.

much larger than those of a butterfly) whether it should raise the
larger to a Heaven it points to, hardly big enough to contain the
great toes of either.

Thou wilt say, perhaps, that the Dame's figure in *stone* may do
credit, in the comparison, to thine, both in grain and shape, *wooden*
as thou art all over: But that the Lady, who, in every-thing but in
the trick she has plaid me so lately, is truly an Angel, is but sorrily
represented by the fat-flanked Cupid. This I allow thee. But yet there
is enough in thy aspirations, to strike my mind with a resemblance
of thee and the Lady to the Figures on the wretched monument; for
thou oughtest to remember, that, prepared as she may be to mount
to her native skies, it is impossible for her to draw after her a heavy
fellow who has so much to repent of as thou hast.[1]

This interesting passage tells us something about Richardson's own artistic perception—his memory for detail, and his
sense of the incongruous. His field for observation would have
been limited to the works of art available in public places, and
he shared his contemporaries' interest in funerary monuments.[2]
There are some interesting and amusing comments on the monuments in Westminster Abbey in *Familiar Letters*.[3] Here Richardson makes his hero choose and describe a particular effigy
because it is relevant to the theme of the story as a kind of anti-
symbol. Lovelace, remembering the monument, seizes upon it
as an objective visual symbol of which the meaning can be
perverted. The attention to detail, shape, dimension, and
attitude ensures that the reader has no difficulty in visualizing
it, but the statuary group is inseparable from the ideas of
clumsiness and heaviness so constantly emphasized. It is
ludicrously earthbound, stony, heavy, lacking in proportion;

[1] *Clarissa*, vii. 331–2.
[2] Katherine A. Esdaile has pointed out that sculpture in mid eighteenth-century
England was almost entirely funerary, and that public interest in sculpture of this
type was reflected in newspaper comments on monuments or busts, and in the
popularity of tours of Westminster Abbey. See 'Sculpture', chapter xvii of *Johnson's
England*, ed. A. S. Turberville, 2 vols., 1933, ii. 72–92.
[3] See Richardson's *Familiar Letters*, letters clv, clvi, pp. 205–11. These two letters
are interesting not only as indications of contemporary taste, but also as examples
of the author's own observation and humour, viz. the description of General Monk
'in a posture so very fierce, as to seem rather intended to scare children, than for any
other purpose' (p. 207). The remarks of his young lady sightseer display in a
simpler form the kind of wit on such subjects, and the perception of incongruous
detail, later to be developed in Lovelace. The magnificent monument 'of a lady,
whose name is Cartaret' is alluded to *en passant* (p. 209).

the movement expresses not ascent but ignoble tension and imminent collapse. It will be noted that the pose of the statue on the Carteret monument closely resembles the attitude of the Lady on the frontispiece of *The Ladies Calling* (Plate 1). The Dame on the monument is suggested to Lovelace by Belford, with his mournful hopes, but it, as well as the 'fat-flanked Cupid', is closely associated with Clarissa. It is as if Lovelace feels compelled to mock any image of feminine spirituality as a comic untruth. He always inwardly denies that 'God . . . gave the feeblest woman as large and capacious a Soul as that of the Greatest Hero'.[1] A woman reaching heavenwards seems a ridiculous figure in an awkward plight, doomed to failure as it is 'riveted to its native earth'. At the same time, he associates any idea of spiritual aspiration with femininity, that is, with weakness and conventionality. The monument he describes, as he describes it, mocks the theme of redemption, aspiration, and ascent, which is so powerful a theme in the novel itself. Belford's status is reduced from that of a candidate for heaven to that of a heavily-built doleful figure 'looking up to its Corn-cutter'; implicitly, Clarissa's aspirations are similarly reduced.

Lovelace has to mock death and heaven because they frighten him; this monument, which crudely represents such things, is an artistic failure which can be burlesqued. Lovelace's ridicule is an expression of his attempt to avoid reality; he flies to aesthetic standards, where he can be sure of his ground. By transforming Belford (and Clarissa) into the monument and then criticizing that in aesthetic terms, Lovelace, by a kind of metaphorical logic, can dismiss what Belford has tried to say. The monument as he describes it bears the same relation to the original idea as a cartoonist's lumpy and squat Britannia does to the sculpted figure. Like the cartoonist's figure, it criticizes the original intention, and is sufficiently complete to exist in its own right.

The theme of redemption, of aspiration for the divine, is part of the essence of the novel, and is summarized in artistic terms which Richardson intends to be read as 'true' in Lovelace's dream. But Richardson also balances his presentation of the theme in grand baroque images by introducing a baroque grotesque. The introduction of the startling grotesque visual

[1] Allestree, *The Ladies Calling*, p. c_1^v.

image may perhaps be taken as a test, of whether the theme of the novel could support such internal ridicule. The strength of the novel is such that it can, and that Lovelace's image helps to complete the theme instead of distracting us from it.

There are in the novel other images from art which are not subject to Lovelace's interpretation, and which exist solely as statements. Clarissa is presented in a series of paintings. The first painting to represent Clarissa is her portrait, the 'whole-length picture, in the Vandyke taste' possessed by the Harlowes. In mentioning the style of the painting, Richardson is endeavouring to express something about Clarissa's appearance and type of beauty. The young Clarissa, still untouched by tragedy, is presented in the suggestion of the elegance and grace of a Vandyke portrait of a lady. The picture itself is not described; Richardson always avoids describing her in very precise detail, even in Lovelace's amorous catalogues. The association of his heroine and a Vandyke subject conveys an impression of the Clarissa of the world, in her health and beauty, with all her worldly prospects before her. It is this Clarissa that the Harlowes have destroyed when they take the portrait down and nail it in her closet 'to perish'.[1]

The next painting represents Clarissa indirectly. Lovelace, in the guise of an old man, is stumbling through the apartments at Moore's; he is determined to open the closet which conceals Clarissa and moves towards it:

> Then stumping towards the closet, over the door of which hung a picture—What picture is that—Oh! I see: a St. Cæcilia!
> A common print, Sir!—
> Pretty well, pretty well! It is after an Italian master.[2]

The economy with which this image is used, and its ironic significance implied, is admirable. Richardson does not tell us from which picture the print is taken; it seems probable that he had in mind (and intended his readers to imagine) a print of Raphael's picture.[3] Cecilia is one of the most sympathetic

---

[1] *Clarissa*, iii. 283.   [2] Ibid. v. 86.

[3] It would be tempting to believe that it might be a copy of Domenichino's scene, or of Gentileschi's *I Martiri Valeriano, Tiburzio, e Cecilia* (which shows the descending angel bearing the martyr's crown), but I have not found copies of these, whereas seventeenth- and eighteenth-century prints and engravings of Raphael's picture are still easy to find. Émile Mâle says that Marc-Antoine's engravings from

images of beauty and chastity.[1] She represents harmony, earthly and divine. In Dryden's ode she brings beauty and order to the earth, informing it with new meaning. Raphael's Saint Cecilia, a symbol of virginity, purity, and love, turns in rapture to the celestial harmony of the spiritual world. Clarissa too turns to the world of the soul, not that of the senses. Like the saint, she introduces a higher, heavenly order into the world of chaos. Like the saint, she is to undergo martyrdom. The image of Clarissa in the world, represented in her portrait, is replaced by this new iconographic representation. Once Lovelace has found her at Moore's, her martyrdom is sure. Lovelace does not comment on the picture, or interpret it; it is not in his interest to do so (an interpretation would not be favourable to him), nor does Richardson wish to labour the point.

The picture also has an immediate ironic significance in the scene in which it occurs. According to the Saint Cecilia legend, her marriage to Valentinian was one of complete chastity, after she had converted her noble wooer to her exalted views.[2] The chaste wedding of Cecilia and Valentinian is in direct opposition to the relationship which Lovelace wishes to exist between himself and Clarissa. However, it is in this same scene at Moore's that Lovelace cleverly tells the women that he and Clarissa are in fact married, but that he has acceded to her wishes, and vowed not to consummate the marriage until she is reconciled with her family.[3] That is, he is able to persuade them that he and Clarissa have been living a life of wedded chastity which would be an equivalent to the marriage of Saint Cecilia. Lovelace's plausible story and the image of the saint which guards Clarissa in her closet are ironic comments on each other.

Raphael's picture made it widely known throughout Europe; in the copies, St. Cecilia is often represented alone, but the posture and air of ecstasy in the original were carefully preserved. (See Mâle, *L'Art religieux de la fin du XVIe siècle, du XVIIe siècle et du XVIIIe siècle*, 1951, pp. 187–9.)

[1] The popularity of this theme in baroque art is discussed by Mâle (as above, chapter iv), and the relation of this theme in art to Dryden's 'A Song for St. Cecilia's Day' is developed by Jean H. Hagstrum in *The Sister Arts*, 1959, pp. 203–5.

[2] The legend can be found in a dramatized version, *St. Cecily: Or, The Converted Twins*, by 'E. M.', 1666; it was evidently known in England.

[3] *Clarissa*, v. 101–2.

The scene is further amplified by an accumulation of religious imagery. Clarissa blazes upon Lovelace 'as it were, in a flood of light, like what one might imagine would strike a man, who, born blind, had by some propitious power been blessed with his sight, all at once, in a meridian Sun'.[1] She is valued far above 'jewels of high price'.[2] Lovelace starts up in his own form 'like the devil in Milton',[3] and the maid 'could not keep her eye from my foot; expecting, no doubt, every minute to see it discover itself to be cloven'.[4] Before his metamorphosis, Lovelace, disguised as an old man 'hobbling with his gout, and mumbling with his hoarse broken-toothed voice',[4] resembles his later image of Death the Wooer. Clarissa is placed at the centre of a religious drama, and is, as implied by the presence of the 'common print', identified with the virgin martyr.

The image of Clarissa as Saint Cecilia prepares us for the great picture of Lovelace's dream, in which Clarissa is clearly visualized as a saint ascending into heaven. Richardson has, with great skill, prepared us for this set piece in the grand style. It has been seen to be natural for Lovelace to think in terms of visual images. His acute imagination constantly combines disparate objects of his own experience to produce a new whole. He is sensitive to the impressions made by works of art and artifacts. This combination of qualities makes his vision seem not unnatural. The picture of his vision is subjective, in that it arises from his subconscious mind, but he does not consciously control it, and it seems objective, like a painting. Lovelace's description conveys the sensation of being a central figure in a world usually safely confined to canvas, a looking-glass feeling of merging into a picture which refuses to remain static, and in which the movement usually suggested by an artist actually takes place.

Methought I had an interview with my Beloved. I found her all goodness, condescension, and forgiveness. She suffered herself to be overcome in my favour by the joint intercessions of Lord M. Lady Sarah, Lady Betty, and my two Cousins Montague, who waited upon her in deep mourning; the Ladies in long trains sweeping

[1] *Clarissa*, v. 88. See Mark 8: 22–5; John 9: 1–12.
[2] Ibid. See Matthew 13: 46; Proverbs 31: 10.
[3] Ibid.   [4] Ibid., p. 89.

after them; Lord M. in a long black mantle trailing after *him*. They told her, they came in these robes to express their sorrow for my sins against her, and to implore her to forgive me.

I myself, I thought, was upon my knees, with a sword in my hand, offering either to put it up in the scabbard, or to thrust it into my heart, as she should command the one or the other.

At that moment her Cousin Morden, I thought, all of a sudden, flashed in thro' a window, with his drawn sword—Die, Lovelace, said he! this instant die, and be damned, if in earnest thou repairest not by Marriage my Cousin's wrongs!

I was rising to resent this insult, I thought, when Lord M. ran between us with his great black mantle, and threw it over my face: And instantly, my Charmer, with that sweet voice which has so often played upon my ravished ears, wrapped her arms round me, muffled as I was in my Lord's mantle: O spare, spare my Lovelace! And spare, O Lovelace, my beloved Cousin Morden! Let me not have my distresses augmented by the fall of either or both of those who are so dear to me!

At this, charmed with her sweet mediation, I thought I would have clasped her in my arms: When immediately the most angelic form I had ever beheld, all clad in transparent white, descended in a cloud, which, opening, discovered a firmament above it, crouded with golden Cherubs and glittering Seraphs, all addressing her with, Welcome, welcome, welcome! and, encircling my charmer, ascended with her to the region of Seraphims; and instantly, the opened cloud closing, I lost sight of *her*, and of the *bright form* together, and found wrapt in my arms her azure robe (all stuck thick with stars of embossed silver) which I had caught hold of in hopes of detaining her; but was all that was left of my beloved Clarissa. And then (horrid to relate!) the floor sinking under *me*, as the firmament had opened for *her*, I dropt into a hole more frightful than that of Elden; and, tumbling over and over down it, without view of a bottom, I awakened in a panic; and was as effectually disordered for half an hour, as if my dream had been a reality.[1]

This is a most extraordinary passage. It is not, of course, extraordinary that Richardson should have used the device of the dream; this was popular with dramatists, and with earlier novelists. What is surprising is that Richardson creates the background and context of a particular type of painting. The descending angel, the ascending sainted figure, the 'golden Cherubs and glittering Seraphs', the azure robe 'all stuck thick

[1] Ibid. vii. 158-60.

with stars of embossed silver'—these are the trappings of the traditional religious picture of the assumption of the Virgin, or the reception of a saint's soul. Not only does it possess these trappings, but the description captures some of the qualities of the baroque religious picture, with the strong dark figures massed in the foreground, the lighter ascending figures spiralling upwards through space, in an irresistible energetic motion towards an infinity suggested beyond the clouds.

At least at the outset, Lovelace's account seems like a description of an ordinary dream-state. Lovelace meets Clarissa (as he desires intensely to do in his waking life, since for a long and frustrating interval he has not been able to see her) and is assured that all will be as he wishes. Just when he is reassured by this wish-fulfilment (having offered, as before in reality, to kill himself) dream-like irrationality enters. Morden, a symbol of all his fears, enters strangely through a window—ordinary walls and boundaries are dissolved—and threatens him. Lord M. throws his mantle over him, a black mantle which is blinding and suffocating him, a symbol of death. His vision of Clarissa is cut off, and he can feel her long-desired embrace only through the heavy cloak. When he tries to clasp her, she is snatched away from him. The suggestions of violence and death, present from the dream's outset, now become expressed in his final fear of separation from her. The idea of her death, which the first part of her dream tried to obliterate, is now expressed in her ascent into heaven, and this part of the dream is vividly stated in traditional pictorial terms. The azure robe (which in pictorial convention distinguishes the heavenly soul)[1] falls from her, and is all that can be grasped by his detaining arms. The robe which she discards also symbolizes the outward and visible; throughout the novel Lovelace has been trying to seize Clarissa, and at the height of his victory, in the rape itself, has been able to seize only her body, while Clarissa herself has eluded him. He drops into bottomless space, in a motion equal and opposite to that of her ascension, like the damned souls falling to hell while

[1] Cesare Ripa in his useful late-Renaissance manual on emblems and symbolic figures recommends that 'Benignità' should appear as 'Donna vestita d'azurro stellato d'oro' and discusses the meaning of such a vesture; the sky with its many stars signifies divine bounty and grace, qualities which the good man imitates, without worldly considerations. (Ripa, *Iconologia, o vero descrittione d'imagini delle virtv', vitii, affeti, passioni humane, corpi celesti, mondo e sue parti*, 1611, pp. 49–50.)

the blessed enter heaven, in pictures of Judgement Day. The dream of falling is a well-known phenomenon, a sufficiently horrible symbol of failure and fear, even if unconnected with eschatological symbolism. Lovelace's dream is psychologically convincing; he tries at first to reassure himself that his hopes will be realized, and what he fears avoided, but his fears dominate him.

As usual, Lovelace cannot resist mocking and reinterpreting an artistic representation, even if this representation is his own dream, and has powerfully affected him. When first under its impression, he shuns any interpretation, but a short time later, deluded into optimism by Clarissa's metaphorical letter,[1] he works upon the 'visionary stuff' to produce a satisfactory meaning:

> I shall now be convinced that there is something in dreams. The opening cloud is the Reconciliation in view. The bright Form, lifting up my Charmer through it to a firmament stuck round with golden Cherubims and Seraphims, indicates the charming little Boys and Girls, that will be the fruits of this happy Reconciliation. The welcomes, thrice repeated, are those of her family, now no more to be deemed implacable. Yet are they a family too, that my Soul cannot mingle with.

> But then what is my tumbling over and over thro' the floor into a frightful hole, *descending* as she *ascends*? Ho! only This; it alludes to my disrelish to matrimony: Which is a bottomless pit, a gulph, and I know not what. And I suppose, had I not awoke, in such a plaguy fright, I had been soused into some river at the bottom of the hole, and then been carried (mundified or purified from my past iniquities) by the same bright Form (waiting for me upon the mossy banks) to my beloved Girl; and we should have gone on cherubiming of it and carolling to the end of the chapter.[2]

Lovelace reassures himself by turning the original baroque picture into an allegory of love. The cherubim of the religious picture become *amorini*, just as they do in the paintings of the eighteenth century in which the serious baroque is parodied.[3] Lovelace has a genius for turning other images into erotic ones. The impression of the original 'picture' of the dream is, however, too strong for Lovelace's interpretation to change its effect.

---

[1] *Clarissa*, vii. 189–90.   [2] Ibid., p. 191.
[3] Notable examples of this type of parody in English art are Reynolds's portraits of Mrs. Billington, and of Mrs. Sheridan, as Saint Cecilia.

The dream is part of the novel's symbolic structure. It is a parallel to Clarissa's dream at the beginning of the novel, when she too dreams of suffocation, falling into a pit, death.[1] It is a focal point for the symbols of the book: Clarissa, metaphorically always an 'angel', is now visibly and explicitly a saint, soaring heavenward, whereas Lovelace, shrouded in black, is fallen, damned. Clarissa has always been elevated; Lovelace has felt her superiority to him. Lovelace has always been 'base', 'low', a 'devil'. Their true relationship is expressed once for all. From the beginning, he has been desiring to dig a pit for her,[2] and he is the ultimate prey of the everlasting pit, 'a hole more frightful than that of Elden'.

The visual impact is important in the dream scene, and it contains what is for Richardson an unusual amount of light and colour. There are few colours mentioned in the whole of the story; black and white are the predominant tones, both literally and metaphorically. Black and white occur in the dream, in the black of Lord M.'s robe and the 'transparent white' of the angel—but all is now illuminated by flashing light. The words 'transparent', 'bright', 'golden', 'glittering' amassed together are unusual for Richardson. The effect is of a picture of the heavens and middle space electrified by light; only the figures at the foreground remain in darkness, gesticulating, heavily massed and sombrely coloured, an effect like that in, for example, Guido Reni's *Assumption of the Virgin*.[3]

This set piece is related to the other strongly visual pieces in the novel. The more static, realistic groups around Clarissa are replaced by this symbolic grouping. (The group of Lovelace's female relatives, dressed in black, around Clarissa in his dream replace his mock relatives, the gaily dressed prostitutes who surround Clarissa at Hampstead and convey her in the coach to the brothel.) The pictorial images used throughout the

---

[1] *Clarissa*, ii. 283.   [2] Ibid. iii. 183.

[3] Probably Richardson had seen a religious picture or a copy which had suggested the dream vision to him. Certainly public buildings in and around London contained examples of baroque paintings in which rejoicing figures move through vaulting clouds to sport in realms of endless day. A well-known example of excellent work in the baroque mode which Richardson could easily have seen is the ceiling by Rubens in the Banqueting Hall at Whitehall. A direct experience of the baroque manner in painting would have enabled him to comprehend even in a poor copy or print of a religious painting in the same mode something of the effects of colour and motion in its original.

novel contribute to the effect of this one. The garish picture of the fair complements it, as Clarissa, in accordance with her calling, has rejected the toys of this world for the heavenly crown. The dizzy fall expressed in Lovelace's flying coaches is reinterpreted by the rise and fall in this picture. The mock-assumption in his description of the Carteret tomb, which comes later, serves only to recall and reinforce the image of the true ascent. The suggestions implicit in the Saint Cecilia print are made explicit in this vision of a saint's destiny. This is Richardson's version of something he could not allow Clarissa herself to express directly—the glory awaiting the sainted soul at death: 'instantly it passes into the throngs of Spirits, where Angels meet it singing . . .'[1]

The theme of the novel is summarized in a brilliant picture that stands out from the sombre background, a picture that emerges strangely and yet naturally through the workings of the mind of Richardson's most aesthetically conscious and most involved and tormented character. The picture is an expression of heroic triumph, appropriate to the theme, an expression of the same kind of triumph as that of the heroine in the baroque tragedies on which Richardson drew. It captures the same mood as that in, for example, *Tyrannick Love*. The imagery of death, so prevalent in the novel, is here sublimed into a complete expression of the beauty of heroic virtue. There is nothing cold or 'Puritanical' in this revelling in glory. The religious theme is here expressed with the striking confidence and boldness we associate with seventeenth-century art and literature. Clarissa is visualized with the same kind of grandeur as that with which Dryden depicts Mrs. Anne Killigrew, the 'Youngest Virgin-Daughter of the Skies' who treads 'with Seraphims, the vast Abyss'.[2]

It seems that Richardson wanted some great expression, some extravagant gesture, to release the built-up tensions. Towards the end of a novel in which the tensions are created in horrifying scenes of enclosure, of frantic movement surrounded by narrowing walls, in which light is always surrounded by darkness and decay, he chose to inset a bright picture in which

---

[1] Taylor, *Holy Dying*, ch. 2, sect. 4, p. 75.
[2] Dryden, 'To the Pious Memory of the Accomplisht Young Lady Mrs. Anne Killigrew', *The Poems of John Dryden*, ed. James Kinsley, 4 vols., 1958, i. 459–60.

virtue explicitly triumphs over darkness and evil in an affirmation of limitless space and glowing light. The introduction of such a picture is a daring device; if it stood alone, the effect would be merely falsely florid and meretricious. Richardson would not have been able to introduce such a picture effectively, had he not made such use of visual imagery throughout the novel. His use of imagery is a means whereby he controls his massive material, and unifies his lengthy tragic tale.

X

The Godlike Hero: Sir Charles Grandison as an Eighteenth-Century Model of Virtue

THE last novel is the only one of Richardson's novels with a masculine character in the title role. One might ask why Richardson felt it necessary to write a novel which is, at least ostensibly, about a hero. An obvious and not untrue answer is that he was stimulated by a certain grudging rivalry with Fielding, whose *Tom Jones* had met an enthusiastic public response equal to that accorded to *Clarissa,* and decided to write his own novel about a young man. More important, he wished to reply to *Tom Jones* by presenting a parallel and opposite case, in showing that a young man of principle, intelligence, and sensitivity could be as good a subject as a happy-go-lucky scapegrace. His story could be used to present a broad examination of society, its ranks, customs, and manners—a survey that would challenge Fielding's in both its similarity and difference. The more laudible masculine attributes of Fielding's character could be those of Richardson's as well (it is noticeable that Richardson makes Sir Charles a master of Greek and Latin and a champion of classical education).[1] The good young man could feel and inspire a passion as intense as, but more refined and complex than, the love of Sophia and Tom. Indeed, there is no reason to think that the natural passion of a good man could not be a subtle and complex subject.

Richardson also wanted to redress the balance; after presenting strong heroines persecuted by faulty or wicked men, he felt it necessary to say to himself and his audience that a man

---

[1] e.g. *Sir Charles Grandison,* v. 415–17.

could be as virtuous as a woman, that a hero could be as 'heroic' as a heroine. Yet this is the interesting thing—Sir Charles is not heroic in at all the same way as Clarissa. He undergoes nothing more terrible than the sentimental embarrassment of being loved by a number of women; the hero himself always powerful, always in control.

It might be argued that this is so because *Sir Charles Grandison* is a comedy. But indeed the notion of a central male character entails, in this period, the notion of comedy. It is appropriate that, in Richardson's two greatest novels, a male character should have the title role in the social comedy, and a female in the tragedy.

The idea of tragedy involves suffering, and a character's conflict with uncontrollable circumstances, difficulties brought on by something within that character, and yet in consequence exceeding any notion of desert, commonly or rationally conceived. Such a concept is at odds with the eighteenth-century idea (or perhaps one should say feeling) about the nature of man, which is grounded on social possibility. The rejection of the old ideal of the noble warrior-hero in favour of the ideal of the benevolent gentleman may be regarded as part of a concerted effort of a whole society to make an adjustment to a kind of communal life other than that of the small self-contained unit, sustained and protected by the leader who can wield the sword. The new developing society is broader-based, with more visible social and economic control and interdependence. Each for the good of all must assist in the achievement of peace, order, and prosperity.

The explicit rejection of the old military heroic ideal is to be found in a number of literary works of the eighteenth century; it emerges with great clarity in Pope's *Essay on Man*. When Harriet says of Sir Charles 'How much more glorious a character is that of *The Friend of Mankind*, than that of *The Conqueror of Nations*!'[1] she expresses a common sentiment of the period. Lovelace has also questioned the traditional heroic ideal:

Hannibal is called *The father of warlike stratagems*. Had Hannibal been a private man, and turned his plotting head against the *other Sex*; or had I been a general, and turned mine against such of my fellow-creatures of *my own*, as I thought myself entitled to consider

[1] *Sir Charles Grandison*, ii. 383.

as my enemies, because they were born and lived in a different climate; Hannibal would have done less mischief; Lovelace more.— That would have been the difference.

Not a Sovereign on earth, if he be not a *good man*, and if he be of a warlike temper, but must do a thousand times more mischief than I.[1]

Lovelace's mocking attack upon the military hero (although contrived, like most of Lovelace's wit, in ingenious self-defence) has, like Swift's attack on warlike kings in *A Tale of a Tub*, and on military and imperial glory in *Gulliver's Travels*, more than a little sharp truth in it. Unlike Swift, however, Lovelace directly ridicules the classical ideal:

Dost thou not think, that I am as much entitled to forgiveness on Miss Harlowe's account, as Virgil's hero was on Queen Dido's? For what an ungrateful varlet was that vagabond to the *hospitable* princess, who had *willingly* conferred upon him the last favour?— Stealing away (whence, I suppose, the ironical phrase of *Trusty Trojan* to this day) like a thief—Pretendedly indeed at the command of the gods; but could that be when the errand he went upon was to rob other princes, not only of their dominions, but of their lives?— Yet this fellow is, at every word, the *pius* Aeneas with the immortal bard who celebrates him.[2]

Lovelace's satiric view, shared by the author in *Clarissa*, emerges from a belief in the natural depravity of man—the simple reason why the sovereign does more harm than Lovelace is 'Because he has it in his *power* to do more'.[3] It is not so much that power corrupts as that it gives the corrupt will a larger opportunity for action. In *Grandison* the old heroic ideal is rejected, the new ideal specifically endorsed. In this novel, the attitude to the heroic does not arise from a vision of man's natural depravity; the emphasis is on the social heroism which is congenial to the nature of all men. Power is not, as Lovelace

---

[1] *Clarissa*, iv. 380.

[2] Ibid. vii. 2. Lovelace here echoes Farquhar's rake, Mirabel, who reads Virgil aloud to Bisarre, insisting that they must 'rail by Book', and then comments: 'I'll write the Tragedy of *Dido*, and you shall act the part; but you do nothing at all unless you fret your self into a fit; for here the poor Lady is stifled with Vapours, drops into the Arms of her Maids, and the cruel barbarous deceitful Wanderer is in the very next line call'd *Pious Æneas*—there's Authority for you.' (George Farquhar, *The Inconstant: or, The Way to Win Him*, 1702, iii. i, pp. 34–5.)

[3] *Clarissa*, iv. 380.

pessimistically sees it, an almost inevitable stimulus to natural viciousness. The exercise of power combined with respect for the freedom of all makes possible the advancement and refinement of social life.

At the same time as social control was becoming more diffused and more coercive (and while philosophically man is more frequently regarded as determined, his actions the result of certain observable processes), the eighteenth century also passionately held the belief that Man is individual, and (more of a novelty) that Man is free. That Man is free means that he is socially free to participate in a society of his own creation. He is also economically free (if he tries hard enough) to win what he wants and to keep what he has gained, through means society provides. There is iniquity and injustice in the organization of things, but these can be counteracted through the exercise of will and reason.

If Man is thus free, the idea of his being overthrown by uncontrollable circumstances becomes repellent. If he comes to grief through his own choice, this must be through his own fault, and faults are either venial and corrigible (as with Tom Jones), or desperately wicked (as with Blifil) in which case the importance of a character is his danger to society, not his own nature as an individual. If a man is overwhelmed by circumstances, this is weakness, and he becomes, at best, only pathetic. Eighteenth-century literature is strewn with figures of pathetic men (old soldiers, beggars) who are there as the objects of concern of the free man, who will manœuvre them back into social position and usefulness. But these pathetic, weak characters have little individuality. To be a failure is not to be interesting, not to be totally a Man. Poverty need not necessarily mean failure, as long as some social position and self-assertion are maintained. Parson Adams is free to use his fists when he chooses.

It does not seem a coincidence that in the England which developed the 'free enterprise' economy and the political ideas so succinctly to be expressed in the American Constitution, it was at the same time impossible to provide a viable tragic play.[1]

---

[1] Lillo's *George Barnwell* (1731) is the only possible exception, but this play, with its roots in folk art, is about a villain, whose end at the hands of the law we are to acknowledge to be just—the play exalts society at the expense of the individual.

If man is free in society he achieves either failure (through censurable error or gross mischance) or success. Writers continued to give formal allegiance to the idea of dramatic tragedy, and a number of tragedies were written, but they kept to the form and matter of a dead art, and lack any true imaginative concern. Who but a scholar can name a tragic drama of the Georgian period?[1]

However, if Man is free, Woman is, in this period, not free. Woman is recognizably, like Man, individual, but she is not free to engage in the social struggle, to order the exterior world according to her wishes, nor even free to correct the effects of her own mistakes. It is no dishonouring sign of disqualifying weakness in a woman to be overcome by social pressure or the power of others. Since she is not free in the realm of action, even a slightly wrong choice of attitude on her part could have immense consequences. Suffering is possible for woman without her losing the admiration and sympathy that go out to a heroic or tragic character. Hence it is possible to create the tragedy of Clarissa, although to do this Richardson still found it necessary to emancipate himself from his own age to some extent, by drawing upon the seventeenth century not only for literary devices but also for a theological view. However, in *Grandison* as well as in *Pamela* and *Clarissa* the heroines develop through suffering caused by love, and it is there that the interest really lies.[2]

[1] This does not, of course, mean that the amount of suffering or tragic circumstance in the life of real men was any less or more in the eighteenth century than at any other time—the tears of the world being, as Beckett's character remarks, a constant quantity (although the population increases). It is only that in that century the view of life which makes tragedy popular was largely abandoned, at least temporarily. Its abandonment in our own age would seem to be for almost exactly opposite reasons.

[2] It is interesting that the greatest and most popular tragic story of Europe in the eighteenth century shows a hero-villain revolting against society and achieving grandeur by the abuse of the one power which fully remains to him in society, the power over women. His course of action results in the loneliness of self-regarding power usually seen in a military or political context in the previous century. The hero sees his individuality only in conquest. The individuality so achieved is egotistical, brilliant, self-divided, and doomed. This is the tragedy of Don Giovanni, which is also the tragedy of Robert Lovelace. The true tragic hero of that age, an impressive variation of the Faust figure, is the sexual villain whose use of lust is his rebellion against the social ideal. This only available form of revolt is self-defeating, absurd. Both Mozart's Don Giovanni and Richardson's Lovelace are conceived in terms brilliantly and frighteningly comic, but in ordinary comedy the rakes never really rebel against society.

The eighteenth-century ideal of virtue in man is inseparable from the notion of strength and social desirability. Divines and secular moralists alike were endeavouring to unite the idea of the true gentleman with that of the Christian and virtuous man. This fusion had been systematically attempted in a Restoration conduct book, *The Gentleman's Calling* by the author of *The Whole Duty of Man*; his later work, *The Ladies Calling*, is a companion piece to this. In *The Gentleman's Calling*, Allestree set out to examine the moral code as it applies to the gentleman possessing wealth, rank, and leisure. He caught the tone of a morality which was to prevail in the next century, and the social system he envisages in *The Whole Duty of Man* and *The Gentleman's Calling* is in alignment with the social system that was to prevail in the Georgian period.

The word 'gentleman' has always been fraught with connotations. Throughout the Christian centuries in the west since the Middle Ages, real inspiration has been derived from the idea that the true gentleman is a Christian, that gentilesse comes from God alone. Being a Christian man includes the qualities of a true gentleman—magnanimity, generosity, self-control, humility, sensitivity to the needs and feelings of others. These are 'gentle' virtues as the man of good birth has more opportunity to learn and practise them, but he may fail, may be boorish, egotistical, or cruel, and true gentilesse may be found in a man of lower degree. Chaucer and Spenser both support this view, which, *mutatis mutandis*, was as important to the nineteenth century as to the sixteenth. The confusion about the use of the word 'gentleman' is not subject to etymological correction; it arises from a laudable human desire to define the good, and should not be sneered at as snobbery.

However, such is the illogicality of the human mind that there has been a perpetual temptation to feel that, if the true Christian is a gentleman, then all the typical qualities of a man of good birth of a given period must be consummately Christian, and a tendency to confuse secular and spiritual values which sometimes are not really reconcilable. (The secular concept of 'Honour' has in the past proved a notable stumbling-block.) This tendency undoubtedly manifests an unconscious desire to support the *status quo*, rather than to summon it to judgement; whereas the idea of 'gentilesse' can be a source of inspiration, the confounding of secular and spiritual concepts can lead to stuffy orthodoxies, limited moral and spiritual views. (Temptation to such confusion is always present; anyone who thinks we can get rid of stuffy orthodoxies, the rigid views which arise from confusion between secular fact and moral value, by ridding ourselves of both Christianity and gentlemen is in for a surprise.)

Latitudinarian moralists were writing for a highly secular society in which the most important figure was still the landed proprietor, who possessed new duties and responsibilities. They tended to temporize unwittingly, and to try to contain the greater within the less. The danger, of which the moralists were apparently unaware, lay in confusing the conventional qualities of the successful gentleman with the commands of Christianity. (It is slightly disturbing to find Steele insisting that St. Paul was a gentleman,[1] and Addison calling Job 'a good-natur'd Man'[2].)

According to Latitudinarian morality, virtue brings self-approval and popular acclaim. There is a marked difference between Allestree's picture of an ideal gentleman and Clarendon's description of a gentleman who seemed to him a type of Christian hero. Lucius Cary, Viscount Falkland, possesses all the virtues—love of learning, temperance, chastity, sweet nature, generosity, integrity—on a scale beyond the ordinary, and these virtues are the more striking because of the role forced upon him by inexorable fate. He is born into times out of joint, corrupt times by which he remains uncorrupted. This perfect young life is ended at Newbury:

In this unhappy Battle was slain the Lord Viscount *Falkland*; a Person of such prodigious parts of Learning and Knowledge, of that inimitable sweetness and delight in Conversation, of so flowing and obliging a humanity and goodness to Mankind, and of that primitive simplicity and integrity of Life, that if there were no other brand upon this odious and accursed Civil War, than that single loss, it must be most infamous, and execrable to all Posterity.[3]

[1] Richard Steele, *The Christian Hero: An Argument proving that no Principles but those of Religion are sufficient to make a Great Man*, 2nd ed., 1701, pp. 55, 61.
[2] Addison, *Spectator*, vol. ii, number 177, p. 200.
[3] Edward Hyde, Lord Clarendon, *The History of the Rebellion and Civil Wars in England, Begun in the Year 1641*, 3 vols., 1702–4, vol. ii, book vii, p. 270.

Compared to such a picture, Allestree's gentleman seems
pedestrian, self-satisfied, self-interested. Clarendon's Falkland
is one of the last of the Renaissance heroes. The virtue which
Clarendon sees as heroic he also sees as doomed to suffer in a
world which is rarely friendly to perfection. The experience of
the Civil War had itself profoundly affected English society and
had stimulated a desire—certainly not ignoble—to create a
world in which the Christian man, the good man, need not be
doomed. Men aspired to mould a society which, far from
fostering division and destruction, is not only a friend to virtue
but also itself the nurse of virtue. The community itself should
be, through men's constant endeavour, a reflection of the love
of the good, and the benefaction of society a primary virtue.
To the moralists who preached to the eighteenth century, the
criterion of virtue becomes, not its loneliness in the world, but
its usefulness to society. The 'Heroick' becomes that which is
generous and amiable in private life (see, for example, the
description of a 'heroic' action in *The Spectator*, no. 240[1]). The
virtuous gentleman, living on his estate, bountifully discharging
his social duties in the full enjoyment of his own benevolence,
is familiar to us in Pope's praise of Bathurst, Kyrle, and Allen,
and in Fielding's picture of Allen as Mr. Allworthy in *Tom
Jones*. Christianity is rational, and 'practical divinity' entails
strict adherence to the performance of social duties, which
duties are inherently reasonable, and, strictly performed, conducive to the good of all.

Richardson, in drawing his hero, was trying to embody the
abstraction that can be seen in Allestree's gentleman and
Steele's Christian hero. He attempts to show that a perfect
Christian life in this world is not only possible, but attractive.
Sir Charles was intended to be the irresistible combination,
'a decent Rake in his address, and a Saint in his heart'.[2] The
moralists had spoken of the attractiveness of Christianity in a
gentleman, and Richardson could assume that the ideal of his
time, the Christian gentleman possessing rank, wealth, education, as well as good looks and elegant manners, would be
incontrovertibly impressive. Allestree in *The Gentleman's Calling*,
and later moral writers following his lead, had dilated on the

[1] Steele, *Spectator*, vol. ii, number 240, pp. 432-3.
[2] *Grandison*, v. 169.

good uses to which such undoubted advantages could be put, and Richardson generously endows his hero with all of them, and shows him putting these qualities to a right use in a variety of situations.

The advantages of birth, as well as the gifts of nature, are of great importance. Sir Charles's rank is, although not exalted, high. Harriet's grandmother Mrs. Shirley reminds Harriet that, compared to her own family, Sir Charles is 'as the public to the private'.[1] Sir Charles himself, although benevolent and condescending, is not a leveller and subscribes completely to a social structure which keeps the lower classes in their place; Providence has designed the system 'that all might become useful links of the same great chain'.[2] He is faintly contemptuous of the mere merchant, as represented by Danby's nephews. ('A *true* merchant this already!' he remarks to himself on Edward's flippant remark about marriage.[3]) The very names used in the novel suggest rank and station. 'Grandison' is a felicitous choice, because of what the name itself suggests (*true* grandeur, greatness of mind, noble lineage), and because of its historic associations. William Villiers, Viscount Grandison, was one of the leading Royalists in the Civil War. Clarendon in his *History* praises him as 'a young Man of so virtuous a habit of mind, that no temptation or provocation could corrupt him . . . and of that rare Piety and Devotion, that the Court, or Camp, could not shew a more faultless Person . . .'[4] 'Byron' is likewise a distinctly Royalist name. Clarendon describes Sir John, afterwards Lord Byron, the commander in the King's army, as 'a person of a very Ancient family, an honourable extraction, and good Fortune, and as unblemished a Reputation, as any

---

[1] Ibid. ii. 23. Richardson makes the social difference between hero and heroine one of the factors that contribute to the tensions of their love relationship. The difference is not broad (as in *Pamela*) but subtle; Richardson is the first novelist to treat such a subject with finesse. He also gives his hero a marked advantage over the heroine from the outset.

[2] Ibid. iv. 156.

[3] Ibid. ii. 254.

[4] Clarendon, *History of the Rebellion*, vol. ii, book vii, p. 231. His descendant was Richardson's contemporary, John Villiers, 5th Viscount Grandison and 1st Earl (d. 1766), husband of the Honourable Frances Carey, daughter of Viscount Falkland. (Their daughter, Lady Elizabeth Mason, Viscountess Grandison, was a friend of the Delanys.) It was a trifle daring of Richardson to use a name so like a real title.

Gentleman of England'.[1] Greville, Beaumont, and Beauchamp are noble names also.[2]

In using names of such Royalist association Richardson is suggesting a continuity between the old types of 'honour', 'nobility' and 'gentleness', and the newer ideal which is non-military and non-political. A family name distinguished by honour in the past is not to be despised, and in Sir Charles Richardson may have meant his readers to see the true eighteenth-century descendant of the incorruptible young man presented in the pages of Clarendon, whose Viscount Grandison would certainly be a happy choice as ancestor for an Anglican hero.

A good education, as well as gentle birth, is the attribute of a true gentleman. Richardson, who had been excluded from the conventional classical education, was rather suspicious of it, and perhaps slightly sensitive about his own lack of knowledge of Latin and Greek. Learned dullness is exemplified in the novel by Mr. Walden, a conceited scholar from Oxford, who is Harriet's opponent in the important debate upon education, which is a battle between ancients and moderns.[3] (Harriet, herself well-educated, champions the moderns.) Narrow-minded pedants were safe game; the age disapproved of such ungentle creatures. The polished Chesterfield says of such as Walden:

> These are the communicative and shining Pedants, who adorn their conversation, even with women, by happy quotations of Greek and Latin, and who have contracted such a familiarity with the Greek and Latin authors, that they call them by certain names or epithets denoting intimacy . . . Wear your learning, like your

[1] Clarendon, *History of the Rebellion*, vol. i, book iv, p. 312. It is interesting to note that Selby in Yorkshire, site of a Royalist defeat, is mentioned in Clarendon's *History* in close proximity to the account of Lord Byron's actions in the war. It is possible that Richardson, when thinking of a name for Harriet Byron's relatives, hit upon the name 'Selby' by process of association.

[2] Several other names in the novel are those of historical personages, and can be found in the pages of Bishop Gilbert Burnet's *History of His Own Times*. It is hardly necessary to mention Danby; Mansfield, Beaumont, Fenwick, Fowler, and Pollexfen can also be found. Sir John Fenwick was a Jacobite; Burnet comments upon the irregularity of his life (Burnet, *History*, 2 vols., 1724–34, vol. ii, 1734, p. 193). Oddly enough, 'Pollexfen', the name of the rakish villain in *Grandison*, is a name connected with the City. A lawyer Pollexfen argued against the forfeit of the Charter of the City of London in 1682 (ibid., pp. 533–5).

[3] *Grandison*, i. 65–87.

watch, in a private pocket; and do not pull it out, and strike it, merely to show that you have one.[1]

Richardson's hero is a master of both ancient and modern learning. He is not one of the idle heirs who waste their educational opportunities. Sir Hargrave, his enemy, is under-educated, and Lord G. not very knowledgeable (Charlotte says 'he spells pretty well, for a Lord'[2]). Sir Charles knows ancient and modern languages, is interested in men, manners, art, antiquities, music, science, and mathematics. He is no cloistered scholar, and has been on the Grand Tour to good purpose. His good example is emphasized as Dr. Bartlett describes to Harriet the different behaviour of the vicious, ignorant Lorimer and the virtuous and thoughtful Sir Charles:

> While Lorimer was passing thro' but a few of the cities in Lombardy, Mr. Grandison made almost the tour of Europe; and yet gave himself time to make such remarks upon persons, places, and things, as could hardly be believed to be the observations of so young a man. Lorimer, mean time, was engaged in shews, spectacles, and in the diversions of the places . . .[3]

We may remember Chesterfield, constantly nagging his son with requests to observe the laws and taxes of Saxony, and the civil, military, and ecclesiastical government of Prussia, and to commit his observations to paper. If we think of Richardson's emphasis on the right use of time as essentially middle-class, it is a good corrective to read Chesterfield's lectures on the same theme: 'The value of moments, when cast up, is immense, if well employed; if thrown away, their loss is irrecoverable.'[4] There is a slight similarity in the relation of Chesterfield to Stanhope and Richardson to Sir Charles. Each is trying to bring into being his idea of a perfect gentleman—but Chesterfield had only live material to work upon.

If high rank and the best education offer no impediment to

---

[1] Philip Dormer Stanhope, Lord Chesterfield, *Letters Written by the Late Right Honourable Philip Dormer Stanhope, Earl of Chesterfield, to His Son, Philip Stanhope, Esq., late Envoy Extra-ordinary at the Court of Dresden*, 2 vols., 1774, i. 263–4.
[2] *Grandison*, iv. 66.   [3] Ibid. ii. 263.
[4] Chesterfield, *Letters to his Son*, i. 258. There is a good measure of priggishness in the little imaginary dialogue which Chesterfield writes out for his son's benefit, in which he imagines a conversation between an earnest young Stanhope, improving his time in Rome, and an idle young Englishman trying to tempt him to waste time in foolish and profitless amusement.

the virtuous life, Richardson could also be well assured that
wealth could be of positive assistance in the expression of
virtue. Sir Charles makes proper use of this advantage; he
takes care of his estate, fulfilling a duty required by God as well
as a duty to his tenants and to his own posterity (duties which
his father scandalously neglected). He maintains handsome
houses and equipage, dresses well, and is hospitable, thus
exhibiting 'a *chearfull enjoyment* of so much of his Wealth, as may
decently . . . support him in that quality wherein he is placed'.[1]
He is no ascetic, nor is this required by the cheerful moralists:

> To have a plentiful Portion of the good Things of this Life, and
> not to have the Heart to make use of them for the Enjoyment of
> Ourselves and Friends . . . for the promoting Acquaintance and
> Society, and the rendring our Condition as easie as may be, is as
> unaccountable a Folly as we can be guilty of . . .[2]

His wealth enables Sir Charles to turn benevolence into action,
which is commonly extolled as one of the chief opportunities
and chief joys of the Christian gentleman.

Sir Charles enjoys the pleasures of the feeling heart, but he
does not act from feeling alone. Bishop Butler says that the
moral faculty can be observed 'whether considered as a Sentiment of the Understanding, or as a Perception of the Heart, or,
which seems the Truth, as including both'.[3] If both intelligence
and emotions are cultivated and refined, the moral faculty in
the individual will function with greater justice and sensitivity.
Butler says that 'the object of this faculty is actions'[4] and adds
that 'Intention of such and such Consequences . . . is always
included; for it is Part of the Action itself'.[5] The enlightened
understanding must perceive the nature of his act, and consider
its consequences and implications. Sentimental and indis-
criminate benevolence is not necessarily virtuous. Butler says
that 'Benevolence, and the Want of it singly considered, are in
no sort the Whole of Virtue and Vice',[6] and argues the point by
showing that injustices, repugnant to the nature of society,

---

[1] Allestree, *The Gentleman's Calling*, 1660, p. 56.

[2] John Sharp, *Fifteen Sermons Preached on Several Occasions By the most Reverend
Father in God, Dr. John Sharp, late Lord Arch-Bishop of York*, 5th ed., 1722, Sermon iii.
p. 99.

[3] Joseph Butler, *Dissertation of the Nature of Virtue*, published with *The Analogy of
Religion, Natural and Revealed*, 1736, p. 310.

[4] Ibid.   [5] Ibid., p. 311.   [6] Ibid., p. 316.

could ensue were benevolence exercised without consideration of the desert of the object and the ultimate social consequence of such a pattern of action.[1] Sir Charles is an example of benevolence arising from fixed principle, rather than of sentimental benevolence as that is usually understood. From the point of view of rational benevolence, Tom Jones's self-sacrifice in endeavouring to relieve the conditions of Black George and his family could be censured as improper and useless giving.[2] Richardson, and Sir Charles, would probably have taken Thwackum's side of the argument about this action.

Such a statement sounds a harsh judgement on Sir Charles and his creator, but it need not seem so if a context of moral complexity is considered. After all, the careless Shaftesburyan hero is ideally suited to the comic picaresque novel, where comic tone, and rapid action and change of scene combine to create the impression of irresponsibility. The hero is not primarily a moral agent. Reader (or audience) is liberated from feeling moral considerations to be primary in this spree of event in which *ad hoc* reactions are the only ones possible. 'Things keep happening to me!' might be the defining statement of picaresque heroes such as Gil Blas or Tom Jones (or the Marx Brothers in their various roles), not 'I am seriously involved in making things happen to and for myself and others; I must decide what I wish to happen, and take on myself the onus of my intentions and their result.' In picaresque comedy the reader's moral instinct is satisfied with a loose moral definition which allows him to sympathize with a character; 'good-nature' will suffice as the magic talisman which permits the hero to be rewarded, as merely being the youngest son permits the Hero of folk-tale (often amoral, cunning, or brutal) his success. Good-nature is a sympathetic concept, so we shall not inquire too closely into how it is applied. The *ad hoc* benevolence of a Tom Jones satisfies a wish in ourselves that the good and the spontaneous should be combined.

In moral domestic comedy, once it reaches the maturity of form which Richardson himself established, such a criterion could not answer—one has only to think of *Emma* or *Middlemarch*. The kind of comedy of character which depends on the

---

[1] Ibid., pp. 316–18.
[2] Fielding, *Tom Jones*, vol. i, book iii, ch. v, p. 114.

human claim not to be at the mercy of events cannot allow a pleasant instinctive quality such as 'good-nature' the status of absolute value. The good and the spontaneous are not one, and moral action involves accountability for understanding and choosing personal and social good. Butler's concept that 'Intention . . . is part of the action' must always be present in the thoughtful art which takes character in society as its subject. In such a novel the virtue of prudence, even if not named, must be invoked. Prudence is the ability to see connections between choice, action, consequence, and responsibility. The word, because of pejorative connotations of self-interest, became unfashionable by the end of the eighteenth century, but interest in the quality certainly did not diminish. Kant rejects maxims of self-interest, but his Categorical Imperative is the highest type of prudence. Kant's noble declaration of the connection between intention and responsibility had been anticipated by Butler's subtle statements about the moral faculty.[1] Eighteenth-century novelists endeavoured to present the moral faculty and to discuss the implications of action. In *Amelia*, which is a different kind of comedy from *Tom Jones*, Fielding himself questions the validity of sentimental 'good-nature'. The existence of a more complicated morality is signified by a practical circumstance. The fact that Booth is married means that he is visibly responsible, not free to pretend that the spontaneous and the good are the same thing. His intentions are subject to question, and his actions entail recognition of consequences to himself and to others.

Richardson does not wrong the spirit of his moral comedy by invoking prudence and principle. Yet he seems to try to have his cake and eat it, in endeavouring to create the same ease of effect in the actions of a character of principle as the creators of other masculine heroes had obtained in the actions of characters of impulse. The perfunctory smoothness of Sir Charles's responses is a kind of caricatured spontaneity. When it came to it, Richardson found it nearly impossible to present a *man* fully exercising the moral faculty 'whether considered as a Sentiment of the Understanding or as a Perception of the Heart'. Perhaps the author feared that a male character involved in

[1] That is, in the thesis of the whole treatise *Of the Nature of Virtue* (inadequately represented by short passages quoted above) Butler closely approximates Kant.

complex moral processes might appear too introverted or over-subtle, lacking in straightforward masculine authority and appeal. Too strong a capacity for thought and feeling on the part of the character might detract from the desirable impression of his strength, a quality better exhibited in effortless control of situation. His hero might even be condemned, as Clarissa had been condemned by some readers, no matter how much the author subscribed to his actions and rewarded him in the end. The way to avoid condemnation is to exhibit the hero acting entirely and unhesitatingly in accordance with an unquestionably valid and acceptable code of conduct. The process of exercising the moral faculty usually involves inner conflict and some error; Richardson feared that one mistake would cost his hero his commanding position as an invincible champion of Christianity and masculine virtue.

Sir Charles is 'the Example of a Man acting uniformly well through a Variety of trying Scenes, because all his Actions are regulated by one steady Principle . . .'[1] His greatness lies in his applying principle to experience, instead of learning more about the principles of conduct through experience. In drawing his hero, Richardson is most cautiously attentive to the most literal application of the accepted code. If the duties entailed in the Christian system are, as was often said, rationally satisfactory and conducive to happiness, they should be shown as capable of performance. If his hero is Christian, he must be shown to be totally Christian, performing every duty satisfactorily. Moral problems are readily soluble by application of the rule, as the answer already exists, like the answers to the problems at the back of a child's arithmetic book.

At the beginning of the novel, Richardson carefully makes the casuistical lines on which Sir Charles is drawn unmistakably clear. In the Grandison girls' account of their family life before their father's death, Sir Charles is presented as the model son in his behaviour to his father, fulfilling a basic familial and social relationship with text-book correctness.

After Lady Grandison's death, when Sir Charles is sixteen, he goes abroad to complete his education on the Grand Tour. His father, the libertine Sir Thomas Grandison, gives himself over to an abandoned course of life; he desires to keep his son

---

[1] Richardson, Preface to *Grandison*, i. viii.

abroad, as he is afraid of losing the virtuous son's respect by his own loose behaviour. Sir Charles not only obeys his father's command to remain in Europe, but also acquiesces cheerfully in his parent's demands upon the estate, even though his patrimony is being wasted. He voluntarily asks his father to reduce his own allowance. While his son is away, Sir Thomas treats his daughters carelessly and cruelly, even forbidding them to correspond with their brother, or their brother with them. He is particularly unkind to Caroline when Lord L., an exemplary young man, makes her an offer of marriage. Sir Thomas hopes to recoup the family fortunes by marrying the girls into wealthy families, and does not wish to spend any money at the moment on a dowry. Richardson carefully keeps the son away from the family at this trying period. Compared to his sisters, Sir Charles has no injustice to undergo, and little incentive to disobedience. His letters to his father, produced by his admiring sisters, are almost slavishly meek and obedient. He is commended by Harriet, and by his sisters, who are supposed to have been educated into a finer moral perception by their brother's example. Sir Charles obeys his father's command not to correspond with his sisters, even though they transgressed and wrote to him. Harriet comments sententiously: 'I should have been concerned, I think, that my brother, in a point of duty, tho' it were one that might be *disputable*, should be more *nice*, more *delicate*, than I his sister.'[1] Sir Charles's niceness and delicacy consist simply in his adherence to a categorical code (as succinctly stated in, for instance, *The Whole Duty of Man*) which prescribes absolute obedience to the command of a father. A parent's command is, unless contrary to God's law, an absolute law. None of the complexities is to be taken into consideration—even though his sisters, younger than he, and motherless, are left at the mercy of a man whom he knows to be extravagant, unreasonable, and licentious. When Lord L. (whom he esteems) writes to him asking his favour in his addresses to Sir Thomas, Charles recoils modestly from the prospect of being of any use, on the plea of his sisters' and his own required obedience to a father.[2]

The example of obedience is thought to be, in itself, sufficient moral assistance. Sir Charles fulfils the duties of a child to

---

[1] *Grandison*, ii. 47.   [2] Ibid., p. 55.

a parent in a 'model' manner. We are never invited to examine the complexities of the situation, as we are in *Clarissa* (although in the scene between Caroline and her father, Richardson's own sympathies and dramatic powers got the better of him, and he allows us to see, very sharply, the misery of the daughter[1]). We are not supposed to wonder what would have happened to the girls, had Sir Thomas lived to a ripe age, instead of dying so conveniently, and had his son's virtuous obedience kept him away from his sisters for much of their lives. When Sir Charles has succeeded to the title and property and returns to his sisters (in a completely unapologetic aura of moral superiority), he is a benevolent brother and model guardian, in marked contrast to the bad example of familial authority seen in Sir Thomas. But Sir Charles is never presented as having felt the conflict of opposing duties and the pain attendant upon choice.

Since he acts according to preconceived formulas, the character of Sir Charles is bound to be static. He cannot develop morally, being already perfect, which means that, in the terms of the novel, he cannot be developed at all. It is the characterization of the women in *Grandison* which makes the depth and interest of the novel. As they have no commanding position to lose, women may be shown exercising the moral faculty and learning with the heart. In place of the development which we find in the female characters, Richardson revolves the hero before us, displaying each of his qualities in their irrefragable correctness. As far as Sir Charles is concerned, there is nothing unknowable about the consequence of moral action, as there is for Clarissa—and for Harriet and Clementina, the two good women in love with Sir Charles. Right intentions and right consequences belong to the public domain, and are known with certainty, so Sir Charles's motives require little examination; the dial of his intentions has been previously adjusted to the correct point. Masculine virtue is official; feminine virtue is unofficial, a private matter, 'off the record', as it were. Despite Sir Charles's supposed delicacy of feeling,

[1] Ibid., pp. 66–90. The younger sister, Charlotte, is very sympathetic in her endeavours to protect her sister and to fight back. We see from this account how her early life, her endeavours to take care of her softer sister and do battle with her father (whose fiery temperament she has inherited) have contributed to her defensive toughness, shrewd wit, and tendency to try to dominate men when she can.

emotion is not allowed to interfere with his actions. The object of the moral faculty is actions; a description of right actions dispenses with the necessity of exhibiting the inward working of the Sentiment of the Understanding. Benevolence so described becomes a programme of events. Sir Charles is not shown as feeling benevolence; rather, he is involved in a series of text-book cases of benevolence, the grandest and most powerful social virtue.

The structure of much of the novel is explained by a considera-tion of the headings and subdivisions of divines and moralists in their treatment of 'doing good'.[1] According to their analysis of benevolence, a man does good to others in two main ways: materially (with money, practical advice, labour) and spiri-tually (with instruction, reproof, endeavour to reclaim neigh-bours from vice). The gentleman's authority holds sway not only over servants and family, but also over his friends, to whom he should recommend virtue by 'friendly stratagems'[2] or whole-some reproofs. Authority and charm should be combined. Christian charity fully considered is the complete fulfilment of social duties and the best of good manners:

A Man doth Good, not only by Acts of Charity properly so called, but by every Courtesie that he doth to another; he doth Good, by shewing his Respect and good will to all about him, by reconciling Differences among Neighbours, and promoting Peace, Friendship and Society, as much as he can; by being Generous, and Liberal, and Hospitable . . . by forgiving Injuries, and, if it be possible, making Friends of those that did them; by being easy of Access, and sweet and obliging in his Carriage; by complying with the Infirmities of those he converseth with; and, in a Word, by contributing any way to make the Lives of others more easy and comfortable to them.[3]

A man is also 'doubly a Benefactor' when he stirs others to do good,[4] and setting a good example is the highest type of bene-

---

[1] Both phrase and idea are popular with moralists of this period. See for example Allestree, *The Practice of Christian Grace or the Whole Duty of Man*, 1658, Partition xvii, 'Of Charity', pp. 358–82, as well as *The Gentleman's Calling*, Tillotson's *Sermons*, vol. i, Sermons iii–vi, and Sharp's *Sermons* (see below). For a discussion of the concepts of duty and benevolence in Anglican thought in this period see H. R. McAdoo, *The Spirit of Anglicanism*, 1965, pp. 172 ff.

[2] Allestree, *The Gentleman's Calling*, p. 121.

[3] Sharp, *Sermons*, vol. i, Sermon iii, p. 84.

[4] Ibid., p. 85.

volence. Of such a virtuous gentleman this writer says admiringly 'his Life will be a constant Sermon'.[1]

Grandison is so planned that the hero may be seen as an example of benevolence in almost all possible instances. He is moved from one episode invoking his benefaction to the next; almost every case could be categorized according to the outlines of sermons and conduct books. He does good materially in rectifying the Danby will, giving money and his own labour and counsel in order to ensure that the Danby niece and nephews will obtain what they need, but not enough to make them rich and idle, and that 'the industrious poor'[2] will be assisted. He does good to his irritable uncle, Lord W., spiritually (by offering forgiveness and good counsel), and materially (by helping Lord W. to get rid of his odious kept woman, and by promoting the marriage to the virtuous Miss Mansfield). (As the Mansfields are poor and Lord W. rich, Sir Charles has been a material benefactor to the Mansfields as well.) The reader is meant to feel that Sir Charles's reforming assistance to Lord W. has been of immense value to that irascible nobleman's soul; as Harriet rather absurdly puts it, Sir Charles has been 'a father to his *uncle*'.[3]

He is most busily employed in stirring others to reform their manners and perform right actions; it is a rare case in which he could not claim to be 'doubly a Benefactor'. We see him as exemplar, instructor, and peacemaker when he intervenes in the Beauchamps' family affairs, bringing ill-tempered Lady Beauchamp to a better sense of her duty to her husband and stepson. Richardson is at pains to contrive an illustration of the gentleman's combination of charm and authority. Sir Charles plays slightly on his attractiveness for the middle-aged female, dominates her with his masculine presence, and (one of the gentleman's 'friendly stratagems') appeals with elaborate assurance to her nearly non-existent goodness of heart. Impressed by his 'air of vivacity',[4] she begins to thaw, and is able to accept his counsel.

We may sympathize more than the author intended with Lady Beauchamp's peevish question: 'But, pray, Sir, are good men always officious men?'[5] The implied answer is that good

[1] Ibid.   [2] *Grandison*, ii. 291.   [3] Ibid., p. 333.
[4] Ibid. iii. 262.   [5] Ibid., p. 254.

men must be what the badly behaved call 'officious' because
the obligations of friendship include attention to the moral and
spiritual welfare of others, and service to the community at
large. The gentleman who follows his highest calling is occupied
in a perpetual reformation of society, which all his advantages
and power enable him to effect. Good example and rebuke are
means of shaming others into good behaviour, and Sir Charles
never flinches from working on other people's sense of shame,
as he does, indirectly, with Lady Beauchamp. (Another example
is the way he forces the villains Sir Hargrave and Merceda into
giving money to Wilson, so that their former tool can reform
and lead a useful life.) It would be a cavil to point out how
many times Sir Charles makes others part with their money.
This is not a reflection on his own generosity, but a sign of his
heroic virtue, which makes others benevolent. He is not at all
soft-headed about money; as Emily's guardian, he is a careful
manager of her fortune, bringing it up to £50,000 by recovering
some money which her father, an experienced merchant, had
given up for lost.[1]

Perhaps the only attractive instance of Sir Charles's benevolence is his kindness to Mrs. Oldham, his father's mistress,
when she has been treated most unkindly by the family after
her keeper's death. The behaviour of Sir Charles, and his
haughty sisters, to Mrs. Oldham is presented in a series of well-
drawn little dramatic scenes.[2] Sir Charles, in his kindness to the
poor woman, is not acting from mere impulsive good-nature.
Mrs. Oldham has a claim on his filial piety, since she has had
children by Sir Thomas; secondly, she has a claim on his social
duty, since, if properly cared for, she and her children can
become worthy members of society, and useful in their station.
Finally, she is an unhappy and repentant woman. Sir Charles
is quite gracious, in a condescending fashion, to sinners if they
are truly humbled, unable to meet his pure gaze.

Except in the embarrassing case of his duty to his father,
most of the duties brought on by relationship are, for Sir
Charles, the duties of authority. As the friend of Jeronymo
della Porretta, he feels obliged to give him serious counsel when
the young Italian lapses into a vicious course of life. This piece
of 'benevolence' is the exercise of one of the kinds of authority

[1] *Grandison*, iii. 148.   [2] Ibid. ii. 112–13.

which Allestree discusses, the authority of friendship.[1] The only obvious touch of nature in this incident is that Jeronymo is annoyed by Sir Charles's lengthy moralizing letter, and the two are estranged. (Nemesis soon overtakes the heedless Italian, and the reader is meant to reflect that, if he had attended to timely warning, Jeronymo would not have met with the assault in the Cremonese which cost him his health and (presumably) his manhood.)

What Sir Charles is supremely capable of giving the world at large, and what nobody is able to give him, is a good example. His virtue, as well as his rank and fortune, gives him authority, and he uses that authority in the way Allestree had said a gentleman ought—in refraining from duelling.

Sir Charles's arguments against duelling are a series of truisms; much is a repetition of the precepts in *The Gentleman's Calling*[2] restated in *The Christian Hero*. The moral courage of a virtuous hero who refuses a challenge had already been represented in fiction. In Steele's *The Conscious Lovers*, the sentimental hero Bevil, in refusing a challenge, eventually convinces the challenger, his friend Myrtle, that 'there is nothing manly, but what is conducted by Reason, and agreeable to the Practice of Virtue and Justice'.[3] Bevil adopts a tone of arrogant superiority:

Sir, shew me but the least Glimpse of Argument, that I am authoriz'd, by my own hand, to vindicate any lawless Insult of this nature, and I will shew thee—to chastize thee—hardly deserves the Name of Courage—slight, inconsiderate Man!—There is, Mr. *Myrtle*, no such Terror in quick Anger; and you shall, you know not why, be cool, as you have, you know not why, been warm.[4]

Sir Charles's speech to Sir Hargrave has much the same moral bluster:

Were I as violent as you, Sir Hargrave, you might carry those marks to your grave, and not wear them long.—Let us breakfast, Sir. That will give you time to cool. Were I even to do, as you would

---

[1] Allestree, *The Gentleman's Calling*, pp. 121–3, 125–6. Cf. *Grandison*, iii. 43–51. If one thinks that only Richardson could present such an office of friendship, it is well to remember that Fielding shows Tom Jones performing a comparable act of benevolence when he takes the liberty of a friend to rebuke Nightingale for his desertion of Nancy, reminding him of 'the very best and truest honour which is goodness' (Fielding, *Tom Jones*, vol. iii, book xiv, ch. vii, p. 123).

[2] Allestree, *The Gentleman's Calling*, pp. 150 ff.

[3] Steele, *The Conscious Lovers*, 1723, ed. iv. i, p. 60.   [4] Ibid., p. 58.

have me, you will best find your account in being cool. You cannot think I would take such an advantage of you, as your passion would give me.[1]

Bevil's friend Myrtle, like Sir Charles's antagonist, is overpowered by the calm superiority of his opponent, and acknowledges his 'Superior Spirit'.[2] Virtue always triumphs; the wrong-doer must be brought to admit that he is wrong, and the righteous must win the praise even of his enemies and spiritual inferiors.[3]

Steele is content to present Bevil's exhortations; Richardson is unsatisfied to leave a situation that might provoke mocking doubt as to his hero's physical prowess and daring. He provides instance after instance of Sir Charles's physical courage. Lady Bradshaigh complained that Sir Charles's acts of heroism were 'too much of a Piece', asking ironically how many lives Sir Charles was supposed to have saved. Richardson responded by pointing out modestly that his hero had saved only four lives 'in the Course of Eight or Nine years'.[4] His hero is strong enough not to have to depend upon his sword. When he rescues Harriet, he is able to rush under Sir Hargrave's sword arm, seize him by the collar, and hurl him under the wheel of the chariot.[5] In Sir Hargrave's garden, when the wicked baronet tries to force him into a duel, Sir Charles disarms him by superior physical force, without himself drawing his sword.[6] He boasts to the company in Sir Hargrave's house of the methods he has for avoiding duels, and 'modestly' indicates his method of retaliation upon the young Venetian nobleman who boxed his ears to provoke him to draw.

> *Sir Har.*   What a plague—You did not cane him?
> *Sir Ch.*   He got well after a fortnight's lying-by.[7]

Sir Charles is careful to let it be known that he is a master of the

---

[1] *Grandison*, i. 382.

[2] Steele, *The Conscious Lovers*, IV. i, p. 60.

[3] For an interesting discussion of Steele's *The Conscious Lovers* and other eighteenth-century fictional works in which sentimental virtue dominates and controls others, and a criticism of such virtue as morally ambiguous, see Paul E. Parnell, 'The Sentimental Mask', *PMLA*, lxxviii (1963), 529–35.

[4] See Richardson's letter to Lady Bradshaigh, 8 Dec. 1753, in which he quotes his correspondent's objection, *Selected Letters*, p. 258.

[5] *Grandison*, i. 212.   [6] Ibid., p. 388.   [7] Ibid., p. 399.

science of swordsmanship, and proves this when he disarms O'Hara and Salmonet,[1] and again when he encounters Greville.[2]

There is no better criticism of Richardson's management of the question of duelling in *Sir Charles Grandison* than that of Mrs. Barbauld:

> Sir Charles, as a Christian, was not to fight a duel, yet he was to be recognised as the finished gentleman, and could not be allowed to want that most essential part of the character, the deportment of a man of honour, courage, and spirit. And, in order to exhibit his spirit and courage, it was necessary to bring them into action by adventures and rencounters . . . How must the author untie this knot? He makes him so very good a swordsman, that he is always capable of disarming his adversary without endangering either of their lives. But are a man's principles to depend on the science of his fencing-master? Every one cannot have the skill of Sir Charles; every one cannot be the *best* swordsman; and the man whose study it is to avoid fighting, is not quite so likely as another to be the best. Dr. Young, indeed, complimented the author upon his success in this nice point, in a flourishing epigram, which is thus expressed:
>
> > What has thou done? I'm ravished at the scene;
> > A sword undrawn, makes mighty Cæsars mean.
>
> But, in fact, it was not undrawn . . . Can, then, a better expedient be suggested? If not, must we not fairly confess that, in certain cases, the code of the gospel and the code of worldly honour are irreconcileable, and that a man has only to make his choice which he will give up.[3]

Richardson is not keeping to the code of the gospel, but to the code of rational virtue. If virtue is social in its effect there must be some resort against bullies and ruffians; what would society come to if the bullies were allowed to have their way? It is not only the code of worldly honour which is involved; justice and orderly social life demand the humiliation of vicious braggarts. Richardson may not feel that the code of worldly honour as usually understood is compatible with the Christian religion; he does feel that the best social values and the code of the gospel must be one and the same, in the case of his hero, and refuses to investigate the possibility of their conflict.

---

[1] Ibid. ii. 378–9.   [2] Ibid. v. 135.

[3] Anna Lætitia Barbauld, 'Life of Samuel Richardson, with Remarks on his Writings', *Correspondence*, i. cxxvii–cxxix.

The code of the gospel, as we are shown it here, ensures both power and pleasure. Sir Charles is an illustration of the cliché of the divines, that the Christian is the 'true Epicurean'. We are meant to understand that control of his passions has made him more capable of enjoyment. The passions when controlled by reason are good. Sir Charles has no wish to overcome 'the tender susceptibilities, which, properly directed, are the glory of the human nature'.[1] These susceptibilities find their proper reward when he takes Harriet to wife. Dr. Bartlett remarks on the 'Sameness' of the lives of libertines, and the '*variety* there is in goodness'; if libertines only realized this, they would 'endeavour to give themselves solid joy, by following . . . so *self-rewarding* an example'.[2]

Besides the innocent delights, Sir Charles tastes the supreme pleasure of conscious goodness, a pleasure recognized by his age, almost as a compensatory substitute for the 'false' glory of the old heroic ideal:

> One self-approving hour whole years out-weighs
> Of stupid starers, and of loud huzzas;[3]

Not that Sir Charles has to remain merely self-approving; he has his starers, and others approve him loudly and often. The vicious confess themselves converted to admiration; the mouths of the virtuous show forth his praise. He is supposed to be universally popular: 'the man whom every-body loved'.[4] The other characters constantly say such things as 'His noble spirit has awakened mine'.[5] As Charlotte observes, 'It is . . . true policy to be good.'[6]

Because Sir Charles is always in a position to bestow money, counsel, good example—he is never the beneficiary—his goodness is a form of sovereignty. Olivia asks what can be said of 'A man, in short, who takes pleasure in conferring obligations, yet never lays himself under the necessity of receiving returns? Prince of a man! What Prince, King, Emperor, is so truly great as *this* man?'[7] His power is in a sense as great as that of Lovelace, who could say 'The Law was not made for such a man as me.'[8]

---

[1] *Grandison*, iv. 400.   [2] Ibid. v. 21–2.

[3] Alexander Pope, *Essay on Man*, Epistle iv, ll. 255–6.

[4] *Grandison*, iii. 404.   [5] Ibid., p. 363.   [6] Ibid. iv. 258.

[7] Ibid., p. 420.   [8] *Clarissa*, iv. 45.

'The Law was not made for a man of conscience',[1] says Sir Charles. Sir Charles is above the law because he more than fulfils it, in spirit as well as letter, transcending it in his own authoritative goodness. He needs no spiritual counsel, even from Dr. Bartlett, who follows humbly in his patron's beneficent wake. Sir Charles perfectly exemplifies the ideal represented on the frontispiece of *The Gentleman's Calling* (Plate 1), and its Biblical caption: 'When I prepared my seat—the Aged stood up: Princes lay'd their hand on their Mouth.'[2] When Sir Charles does his wooing, the young ladies who are (almost simultaneously) the objects of his affection are aware that he is conferring a benefit upon them, and, in each case, it is the lady who is humbled by having been the first to feel the pangs of love. As a suitor, Sir Charles has little to ask and much to confer. The life of the Christian gentleman may be social in its basis, but the result of such a life lived in perfection is a splendid eminence, and oppressive power. Who would suppose that the object of Christian life was such a state of emancipation from any humbling claim on others, such potent self-sufficiency?

Richardson realized, at least in theory, that Sir Charles must be allowed to have some faults, so that he should not be a 'faultless *monster*'.[3] Sir Charles has two main faults, which he alone mentions; he is naturally choleric, and he is proud. In such a person, enjoying all the distinctions of wealth, rank, authority, unblemished conscience, and universal favour, this fault, the 'pride of spirit'[4] which he notices in himself, seems natural enough. Indeed, it is only too natural, and goes deeper and strikes us as more serious than Richardson intended. He obviously admired his characters' spirit, and allows him to explain his pride, distinguishing it from the baser varieties. Sir Charles explains to Olivia that there is a proper pride, 'Not the odious vice generally known by that name (the fault of fallen angels) but that which may be called a prop, a support, to an imperfect goodness . . .'[5] Yet Sir Charles seems to be upholding the baser kind of pride in his interviews with Clementina's choleric brother, the General: 'Insolence in a great man, a rich man, or a soldier, is a *call* upon a man of spirit to exert

[1] *Grandison*, ii. 127.   [2] Job 29: 7–9.
[3] Richardson, letter to Hester Mulso, 11 July 1751, *Selected Letters*, p. 185.
[4] *Grandison*, iv. 127.   [5] Ibid., p. 416.

himself.'[1] His lofty speeches to the Porretta family often seem scarcely calculated to endear, as he insists upon trumpeting forth his own conscious merit.[2] Sir Charles also appears to enjoy the opportunity of delivering a crushing rebuke to the good Father Marescotti,[3] and reflecting complacently upon the good man's conscious shame and humiliation before him.[4] Sir Charles's spiritual pride, particularly in his behaviour to the Porretta family, becomes more and more evident, and it is the 'odious vice generally known by that name'. Several kinds of pride are apparent in this rumination upon his behaviour and that of the Porrettas:

When, when shall I meet with the returns, which my proud heart challenges as its due? But then my pride (shall I call it?) came in to my relief—Great God! I thank thee, thought I, that thou enablest me to do what my conscience, what humanity tells me, is fit and right to be done, without taking my measures of right and wrong from any other standard.[5]

Somewhere, do we not hear a voice intoning 'Lord, I thank thee that I am not as other men'? Sir Charles's pride is as grand as any of his other qualities; it is 'the fault of fallen angels'.

The dominant morality of the age encouraged pride. Self-approval is offered as an incentive to virtue by Christian moralists and Deists alike. Shaftesbury intimates that one of the greatest pleasures of a good man is the contemplation of his goodness.[6] Christian moralists and Deists both stressed the rationality and amiability of the moral law, and both alike fell into the trap which Mandeville sprung in *The Fable of the Bees* (1714), and in his ensuing essays. Mandeville ruthlessly exposes the pride which lies at the root of the accepted morality of good conscience and self-approval.[7] The idea of the heroically virtuous gentleman is built on the assumption that there is nothing in the truly Christian life to conflict with wealth, rank, authority, or pleasure; Mandeville attacks this morality in his mocking picture of the epicurean gentleman 'wallowing in a

---

[1] *Grandison*, iii. 187.   [2] e.g. ibid. iv. 137, 146.
[3] Ibid., p. 313.   [4] Ibid., p. 314.   [5] Ibid., p. 169.
[6] Anthony Ashley Cooper, Lord Shaftesbury, *Characteristicks of Men, Manners, Opinions, Times*, 3 vols., 1711, *An Inquiry Concerning Virtue*, ii. 118–19.
[7] Bernard Mandeville, *The Fable of the Bees: or, Private Vices Publick Benefits, An Enquiry into the Origin of Virtue*, 1714, pp. 23–41.

sea of lust and vanity'.[1] Taken in the context of the prevailing doctrines, his attacks are highly successful. The 'natural law' and the law of society may produce happiness and esteem for the individual, but there is no need to pretend that such happiness and such esteem have much to do with the story of the New Testament.

Christian moralists, professing Anglicans as well as avowed Socinians, had enervated their belief by rationalizing the mission of Christ. They endeavoured to remove the 'mysterious' elements in the doctrine, leaving nothing that is not rational and reasonably moral; the purpose of Christ's coming was to issue 'a republication of natural law'.[2] Once the essence of Christianity is seen as a rational moral code, there is little need or use for 'mystery'. Addison's description of churchgoing, at which people 'hear their duties explained to them, and join together in Adoration of the supreme Being'[3], could describe a group of socially-minded Deists.

Harriet, with complacent pride, reflects upon the propriety of Sir Charles's appearance in church:

> Sir Charles edified every-body by his chearful piety. Are you not of the opinion . . . that wickedness may be always put out of countenance by a person who has an established character for goodness, and who is not ashamed of doing his duty in the public eye? Methinks I could wish that all the profligates in the parish had their seats around that of a man who has fortitude enough to dare to be good. The text was a happy one to this purpose: The words of our Saviour: 'Whosoever shall be ashamed of me and of my words, in this adulterous and sinful generation, of him also shall the Son of man be ashamed, when he cometh in the glory of his Father, with the holy Angels.'[4]

There is nothing mysterious or awesome in this picture of churchgoing; it is another social duty which Sir Charles perfectly performs. He publicly and handsomely exhibits the good

---

[1] Ibid., *Remarks* (*N.*), pp. 114–17.

[2] This idea can be found in John Locke's *The Reasonableness of Christianity* (1695) and Matthew Tindal's *Christianity as Old as Creation, or the Gospel a Republication of the Religion of Nature* (1730). Butler, although he acknowledges the doctrine of the Atonement, lists first among the three chief parts of Christ's office his role as moral legislator: 'He published anew the Law of Nature . . .' (See *The Analogy of Religion*, part ii, ch. v, p. 206.)

[3] *Spectator*, vol. i, number 212, p. 460.

[4] *Grandison*, v. 156–7.

terms he is on with the Almighty, and this affords an edifying moral example to the less perfect. Sir Charles's churchgoing seems far removed from that of Clarissa, lonely, defamed and disinherited, seeking her salvation when all else is denied her, attending St. Paul's, Covent Garden, to be taken from the very steps of the church to her prison room. As a picture of a spiritual state, it is also far removed from the spiritual emotions undergone by the heroes and heroines of the High Church Victorian novelist Charlotte Yonge, who, like Richardson, in her own time proclaimed the advantages of sincere and pious Anglicanism. (Indeed, a social historian could learn much about the difference between eighteenth-century and nineteenth-century Anglicanism by comparing *Sir Charles Grandison* with, say, *The Heir of Redclyffe*.)[1] In his churchgoing, as in all else, Sir Charles is completely of his time.

Since virtue, in this novel, is primarily social it is not surprising that the life of religious seclusion is presented with disfavour. Clarissa persuades us that she understands the life of contemplation and religious retirement; when she half wishes she could enter a convent, she means what she says.[2] In *Grandison*, Clementina must be argued out of the notion. The argument was partially necessitated by the demands of comedy; the assumption of the veil would have been a convenient method of disposing of an extra heroine, and was traditional in novels, but such a sombre conclusion would have cast a slightly melancholy shade over the rest of the book. Equally important, as the tenor of the novel is to encourage virtue as action in the world, the argument must dispose of the claims of the secluded life as a higher form of virtue. That cheerful Latitudinarian, Dr. Sharp, dismisses the life of secluded contemplation:

But whatever Excellence may be pretended in this Course of Life, it certainly falls much short of that, which is led in a Publick Way. He serves God best, that is most Serviceable to his Generation. And no Prayers, or Fasts, or Mortifications, are near so acceptable a Sacrifice to our Heavenly Father, as to *do Good in our Lives.*[3]

---

[1] There is an implied comparison between the self-satisfied Philip, the 'villain' of Charlotte Yonge's novel, and Sir Charles Grandison. (See *The Heir of Redclyffe*, 1853, ch. iii. pp. 32–3.)

[2] *Clarissa*, i. 90.

[3] Sharp, *Fifteen Sermons*, Sermon iii, p. 92.

Sir Charles arguing with Clementina is an exponent of the *vita activa*:

> May it not be justly said, that to obey your parents, is to serve God? Would the generous, the noble-minded Clementina della Porretta, *narrow*, as I may say, her piety, by limiting it (I speak now as if I were a Catholic, and as if I thought there were some *merit* in secluding one's self from the world) when she could, at least, *equally* serve God, and benefit her own soul, by obeying her parents, by fulfilling the will of her deceased grandfathers, and by obliging all her other near and dear relations? . . . Shall I say, there is often cowardice, there is selfishness, and perhaps, in the world's eye, a too strong confession of disappointment, in such seclusions?[1]

Clementina might have retorted that, after her mental breakdown, she had a right to some cowardice, and, after losing Sir Charles, a claim to disappointment. Sir Charles does not face these possibilities; he preaches to the sick as if they were sound. It is he who draws up the 'Articles' of Clementina's agreement with her parents, and includes the pointed remark that, as she now agrees not to be a nun, she can realize the profits of her estate 'that she may be enabled to do that extensive good with the produce, that she could not do, were she to renounce the world'.[2]

None of these arguments is seriously applied in Clarissa's case, although, if Sir Charles's premises are correct, that heroine's complete renunciation of the world, in her repentance and longing for death, is extravagant and wrong-headed. According to standards whereby virtue is measured in terms of social beneficence, Clarissa is a signal failure.

Such a view of Christianity, which emphasizes the reasonableness of the moral code, and its compatibility with the ways of the world, is based on an optimistic view of the world itself and of human nature. It also places a terrifying emphasis upon the power of the human will. If natural reason shows us the moral law, there is no excuse for perversity, once reason is enlightened. The penalties of failure must be harsh, if the standard is so simple to perceive, and so easy to live up to, if it is in accord with our natural desires. The estimate of others depends upon how well or ill they behave according to the code of conduct

---

[1] *Grandison*, iv. 379–80.   [2] Ibid. vi. 185.

which Christianity and right reason both show to be correct.
Sir Charles tells Jeronymo that he cannot say

> —*Video meliora, proboque;*
> *Deteriora sequor.*—[1]

This attitude, that the will and reason of a Christian must be
always and uniformly in accord, is an inheritance from the
divines of the seventeenth century who insisted that in Romans
7: 19–25 ('the good that I would, I do not; but the evil that I
would not, that I do') Saint Paul could not have been speaking
of a regenerate person, and certainly not of himself.[2] If the
moral code is simple and reasonable, we must behave uniformly well, or God will withdraw his love. There is a harsh
undertone to the Latitudinarian appeals to reason and profit.
This strict Pelagian morality is what Richardson has completely adopted in *Sir Charles Grandison*. Sir Charles is not to be
allowed to transgress, even in the least degree, and in his
imitation of the Divinity, he imitates the Latitudinarian
Deity who rewards merit with love, and withdraws love as soon
as merit lapses. He threatens Charlotte with a total withdrawal
of his love should she treat Lord G. badly: 'I should be apt to
forget that I had more than *one* sister: For, in cases of right and
wrong, we ought not to know either relation or friend.'[3]

Even if we believe that God acts in this manner, there seems
little reason why one sinner should take it upon himself to
withdraw his love in proportion to the misbehaviour of his
friends, still less why he should boast about it as a principle of
virtue. It is part of human weakness to bend with the remover
to remove, but to take pride in this tendency, and encourage it,
can be a dangerous expression of selfishness. Perhaps the
belief about the nature of God explains the priggishness of
other virtuous heroes in later novels—Edgar Mandlebert in
Camilla, or Lord Elmwood in Mrs. Inchbald's *A Simple Story*.
The virtuous hero is an image of the Deity.

In Allestree's *The Gentleman's Calling* we meet the most ful-
some praises of the noble moral ambition by which 'we may
not onely innocently, but successfully entertain *Lucifers* disigne,

[1] *Grandison*, iii. 45.
[2] For a discussion of the controversy on this text, and its implications in the
doctrine of Taylor, Hammond, Bull *et al.*, see C. F. Allison, *The Rise of Moralism*,
1966.   [3] *Grandison*, iii. 7.

of being *like the Most High*. It really makes Men what the Heathens vainly fancied their *Heroes*, even *Demy-gods*.'[1] Sir Charles is described as godlike. '*The godlike man . . . has nothing to conceal*', one of the characters says of him, quoting Dr. Young.[2] Sir Charles is the 'divine Philanthropist' who imitates the Deity in his benevolence.[3] The imitation of the Divinity in the eighteenth century means the imitation of the Creator, in power, righteousness, benevolence, and justice; the Christian gentleman with his wealth and estates is in a perfect position to imitate the Almighty. Of course no woman could imitate the Deity, ruler, benefactor, and law-giver. A woman might be saintly (might even, like Clarissa, read and practise *The Imitation of Christ*) but it would obviously be preposterous to call a woman 'God-like'. In this world, the wide dispensation of Justice and Charity, the support of Nobility and Religion, emanate from the kingly virtue and authority of Man (Plate 1).

Sir Charles, the best possible human image of the Almighty, is always superior to all others around him, including the women he loves. They are conscious of his condescension, and his love is a most precious reward of merit. Such a central character creates difficulties in the course of a romantic novel: Richardson himself was struck by the incompatibility of strict moral virtue and ardent gallant love in his hero. The difficulty is brought out by Harriet's comparison of Sir Charles and Milton's Adam:

Do you think, my dear, that had he been the first man, he would have been so complaisant to his Eve as *Milton makes Adam* . . . To taste the forbidden fruit, because he would not be separated from her, in her punishment, tho' all *posterity* were to suffer by it?—No; it is my opinion, that your brother would have had gallantry enough to his fallen spouse, to have made him extremely regret her lapse; but that he would have done *his own duty*, were it but for the sake of posterity, and left it to the Almighty, if such had been his pleasure, to have annihilated his first Eve, and given him a second . . .[4]

---

[1] Allestree, *The Gentleman's Calling*, p. 116.

[2] *Grandison*, i. 447. See Edward Young, *The Complaint, Or Night Thoughts on Life, Death and Immortality, Night the Eighth. Virtue's Apology: Or, The Man of the World Answer'd*, 1745, p. 60. A lengthy passage of this poem is later quoted by Harriet, who refers to the (unnamed) poet as 'my favourite author'. (*Grandison*, ii. 10; see *Night Thoughts, Night the Eighth*, p. 52.) Richardson was complimenting his friend.

[3] *Grandison*, iv. 296.   [4] Ibid., p. 362.

This is an extremely telling passage, and it is written by Harriet in a mood which is not completely happy; the tone is not that of entire approbation. When examined, it is a very severe criticism of Sir Charles, although that is not Richardson's intention. Unfallen man and fallen sinful man cannot be compared. In the Christian belief, the life, death, and Resurrection of Jesus Christ have superseded the life of unfallen Adam. Sinners and sufferers in this world, we have Christ's example and his intercession before us. There is no condition now which we can imagine which allows us to turn away, totally clear of guilt, while we hug our righteous merit to our bosoms. Richardson's hero is almost an unfallen Adam, in a world which is still near Paradise. By the discipline of the right will, man can achieve near-perfection, in a life of virtue which is directed to the well-being of society (Adam ought to have considered 'posterity'). Since virtue is social in its effects, the world of human society will respond to it, because that world is essentially good, and its defects are corrigible by instruction and example. This is an optimistic view of man and society which Richardson in this work shares with the Deists; indeed, sin and suffering alike can be nearly eradicated without the necessity of the agony on the Cross. Man and God are in harmony already if man will only realize that self-love and social are the same. Christianity in *Grandison* is a system of rules for right living which, if obeyed, bring instantaneous personal satisfaction and social harmony. If virtue is so suited to the nature of things, what need is there of Christ, or of mysteries? The theme here is true virtue as it can be practised by all the children of the Deity. Richardson gives himself away when he makes Harriet say that she and Dr. Bartlett have serious talks about religion, in which they begin by discussing Christianity, and continue by discussing the virtue of Sir Charles.[1] It should be, at least, the other way around.

Morality is not so simple in *Clarissa*. Hooker has said:

I am not afraid to affirm it boldly, with St. Augustine, that men puffed up through a proud opinion of their own sanctity and holiness receive a benefit at the hands of God, and are assisted with his grace, when with his grace they are not assisted, but permitted, and that grievously, to transgress; whereby, as they were in over-

[1] *Grandison*, ii. 235.

great liking of themselves supplanted, so the dislike of that which did supplant them may establish them afterwards the surer. Ask the very soul of Peter, and it shall undoubtedly make you itself this answer: My eager protestations, made in the glory of my ghostly strength, I am ashamed of; but those crystal tears, wherewith my sin and weakness was bewailed, have procured my endless joy; my strength hath been my ruin, and my fall my stay.[1]

This is akin to the view Clarissa comes to take of her own transgression (her flight from her father's home) and of her ensuing suffering, when she writes in her Meditation '*There is a shame which bringeth sin, and there is a shame which bringeth glory and grace*'[2], when she says that God would not allow her to depend on any but Himself[3], and when she says, in her last moments, '*It is good for me that I was afflicted!*'[4]

In *Clarissa*, the world is not sympathetic to virtue, and virtue is not triumphant in it. In *Grandison*, all the vicious and faulty characters are converted to admiration and love of higher things by the light of Sir Charles's countenance. In *Clarissa*, most of the characters are *not* converted by the light of the heroine's countenance. In that novel, the 'mysterious' elements in Christianity are retained; there is something mysterious about the heroine herself. She is a saint, a martyr, a redeeming force in an evil world. Her 'heroic' virtue transcends the laws of prudence, and for her problems 'right answers' are not readily available. Simple conformity to an accepted code of behaviour can on occasion be a sin. Neither Richardson nor Clarissa herself is ever brought to say that Clarissa should have obeyed her parents and married Solmes. Society cannot be depended upon to enforce Christianity. It does not give ready approval to saints and martyrs. The emotion aroused in the vicious, or even the mediocre, by the sight of unusual and persistent virtue is the desire to smash and destroy it.

In *Grandison*, Richardson affirms what he denied in *Clarissa*. Here, the heroic is the triumphantly successful. We may resent such flagrant success, but there is something impressive about success. The defects in the presentation of a static character are

---

[1] Richard Hooker, *The Works of that Learned and Judicious Divine Mr. Richard Hooker*, ed. John Keble, 7th ed. (revised by R. W. Church and F. Paget), 3 vols., 1888, vol. iii, Sermon iii, pp. 609–10.

[2] *Clarissa*, vii. 136. [3] Ibid., p. 459. [4] Ibid. viii. 3.

easy to find. Yet this does not mean that Sir Charles does not exist as a character. He is not a man made after supper out of parings from the moralists; we are aware of his presence. The hero controls and directs the world with the authority of virtue, in contrast to Lovelace's control of his world through perverted ingenuity. It is easy to mock Sir Charles, as Meredith did in his parody of him as Sir Willoughby Patterne in *The Egoist*. However, unlike Willoughby, Sir Charles is not weak—despite the chorus of praise, he is not dependent upon it. Indeed, the frightening thing about him is that he is too independent, too invulnerable. Meredith's anti-hero is easily deluded, but Sir Charles's vision of others is extremely clear. It would be easy to see him as a successful politician, which, in a way, is just what he is.

Indeed, Sir Charles is so credible that he could easily be intolerable. Fortunately he does not dominate the novel. The emphasis is thrown on the female characters, and our impression of the hero is softened because it is largely conveyed to us through Harriet, a highly sympathetic character. Also, she is in love, and enthusiastic praise of the man she loves is natural, and does not affront the reader.

In *Clarissa*, Christianity exists as subjective experience. The religious literature on which it draws is that which explores the confrontation of the soul with itself, and the inward apprehension of life and death. But in *Grandison*, Christianity, of an entirely different kind, almost one feels a different creed, is objective law, manifested in the outer world of social life and moral behaviour. The validity of this law, this outer world, is represented in the hero who establishes a stable moral norm. Sir Charles is the less frightening because he is usually observed by someone else (if he were seen subjectively like Lovelace the result would be something quite different, and probably as fearsome as that hero). We know him as object, we feel that he is acceptable as representing the secular as the possible. Sir Charles does not transcend the things of the world—he uses them, displaying, with consummate confidence, that in these we live and move and have our being. Through him, Richardson creates a philosophical background which ensures our belief that the inward and moral life of the heroines, as they struggle towards happiness, is of importance. Sir Charles has achieved freedom without injuring himself or disrupting society. The Grandisonian ethos means that the women can also attain a wider freedom, as neither conscience nor desire is antagonistic to the social life. Because he assures us of the goodness of human nature and of social life, the other characters are free to live and move and develop within this optimistic moral setting. (Sir Charles's righteousness is a setting; Clarissa is a vital expression of a belief, but her existence is not a setting—she is the novel.) Richardson is able to examine his characters, and the delicate *minutiae* of their heart's affections, and his humour has free play. The wit and humour of *Clarissa* is usually grotesque or macabre; that in *Grandison* is charming and subtle. The novel teems with good characters who are both interesting and amusing—Uncle and Aunt Selby, Mrs. Shirley, Sir Rowland Meredith, Lord G., Emily, Charlotte, Harriet. Few comic novelists could present a longer list of characters in one novel who were both virtuous and entertaining.

The social virtues for which the hero stands have a charm when put into practice within the novel, and the morality is not oppressive when, as with the female characters, difficulties and conflicts are allowed to exist. Even the most modern reader usually has no difficulty in accepting much the same system of virtues as those in *Grandison* when they are presented in the social comedies of Richardson's great successor, Jane Austen. The discovery that Darcy fulfils so admirably his duties as brother, landlord, and master of a household raises him in the estimation of Elizabeth Bennet. The morally enlightened Mr. Knightley performs his duty as a friend in rebuking Emma for her behaviour at Box Hill. In Jane Austen's novels we are aware of the charm of a world in which the code of conduct is clearly defined, and in which goodness is seen as possible within the framework of society as it exists, by adhering to the code of right conduct and developing the perceptions of head and heart together. Richardson, the first English author of a major domestic comedy, had to affirm more emphatically what Jane Austen could take for granted. Perhaps true social comedy can exist only when there exists some framework of moral values accessible to all, and practicable within the world of ordinary contemporary life. Without an offered norm, comedy turns into caricature, or satire.

Richardson's 'hero' is the perfect example of the moral excellence most admired by his age, a union of intelligence and heart which benefits the whole of society and allows that society to realize what it could and ought to be. It is easy to question the rational virtue admired by Richardson's century; it must be remembered that that century was capable of producing an Oglethorpe, and a John Howard, and of admiring them. Sir Charles is another picture of the idea of his age, the rationally virtuous man whose goodness moves from self-love to love of all humanity, and benefits all, the ideal man whom Pope describes so well in the *Essay on Man*, and whose goodness is rewarded by the approval of God and man:

> Earth smiles around, with boundless bounty blest,
> And Heav'n beholds its image in his breast.[1]

[1] Pope, *An Essay on Man*, Epistle iv, ll. 370–2, p. 164.

XI

'Love and Nonsense, Men and Women':[1] *Sir Charles Grandison* as Comedy

DISCUSSING his last novel, 'The History of my Good Man', Richardson said of it: 'It is entirely new and unborrowed, even of myself . . . It is said to abound with delicate Situations. I hope it does; for what indelicate ones can a good Man be involved in?—Yet he must have his Trials, his Perplexities— And to have them from good Women, will require some Management.'[2] Many have felt that the central 'perplexity' has not been managed entirely satisfactorily. There is something absurd in Sir Charles's Macheath-like situation; we are meant to believe that he is truly in love with both Harriet and Clementina. The main interest of the novel, however, centres upon Harriet; the reader becomes aware of her love for Sir Charles before she will admit to it herself, and then shares with her the shock of learning of his entanglements in Italy. The most interesting 'delicate Situations' are those involving Harriet, and the complexities of her emotional state as she constantly endeavours to come to terms with her own heart; we realize what those complexities are, even better than she does herself, through her constant stream of confidences to her sympathetic friends and relatives, who offer their comments in return.

The structure of the novel is quite different from that of

---

[1] Speaking of *Grandison*, then in progress, Richardson told Lady Bradshaigh 'I think the characters, the sentiments, are all different from any of those in my two former pieces, though the subjects are still love and nonsense, men and women.' (20 Nov. 1752, *Selected Letters*, p. 221.) Richardson's tone when speaking of his new novel is lighter and more jocose than that in which he was wont to discuss *Clarissa*.

[2] See Richardson's letter to Johannes Stinstra, 2 June 1753, *Selected Letters*. p. 234.

Clarissa, as the new kind of complexity, the delicate emotional situation, requires a new use of the letter narration. Richardson himself comments acutely upon the difference in narration between *Clarissa* and *Grandison*:

In Clarissa, my Favourite Clarissa, there is a two-fold Correspondence necessary, one between her and Miss Howe; the other between Lovelace and Belford. The Subject of one Letter arose often out of another. It was necessary it should. In the new Work (except one or two Letters of each of the Respondents, as I may call them) the Answers to the Letters of the *Narratist* are only supposed, & really sunk . . .[1]

In *Clarissa,* as the differences between the two main characters are stressed, the true thoughts of each are largely guarded from each other. The same scene is described by the two main characters from two entirely different points of view—a masterly device which Richardson refrains from using in *Grandison.* One of the ironies of *Clarissa* is that, although it is a novel in letters, one of the main themes is the lack of communication between the two characters most concerned with each other. Truth—total knowledge of the situation—arrives only at the end, too late to serve anybody. If Clarissa's family had read her letters to Anna, and had known what was really happening, they could not have remained so hostile. If Clarissa had read Lovelace's letters to Belford, and thus known what he really thought and hoped, she would never have gone with him. In *Sir Charles Grandison,* everybody seems to know what everbody else is doing, saying, thinking, feeling—almost everybody. Clementina does not know about Harriet's love for Sir Charles until after her own crisis has passed. Letters are prized by a large number of good people who are involved in each other's lives and capable of sincere sympathy. Social life at its richest depends upon openness of heart, in the ability to understand and sympathize. If this is attained, as Richardson here implies it is among the truly good, then feelings can be communicated: 'The mutual unbosoming of secrets is the cement of faithful Friendship, and true Love.'[2] Each 'Narratist' in the novel is involved in unbosoming his inmost secrets to a large company. Feelings are to be shared; it is safe to allow one's feelings to be

---

[1] Richardson to Johannes Stinstra, 2 June 1753, *Selected Letters*, pp. 234–5.
[2] *Grandison,* iii. 87.

known, as one can be confident, in the world of *Grandison* as not in *Clarissa*, that they will not be exploited or misunderstood.

The narration in *Grandison* is, as it can afford to be, much more straightforward and more relaxed than that in *Clarissa*. The education of the heart, as it is shown in Harriet's immediate experience and perceptions, involves the exploration of several large themes: the nature of relationships in society, the relationships between men and women, and the meaning of love. As the author is not working within the limitations of tragic suspense and tragic irony, the structure need not be so strictly controlled. Every incident in *Clarissa* is appropriately placed where it will best contribute to mounting tension; very few incidents could be removed or transposed without weakening the novel. Almost all the characters, even the most minor ones, contribute directly to the main plot. In *Grandison*, the kind of suspense is different; the author could allow sub-plots and incidents to assume some of their own control, and could let his imagination go in describing and developing numerous minor characters. The novel's unity is thematic, rather than structural.

The novel is not entirely 'new and unborrowed' (no work can be that) but to Richardson the craftsman much of the creative excitement in writing it consisted in discovering how to adapt conventional comic and romantic modes, as well as moral and instructive material, to the form of the domestic novel in order to create a new kind of novel, the domestic comedy, as he had previously adapted material from dramatic and religious literature to create the first tragic novel in *Clarissa*.

In writing his comedy, Richardson had stage comedy in mind.[1] He realized he was writing for a public used to perusing play-books. Harriet explains her method of narration to Lucy: 'By the way, Lucy, you are fond of plays; and it is come into my head, that, to avoid all *says-I's* and *says-she's*, I will henceforth, in all dialogues, write names in the margin: So fansy, my dear, that you are reading in one of your favourite volumes.'[2] Richardson had used this play-book narration in *Clarissa*, but he draws

---

[1] A few of the following points are made by Ira Konigsberg in *Samuel Richardson and the Dramatic Novel*, 1968.

[2] *Grandison*, i. 419.

upon it even more extensively in *Grandison*. The 'play-book' element in the narration helps to overcome the limitations of the letter form; by allowing his readers to be present, as audience, at the performance of a lengthy scene, the author lets us forget the impossibility of such long conversations being remembered by one narrator, and the point of view is brought in as a comment on a scene we have experienced at first hand. In *Clarissa*, the drama is in the main structure of the novel; few scenes exist objectively; we see most in turn, first from Clarissa's point of view, then from that of Lovelace, and note the difference. In *Grandison*, the dramatic elements are the constituents of each scene and conversation; the tensions are in the open, and do not depend on the irony of widely divergent points of view. Richardson permits himself a leisurely unfolding of character and theme in conversation, debate, and verbal by-play. In doing so, he is deliberately aiming at a resemblance to the genteel comedy, and must have felt gratified when the ingenuous Lady Bradshaigh remarked on the novel: 'What a delightful play might be form'd out of this piece. I am sure Mr. Garrick will have it upon the Stage.'[1]

There are a number of comic types and characters within the novel, presented as they are seen by the main narrators. Harriet, the heroine, has a keen perception of the ridiculous; her youthful elasticity, vitality, and sense of humour make her from the beginning an interesting and amusing character. There is a subacid quality in some of her comments, even more noticeable in Charlotte's observations. The witty observations of these heroines provide a necessary balance to the serious and sentimental tone of the central romantic tale. The astringent quality of the heroines' comic perceptions is akin to the same quality, refined and made more subtle, which we find in the heroines of Jane Austen's novels. The kind of 'wit' directed upon the humorous characters, the fops and fools, in Richardson's comic novel is directly related to the wit of Restoration comedy.

At the beginning of the novel, we are introduced to a number of characters, many of whom make their appearance only to swell a scene or two. At the beginning of *Pamela II* the heroine

---

[1] Lady Bradshaigh, letter to Richardson, 20 Nov. 1753, Forster MSS., Vol. xi, p. 48ʳ.

presents her new acquaintance, but there the value of such description consists only in whatever entertainment these minor characters can supply in themselves. At the beginning of *Grandison*, Harriet's character is yet to be known, and her emergence into town life reveals her personality, her responses to people and events. Unlike Pamela the matron, Harriet is in a situation of suspense, her choice of suitors not yet made. Her reaction to her male acquaintance is interesting because it tells us what she is, not always consciously, looking for in a husband, and makes us, more than the cheerful heroine, aware of the difficulty of finding the love she needs. Her female acquaintance are a contrast to herself and to her later friends, Charlotte, Caroline, and Emily. Harriet is in the position of the heroine of dramatic comedy—the girl on the point of choice—and the minor characters who emphasize her position are presented in a comic mode.

On her first visit to town, Harriet meets a variety of fops and would-be wits, such as Mr. Somner, whose head has been turned by marriage to a rich young widow, who 'gave him consequence by falling in love with him',[1] and Mr. Walden, the pedant who quotes the classic authors in season and out. Mr. Singleton is a harmless fool, who, to be agreeable, laughs at every jest, 'tho' it must be owned, he now-and-then mistakes for a jest what is none'.[2] Since he is a fool by nature, whereas others aggravate their folly by vanity, his lack of affectation should allow him to be, as Harriet admits, not despicable, although she delightedly notices that, unlike the others of the party who are over-talkative, he is unable to say anything at all: 'Once, indeed, he tried to speak: His mouth actually opened . . . as sometimes seems to be his way before the words are quite ready: But he sat down satisfied with the effort.'[3] Mr. Barnet is a loquacious fop:

At first, I thought him *only* a fop. He affected to say some things, that, tho' trite, were sententious, and carried with them the air of observation. There is some degree of merit in having such a memory, as will help a person to repeat and apply other mens wit with some tolerable propriety. But when he attempted to walk alone, he said things that it was impossible a man of common sense could say.[4]

The collection of fools at the dinner-party at Lady Betty

[1] *Grandison*, i. 21.   [2] Ibid., p. 57.
[3] Ibid., p. 60.   [4] Ibid., p. 22.

Williams's house is reminiscent of the gallery of such types found in the drama, and Harriet's comments on them are like the remarks passed by some dramatic characters on others. Her remarks on Mr. Barnet are, for instance, similar to those of Mirabell and Fainall on Witwoud:

> *Fain[all]*. . . . . To give the t'other his due; he has something of good Nature, and does not always want Wit.
> *Mira[bell]*. Not always; but as often as his Memory fails him, and his common place of Comparisons. He is a Fool with a good Memory, and some few Scraps of other Folks Wit.[1]

As well as the minor fools, there is the more important character Sir Hargrave Pollexfen, affected town-beau and rake, who betrays his conceit about his appearance:

> The taste of the present age seems to be dress: No wonder therefore, that such a man as Sir Hargrave aims to excel in it. What can be misbestowed by a man on his person, who values it more than his mind? But he would, in my opinion, better become his dress, if the pains he undoubtedly takes before he ventures to come into public, were less apparent: This I judge from his solicitude to preserve all in exact order, when in company; for he forgets not to pay his respects to himself at every glass; yet does it with a seeming consciousness, as if he would hide a vanity too apparent to be concealed; breaking from it, if he finds himself observed, with an half-careless, yet seemingly dissatisfied air, pretending to have discovered something amiss in himself. This seldom fails to bring him a compliment . . . [2]

Sir Hargrave cannot resist looking in the glass, even when he is announcing to Mr. Reeves his intention of continuing as Harriet's suitor:

> He was determined I should be his; and swore to it. A man of his fortune to be refused, by a Lady who had not (and whom he wished not to have) an answerable fortune, and no preferable liking to any other man [There Sir Hargrave was mistaken; for I like almost every man I know, better than him]; his person not contemptible [And then, my cousin says, he surveyed himself from head to foot in the glass]; was very, *very* unaccountable.[3]

Behind Sir Hargrave is a long line of fops in Restoration comedy, who distinguish themselves by their vain gazing in

---

[1] William Congreve, *The Way of the World*, 1700, I. i, p. 7.
[2] *Grandison*, i. 62.   [3] Ibid., p. 145.

looking-glasses—Sir Fopling Flutter, Sir Courtly Nice, Duretete in Farquhar's *The Inconstant*. It is no wonder that a rival suitor, Greville, bitterly refers to Sir Hargrave as 'this Sir Fopling'.[1] The vain fops are used by the dramatists to set off the heroes, the men of sense, and Richardson follows the pattern by using this type of vain fool as a foil to Sir Charles. A disgust for the shallow fellows distinguishes the sensible heroine from lesser women. Harriet dislikes Sir Hargrave, although other women like him; the silly Miss Cantillon endeavours to flirt with him.[2] In *Sir Courtly Nice*, the hero Farewel remarks that he need fear nothing from the addresses of Sir Courtly to his beloved Leonora: 'Hang him, he secure's himself by his Foppery's, she despises him.' The lovers' mutual friend Violante thoughtfully responds. 'Not many Lady's do so.'[3] The introduction of the fop to point up the good sense of the hero and the heroine is a conventional dramatic device. Sir Hargrave is, from the beginning, a light and foolish character, who is, unlike Lovelace, incapable of bringing events to any serious catastrophe. It is safe to laugh at him.

Everard Grandison, Sir Charles's cousin, is another example of the vain fop and stupid rake. His weak attempts at wit, and his use of slang, mark him as of but poor understanding. This would-be leader of fashion and gallantry is more weak-willed and less daring than Sir Hargrave and, in his excursions into fashionable rakishness, proves himself a complete gull, falling into a trap set for him by a designing woman of the town, from which he is rescued by his sensible cousin. The rest of the Grandison family are fairly tolerant of Everard, who provides them with an object of mirth; his folly is to be laughed at as much as reproved. It is Richardson's intent throughout the novel to equate the rake with the fop and fool. The intelligent and attractive rake, the hero of so many comedies, and from whom Lovelace is partly drawn, is here sunk to the level of the Foplings, and empty-headed Froths, to set off the hero whose virtue is to commend itself by sober and masculine good sense.

Richardson also drew upon the comic buffoons of the stage. Major O'Hara and Captain Salmonet are comic, not only because they assume military airs 'which not sitting naturally,

---

[1] Ibid., p. 147.   [2] Ibid., p. 86.
[3] John Crowne, *Sir Courtly Nice: or, It cannot Be*, 1685, II. i. p. 11.

gave them . . . The swagger of soldierly importance',[1] but also because they are foreigners with heavy stage accents. O'Hara is the blustering Irishman; the underbred and swaggering 'Teague' had long been a stock dramatic figure of fun. The O'Haras' invasion of Sir Charles's house with the half-French Captain Salmonet is narrated in the mode of comic drama, even to the way in which most of the speeches are set out, in a play-book manner.

Capt. De man of honour and good-nature be my broder's general cha-*ract*-er, I do assure your Lordship.
    He spoke English as a Frenchman, my Lord says; but pronounced the word character as an Irishman.
Major (bowing). No need of this, my dear friend. My Lord has the cha-*ract*-er of a fine gentleman himself . . .
Mrs. O'Hara . . . Sir Charles Grandison is a very fine gentleman.
Capt. De vinest cha-*ract*-er in de vorld. By my salvation, every-body say so.[2]

The party become less polite when Lord L., acting for the absent Sir Charles, refuses to give Mrs. O'Hara and her new and dubious husband the custody of Emily, her daughter and Sir Charles's ward. '*Capt.* Very surprising, indeed!—Ver dis to be done in my country—In France—English liberty! Begar ver pretty liberty!—A daughter to be supported against her moder—Whew! Ver pretty liberty, by my salvation!'[3]
    This is stage-speech, and these are stage characters. Captain Salmonet's mixture of pronunciation, part French, part Irish, is not unlike that of Foigard in *The Beaux Stratagem*. Foigard wishes to pass for French, concealing his Irish pronunciation by an exaggerated French accent: 'Upon my Shoul, Noble Friend, dis is strange News you tell me, Fader *Foigard* a subject of *England*, de son of a *Burgomaster* of *Brussels* a Subject of England! . . . I vil never spake *English* no more.'[4]
    Another character who has some of the qualities of the stage buffoon is Sir Rowland Meredith, the Welsh country knight, but he is treated sympathetically, and his foibles are endearing. His nephew, Mr. Fowler, falls in love with Harriet, and Sir Rowland comes to see Harriet and her cousins the Reeves to

[1] *Grandison*, ii. 306.   [2] Ibid., p. 305.   [3] Ibid., p. 310.
[4] George Farquhar, *The Beaux Stratagem*, 1707, IV. i, p. 52.

inspect the young lady and make a proposal of marriage. He comes to breakfast, where the group of pretty and fashionable young ladies sit daintily drinking tea, and peers short-sightedly at them, jogging Mr. Reeves with his elbow, and whispering 'Hay, Sir?'[1] Satisfied that Harriet is the prettiest of the ladies, he decides at once 'My boy *shall* have her',[2] and makes the offer upon the spot: 'Be all this good company witnesses for me. I am no flincher . . . I love these open doings. I love to be above-board. What signifies shilly-shally?'[3] His bluntness and his approval of his own decisiveness resemble the qualities of that other country gentleman, Sir Wilful Witwoud: 'I am somewhat dainty in making a Resolution,—because when I make it I keep it, I don't stand still I, shall I, then; if I say't, I'll do't . . .'[4]

The introduction of the country gentleman, unsophisticated amid the sophistication of the town, is a device often used by the dramatists. Sir Rowland's countrified ways are seen in his gauche manners, his old-fashioned finery (with his 'full-buckled wig'[6]), his language and expressions, such as 'Ad's-my-life',[6] 'alamort',[7] 'all in the *suds*'.[8] He slightly resembles the country parent, Sir Harry Gubbin, in his desire to do all the young man's courting for him, but Sir Rowland is motivated only by benevolence to his nephew, once the bashful youth has fallen in love with Harriet. Sir Rowland is also unmercenary, which Steele's country character is definitely not. Sir Harry's ungallant view of women and marriage, 'The whole nation is over-run with Petticoats; Our Daughters lye upon our Hands, Brother *Tipkin*; Girls are Drugs, Sir, mere Drugs'[9], is, in Richardson's novel, attributed to the young merchant, Mr. Edward Danby: 'Women are a drug, Sir. I have no doubt of offers, if once I were my own master.'[10]

In *Grandison*, the landowning class is not seen as materialistic or mercenary; the bourgeoisie do not come off as well. The disgraceful but irrepressible Everard Grandison retrieves his broken fortunes by marrying into the merchant class. Our last

[1] *Grandison*, i. 46. [2] Ibid. [3] Ibid., p. 49.
[4] Congreve, *The Way of the World*, III. i, p. 47.
[5] *Grandison*, i. 105. [6] Ibid., pp. 49–55 *passim*.
[7] Ibid., p. 117. [8] Ibid., p. 109.
[9] Steele, *The Tender: Husband Or, The Accomplish'd Fools*, 1705, I. i, p. 9.
[10] *Grandison*, ii. 254.

glimpse of him is a comic picture of his married life. The rich
merchant's widow is a snob, stupid enough to take all her new
husband's follies as manifestations of high birth: 'He is gay,
fluttering, debonnaire; and she thinks those qualities appen-
dages of *family*. He has presented her with a genealogical table
of his ancestors, drawn up and blazoned by heraldry art. It is
framed, glazed, and hung up in her drawing-room. She shews
it to every one.'[1] Sir Charles then makes appropriate remarks
about the value of trade and commerce compared to mere
gentility, but we, acquainted with the Grandison way of life,
know better. Sir Charles's magnanimous observations themselves convey the opposite import—who but the large-minded
modern gentleman would be so free from bias, so concerned
with the good of the whole of society? Sir Charles has neither
the rustic manners of the antique gentry, like Sir Rowland,
nor the vulgarity of the *nouveaux riches*. Richardson provides
his own variation on a constant theme of Restoration and
eighteenth-century comic drama, the contrast between gentle
and mercantile values.

It is natural that Richardson, who had little or no personal
knowledge of high life, should have turned to the conventions of
stage comedy in creating a stylized *beau monde*. The character in
Grandison who is most fully drawn from the conventions of
dramatic comedy is, however, also one of Richardson's most
fully developed, original, and delightful creations.[2] Charlotte

---

[1] *Grandison*, vi. 143.

[2] For another commentary on Charlotte's resemblance to the gay heroines of
comedy, see pages 52–3 of Ira Konigsberg's article, 'The Dramatic Background of
Richardson's Plots and Characters'. The plays to which Konigsberg refers are
Miller's *The Humours of Oxford* (1730), Catherine Trotter's *Love at a Loss* (1700),
Odingsells's *The Bath Unmask'd* (1725), and Moore's *The Foundling*(1748); the last
is the only one from which he quotes. The other examples are too obscure to be
satisfactory, and I have thought it more relevant to choose some of the earlier and
better-known plays which treat the same themes and have the same kind of lively
heroines. It is not necessary to assert that Richardson has particular passages from
any of these plays definitely in mind; what is striking is the resemblance between
passages and characters from his comedy and scenes and characters in a well-known
type of social comedy. It is not possible to prove, for instance, that he knew Congreve's comedies (he did know *The Mourning Bride*—see *Clarissa*, vi. 433, vii. 5) but
the plays of that dramatist provide the best examples of certain character-types and
scenes which were common to many stage plays of the period. Cibber was Richardson's friend over many years, and it does not seem unlikely that Richardson would
have had some acquaintance with his plays. He disagreed entirely with Cibber's
idea of a virtuous hero, in a discussion they had when Richardson was beginning

Grandison is a real and lively character. Richardson's ostensible purpose was to exemplify in her a mildly improper mode of conduct requiring reproof and correction, but he obviously enjoyed Charlotte's wit and gaiety immensely, and most of his readers have felt about her as did Lady Bradshaigh:

> Your Caution signifies nothing, Sir, for I *must* and *will* be entertain'd with the inimitable humour of Charlotte. Pray do not you Expect your readers to laugh, when, I am Sure, you cou'd not help laughing your Self, at the time it was writt. it is impossible not to be pleas'd. I must love her *with* your *leave*, or *without* your leave.[1]

The witty, teasing, independent heroine, whose head rules her heart in the game of love, is an established character-type in Restoration comedy. In the earlier more 'witty' plays, the lively lady is the central heroine, although she is often given a foil in a more serious friend, and two love stories, the serious and the witty courtship, are interwoven (e.g. the courtship of Dorimant and Harriet, and Bellair and Emilia, in *The Man of Mode*). In the later, more sentimental comedies the relationship between the more serious couple is emphasized; the giddy heroine is often given a sensible lover, instead of a witty rake, and she must learn to model her behaviour on that of her more right-thinking friend, the sober heroine. For example, in Steele's *The Funeral*, the sisters Harriot and Sharlot are in contrast; Harriot is coquettish and giddy, Sharlot more grave and serious. Harriot enjoys teasing her lover, Campley, and has to be scolded by him into more rational conduct.[2] In Cibber's *The Careless Husband*, Lady Betty Modish is a coquette, who teases her serious suitor Morelove, until she is scolded by her grave and virtuous friend Lady Easy, and worked upon by the other characters so that she comes to see the error of her ways.

Although coquettes reform, their behaviour and their wit

this novel and asked the dramatist's advice (see Richardson's letter to Lady Bradshaigh, 1750, *Selected Letters*, p. 171), but Richardson's idea of a lively heroine is certainly similar to Cibber's.

[1] Lady Bradshaigh, letter to Richardson, 30 Nov.–11 Dec., 1753, in section dated 4 Dec., Forster MSS., vol. xi, p. 55ʳ.

[2] See Steele's *The Funeral: Or, Grief A-La-Mode*, 1702, II. i, pp. 29–31. It is interesting that Richardson gives his heroines the same names, with reversed roles—his Harriet is serious in affairs of the heart, and it is his Charlotte who is flippant.

and raillery furnish much of the entertainment of such plays. The dramatists enjoyed exhibiting such airy indifference and witty comment, and such roles offered excellent opportunities for actresses. Mrs. Oldfield appeared most successfully in such roles in Cibber's plays, as Lady Betty, Maria, and Narcissa, and the character of Charlotte Grandison is just such another part for Mrs. Oldfield.

Charlotte has most of the characteristics of the giddy heroine of the stage. Her head rules her heart. She is suspicious of marriage, as implying subordination, and delights in independence. She is a coquette who loves her own power, and, however much she may protest contempt for the follies of men, she is not averse to compliments and adulation.

Like the stage heroines, she enjoys the admiration of her lovers, while professing to treat them as idle vanities, easily forgotten. She entreats Harriet to tell her about her lovers: 'you must encourage me by your freedom, and we will take up our fellows and lay them down again, one by one, as we run them over, and bid them lie still and be quiet till we recal them to our memory'.[1] She resembles Millamant, who says that lovers are 'vain empty things if we are silent or unseen, and want a being'.[2]

She enjoys her power, and when her brother presses her to make a decision between her two suitors, Charlotte treats the matter flippantly: 'The fluttering season is approaching. One wants now-and-then a *dangling* fellow or two after one in public . . .'[3] Charlotte is soundly berated by the rest of her family for a remark which they consider in bad taste, but after she is forgiven, her brother has to confess that he loves her '*With all your faults, my dear*; and I had almost said, *for* some of them.'[4] His remark perhaps indicates that we are to feel about Charlotte somewhat as Mirabell does about Millamant: 'I like her with all her Faults; nay, like her for her Faults. Her Follies are so natural, or so artful, that they become her; and those Affectations which in another Woman wou'd be odious, serve but to make her more agreeable.'[5] Charlotte's coyness in

---

[1] *Grandison*, i. 292.
[2] Congreve, *The Way of the World*, II. i, p. 28.
[3] *Grandison*, ii. 408.
[4] Ibid., p. 429.
[5] Congreve, *The Way of the World*, I. i, p. 6.

replying to a proposal which she means to accept also resembles the coyness of such heroines as Millamant:

Sir Ch. Well, And what shall I say to Lord G.?
Miss Gr. Why that's the thing!—I was afraid it would come to this—Why, Sir, you must tell him, I think—I profess I can't tell what—But, Sir, will you let me know what you would have me tell him?¹

Like many of the light-hearted heroines of comedy she is a sceptic about marriage; she feels rather as does Cibber's Lady Betty Modish:

L[ady] Bett[y Modish]. Prithee tell me. You are often advising me to it, are there those real Comfortable Advantages in Marriage, that our Old Aunts, and Grand-mothers wou'd persuade us of?
L[ady] Ea[sy]. Upon my word, if I had the Worst Husband in the World, I shou'd still think so.
L. Bett. Ay, but then the Hazard of Having a good one, my Dear.
L. Ea. You may have a good one, I dare say, if you don't give Airs till you spoil him.
L. Bett. Can there be the same Dear, full Delight in giving Ease, as Pain? O! my Dear, the Thought of Parting with ones Power is Insupportable!
L. Ea. And the keeping it, till it dwindles into no Power at all, is most Rufully Foolish.
L. Bett. But still to marry before One's Heartily in love—
L. Ea. Is not half so Formidable a Calamity . . .²

Charlotte condemns the 'free-masonry' of married women, and her scorn of 'comfort' causes Harriet to compare her to Steele's Biddy Tipkin.³ She protests, even after she has accepted Lord G., against being hurried into marriage: 'Pride and petulance must go down by degrees, sister. A month, at least, is necessary, to bring my features to such a placidness with him, as to allow him to smile in my face.'⁴ She is like such whimsical heroines as Farquhar's Bisarre who says: 'I do love a little Coquetting with all my heart . . . He shou'd have my consent to buy the Wedding Ring, and the next moment wou'd I

---

¹ *Grandison*, ii. 432.
² Colley Cibber, *The Careless Husband*, 1705, v. i, p. 49.
³ *Grandison*, iii. 240; see *The Tender Husband*, ii. i, p. 19.
⁴ *Grandison*, iii. 320–1.

Laugh in his face.'[1] Charlotte, like many of the comedy heroines, makes conditions and provisos with her husband-to-be. She is almost rudely blunt to her bashful fiancé about the conditions under which she consents to enter the married state: 'But marriage itself, Sir, shall not give you a privilege to break into my retirements.'[2] Even at her wedding (which is, unlike Harriet's, a comic occasion) Charlotte cannot forbear conditioning: 'I overheard the naughty one say, as Lord G. led her up to the altar, You don't know what you are about, man. I expect to have all my way: Remember that's one of my articles before marriage.'[3]

Richardson varies the usual dramatic pattern by allowing his coquette to remain unreformed after marriage. Charlotte has the advantage of her bashful husband, the slightly absurd Lord G., who is very much in love with her. Her conversion to better behaviour takes place only by fits and starts, and the explosions of her unkind wit after marriage sound like the ruthless raillery indulged in by the heroines of comedy at the expense of their suitors. This kind of sparring between a *married* couple is not the usual subject of stage comedy, where married differences, if they are shown, are more serious than those between the unmarried couples; marital disharmony in stage comedy usually involves adultery and cruelty. Richardson determined to show a lighter kind of matrimonial difference, letting the witty girl continue her career as an unkindly witty married woman who reforms slowly, and then not so much through the influence of advice or even of love as because of experience of married life.

One of the things that provokes Charlotte is that her husband forgets to abide by her conditions and 'articles'. She insists that Lord G. is taking unwarrantable liberties in breaking into her retirements. It is as if we were called upon to watch the behaviour of a Millamant, married, but not to a Mirabell. It is implied in the novel that the couple's disharmony arises partly from the sexual relationship. Charlotte resents being Lord G.'s property; it is galling to her to realize that her husband feels he may make love to her when he pleases. Since she is not the one deeply in love, she finds his 'raptures' difficult to understand. Richardson means the reader to agree with Harriet, and Aunt Nell, and the

---

[1] Farquhar, *The Inconstant: or, The Way to Win Him*, II. i, p. 14.
[2] *Grandison*, iii. 341–2.   [3] Ibid., p. 360.

rest, in thinking Charlotte's conduct wrong, and not becoming in a wife. Still, her behaviour is of a piece with her emphasis on her 'articles' (or as Congreve put it, 'provisos'), and it is hard to understand quite why Lady Mary Wortley Montagu was so infuriated:

> Charlotte behaves like a humorsome child, and should have been used like one, and *** whipped in the presence of her friendly confidante Harriet. Lord Halifax very justly tells his daughter, that a husband's kindness is to be kindly received by a wife, even when he is drunk, and though it is wrapped up in never so much impertinence.[1]

Lady Mary conveniently forgot, in this instance, that she herself was living entirely separated from her husband, and beyond the reach of any of his 'kindness' except the financial sort. There is no reason why Charlotte, with her somewhat haughty and independent nature, might not feel as she does. Harriet's reception of her husband's 'kindness' will be different, but then she will be wholly in love with the man she marries, and he will have rather more tact than Lord G. Most of Charlotte's offences arise from her enjoyment of teasing her husband, whose stiffness and earnestness make him, for her, an irresistible target. As she says on her wedding day: 'I have been so much accustomed to treat him like a fool, that I can't help thinking him one. He should not have been so tame to such a spirit as mine. He should have been angry when I played upon him. I have got a knack of it, and shall never leave it off, that's certain.'[2] Her contrary spirit is like that of Cibber's Lady Betty, who says, referring to her suitor Morelove, that she is 'pleas'd when he lets me use him ill; and if ever I have a favourable Thought of him, 'tis when I see he can't bear that Usage'.[3] Like the witty heroines of the comedies, Charlotte provokes her lover (in this case her husband) until he lets her see that he will not bear that usage, and she begins to reflect upon her own wrong behaviour. Her descent is gradual, and she refuses to be abject. Like Cibber's Lady Betty, she waits for the man to make the first apology before she too will apologize

---

[1] *Letters of Lady Mary Wortley Montagu*, ii. 290.
[2] *Grandison*, iii. 328-9.
[3] Cibber, *The Careless Husband*, iv. i, p. 36.

and make amends.[1] Charlotte explains to her sister how she reasoned with herself:

> Make your retreat while you can with honour; before you harden the man's heart and find your reformation a matter of indifference to him . . . At present the honest man loves you . . . I shall make him appear weak in the eyes of every-body else, when I have so much grace left, as would make me rise against any one who should let me know they thought him so . . . My wit will be thought folly . . . I will be good of choice, and make my *duty* received as a *favour*.[2]

Her argument with herself resembles that of Cibber's Clarinda when she decides that she must behave better to her lover: 'I have us'd him Ill . . . and he may e'n thank himself for't—he wou'd be Sincere . . . Well (begging my Sexes Pardon) we do make the silliest Tyrants—we had better be reasonable . . .'[3]

In the plays the female tyrant subsides gracefully, acknowledging the claims of good nature, principle, and social duty. Richardson explores this theme further by showing his spirited Charlotte in the process of dwindling into a wife. She never reforms completely; she asks her sister to 'Allow a little for constitution now-and-then'.[4] Her shrewd comments sometimes hit on a truth that the others do not wish to acknowledge; her wit and high spirits allow her to make the remarks that the others, with their more serious outlook, cannot make, and the sheer fun in some of her comments reminds us of the heroine of stage comedy at her unreformed best. For instance, when Harriet gravely censures the masquerade, with its crowd of costumed apparitions including 'Witches and Devils', at which every one seemed to be 'endeavouring to be thought the direct *contrary* of what he or she appeared to be!' Charlotte airily observes, 'Well then, the Devils, at least, must have been charming creatures!'[5] Her sister's scolding meets with an airy response:

> You, Charlotte, said Lady L. have odder notions than any-body else. Had you been a man, you would have been a sad rake.
>
> A rake perhaps I might have been; but not a *sad* one, Lady L.[6]

Her answer is in the spirit of Farquhar's robust and unrepentant

---

[1] Cibber, *The Careless Husband*, v. i, p. 64, and *Grandison*, iv. 203.
[2] *Grandison*, iv. 220.
[3] Cibber, *The Double Gallant: or, The Sick Lady's Cure* [1708], v. i, p. 69.
[4] *Grandison*, iv. 221.   [5] Ibid. ii. 215.   [6] Ibid. iii. 375.

Silvia, to whom her friend Melinda says: 'had'st thou been a Man, thou had'st been the greatest Rake in Christendom.'[1]

The presence of the lively Charlotte ensures that the conversation of the virtuous in *Grandison* will never be allowed to become too tedious. In the world of sentimental love and high principles, she speaks for the world outside, where it is often necessary to combine some cynicism with principle, and defensive wit with good nature. Because she is there, Richardson can persuade the reader that his perception of the social world and the logic of the heart is well-balanced and complete.

Harriet herself is a more sentimental heroine, but this does not mean she is dull as a character. Much of the comedy emanates from her; she has a keen sense of humour, except when her feelings are deeply involved. When we first meet her, she is heartfree, and full of gaiety and harmless impudence, as can be seen when she mischievously stands 'making mouths in the glass' in an endeavour to imitate Mr. Walden's extraordinary grimaces.[2] Because she has this native insouciance, it is the more interesting to watch her fall in love, in spite of herself; she, who has been able so lightly to dispose of her suitors, is brought to the condition her uncle once wished upon her, 'heartily in love: Ay, up to the very ears', and unable to help herself.[3] Her love, which she at first refuses to recognize, involves her in the agony of suspense, especially during Sir Charles's visit to Italy.

The theme of the novel, which is centred upon Harriet and radiates from her, is the nature of love. Within the novel, love is perpetually analysed and examined. The various groups in different ways illustrate good and bad love between men and women. There are several examples of the abuses of love, or love which is not worthy of the name, in the examples of Sir Thomas Grandison and Mrs. Oldham, Lord W. and his kept woman, Mrs. Giffard, Everard Grandison and the woman of the town. Less guilty but still dishonourable is the avaricious and deceitful Captain Anderson's pursuit of Charlotte with her rank and fortune. There are examples of marriages which have gone sour, or are only partially satisfactory, because one or both of the parties will not learn to love aright, or act according

---

[1] Farquhar, *The Recruiting Officer*, 2nd ed., 1706, I. ii, p. 10.
[2] *Grandison*, i. 63.   [3] Ibid., p. 36.

to his duty, as in the case of Mr. and Mrs. Jervois, or Sir Harry Beauchamp and his termagant wife. To balance such instances, there are examples of happy and harmonious married life, like that of the Reeves, Selbys, and Lord and Lady L. There are also the marriages which begin with esteem and prudence rather than rapturous love, in which love ripens during marriage, as is the case with Lord W. and his new bride, and with Charlotte and Lord G. To crown all, there is the ideal, the passionate yet reasonable love which finds its complete fulfil-ment in marriage, which we see in the case of Sir Charles and Harriet.[1] This is the kind of love which can exist only when there is true magnanimity of heart, which desires the happiness of its beloved above its own. Harriet, Clementina, and Sir Charles prove they possess this magnanimity. In the refined atmosphere in which the chief characters live and move, love is perpetually discussed, rediscussed, and defined. The cumulative effect of discussion and example is the appearance of achieving a defini-tion of love which has taken all possibilities into account.

This atmosphere, in which the main characters spend much of their time analysing themselves, their emotions, and the nature of love in its various aspects, would not be unfamiliar to those of Richardson's readers who were familiar with the French romances. There would still have been many such, despite the improving influence of *The Spectator*.[2] In Mlle

---

[1] Richardson intends to mock the false romantic, and to suggest that the charm of true love must be sought in everyday life. There is a parody of the romantic-pastoral style in Sir Charles's words to Charlotte: 'The subject we are upon, *courtship* and *marriage*, cannot, I find, be talked seriously of by a Lady, before company. Shall I retire with you to solitude? Make a Lover's *Camera Obscura* for you? Or, could I place you upon the mossy bank of a purling stream, gliding thro' an enamelled mead; in such a scene, a now despised Lord G. or a Sir Walter, might find his account, sighing at your feet. No witnesses but the grazing herd, lowing Love around you; the feathered songsters from an adjacent grove, contributing to harmonize and fan the lambent flame—'. (*Grandison*, ii. 427–8.) This gentle mockery resembles Steele's in his picture of Biddy Tipkin, as Pounce describes her to Clerimont Sr.: 'She has spent all her solitude in Reading *Romances*, her Head is full of Shepherds, Knights, Flowery Meads, Groves and Streams, so that if you talk like a Man of this World to her, you do nothing.' (*The Tender Husband*, i. i, p. 7.) Richardson, however, makes Sir Charles Harriet's rescuer in true romantic style, and endows him with a heroism which is the counterpart of the older heroes' exaggerated nobility.

[2] See Mrs. Shirley's speech to the young ladies: 'The reading in fashion when I was young, was Romances. You, my children, have, in that respect, fallen into happier days. The present age is greatly obliged to the authors of the Spectators.' (*Grandison*, vi. 223.) But the romances were still read in the eighteenth century; see

de Scudéry's *Clélie* (1654–60), the characters constantly discourse upon the nature of love in its various guises. Love is not divorced from marriage in this romance. The characters, who like the characters in *Grandison* choose illustrative *exempla* among their acquaintance, cite the contrasting cases of two married couples; in one case, the man married for love but fell out of love after marriage, while in the other, the man who married without being in love came to love his wife after the wedding.[1] The second example is the same as Mrs. Shirley's experience in her own marriage: 'Esteem, heightened by Gratitude, and enforced by Duty . . . will soon ripen into Love.'[2]

The characters of *Clélie* argue about the worth of love at first sight; the heroine decides against it:

> Pour moy, dit alors Clelie, ie n'ay iamais pû comprendre qui'l fust possible d'aimer ce qu'on n'a pas eu le loisir de connoistre . . . & ie suis fortement persuadée, qu'on ne peut tout au plus la premiere fois qu'on voit vne Personue [*sic*], quelque aimable qu'elle puisse estre, sentir autre chose dans son cœur, que quelque disposition à l'aimer.[3]

Clélie is supported by Aronce:

> ie suis pourtant persuadé qu'vne amour qui n'a pas vn commencement si subit, & qui est deuancée par vne grande estime, & mesme par beaucoup d'admiration, est plus forte, & plus solide, que celle qui naist en tumulte, sans sçavoir si la personne qu'on aime, a de la vertu, ny mesme de l'esprit . . .[4]

The same topic is canvassed in *Grandison*, with a similar conclusion: 'Love at first sight, answered Sir Charles, must indicate a mind *prepared* for impression, and a sudden gust of passion,

Margaret Dalziel's Introduction to Charlotte Lennox's *The Female Quixote*, Oxford English Novels, pp. xvii–xviii.

[1] See Madeleine de Scudéry, *Clélie, Histoire Romaine*, 10 vols., Paris, 1660–1, i. 195–6. This reference, and the ensuing quotations, can be found in the translation, *Clelia, an excellent New Romance*, 1678, pp. 21–3. The translators, J. Davies and G. Havers, had Englished the work when it first came out, but the later edition is easier to find. Their version of the *Carte du Tendre* can be seen in Plate 4. Quotations in the original preserve the delicate flavour of the French romance, and heighten our awareness of the relationship between apparently antique works and the new, eighteenth-century 'sensibility'; we are often rash in assertions about the causes and origins of the latter.

[2] *Grandison*, vi. 224.
[3] Scudéry, *Clélie*, i. 196.
[4] Ibid., p. 198.

and that of the least noble kind; since there could be no opportunity of knowing the *merit* of the object.'[1]

The relative merits of love and friendship are debated in
Grandison. Harriet comforts herself by professing to believe that
'True friendship . . . being disinterested, and more intellectual
than personal, is nobler than Love.'[2] She is afraid of the self-
seeking in her own love, and avers that 'Love is a narrower of
the heart.'[3] The criterion for judging a person's capacity for
either friendship or love is the 'feeling heart'; this the hero is
supposed to possess:

> How nobly does Sir Charles appear to support himself under
> such heavy afflictions! For those of his friends were ever his. But his
> heart bleeds in secret for them. A feeling heart is a blessing that no
> one, who has it, would be without, and it is a moral security of
> innocence; since the heart that is able to partake of the distress of
> another, cannot wilfully give it.[4]

Just so do the characters in *Clélie* argue the relative merits of
'amour' and 'amitié' in terms of 'tendresse'; 'tendresse' is, as
the heroine defines it,

> vne certaine sensibilité de cœur, qui ne se trouue presques iamais
> souuerainement, qu'en des personnes qui ont l'ame noble, les inclina-
> tions vertueuses, & l'esprit bien tourné; & qui fait que lors qu'elles
> ont de l'amitié, elles l'ont sincere, & ardente; & qu'elles sentent si
> viuement toutes les douleurs, & toutes les ioyes de ceux qu'elles
> aiment, qu'elles ne sentent pas tant des leurs propres.[5]

Clélie says that 'tendresse' applies to friendship, but not to love,
but Aronce claims that it is a quality even more necessary in
love than in friendship:

> En effet, vne amour sans tendresse, n'a que des desirs impetueux,
> qui n'ont n'y bornes ny retenuë: & l'Amant qui porte vne semblable
> passion dans l'ame, ne considere que sa propre satisfaction, sans
> considerer la gloire de la Personne aimée: car vn des Principaux
> effets de la veritable tendresse, c'est qu'elle fait qu'on pense beaucoup
> plus à l'interest de ce qu'on aime, qu'au sien propre.[6]

Harriet and Sir Charles each prove that they possess the
rarest, most refined sensibility of the heart and nobility of soul;

---

[1] *Grandison*, iii. 386.   [2] Ibid. iv. 218.   [3] Ibid. iii. 34–5.
[4] Ibid., p. 231.   [5] Scudéry, *Clélie*, i. 211.
[6] Ibid., p. 216.

they are thus meant for each other. As her grandmother says of Harriet's case, 'is it to be wondered at, that a heart, which never before was won, should discover sensibility, and acknowledge its fellow-heart?'[1]

It is not possible to estimate how much Richardson knew of the French romances: he could not read French, but it is not impossible that he might have come upon translations, or heard pieces translated in reading aloud. What is remarkable is that he manages to recreate some of the qualities that made the long French *roman* so popular in its time, and transpose the delicate precious sensibility into terms suited to the drawing-rooms of Georgian England. The civilized and civilizing progress of Harriet's love for Sir Charles, Emily's for Beauchamp, or Clementina's probable tenderness for the Count of Belvedere, could be mapped on the celebrated *Carte du Tendre* of Mlle de Scudéry (see Plate 3 for the English version)—except that there is, as in all cases of love fully explored by Richardson, a kind of violence in Harriet's passion which the writers of romances do not comprehend in presenting true and lofty feminine love. Structurally, *Grandison* resembles the French romance in its leisurely episodic narration, in which the main love stories and the discussions of sensibility support and complement one another.

There is a French work which Richardson did know in translation, which may have been of some help to him in creating an atmosphere which would provide a satisfactory reflection of high life and manners while remaining in accord with the novel's moral themes and emphasis on sentiment. A translation of the *Letters* of Mme de Sévigné was published in England in 1727, and Richardson seems to have read it.[2] We know that Richardson was conscious of the difficulties in presenting the life of the upper classes when he himself was only an 'obscurely situated' man of business: 'How shall such a

[1] *Grandison*, ii. 18.

[2] See Richardson's letter to Lady Bradshaigh, 14 Feb. 1754: 'Have you read Mad. *Sevigne's* Letters . . .? Fine passages and Sentiments there are in it, & a notion given of the French manners . . .' (*Selected Letters*, p. 293.) He also mentions Mme de Sévigné's *Letters*, in an unpublished letter to the same correspondent, dated 12 July 1757: 'I shᵈ have been glad to have seen yᵉ Answers of yᵉ Countess of Sevigne's Daughter to her Mothers admirable Letters, such Loverlike ones! I shᵈ then have been better able to judge of yᵉ Propriety of yᵉ Mothers Stile in hers.' (Forster MSS., vol. xi, p. 209ᵛ.)

one draw scenes of busy and yet elegant trifling?'[1] In the letters
of Mme de Sévigné he would find a bona fide utterance of a
member of a very high aristocracy, and the tone of the letters
is close to that which Richardson wished to achieve in the
letters in *Grandison*.

The world which Mme de Sévigné inhabits is elegant and
leisurely. The letters depict this world, in its 'genteel' scenes,
without saying anything that would offend Richardson's moral
feelings. Indeed, they are full of moral and pious reflections,
but the writer is neither severe nor gloomy; she has a witty
pen, and can be a trifle sharp, though not disagreeably so, in
her descriptions: 'Your Brother is a Treasure of Folly, which
delights us much here. We have here sometimes very good
Conversations, which he might make his Advantage of; but
his Wit is a little rarefied into a sort of whipt Cream; he is
in other Respects very agreeable.'[2] Mme de Sévigné enjoys
recounting incidents in the manner which Richardson particularly approved: 'I have sent you, my Dear, a tedious Account of
little Particularities, but you tell me sometimes that you like
such minute Histories.'[3] The world which she describes is a
little circle which shares mutual tenderness and admiration:

> We talk of you without ceasing; it is a Subject that leads us far,
> and touches us very nearly.[4]

> As for your Wit, these Ladies have seen nothing superior to it;
> your Conduct, your Prudence, your Judgment, every thing, was
> celebrated; I have never seen any One commended in a handsomer
> Manner. I had not the Power to constrain myself to say one modest
> Thing for you, nor to speak against my Conscience.[5]

Letters are the medium by which more sensibility can be
expressed, and more praise won. The world of the *Letters* is one
of letters; as in *Grandison*, letters are passed about, discussed and
admired: 'Mr. *de la Rochefoucault* . . . shewed me the Letter you
writ to him, which is a very fine one: In his Opinion, Nobody
writes better than you; I believe his Taste will not be dis-
puted.'[6]

---

[1] Richardson to Lady Bradshaigh, 24 Mar. 1751, *Selected Letters*, p. 180.

[2] Mme de Sévigné, *Letters of Madame de Robertin Chantal, Marchioness de Sevigne, To the Comtess de Grignan, Her Daughter*, 2 vols., 1727, i. 61–2.

[3] Ibid. ii. 11.   [4] Ibid., p. 28.

[5] Ibid. i. 148.   [6] Ibid., p. 196.

The world which Mme de Sévigné describes is the world
Richardson wanted for Harriet: a world of polite raillery
mingled with serious reflection, a world consisting of a small
circle of mutual admirers, ready to study a letter for wit, truth
to nature, and sensibility, and eager to cover an absent heroine
with praise. In the world which Mme de Sévigné creates, as in
Richardson's artifact, letters are the substance of life, and the
reading of a letter received can be described in the next
epistle. Not only in the France of Mme de Sévigné, but in
Georgian England, family letters were passed around, quoted,
and admired. Richardson depended much on real life for his
material. His own correspondents were necessary to his art,
especially Lady Bradshaigh, who provided an unconscious
example of epistolary style in a higher social sphere, and Hester
Mulso, who provided a model for the style of a witty and sensitive young girl—for a heroine in fact.[1] By the time he wrote
Grandison, Richardson had acquired friends and correspondents
of superior rank, such as Mrs. Donellan and Mrs. Delany. He
borrowed a packet of Mrs. Delany's letters to Mrs. Dewes
from the latter. Mrs. Delany was a trifle annoyed with her
sister:

> I am angry with you that you sent my letters to Mr. Richardson.
> Indeed, such careless and incorrect letters as mine are to you, should
> not be exposed: were they put in the best dress I could put them into,
> they have nothing to recommend them but the warm overflowing of
> a most affectionate heart, which can only give pleasure to the partial
> friend they are addressed to.[2]

But the natural 'careless' style of an elegant lady writing long,
affectionate chat about family, neighbours, dances, houses,
dress, music, and the minutiae of daily life was exactly what
Richardson wanted. (Neither lady seems to have suspected
that she was being used as material.) The manner of Mrs.
Delany's letters is very like that of Harriet and her family. As
often happens, 'real life' and art refuse to keep rigid boundaries,

---

[1] Mrs. Donellan thought Richardson mistaken in his model: 'she admires her
sense and ingenuity, but thinks her only *second rate* as to *politeness of manners*; and that
Richardson's *high admiration for her* has made him take her *as a model* for his genteel
characters, and that is the reason they *are not* so really polished as he thinks them to
be.' (Mrs. Delany to Mrs. Dewes, 16 Nov. 1751, *The Autobiography and Correspondence of Mrs. Delany*, iii. 60.)

[2] Mrs. Delany to Mrs. Dewes, 17 Nov. 1750, ibid. ii. 617.

but intermingle: 'It was proposed by Mrs. Van Luen that everybody should own what quality they valued themselves most for, and afterwards, what they most disliked in themselves; this fancy made us very merry, and made our conversation not unlike some in Clelia.'[1]

Those who think Richardson's style in *Sir Charles Grandison* vulgar, because certain locutions have become debased fifty years later in Jane Austen's period, could correct this impression by perusing some of the letters of Mrs. Delany, who was not vulgar in rank or taste. It is interesting that Mrs. Delany on reading *Grandison* thought 'The style is better in most places than that of "Clarissa" '[2]; perhaps she herself had contributed to the improvement.

The climate of wealth, breeding, and leisure inhabited by a Mme de Sévigné, or a Mrs. Delany, was not Richardson's personal habitat, but he was fascinated by this kind of life and its possibilities. As an artist, he was capable of taking the hints he needed to create the world of *Grandison*—not only, or primarily its physical environment, the material expressions of wealth, but its customs, tone, forms of thought and feeling. Had he depended for his comedy only upon figures from comic drama superficially adapted to the novel (like Mrs. Haywood in her later stories) he would not have achieved his object, and his large work would have fallen in pieces. The adopted devices of stage comedy allow a variety of wit and humour, but the variety is unified here, so that nothing seems arbitrary or out of place. All the comic incidents, all the comic characters from the broadest (such as Salmonet, Sir Rowland, and, at times, Charlotte) to the most subtle (such as Harriet) belong in the same recognizable environment, spring, as it were, from the same soil.

The narrative manner which fuses elements of romance and stage comedy gives *Grandison* the inner consistency which is so lacking in the *Pamela* sequel. The apparently casual control of the author allows the reader to feel he is absorbed in the meanderings of daily life, with all its random particularity, and yet there is no scene that does not reflect and amplify major

[1] Mrs. Pendarves (Mrs. Delany) to Mrs. Ann Granville (Mrs. Dewes), 9 Dec. 1731, *The Autobiography and Correspondence of Mrs. Delany*, i. 327.
[2] Mrs. Delany to Mrs. Dewes, 3 Dec. 1753, ibid. iii. 252.

themes, and render central characters more completely known. At the novel's first appearance, the artistry of this new kind of writing was noted and commended:

> The narrative is judiciously conducted; if the events and adventures be fewer than in other works of this nature, the interesting scenes, the affecting and moving situations are much more numerous, the heart is more frequently and more deeply touched, our curiosity is continually kept up, and continually gratified. Some indeed who desire only a tale, are delighted with nothing but the novelty and multiplicity of events, and read but to kill time, may complain that the narrative stands still too long, and is too much interrupted with minute descriptions and tedious conversations: But these minutiæ and these conversations are indeed the most valuable and instructive part of the work: The minute and exact descriptions of the air, the attitude, the manner, the every motion of every person on every occasion, animates and enlivens the work, and sets the persons before our eyes: We think we see them, and imagine ourselves to be of the company. Besides there is such an energy of expression, such a depth and delicacy of sentiment, such justness of observation, such quickness of repartee, such sudden turns and strokes of wit, all properly divided and appropriated according to the different characters of the persons, as charmingly diversify these conversations and render them highly useful and entertaining . . . In fine this work resembles a *great drama*, unconfined to the narrow limits . . . of time, place, and action, wherein a larger portion and more extensive view of real life is exhibited than in the *small one*, and yet the behaviour, character, manners, and sentiments, of the persons are expressed in a manner not at all less lively and affecting.[1]

Almost every scene is a dramatic scene, and small knots of complexity are unravelled over several successive scenes, so that 'our curiosity is continually kept up, and continually gratified'. This use of suspense does not resemble that in *Clarissa*, where curiosity finds no breathing space. The technique of *Grandison* is like that of a television serial; such a method of maintaining continuous but not acute suspense was to be adopted by the Victorian novelists dealing with domestic life: Thackeray, George Eliot, Trollope, Henry James.

Richardson's novel has its own kind of unity of action. Episodes and subplots are related to the main story and

---

[1] 'Character of Sir Charles Grandison', *Gentleman's Magazine*, xxiii (Nov. 1753) 511–12.

characters, and to each other. The reader does not feel his knowledge of Charlotte's circumstances is any hindrance to his observation of Harriet. *Grandison* also has its own organic unities of character and theme. Richardson took the deliberate risk of venturing into another tone, in the Clementina sections, but the theme, albeit in a new key, is essentially the same as in the passages relating to Harriet; as in a concerto, variations are to be resolved in the last movement. Very rarely does Richardson transgress his own unities, and, when he does, it is almost always his own precedent in *Clarissa* that leads him astray. The section dealing with Sir Hargrave's abduction of Harriet may be considered a somewhat false and hackneyed imitation of the author by himself. Another grating circumstance is the death-bed of Sir Hargrave Pollexfen.[1] Richardson had met with such success in the deathbed scenes in *Clarissa* that he could not refrain from introducing another such scene in *Grandison*. In this novel, such a scene is inappropriate; it is a discordant note in the general harmony of the last part of the book. Earlier, just before Harriet's wedding, Lucy Selby has whimsically remarked that Harriet ought to be grateful to her unwanted lover, who was the accidental cause of her introduction to Sir Charles: 'Poor Sir Hargrave, to whom all this joyful bustle is primarily owing!—I tell Harriet, that she has not, with all her punctilio, been half punctilious enough. She should have had him, after all, on the motive of Prince Prettiman in the *Rehearsal*.'[2] Sir Hargrave, who is really a comic character, ought to have been dismissed on this comic note.

Yet, compared to other novelists of his time working with some of the same material—even compared to Fanny Burney in her later works—Richardson is distinguished by his sense of

---

[1] *Grandison*, vi. 323–4. There are other deaths within the book, but those of Lady Grandison (ii. 36–42) and Sir Thomas (ii. 102) are narrated as events long past, and the Grandison parents exist less as full characters than as *exempla*. Clementina's wicked cousin Lauraena is less substantial, so her death (vi. 300) is unimportant.

[2] Ibid. v. 340. The reference is to a short passage at the end of *The Rehearsal*, in which the Third Player sums up the remaining action: '*Cloris* at length, being sensible of Prince *Pretty-man's* passion, consents to marry him; but, just as they are going to church, Prince *Pretty-man* meeting, by chance, with old *Joan* the Chandlers widow, and remembring it was she that first brought him acquainted with *Cloris*: out of a high point of honour, breaks off his match with *Cloris*, and marries old *Joan*.' (George Villiers, Duke of Buckingham *et al.*, *The Rehearsal*, 1672, v. i, p. 51.)

structure, and of internal consistency. His attitude to the older episodic novel, with its constant introduction of arbitrary events, bearing no relation to a central theme or to the nature of the characters, is seen in his remarks to Urania Johnson about her novel *Almira*.[1] This novel, which Richardson saw in manuscript, has disappeared from view, unpublished and unlamented, but Richardson's notes give us a good idea of what the novel was like, and what kind of corrections he thought most necessary.[2]

Samanders Character and Courtship of Almira, and Rejection by her, to be more enlarged upon in the beginning, if his History is to make so considerable a Figure here after the principle [*sic*] Heroine is made happy . . .

Almira's spirit high, and low, unequal, high in her Resenting her Aunts Design in Favour of her Son; tame in so easily giving up Plays to please such a Woman as Cradelia [Crudelia] . . .

Be so good, as to deny Nerves to your Ladies . . .

In many of the Speeches, and Dialogues, Clearness of Expression seems to be wanting . . .

Ten persons said to be at Almira's Wedding—there are Eleven inumarated [*sic*].

Need Brutus be made so very a Brute? And withal so shockingly Silly? Give the Savage a little Tincture of something *like* Wit if not so.

P. 329, Samanders Raptures on finding Cleone worth 10 000£ too extatic for his Generosity . . .

The whole Story of the Casket Revealment too improbable . . .

Cleone's Refusal to visit the Wounded Samander in his Chamber when Almira did, really Prudish, and not in Character; her Character is above such Prudery . . .

A Lady writer shou'd not, I think, be so particular in describing Florelle's [Florello's] Disposition to retire on the Wedding Night. But be this as it may, as Consummation only cou'd then be in his

---

[1] Urania Johnson was one of Aaron Hill's daughters; she obviously hoped to make money by her pen. She sent her novel *Almira* to Richardson, begging the '*greatest Master of the* PASSIONS' to criticize and correct her 'Trifle'. (Letter to Richardson, 16 Aug. 1758, Forster MSS., vol. xiv, sect. i, p. 11^r). She was indignant at Richardson's (obviously justified) criticism of her work; her letter of 9 Sept. 1758, in reponse to his observations, is most aggrieved (ibid., pp. 20^r–20^v).

[2] Richardson's comments have been copied out by an amanuensis, and are headed 'Observations upon Memory only, on Almira'; see Forster MSS., vol. xiv, sect. i, pp. 15^r–17^r. A few passages of these observations, drafted out in Richardson's own handwriting, can also be found (ibid., p. 19^r).

Thoughts, I won't allow that his Impatience shou'd be introduced by his Yawaing [i.e. 'yawning'] . . .
 . . . Great improbalities [sic] in Crudelia's Character, Catastrophe, &c &c . . .

From Richardson's observations, it can be seen that Mrs. Johnson's novel was of the older variety, depending on conceal-ments and revelations, violence and surprises. The names of the characters, such as 'Crudelia' and 'Florello' belong to the kind of novel in which all the characters are merely types. Richardson's endeavours to improve this farrago indicate how much he values careful construction. He has a keen eye for consistency in detail (ten persons or eleven at the wedding?). He is impatient with elaborate false delicacy; he certainly did not commit any such prudish solecism as having his hero yawn on the wedding night. Above all, he values consistent and believable characters; the author should be careful to judge whether an action or speech is appropriate to the person as originally conceived, and characters must have something life-like about them.[1]

Richardson's own characters were important to him; they took on a life of their own, and, like some nineteenth-century novelists, he enjoyed discussing them as if they were living people. He had the dramatic imagination which saves his characters from being mere types:

Here I sit down to form characters. One I intend to be all good-ness; All goodness he is. Another I intend to be all gravity; All gravity he is. Another *Lady G*—ish; All *Lady G*—ish she is. I am all the while absorbed in the character. It is not fair to say—I, identi-cally I, am anywhere, while I keep within the character.[2]

The development of situation depends upon the characters. They must find their own way to happiness, not find the wedding-bells set a-ringing for them because of sudden dis-coveries or 'Casket revealments'.

The last novel is full of liveliness and gaiety. It is extraordinary that a middle-aged man (indeed, elderly—he was over sixty) should have written a novel dealing with youthful love, and the

---

[1] For an example of Richardson's advice to a rather better novelist than Mrs. Johnson, see Duncan Isles, 'Johnson, Richardson, and *The Female Quixote*', append-ed to *The Female Quixote*, Oxford English Novels, pp. 418–27.
[2] Richardson to Lady Bradshaigh, 14 Feb. 1754, *Selected Letters*, p. 286.

happiness of life, in so spirited a manner. He was, at the time of composition, surrounded by a company of divers young friends, male and female, all amiable and some witty. (Hester Mulso was to become, as Mrs. Chapone, a writer of some repute.) They appear to have been in a mood to appreciate the theme of love, for Richardson's gatherings became a kind of nursery for engagements.[1] These young people asked Richardson to read the novel to them, instalment by instalment, as he wrote it. Nothing could have been more encouraging to a writer who craved a responsive audience as much as Richardson. The prospect of reading each new scene aloud must have called forth his best efforts, and stimulated him to write passages and conversational scenes suitable for semi-dramatic rendering. As much as possible, he seems to have made the atmosphere about him the atmosphere of *Grandison*. It seems fitting that the very writing of *Grandison* was a social event, in a way that the composition of *Clarissa* could not have been.

[1] Hester Mulso married John Chapone in December 1760; Mary Prescott married Thomas Mulso in January 1761; Susanna Highmore (who sketched the picture of Richardson reading to their circle) married John Duncombe in 1763. See Carroll, Introduction to *Selected Letters*, p. 19.

XII

Heroines

RICHARDSON's last novel is a direct development from the courtship novel (see above, chapter ii). Certain new conventions were already evolving in this type of early novel. The worldly-wise heroine of earlier stage-comedy, brilliant and victorious, gives way to a more introspective type of female character, yet the novel heroines possess shrewdness, dignity, and wit, which keep them from resembling the lachrymose female characters of the new sentimental drama. Mrs. Barker's Galesia, for instance, is a bookish country girl who is not entirely at home in the midst of town life: 'What the World there calls Diversion, to me was Confusion. The Parks, Plays, and Operas, were to me but as so much Time thrown away.'[1] She finds that her fashionable London companions mock her country ways and interests, but in describing this she has sufficient sense of humour to see the funny side herself:

> Perhaps some or other of the Company, either out of Malice to expose me, or Complaisance to entertain me in my own Way, would enter into the Praise of a Country Life, and its plentiful Way of Living, amongst our Corn, Dairies, and Poultry, 'till by Degrees, these bright *Angels* would make the *Ass* open its Mouth, and upon their Demand, tell how many Pounds of Butter a good *Cow* would make in a Week; or how many Bushels of *Wheat* a good *Acre* of *Land* would produce; Things quite out of their Sphere or Element.[2]

One can here observe a change in sensibility; the young lady from the country is, in Restoration comic drama, a figure of fun, but now a novelist allows us to see the situation from her point of view, and Galesia is a person who arouses the reader's interest and respect. Such predecessors as Mrs. Barker enabled Richardson to present his country young lady, Harriet, with

[1] Barker, *A Patch-Work Screen for the Ladies*, 1723, p. 43.   [2] Ibid.

her own observations about the town and its characters. The heroine of his domestic comedy need be neither brilliant coquette, nor boorish prude. The female novelists had also begun to portray the inner sufferings of the female heart, the suspense or unhappiness in love; a beautiful heroine may not always feel victorious, or confident of her own charms. The writers of courtship novels had shown how a female could be presented as the observing centre of interest, in social situations which are not lurid or sensational (as in the seduction tales) but governed by a refined and subtle code of moral behaviour. They had also begun to give their histories a thematic unity by dealing with the problems and behaviour of various couples in courtship and marriage.

By the time Richardson wrote *Grandison*, there was a growing demand for a more realistic fiction dealing with the love and courtship themes. That inveterate writer of popular novels, Mrs. Haywood, had already recognized the demand, and her novel *Miss Betsy Thoughtless* appeared on the scene in 1751, while Richardson was still in the early stages of *Grandison*. It is unlikely that Richardson knew any more of the book than that it existed.[1] What is really interesting about the contemporaneity of the two novels is that *Miss Betsy Thoughtless* shows us what the domestic novel of love and courtship was becoming, and gives us some idea of what would have happened to this form of fiction if Richardson had never written, as well as allowing us to perceive to what extent Richardson's own domestic comedy in prose fits into an established contemporary mode.

In *Miss Betsy Thoughtless* the author discards the vague environment of her earlier works, and establishes a definite setting for her character. The time is the present; the place,

[1] See Mrs. Anne Donnellan's letter to Richardson of 11 Feb. 1752, in which she mentions this new novel (not knowing the author) comparing it and Fielding's *Amelia* unfavourably to *Grandison*, and urging Richardson to finish his work: 'Will you leave us to Capt. Booth and Betsy Thoughtless for our examples? . . . Who the author of Betsy Thoughtless is I don't know, but his poetic justice I think very bad: he kills a good woman to make way for one of the worst, in my opinion, I ever read of: but I only mention these, to excite Sir Charles Grandison to rescue us out of their hands. (*Correspondence*, iv. 55–6.) Some readers liked *Betsy Thoughtless*, including Lady Mary Wortley Montagu, who mentions it almost, as it were, in the same breath as *Amelia* and *Ferdinand Count Fathom* (see *The Letters of Lady Mary Wortley Montagu*, ii. 280).

London. There are references to shopping, going to the theatre, attending a sale in Golden Square, hiring carriages from Blunt's, having a wedding breakfast at Pontack's. The characters are also surrounded by convincing detail; we are told, for instance, what Betsy's allowance was, and how much she spends on clothes every year. There are several comic characters adapted from stage comedy, notably Betsy's suitors, the fop Gayland, and the rough sea-dog, Captain Hyson.[1] There are occasionally very good passages of comic dialogue; the colloquial idiom and exaggerated humour resemble the style of Fanny Burney's comic passages more than Richardson's.

The theme of the novel is like that of *The Reform'd Coquet*. Betsy is good-hearted but vain, and her coquettish behaviour displeases the hero, Trueworth. Like the later Edgar Mandlebert, he keeps a critical eye on the heroine's conduct, and is displeased to find her visiting a woman of questionable morals; he is further estranged by hearing a piece of false scandal about her. Trueworth cools towards Betsy, and marries Harriet Loveit, who is virtuous, well-conducted, and high-principled. The unhappy Betsy is eventually persuaded to marry Mr. Munden, whose adoring behaviour disappears rapidly after marriage; his cruel behaviour necessitates a separation. The author cuts the knot by killing off both the unwanted spouses, the virtuous Harriet as well as the vicious Munden, so that the hero and heroine can marry. Betsy, after education in the harsh school of experience, has learned to repent her vanity and earlier flirtatious behaviour; the rigours of a difficult marriage, and the strain of endeavouring to be obedient to a man whom she does not love and who does not love her, have taught her to value a marriage based on true love, as well as to esteem prudence in conduct.

Throughout the novel, the author has displayed, although not as symmetrically as Richardson, examples of prudent and foolish behaviour in courtship, and has set in contrast pictures of bad marriages and good ones. The story is full of choric characters of the highest probity, who give quantities of good advice, repeating the maxims of the conduct books. For instance, Betsy's friend Lady Trusty advises her in her behaviour to her husband: 'I would not have you, for your sake,

[1] Hyson may also have been suggested by Richardson's Anthony Harlowe.

too much exert the wife:—I fear he is of a rugged nature,—
it behoves you, therefore, rather to endeavour to soften it . . .'¹

Although markedly inferior, much of *Betsy Thoughtless* is
compounded of the same elements as *Grandison*. In each novel
the author is examining courtship, love, and marriage from
the female point of view. In the earlier novels Richardson had
dealt with these subjects in a different way; Pamela and Clarissa
are both, for different reasons, outside the ordinary course of
polite society. In *Grandison*, Richardson deals with normal
life in the polite world. The structure of society is not questioned, as it is in *Pamela I* and *Clarissa*: society is good, and the
problems concern the achievement of happiness in a world
which is not unsympathetic—the world is congenial, and at
times very funny.

Richardson intended to instruct, and, in his gallery of marriages and courtships, to point out right and wrong behaviour
according to social duties, and particularly according to the
standards of behaviour relevant to women. Since he here
accepts society as good, the standards are those which society
at its best approves—i.e. the standards of the conduct books.
These are applied perhaps more conservatively here than in
the previous novels. We have seen that Pamela overcame a
marital difficulty by acting somewhat unconventionally. However, Richardson has applied the accepted standards in presenting the marriage of Sir Thomas and Lady Grandison; the
husband is a heartless rake, shamed by his wife's continued
patience.² The correct behaviour of Lady Grandison is in
marked contrast to the married behaviour of her daughter
Charlotte, who inherits some of her father's wilfulness, and
flouts her duty by indulging wanton petulance at the imaginary
offences of her doting husband. That the accepted standard
was there to be appealed to can be seen in Lady Mary Wortley
Montagu's reference to Halifax's *Advice to a Daughter* in criticism of Charlotte's behaviour.³ Lady Mary appears to ignore
the fact that the conduct book has already been represented in
the novel as tacit judgement of Charlotte. The energy of Lady
Mary's comment—she speaks of Charlotte as if she were a

¹ Haywood, *The History of Miss Betsy Thoughtless*, 4 vols., 1751, vol. iv, ch. vi,
p. 52.
² *Grandison*, ii. 30–4.   ³ See above p. 291.

real person—is a compliment to Richardson's ability to create characters who cannot be judged as mere conduct-book types. As Lady Mary senses, the author has a dramatic sympathy with Charlotte—she is not there merely to be proved wrong. The good Lady Grandison does not really exist within the novel except in her children's memory. The main characters have an individual life and temperament of their own. Something new has come into the English novel when Charlotte runs upstairs to Harriet's room at the Reeves', on one of her 'flying visits'[1]: 'Give me some chocolate then; and let me see your Cousin Reeves's: I like them.'[2] A character of such charm and vitality requires to be judged as an individual and no situation involving her can be seen merely in the abstract.

As soon as individual characters and their situations are dramatically investigated, Richardson is far less conventionally didactic, and the problem is seen as more complex than set standards would allow. Men ought, for instance, to be lords and masters, but what of the position of an intelligent girl like Harriet or Charlotte, who must justly find many men her intellectual and moral inferiors, but inferiors sustained by a belief in their native superiority over the opposite sex? What of the position of girls like Caroline and Charlotte, placed at the mercy of a boorish and tyrannical father, and what kind of obedience should they give? The answers to such questions are in the novel, no mere copy-book maxims, but are to be found, at least in part, in the reader's own response. His sympathies, deliberately aroused by the author, point out the complexity of cases which cannot easily be resolved by applying moral schemata.

In the marriage game, Harriet is fortunate, because she meets and marries a man who is more than her intellectual and moral equal, and whom she can treat unironically as her 'lord and master'. It was through Lady Bradshaigh's intervention that Richardson was induced to change 'Chaste conversation coupled with fear' to 'sweet conversation, *un*coupled with fear' in Sir Charles's gallant address to Harriet,[3]

[1] *Grandison*, i. 287.   [2] Ibid, p. 293.
[3] Ibid., p. 219. Lady Bradshaigh and Richardson debated upon the relation of husband to wife and the subordination of women in marriage in a lengthy sequence of letters from December 1751 to November 1752 (See *Correspondence*, vi. 128–228). Richardson claimed that a woman ought to fear her husband; his correspondent

although Richardson's imaginative examination of the best kind of married relationship does show it to be a harmonious partnership.

Charlotte, however, has not married her equal, and the reader recognizes her difficulty. The reason for her wilfulness after marriage is partly disappointment; she now realizes that her fate is decided, and she is out of the game without hope for a higher prize. Lord G. is innocently responsible for the marital dissension; his manner offers to a character like Charlotte a permanent temptation to tease. She realizes that the burden of good behaviour falls on her, not merely because of duty and precept, but because she is the superior in intellect and perception, and on her falls the onus of making things right. Also, we realize, she has more, in a way, to bear than her husband; although he is the more obvious sufferer, she never irritates him in the little exasperating humiliating ways in which he irritates her.

It is essential to Charlotte to preserve her inner freedom, even within marriage, and this is a need to which Richardson is most sympathetic. With Harriet, as with Pamela and Clarissa, the effect of such a desire in a right-minded personality is a degree of eccentricity, seen in behaviour which is moral, but not conformist. Harriet is more conventional than her sister heroines, and yet in one respect saliently unconventional. She breaks the rules in confiding to her friends her love for a man who, she fears, does not return the affection. The liberty she takes in being thus 'indelicate' has seriously affected some readers' estimation of her:

And with respect to Miss Byron, amiable as she is represented, and with qualities supposed to approach almost to those of Clarissa in her happiest state, there attaches a sort of indelicacy of which we must suppose Clarissa, in similar circumstances, entirely incapable.

hotly asserted that, while honour and obedience were demanded of a woman, fear was unnatural and destructive; 'to my husband . . . I must be all love, no mixture of fear' (ibid., p. 140), and took as her text 'perfect love casteth out fear' (ibid., p. 176).
     She obviously remembered this debate when she read the last volumes of *Grandison*; her letter to the author indicates that she felt she had won her point: 'It is worth observing, that Sr Charles tells his Har't. "She must perfect, by her Sweet Conversation *un*coupled with *fear*, what Doc^r Bartlett had so happily begun." Charming Man, *un*coupled with *fear*.' (Forster MSS., vol. xi, Lady Bradshaigh to Richardson, 30 Nov.–11 Dec. 1753, section dated 4 Dec. page 55^r.)

She literally forms a league, in Sir Charles's family, and among his friends, for the purpose of engaging his affections, and is contented to betray the secret of her own love, even when she believes it unreturned—a secret which every delicate mind holds so sacred—not only to old Dr. Bartlett but to all her own relations, and the Lord knows whom besides . . .[1]

Scott misrepresents the case—Harriet does not try to 'form a league' among Sir Charles's family, but is taxed with her feeling by the two sisters and forced to admit it to them. 'Could the most punctilious have paraded more than she did, if they would not have absolutely denied the Truth . . .'[2]

Harriet's frankness could be taken merely as a device necessary for the novelist in telling his story, but it is evident that to Richardson it is more important than that. He defends his heroine against the strictures of the novel's earliest readers; she acts with frankness and truth. 'Was she to be honest, or not?'[3] Harriet does not have the heroic strength of Clarissa, who might not have told; she is an ingenuous and warm-hearted person who needs, and trusts in, communication with others. Yet there is a kind of heroism in her honesty. She takes a great risk because she knows that if Sir Charles were to be led by his family into suspecting her feelings, and could not or did not return them, she could be the victim of his pity or his scorn. She is right to keep feelings from him, but equally right to be honest with others, instead of letting concealment prey upon her, like a worm i' the bud, and bring her to a green and yellow Melancholy.[4] Harriet's frankness is part of her own kind of virtue; her pride will not allow her to keep hidden what she knows to be a most important truth about herself. Her self-respect does not depend on that kind of pride, and nature does not bow to the convention that young ladies do not entertain any such feeling until surprised by the gentleman's proposal. 'Because, says your Ladiship, the Man had made no Declarations; and because she was in Love first.—Is she therefore not to own the

---

[1] Sir Walter Scott, 'Prefatory Memoir to Richardson', Ballantyne's Novelists Library, 1824, vol. vi, p. xxxvii.

[2] Richardson to Lady Bradshaigh, 8 Dec. 1753, *Selected Letters*, p. 255.

[3] Ibid.

[4] This passage from *Twelfth Night* is quoted in *Grandison* and provides a comment on the contrast between the two heroines; Harriet reveals her love, Clementina tries too hard to conceal it (iii. 75–6).

Truth when put to her?—And is Love then a vincible Passion, that a Lady must have an Example set her by the Man?'[1] Love is not easily vincible, and a young lady's denial of her feelings is a yielding to conventional artifice, not to morality, far less to nature. Harriet acts according to her earlier advice to Lucy, given when she herself was still heartfree: 'And why should you deny, that you *were* susceptible of a natural passion? You must not be prudish, Lucy.'[2] Harriet is not prudish, and her capacity to fling prudent discretion to the winds shows that she is a passionate person capable of making her own emotional decision. Her freedom to say what conventionally should not be said, to keep to the truth at the centre of the situation, matters more to her than maintaining her appearance as a cool and heartfree young lady, just as Pamela's truth to her own emotions and the real circumstance matters more to her than maintaining before her husband the guise of a calm and unsuspicious matron. Harriet has the strength to accept her weakness —or rather her own nature. Her response to passion is natural, not artificial, and her frankness, her lack of disguise, are qualities appreciated by the man who loves her.

Not all of our interest is to be centred upon Harriet. The pattern of the novel demands quite otherwise. A striking manifestation of Richardson's originality in this novel is the dual centre. We begin by supposing that Harriet is '*the* heroine', the focus of our attention, the primary source of our experience in the novel. In the centre of the story, we find another heroine, and our sympathies are deliberately divided. At first we share with Harriet her shock at finding out about Clementina and, like her, feel the latter to be an alien threat; then, with Harriet, we are encouraged to enter the Italian girl's world and experience, and she can no longer be considered as an alien, nor her feelings disregarded. In the first Clementina sections, Richardson's use of the time scheme is particularly interesting; time stands still for a while, to allow the past to be retraced. As in the Sally Godfrey episode in *Pamela I* but much more completely, the past of one major character becomes a factor in the present experience of another. The letter mode of narration serves to make us realize that the past is never lost. Incidents flow

---

[1] Richardson to Lady Bradshaigh, 8 Dec. 1753, *Selected Letters*, p. 257.
[2] *Grandison*, i. 96.

by and yet at the same time remain, part of the material of the present. The past is not a constant—it changes and varies, depending on who surveys it, and new experience can display the past in different colours. The rereading of the past is most strikingly shown in *Clarissa*, where earlier experiences are seen again by the heroine, after her painful recognition of the truth, in a new light. In his last novel Richardson uses the relation of past to present in a quieter manner, but we are constantly made aware of it, which is one of the reasons that reading the novel carries such a conviction of participating in the condition of 'real life'. Harriet's own immediate past—her friendship for Sir Charles and his family, her innocent and tremulous hopes, perhaps even expectations—is changed by Sir Charles's explanation of his commitment to the Porrettas, and still more by her reading of the Italian letters. When later she is truly afraid that Sir Charles is lost to her, her emotional education makes a painful advance, as she views the suffering of her own previously rejected suitors with a sadder compassion than hitherto. She suspects a bitter similarity between her insistence on calling Mr. Fowler her brother, and Sir Charles calling her his sister, and the position of such as Mr. Fowler and Mr. Orme in relation to her resembles, she fears, hers in relation to Sir Charles: 'How am I to be distressed on all sides! by *good* men too; as Sir Charles could say he was, by good women.'[1] Present experience changes the vision of the future and modifies the appearance of the past.

Harriet is placed in an unusual position, in that she must vicariously participate in her rival's feelings as well as her own, and cultivate sufficient generosity to value them almost as much. This is her heroism, her victory, as unconventional in effort and achievement as her telling her love. We are made to feel that Harriet is the superior claimant for Sir Charles and by the laws of romantic comedy ought to win him, because she is able to take on the burden of both sets of emotions, whereas Clementina, emotionally insulated, knows nothing of Harriet, but concentrates her attention chiefly on her own struggle. The difference between the two rival heroines is unobtrusively but significantly marked by the novel's narrative method. Harriet is a main narrator: she observes events, analyses and comments

[1] *Grandison*, iv. 41.

upon her own emotions and those of others. Clementina is responsible for no narration within the story: the letters she writes are emotional arguments about Catholicism or convents. She observes and describes nothing, and everything we know about her really comes through her words and actions as they are observed by others. The drama of her situation is one which she does not understand (unlike Pamela, Clarissa, and Harriet) and the reader is thus made to realize that, however delicate and spiritual her nature, she has not that refinement of consciousness which is able to organize and comprehend itself and the outer world which impinges upon it. Her attitude is thus from the beginning incomplete and subject to alteration.

Yet Clementina is meant to be a formidable rival, not only for Sir Charles's hand, but for the reader's affection. Richardson took a bold step in introducing into such a novel a heroine whose situation and sufferings are potentially tragic. As far as his earlier readers were concerned he succeeded almost too well; Clementina was a favourite and in the romantic period was commonly considered to surpass Harriet in excellence and attractions. Hazlitt complained:

There is another peculiarity in Richardson, not perhaps so uncommon, which is, his systematically preferring his most insipid characters to his finest, though both were equally his own invention, and he must be supposed to have understood something of their qualities. Thus he preferred the little, selfish, affected, insignificant Miss Byron, to the divine Clementina . . .[1]

Sir Walter Scott confidently remarked 'The real heroine of the work, and the only one in whose fortunes we take a deep and decided interest, is the unhappy Clementina, whose madness, and indeed her whole conduct, is sketched with the same exquisite pencil which drew the distresses of Clarissa.'[2]

The sense of the pathetic changes far more quickly than that of the comic. Richardson felt he was drawing upon Shakespeare for inspiration. There are several references to *Hamlet* in these sections of the novel, and Clementina is obviously supposed to be a version of Ophelia, run mad for love. Her madness is, of course, more ladylike—she does not run about dishevelled,

[1] William Hazlitt, *Lectures on the English Comic Writers*, Lecture vi, 'On the English Novelists', *Complete Works*, ed. P. P. Howe, 21 vols., vol. vi. 1930–4, pp. 119–20.
[2] Scott, 'Prefatory Memoir to Richardson', p. xxxvii.

singing questionable songs. The mad scenes were highly praised:

> It were superfluous to any one who has perused this work, to remark the masterly manner in which the madness of Clementina is painted. Dr. Warton speaks thus of it:
>
> > 'I know not whether even the madness of Lear is wrought up and expressed by so many little strokes of nature and passion. It is absolute pedantry to prefer and compare the madness of Orestes, in Euripides, to this of Clementina.'
>
> There is such a tenderness and innocence in her wanderings, such affecting starts of passion, such significant woe in her looks and attitudes, such a sanctity of mind, with so much passion, that he who is not moved with it, must resign the pretension of being accessible to fictitious sorrow.[1]

Regrettably, most modern readers must, if this is to be the criterion, resign such a pretension. Clementina seems too innocent and pathetic to awaken sympathy in the hardened modern reader. We also feel we have been transported to the Neverland of earlier novels, a land of myrtle and orange groves, where a young lady's malady can be pronounced by her physicians to be love.[2] Italy was already established as a suitable setting for novelistic adventure, intrigue, and romance. For Richardson it remained a country of the imagination, whatever pains he took to make the travel and Italian sections authentic (he may have consulted Baretti).[3] He was really drawing afresh upon the stock idea of romantic Italy—an idea which seems particularly attractive to the English mind, and which received fresh vigour from writers like Mrs. Radcliffe at the end of the century. We are inclined to dismiss Richardson's Italy as a chimerical land of beauty and passion, and Clementina as a melodramatic figure in this setting.

However, to dismiss Clementina thus lightly is to disregard the novel's balance. In the 'eternal triangle' Clementina is

---

[1] Barbauld, 'The Life of Mr. Richardson', *Correspondence*, i. xcix.

[2] *Grandison*, ii. 25.

[3] Suggested by McKillop, *Samuel Richardson*, pp. 211–12. The reviewer in *The Gentleman's Magazine* is impressed by the description of the passage over Mt. Cenis (*Grandison*, iv. 107–11) and quotes it in full (*Gentleman's Magazine*, xxiii (Nov. 1753), 512–13); Richardson probably had mixed feelings about such praise of a passage for which he must have been indebted heavily to another.

symmetrically opposed to Harriet, and provides, or is meant to provide, a counter-interest. Clementina is the loser in the game of love (which is not the customary game of wits and jealous skill, but, as Scott has lightly indicated, more like a lottery in which Sir Charles figures 'merely as the twenty-thousand prize, which was to be drawn by either of the ladies who might be so lucky as to win it'[1]). It is customary in fiction to make the rival lady who loses the hero to the heroine either insignificant or disagreeable. The heroine's competitors in Restoration comedy are usually rather poisonous *femmes du monde*, jealous cast-off mistresses. Mrs. Haywood in *Betsy Thoughtless* was sufficiently inventive to give her heroine a rival who is sweet and good—but Harriet Trueworth is a nonentity and her convenient death is unlamented by the reader. And on reading later novels few readers are concerned at the loss sustained by Harriet Smith or Louisa Musgrove, or moved by the feelings entertained by Blanche Ingram for Mr. Rochester, or (in different circumstances) by Rosamond Vincy for Ladislaw. In making the rival who is destined not to win the prize both charming and good, and putting the suffering of her passion in such a central position, Richardson is unorthodox. He paves the way to a great romantic and unorthodox novel like *Villette*. The Romantic novel begins to examine the position of the characters who do not win their heart's desire. The totally brilliant, beautiful, and victorious heroines of earlier fiction no longer make their appearance. Clementina marks a change in the study of the heroine.

Harriet is intelligent and beautiful, but she undergoes the humiliation of jealous anxiety, and for a time the desolate sense of loss. Clementina suffers more than Harriet. In her case, even more than in that of her English rival, the 'natural passion', although innocent and laudable, is dangerous, injuring the personality while awakening it.

Because Clementina is presented in a manner so foreign to the modern novel, readers are at once tempted to dismiss her and her situation as mere melodrama. Yet on rereading the book one may be surprised to find how closely she is connected with the rest of the novel, and to what an extent her situation amplifies the theme. In spite of the obvious 'staginess' in some

[1] Scott, 'Prefatory Memoir to Richardson', p. xxxvi.

scenes, Clementina has a character, and a case, and her own psychological validity.

Despite the pseudo-idyllic Italian setting, the relationships among the della Porretta family are sharply drawn. The theme of conflict within the family recurs in Richardson's novels. Pamela is the only heroine who never has to struggle against her family—and her parents are dramatic ciphers. Harriet, a wealthy orphan with loving and good-humoured relations, has more freedom than most of Richardson's girls, but even she has a slight struggle with her relatives over the Earl of D.'s courtship. She is fortunate in her uncle, who prefers humour to dignity and allows her to carry on a comic combat with him. The most notable example of the heroine at odds with her family is of course Clarissa, but Polly Darnford, Charlotte and Caroline Grandison, Emily, Clementina, and Anna Howe are all involved, with various degrees of intensity, in a struggle with one or both parents.[1]

Imaginatively, Richardson sympathizes. One of the reasons Sir Charles seems so rigid, so lacking, is that he is not allowed by his creator, restricted by making him the mirror of conventional virtue, to oppose his father—he escapes the struggle. Richardson's heroines cannot, in social fact, escape, and the strife with the parents is one of the forces that makes them mature. The author's perceptions about the family situation are very acute. Clementina's situation, controlled by her solicitous family, seems at first to represent an ideal comparable to that presented by the Selbys and the Grandisons; as we continue, we realize that this is not true. How serene and elegant (if artificial) the della Porrettas seem—how (apparently) inadequate by comparison is, for instance, the condition of the Howe family in *Clarissa*. Anna and her widowed mother carry on a grumbling series of hostilities, with intermittent periods of truce, and the occasional alliance. Anna, who is, as her mother complains, her 'father's daughter', is sharp-witted and sharp-tempered, dominating rather than obedient. She is able to turn on her mother and give more than she gets in argument, as can be clearly seen in the great debate on Mrs. Howe's possible

---

[1] Hortensia Beaumont, in the unfinished sketch of a story, is also involved in a battle with her wicked uncle and his family over the orphan girl's inheritance. ('History of Mrs. Beaumont', *Correspondence*, v. 301–48.)

remarriage, following Anthony Harlowe's letter of proposal
(itself one of Richardson's finest strokes of broad humorous
comedy).[1] Anna's sharp attack on her parent strikes very
cleverly at all Mrs. Howe's weak points—as it could not do if
Anna, an adult, did not know what was what. Her attack is
veiled in satiric humour; Anna (the narrator here) recognizes
the comedy of the situation:

M[*other*]. . . . Why, indeed, Ten thousand pounds—
D[*aughter*]. And to be sure of outliving him, Madam! . . .
M. Sure!—Nobody can be sure—But it is very likely, that—
D. Not at all, Madam . . . Why, Madam, these gentlemen who have
    used the Sea, and been in different Climates . . . are the likeliest
    to live long of any men in the world. Don't you see, that his very
    Skin is a Fortification of Buff?
M. Strange Creature!
D. . . . But suppose, Madam, at your time of life—
M. My time of life!—Dear heart—What is my time of life, pray?
D. Not old, Madam: and that you are not, may be your danger!
    As I hope to live (my dear) my Mother smiled, and looked not
    displeased with me . . . But dear Madam, if it be to *be*. I presume
    you won't think of it before *next winter*.
M. What now would the pert one be at?
D. Because he only proposes to entertain you with pretty Stories of
    Foreign Nations in a Winter's Evening.[2]

Mrs. Howe's vices are readily apparent, and her virtues less
detectable. She is greedy, complacent, vain, and a bit foolish.
If her daughter is pert, she is undignified. Yet she is not
unamiable. One of her saving qualities is her lack of pride:
because she enjoys the comfort of a retort more than dignified
silence, she treats her daughter as an equal in the fray. Indeed,
she relies on her for assistance and direction. Her temperament
makes it more convenient for her to treat her daughter as an
individual, and the affection between them is the more real
for that reason. The quarrels have helped Anna to define
herself, and have preserved Mrs. Howe, who is inclined to
sluggishness, in emotional animation.

Conventionally, such family conduct is rather shocking, but,
as Richardson shows, it works fairly well. It is better than the

---

[1] *Clarissa*, iv. 168–71.   [2] Ibid., pp. 175–180.

pursuit of power illustrated by the Harlowes. It is also, in its own way, better and healthier than the controlled serenity for which the Porrettas strive, encasing Clementina in a love as smooth as marble.

Clementina's type of character is almost the complete opposite of Anna's. In *Grandison* she is contrasted with Harriet, in whom we can see some of Anna's traits softened in a gentler and more refined but still fairly robust character. Clementina is younger than Harriet (sixteen or so when she first falls in love whereas Harriet is twenty) and her life is more sheltered. Harriet's situation among her relatives allows her some detachment. Clementina is the youngest child of a dominant father and an over-anxious mother, and she is further dominated by three elder brothers, two of whom are obviously aggressive men who prosper in the world of affairs. Unlike the Harlowes, the Porretta father and brothers are worthy of love and esteem, and their daughter deeply, and not unjustly, respects them; she has not had to learn the kind of shrewd judgement that Clarissa has had to employ in self-defence against such men as the two James Harlowes. In such an atmosphere of oppressive masculinity, Clementina's over-docile feminine tendencies have developed at the expense of her true womanliness. She is treated as a pet, a dear plaything, allowed to want nothing, and kept under control. She has remained a child. The family's care for her is too benevolent for her ever to have been taught to exert herself. She thinks and feels as her society dictates, and thus admirably in many ways, but she has thought in narrow categories, especially in regard to her family and her faith, without having to question anything.

It is suitable that she should fall in love with a man who is some years (seven or thereabouts) older than she, and the friend of her favourite brother. Also, Sir Charles acts as her tutor in giving her instruction in English, and Clementina is just the kind of young woman to be affected by the master–pupil relationship—a powerfully charged one for a woman in any case. Sir Charles teaches her to read Milton, the Protestant poet, so her process of intellectual growth begins to show her something of life's complexity. Protestants need not be wicked, nor Protestantism ugly. She falls in love with a Protestant, and her movement from the simple to the complex wreaks havoc within, as she cannot allow herself complete recogition of what has happened.

Her reluctance to face the reality is not ill founded; recognition is to be paid for in loss of security, and the childlike state of being, formless and floating in a communal identity, will have to undergo painful transformation into personal existence. Her family, like Clementina herself, attempt at first to treat her feelings as negligible: 'both my Lord, and self, hope to see her of another mind; and that she will soon be Countess of Belvedere. My Lord's heart is in this alliance; so is that of my son Giacomo.'[1] The nature of her feelings for Sir Charles is recognized with pity and then irritation. The General speaks of her love as 'a passion less excusable' than gratitude,[2] and the Porrettas allow her to be treated harshly by the Sforzas, who assert 'that she was to be shamed out of a love so improper, so unreligious'[3] and 'insisted upon her encouraging the Count of Belvedere's addresses, as a mark of her obedience'.[4] So in fact Clementina was not mistaken in unconsciously fearing that her feelings might be considered punishable.

Her situation can be compared with that of Caroline Grandison during Lord L.'s courtship. Caroline (and with her Charlotte) had to endure the malicious wrath of that tyrannical libertine their father, when Lord L.'s proposals made him realize his daughters are 'women-grown'.[5] His cruel comment to Lord L., 'I will ask her, if she wants for any-thing with me that a modest girl can wish for?'[6] is a sneer at feminine sexual feeling, and he taunts Caroline, calling her 'my amorous girl', 'Sweet impatient soul!'[7] His behaviour to his daughters is more monstrous than the Porrettas' treatment of Clementina (although the Porrettas are not unwilling to let relatives do their dirty work for them). Yet the overt hostility between Sir Thomas and Caroline, the alienation rooted in the fact that he does not really love his girls, is less damaging, as he cannot through love confuse her above her own identity and will. Obedience can be rendered, but not the total submission of all thought and feeling. Caroline also is a Grandison in being fairly strong-willed, although gentle, and she is not ignorant

---

[1] *Grandison*, iii. 59.   [2] Ibid., p. 182.   [3] Ibid., p. 183.
[4] Ibid., p. 184.   [5] Ibid. ii. 83.
[6] Ibid., p. 57.   [7] Ibid., p. 77.

about the nature of her feelings, nor ashamed, nor uncertain within her Protestant conscience (and with Charlotte to back her up) about the extent to which she is in the right.

Clementina's madness shows us a personality usually weak and timid becoming unexpectedly and perversely strong. She is not strong in the manner of Clarissa, because she has no such force of personality or comprehension of events, and it is primarily herself with whom she is at war. Like Clarissa, she is in opposition to her family; however, she does not know this— her hostility is concealed from herself, and she fights back through derangement.[1] Her Catholic faith does not allow her to recognize the force of sexual passion she has for a Protestant, and her madness is a kind of martyrdom to her faith. She has, after all, not only her family to honour; there is also the obedience she owes to Mother Church, and to her spiritual director, Father Marescotti. To the Protestant Richardson, the nurture and admonition offered by the Roman Catholic Church undoubtedly appeared weakening to the highest development of character, suppressing or tacitly discouraging individual moral choice. Such a view of Catholicism is not uncommon among English writers, then or later. Richardson, unlike contemporaries and successors, implies this view, and does not state it categorically. His Anglicanism is not antipathetic to some elements of Catholicism (witness the elements of saint's legend in *Clarissa*), and imaginatively he is surprisingly ready to sympathize and unwilling to condemn. We do not hear from him the fulminations against priestcraft, tyranny, absurdity, and tawdry ceremony which so readily emanate from the pens of Defoe or Charlotte Brontë. Clementina's faith is not ridiculous but real and valuable, and its claim on her is not an appeal to superstition, but to the highest elements of her own nature. Her suffering is seen as an emblem of the sacrificial nature of Christian belief, and in its emotional emphasis provides a counterpoise to the rational 'chearfulness' of the practical Christianity that Sir Charles represents. The various aspects of Clementina's state—suppressed hostility, inadequately recognized sexual desire, and Christian sacrifice—

---

[1] Morris Golden has indicated this in his brief and disdainful discussion of Clementina: 'Madness becomes her medium for forcing her will upon others' (*Richardson's Characters*, p. 71).

are all vividly represented in the scene in which she escapes
from the doctor's lancet, and then allows herself to be bled:

O my mamma! And *you* would have run away from me too, would
you!—You don't use to be cruel; and to leave me with these doctors
—See! see! and she held out her lovely arm a little bloody, regarding
nobody but her mother; who, as well as we, was speechless with
surprize—They did attempt to wound; but they could not obtain
their cruel ends—And I ran for shelter to my mamma's arms
(throwing hers about her neck)—Dearest, dearest madam, don't
let me be sacrificed. What has your poor child done, to be thus
treated? . . .
Her brother begged of her to submit to the operation. Her
mother joined her gentle command—Well, I won't love you brother,
said she: You are in the plot against me—But *here* is one who *will*
protect me; laying her hand upon my arm, and looking earnestly
in my face, with such a mixture of woe and tenderness in her eye,
as pierced my very soul . . .
Dearest madam, said I, submit to your mamma's advice. Your
mamma wishes you to suffer them to breathe a vein—It is no more—
Your Jeronymo also beseeches you to permit them.
And do *you* wish it too, Chevalier?—Do *you* wish to see me
wounded?—To see my heart bleeding at my arm, I warrant. Say,
can *you* be so hard-hearted?
Let me join with your mamma, with your brother, to entreat it;
For your father's sake! For—
For *your* sake, Chevalier?—Well, will it do you good to see me
bleed?
I withdrew to the window. I could not stand this question; put
with an air of tenderness for me, and in an accent *equally* tender.
The irresistible Lady (O what eloquence in her disorder!)
followed me; and laying her hand on my arm, looking earnestly
after my averted face, as if she would not suffer me to hide it from
her—Will it, will it comfort *you* to see me bleed? Come then, *be*
comforted; I *will* bleed: But you shall not leave me. You shall see
that these doctors shall not kill me quite.[1]

The sexual overtones of this scene are obvious. We may
perhaps be reminded of the title of the Jacobean play *Love Lies
Bleeding*, and the emphasis on 'blood' and 'bleeding' is more
like an effect in a late-Jacobean or early Caroline play than
in a typical polite novel. It does seem too that Clementina,

[1] *Grandison*, iii. 126–30.

presenting herself to Sir Charles as the victim, and requiring him to desire that she should be pierced, is, unknown to herself, making a kind of sexual statement. Richardson's contemporaries were greatly impressed with the innocence of Clementina's mind, the fact that in her insanity she never utters anything impure or immodest, but the reader is certainly not left in doubt as to the source of her trouble. The reader is also to be made aware of her presence as a real physical object—literally of flesh and blood.

Clementina is in this scene using the opportunity to make her family suffer. They have been cruel to her, in more than in merely delivering her to the attention of the doctors. She is now being disobedient, and, defended by her illness, reproaching them for their over-protectiveness while at the same time demanding, as a child, more parental love. Her childishness is shown in her whole reaction, and in the atmosphere of rather cloying family relationships. 'Mamma' is a word constantly repeated. One cannot envisage Clarissa using this childlike language, or endeavouring with such earnestness to retreat to infancy. Scott was not quite right in indicating that Richardson drew these scenes in the same way as the sufferings of Clarissa. In tone, shading, meaning the picture is widely different.

The scene quoted also represents Clementina's other passion —equal and conflicting—her dedication to her religion. Her pose, as the blood trickles down her arm, recalls the Catholic images or paintings of saints suffering martyrdom for the Faith. The erotic and mystical are mingled in Catholic symbolism, and Richardson fittingly combines the two in these passages. If Clementina is wooing Sir Charles as a possible love-object, she is also appealing to him to join the true Church. The two instincts—sexual and religious—are equally strong, but Clementina has refused to understand exactly where they are at war within her, and her suffering manifests a conflict of which she herself does not wish to be entirely aware. A short while ago she has strongly denied entertaining love for Sir Charles, quoting to him the Shakespearian passage beginning 'She never told her love' and adding 'Now Chevalier, if you had any design in your pointing to these very pretty lines, I will only say, you are mistaken: and so are all those who affront and afflict me, with attributing my malady to so great a weakness.'[1] The trouble here is that her denial is asserted to herself as much as to anyone else. Harriet's diagnosis seems fairly adequate: 'A flame, the most vehement, suppressed from motives of piety, till, poor Lady! it has devoured her intellects!'[2] It is the suppression (partly what we would call repression) that does the damage. Clementina, in endeavouring to suppress her feeling, clings to the position of the child, with its privileges not only of innocence, but of ignorance.

When Sir Charles returns, and her mind is calmed, she is able to recognize consciously what all her difficulties are; when she realizes that he may marry her, but will never become a Catholic, she has to face reality, and choose between two equal, real, and acknowledged passions—faith and love. Her family pass the freedom of choice to her: like all of Richardson's heroines she violently craves freedom of choice although she is, of all of them, least aware of her own need. Once free, she is able to make a conscious decision—to give up Sir Charles and remain sure of her Catholicism—without breaking down again under the strain of shouldering the consequences. Psychologically, this seems valid—it is not the fully conscious decision, even if painful, which damages the mind, but the unconscious conflict of unrecognized emotions. Clementina has grown up, and is no longer in the childlike state of her first happy, and negative, innocence.

The distress of her experience is not meant to be seen as negative. Love and the conflict it arouses make for maturity. Perhaps a character like Clementina's would never leave the nestling state if no acute crisis were thrust upon it, but that she is capable of this conflict proves her worth. The struggle would not have occurred had she been too phlegmatic a spirit to fall in love, or if she had been facile and worldly, ready to think Sir Charles worth a Mass. Her madness makes her at last an individual; her experience is one which her family cannot share. As her malady progresses, she acquires more dignity. Her mania about her religion has that about it which resembles the romantic imagination, as in Coleridge's famous comparison. Her madness is not delusion; she is almost visionary, and her suffering, her insanity, confer upon her the role of the saint

[1] *Grandison*, iii. 68.   [2] Ibid., p. 84.

and sibyl—much of what she says on the subject of faith is true, and it is deeply true to Clementina who is ardently emotional.

One of the interesting aspects of Clementina's case is the fact that her story appealed so strongly on the Continent, where Catholicism was still the major force in cultural life and religious thought. Richardson's imagined Catholic piety seems to have struck the right note. In Germany, Clementina was greatly beloved. The novelist and dramatist Christopher Martin Wieland wrote a play based on the novel, *Clementina von Porretta* (1760). In this version, Clementina has the story to herself: Sir Charles is devoted to her, and there is no thought of Miss Byron. The end of the story is changed; after sacrificing Sir Charles, she is to be allowed to enter a convent, to devote her last days (she is mortally ill by now) completely to God. The play ends on her exultant celebration of faith, despising the things of the world:

> Die Welt rollt unter meinen Füßen; unbegrenzte Himmel öffnen sich über mir! — Selige Einsamkeit! . . . Willkommen, du werthes Bild des Grabes, worin ich bald diesen, dem Tode geweihten Leib niederlegen werde, um in das unsichtbare Land der Unsterblichen zurückzukehren![1]

The happy ending of the real Clementina, part of whose cure and education is accepting life in the world, is obviously felt unsuitable to such a saint.

Chateaubriand in *Le Génie du Christianisme* (1802) cites Clementina as an example of the beauty and nobility of Christian emotions. Expounding Christianity to an age and a country which had become sickened of the worship of the Goddess of Reason, he emphasizes, not the reasonableness, but the emotional power of Christianity, which ennobles the passions and appeals to man's deepest needs and highest aspirations. Among literary examples expressing the new and noble passions evoked by Christianity, he cites Rousseau's Julie and then adds 'Voulez-vous un autre exemple de ce nouveau langage des passions inconnu sous le polythéisme? Écoutez parler Clémentine; ses expressions sont peut-être encore plus naturelles, plus

---

[1] C. M. Wieland, *Sämmtliche Werke*, Leipzig, 1857, Band 28, *Clementina von Porretta*, VI. xii. 199.

touchantes et plus sublimement naïves que celles de Julie . . .'[1]
There follows a long quotation from the French translation
of the novel.[2] It is interesting that Chateaubriand prefers the
style of Richardson's character to that of Rousseau's. It seems
that Richardson thrilled a nerve now defunct with the accents
of exalted piety. Clementina is pathetic, not tragic like Clarissa,
and our age shrinks from pathos. The fact that she is merely
pathetic makes it relatively easy for the author to change her
situation from misery to moderate happiness and hopeful
prospects. She is not the gallant victim of fate, and, until she
has suffered, her identity as a person is incomplete. Yet her
piety and her derangement had a particular appeal to readers
of the late eighteenth and early nineteenth centuries. Perhaps
an era which had over-emphasized the rational was struck by
Clementina's madness as a symbol of the unconscious world
breaking through, and with the advent of Romanticism was
able to appreciate the picture of emotion's capacity to raise
and solve its own problems. Clementina is a dominantly
emotional character, whereas Harriet, however much her
emotions are involved, is dominantly rational.

Clementina presents something new in the novel. It is not
easy to trace her origin back to drama, as with Pamela,
Clarissa, or Charlotte, or to earlier novels, as with Harriet. Her
affecting qualities, her rhapsodic style, belong to the Romantic
mood to come. Yet Richardson, while fully conscious of the
unusual quality of Clementina and her appeal (and of his own
faculty for creating pathetic scenes), never intended to let her
take possession of the story, or provide the dominant voice and
view in the novel. He did not intend the reader's response to
her to be too simple: '"It appears to you impossible to exalt
Harriet above, or even to an Equality with Clementina."—Yet
calling her Names again in the same Paragraph—"Sweet
Enthusiast; Narrow-principled; Yet cannot blame her"—
Charming Puzzle! how I enjoy it!'[3] She is an ambiguous
character, and our reaction to her 'enthusiasm' is not to be

[1] Francois René, Vicomte de Chateaubriand, *Œuvres complètes*, 36 tomes, tome
ii, 2 ème partie, chap. iv, pp. 202–3.

[2] It is a translation of the passage beginning 'Let me beseech you, Sir, to hate . . .
the unhappy Clementina . . . but, for the sake of your immortal Soul, let me conjure
you to be reconciled to our Holy Mother Church' (*Grandison*, iii. 160–1).

[3] Richardson to Lady Bradshaigh, 8 Dec. 1753, *Selected Letters*, p. 254.

uncritical. Eventually her romantic exaltation is subdued, not to mere prudence or hard common sense, but to a wider social sympathy which Richardson saw as more healthy. Even a modern critic who is extremely impatient with Clementina seems to share Scott's and Hazlitt's disappointment at her fate:

> Her position as an ideal of fantasy is irrevocably undermined, and she is demoted from tragic heroine to girl next door. Though we are supposed to admire her acceptance of social restraint as a triumph it is ultimately unlike the triumphs of the other heroines, a denial of the values of her original attitude ... Such an approach is useful for the conscious moralist, but it completely subverts both artistic consistency of tone and that tragic understanding which is the essence of *Clarissa*.[1]

The artistic consistency of tone is, however established throughout by Harriet, not Clementina, who is not a narrator. The mingling of tones is daring, and has not been perfectly successful, but Richardson's excellence, as an artist and as a moralist, lies here in making the reader's sympathies fluctuate. Clementina's original attitude is neither completely affirmed nor denied as an ideal, but whatever its excellence, it has been seen from the beginning as incomplete. Her essential 'nobility' in her adherence to her faith is not reversed; what she has to do is to find a means of living by her decision. She does not live in a world so harsh and cruel as to drive her into isolation, and standing by her faith does not demand from her any response as absolute as standing by godliness in an evil world demands of Clarissa. If Harriet, the more complex character, supersedes Clementina in our interest, we shall feel her private heroism, in her struggle with her own jealousy, provides a standard by which Clementina's attitude can also be evaluated. Clementina's sufferings, except as they evoke Harriet's generosity and compassion, imply no new standard by which Harriet is to be judged. Harriet is already capable of feeling, and her character is in no way reproached through our vision of Clementina's intensity. Thus, Harriet has what Clementina lacks (judgement, generosity, understanding of others as separate individuals) but Clementina possesses little or nothing that Harriet lacks.

Clementina's capacity for feeling is not to be destroyed or

[1] Golden, *Richardson's Characters*, p. 71.

contemned, but she is invited to withdraw the attention of her feelings from herself and her own circumstances. Even her religious emotions have a certain self-centredness—unlike Clarissa she has the unimpaired chance to serve God in a beneficent world—and her desire to retire into a convent may not be piety so much as an unhealthy tendency to continue fascinated brooding upon her circumstances and a retreat to a sheltered state resembling that of her earlier childlike condition. Having discovered that she has a separate identity, an ego, she had better learn how to live with it. We may be reminded of Imlac's advice to Nekayah, when the latter's self-indulgent mourning, a non-religious fixation, has led her to desire a convent: 'Do not suffer life to stagnate: it will grow muddy for want of motion: commit yourself again to the current of the world . . .'[1] Johnson's appeal is not to dry reason, but to life's natural tendency. Richardson in *Grandison* takes on the whole a similar classical view and in his picture of Clementina tacitly rejects a romanticism which would make intensity of feeling the criterion of its validity.

Clementina needs to be reclaimed into the world—unlike Clarissa (and again in entirely different circumstances) she has a mind that could easily stagnate. Her sympathies need broadening. Harriet has learned, although the lesson is hard, to appreciate Clementina without personal acquaintance: Clementina requires personal acquaintance to appreciate Harriet. Clementina's bolt to England is highly imprudent, and could be taken merely as a sign that her mind is still unhinged, if it were not a flight into, instead of away from, reality. She has to see and know the truth of Sir Charles's marriage, and she is correct in thinking this will reconcile her to the real situation. Everything needs to be proved on her pulses—she has surprisingly little common imagination, despite her capacity for exalted vision. One of the wholesome aspects of her flight is her escape from her family: she knows this can only be temporary, but it provides her with a little of that freedom she needs so much. Her individuality is developing; she is capable of acting independently, and, as she says, rashly. She refuses to be directed as formerly by her family, and

[1] Samuel Johnson, *Works*, ed. Arthur Murphy, 12 vols., 1823–4, vol. iii, *The History of Rasselas, Prince of Abissinia*, ch. xxiv, p. 397.

married off to the Count, but instead of retreating into madness she is able to rebel, and finds expression in action. For a passive soul like Clementina, a little rebellion is an excellent thing. One feels that the proud and over-protective family deserve their shock: 'Good Heaven! could Clementina della Porretta be guilty of such a rashness?'[1] and it may also be that Clementina enjoys administering it: 'I, who am a runaway from the kindest, the most indulgent of parents—God forgive me!— Yet, can I say, I repent?—I *think*, I can.—But at best, it is a conditional repentance only, that I boast of.'[2] That it takes Clementina a long time to develop is understandable, considering her background. She still tends to think and talk only of herself and very seriously, and she cannot look at any circumstance with objectivity. She is the only one of the major Richardson heroines who does not possess a sense of humour. Anna Howe, rational individualist and the opposite of Clementina in most respects, turns to wit almost too readily, as first resort. Meeting a situation through the exercise of a sense of humour, as Anna so ably does, is completely impossible to Clementina because she has no sense of herself as separate from other people, and cannot perceive her world. Outer reality frightens her very much—she is the only Richardson heroine who refuses to recognize the fact of sex. Anna is able to accept it and to joke about it. Clementina refuses to let go of her precious ignorance, and has to be compelled to recognize the sexual fact (and that the instinct is part of her nature) along with the equally important and not unconnected fact that she is a person. Sexual 'innocence' and the lack of humour are not unrelated.

Clarissa possesses a sense of humour, but she is always a strong individual (though her individuality develops) and never relies on ignorance as protection. (This makes it the more ironic that she is so deceived.) Her hold on reality is very strong, and she is brought to suffering for reasons which were not in her control, nor the invention of her own emotions. Nor does Clarissa go to pieces when life becomes hard. Her madness is only momentary; she does not seek it as refuge. In the prison scenes she has lost none of her strength of mind. Clementina (whom one could not imagine in such circumstances anyway)

---

[1] *Grandison*, vi. 109.   [2] Ibid., p. 118.

could never have replied to her tormentors as Clarissa replies to the sneering prostitutes. Clementina tends to disintegrate when things become difficult. Since she herself is the unwitting cause of most of her suffering, her situation can be put right, and she herself can develop naturally as a more complete person. She is brought into the world of Grandison Hall, where life is not suffered to stagnate, and where her friends cultivate her as a woman instead of treating her, as did the della Porrettas, as a child.

The critical response evoked, in the past, by the rival heroines of the novel has resembled a more modern strain of criticism of the heroines of *Sense and Sensibility*. The relative merits of Elinor and Marianne have been similarly canvassed, and there are not lacking those who would award the palm of excellence to Marianne, just as in the past readers like Scott and Hazlitt declared for Clementina. The views of Jane Austen and of Richardson in *Grandison* are markedly alike, and it is probable that the structure of *Sense and Sensibility* with its two heroines was influenced by Richardson's comedy. Both novels stand for restraint, self-command, humour, social obligation, against romantic and self-indulgent attitudes. Yet Richardson takes the romantic attitude seriously, is willing to explore it, and does not see it as ridiculous. What it stands for, at its best, can be included in the vision of natural order. At times, in *Sense and Sensibility*, one feels that Jane Austen thought so too, but one cannot be sure. Her heroines run to extremes; it is a mistake to take Elinor as merely a figure embodying good sense, but she can be read in that way, whereas no one could see Harriet thus. However, both Elinor and Harriet come to terms with themselves, their circumstances, and other people, while Clementina and Marianne tend to remain wrapped up in themselves. In the middle of *Sense and Sensibility* Marianne becomes more interesting than she is at the novel's outset, more like a Clementina figure and far less of a satiric type, but the censure passed on her is more severe, and she is rendered almost abject. She *is* 'demoted to girl next door', her rapturous love for Willoughby exchanged for her excessively prosaic marriage to the lugubrious Colonel Brandon. Clementina is wooed by the young and handsome Count Belvedere, her countryman and fellow Catholic, and her fate is pleasanter than being thrust into the arms of a rheumatic gentleman in a flannel waistcoat, like poor Marianne. It is a piece of literary tact that the Italian heroine is not married at the end of the story, and the union is only a conditional future prospect. Clementina's attitude may be modified but the authenticity of her earlier attitude and experience is never derided. For a generation or two after Richardson, her experience, so power-fully drawn, seemed the only one worth while. To a modern generation, it seems melodramatic, but the statement of the novel as a whole is not that of melodrama. The techniques Richardson uses to show a refined but immature personality undergoing a violent crisis in the process of achieving a fuller identity are not those we should use but the process itself is not incredible. Richardson's vision of madness falls between the two common views of his century; he sees it as neither a fall into absurdity and anti-reason, nor as the inspired source of universal wisdom. He relates it to the individual who suffers it, and considers that the deranged person may have something important to say (especially for and to herself) but not every-thing. His view of breakdown as purposive, of value in assisting attainment of identity, is curiously modern. The world which Clementina flies, and to which she returns, a more competent person, is not that of Clarissa, but of the della Porrettas, of Sir Charles, of Harriet, and it is a world worth learning to live in. The careful subordination of Clementina's responses to those of Harriet, and of the Grandison society, keeps her in a perspec-tive consciously maintained by the author, a perspective which serves somewhat the same moderating purpose (although the means are so different) as the poised irony of Jane Austen.

There are two other female characters in Grandison who are also aspirants for Sir Charles's love. Each is a foil to one of the two major heroines. Olivia, the passionate Italian lady, is supposed to function as comment upon Clementina. The reverse of over-controlled, she is totally independent, financially and morally, and sets up her own will in disregard not only of convention, but of others. She is a slave to her love for Sir Charles, and the result is not mental but moral chaos. Like Clementina, but far less innocently, she is self-centred (and intensely serious about herself) but her egotism is destructive and (as she possesses, instead of too much docility, no docility at all) she cannot be educated by experience into better behaviour. As a concept, the character of Olivia is not altogether bad, but it must be admitted that she is a melodramatic and unconvincing type—despite the fact that Richardson may have been drawing upon his own experience to some degree in presenting this 'violent Roman Catholic' who does her own proposing.[1] Richardson had some fondness for Olivia, and reproached his friends for not liking her, or understanding the 'noble End' for which she was introduced, although he was slightly conscious himself that her actions might not seem perfectly comprehensible: 'Had I had time and room I would have given her History at length, and made this appear probable.'[2] There is little that a lengthy history could do for Olivia's plausibility. She seems to have emerged straight from the pages of the more sensational *novelle* of the 1720s, and could be transplanted back without exciting surprise. Olivia is strikingly like the bold temptress Ciamara, whom Mrs. Haywood's hero, Count D'Elmont, meets in Italy. Ciamara, who has fallen violently in love with the hero, invites him to her home, where she appears in all her beauty, her hair 'black as Jet' adorned with diamond bodkins which glitter 'like Stars darting their fires from out a sable Sky'.[3] Ciamara tries to persuade D'Elmont to love her, although he protests he cannot, as he is already bound in honour to another: '. . . ungrateful and uncourtly Man said she, looking on him with Eyes that sparkled at once with Indignation and Desire . . .'[4] Ciamara becomes alternately more pleading and more indignant. When he endeavours to leave, she gets between him and the door, and throws herself into his arms: 'Pardon me, Madam, answer'd he fretfully, and struggling to get loose from her Embrace . . . Hear me but speak, resum'd she grasping him yet harder; return but for a Moment—lovely Barbarian— Hell has not tortures like your Cruelty.'[5] Olivia is just such another passionate Italian, with her dark hair and her black eyes, which shine with a 'piercing lustre',[6] and her fiery impetuous temper. She falls madly in love with Grandison, and pursues

[1] See above, pp. 7–8.
[2] Richardson to Lady Bradshaigh, 8 Feb. 1754, *Selected Letters*, p. 278.
[3] Haywood, *Love in Excess*, part iii, p. 66.
[4] Ibid., p. 70.   [5] Ibid., p. 73.   [6] *Grandison*, iii. 396.

him, in Italy and in England, with her offers to be his without
any conditions or contract; 'Had Sir Charles been a Rinaldo,
Olivia had been an Armida.'[1] She exhibits her Italianate
temper by attempting to stab her beloved with a poniard.[2]
Her speech is in high novelettish style: 'the moment . . . we
were alone, her eyes darting a fiercer ray, Wretch, said she,
what disturbance, what anxieties, hast thou given me',[3] and
her conduct is after the same manner: 'Her behaviour afterwards was that of the true passionate woman; now ready to
rave, now in tears.'[4] Olivia with her wealth and unbridled
passion and rages is just as artificial as Mrs. Haywood's Ciamara.
Richardson said that he introduced her to show the virtue of
the hero, but this is unnecessary. If we believe the hero was
chaste, we believe it no more for seeing him resist the attentions
of such a cardboard virago. And if we are going to appreciate
Clementina, we will appreciate the scruples of Clementina's
conscience which forbade her to give in to love without such a
tawdry example of an Italian female whose passion had no
measure. Like the earlier novelists, Richardson had some
sympathy with ebullient passion, unwilling to be fettered by
morality, but Olivia's appearance on the scene is an unfortunate
tribute to the excitements of the older novel.

Olivia has been generally, and justly, ignored, but little
Emily Jervois has been a general favourite. None of the characters in *Grandison* is more attractive or more originally conceived than this young girl, shy and pert by turns, who is just
on the threshold of womanhood. The author does not devote
as much space to the development of her character as is allotted
to Harriet, but she is a convincing personality from her first
appearance. A half-orphan, and saddled with a dreadful
raffish mother whose conduct is a source of anxiety, Emily
is emotionally dependent on the Grandisons, and her hero-
worship of her guardian is on the point of becoming a more
tender sentiment. When Miss Byron is introduced to the group,
Emily, who is a trifle afraid of Charlotte's saucy tongue, has a
younger-sisterly adoration for her, until this amiable situation
is threatened by mutual jealousy. Harriet, with unwitting
hyprocrisy, at first pities Emily's condition, but becomes upset

[1] *Grandison*, iii. 415.   [2] Ibid. iv. 5.
[3] Ibid., p. 383.   [4] Ibid., p. 384.

when she fears Emily's affection for Sir Charles might be returned:

I don't love whispering, said Miss Jervois, more pertly than ever: But my guardian loves me; and you, Ladies, love me; and so my heart is easy.
Her heart easy—Who thought of her heart? Her guardian *loves* her!—Emily sha'n't go down with me, Lucy.[1]

The contrast between the two girls is well done, and not over-emphasized by the author: Emily is not really aware of her feelings; Harriet is painfully aware of her own emotions, and has, at least partially, to recognize and conquer her own jealousy, first of Emily, then of Clementina.

Emily herself is tempted by jealousy, but she has less spite in her character than Harriet potentially has. She is hurt by Sir Charles's marriage to Harriet (which she had thought to be the event she desired) but her melancholy is alleviated by her visit to Northamptonshire; the new family relationship has a tonic effect, and she reaches the state of maturity where she can begin to analyse what her feelings have been.

It is true, I was, (or I might have been I should rather say) a forward girl with regard to him: But then my whole heart was captivated by his perfections, by his greatness of *mind*: that was all. May not a creature, tho' ever so young . . . have a deep sense of gratitude for kindness conferr'd? That gratitude may, indeed, as she grows up, engage her too deeply; and *I* found myself in danger; but made my escape in time.[2]

Instead of breaking down from blighted affection, she follows Harriet's pattern of self-control and the application of a good sense which allows for sensitivity and sensibility. The Italian heroines, the good and the bad, get so involved in their own feelings that they are unobservant of anything else, but Emily, like Harriet, is sociable and perceptive about other people. As she grows up throughout the book, her naïve letters become increasingly chatty and observant, and they have the charms of modesty and delicate humour. We feel that she will mature into an attractive woman. Despite her *gaucherie*, her femininity blossoms early. Richardson was criticized for showing so young a girl in love, but his response was an appeal to nature and to

[1] Ibid. ii. 296.   [2] Ibid. vi. 293.

fact: ' "Ashamed for your Sex, when you think of her Age."
O dear! O dear! Ashamed of human Nature! Do all fruits
ripen alike? Ask this Question in your Orangery, Madam.'[1]
Emily's feelings, and their ingenuous manifestations, are natural.
The picture of Emily is of a very nice adolescent growing up.

Emily, like Harriet and Clementina, moves from a limited to
a wider view. Luckily, she is brought up in a family which
encourages her to be a person. When the novel closes, Emily is
still slightly younger than Clementina was when the Italian
girl first met Sir Charles, but she is more mature, if less elegant.
Like the young Clementina, the young Emily is not readily able
to deal with others, but she is taught to do so—her passivity
is not exploited. Her violent mother quite understandably
frightens her (the picture of Mrs. O'Hara is that of a somewhat
deranged personality) and Emily does require protection, but
when this protection and assurance are given, she is not
encouraged to forget her mother's existence. She is not kept
too safe; unpleasant reality is not removed from her horizon.
Sir Charles makes her invite Mrs. O'Hara to the house, and
her daughter must talk to her.[2] Eventually, Emily is able to
make her own generous response to her mother on her own
initiative, when they meet in the mercer's shop, and her
generosity is not the result of ignorance.[3]

Even as Emily comes to terms with her feelings for Sir Charles
and conquers her jealousy of Harriet, new demands are made
on her, and she has to continue to react. She must manage the
attentions of James Selby,[4] and (by the end of the novel) understand her feelings about Edward Beauchamp. She describes the
situation to Harriet:

Here every-body is fond of Sir Edward Beauchamp. He is indeed
a very agreeable man. Next to my guardian, I think him the most
agreeable of men. He is always coming down to us. I cannot but
see that he is particularly obliging to me. I really believe, young as
I am, he loves me: But every-body is so *silent* about him: yet they
slide away and leave us together very often. It looks as if all favoured
him; yet would not interfere . . . His address is *so* gentle: His words
are *so* soothing: His voice—To be sure he is a very amiable man!

[1] Richardson to Lady Bradshaigh, 8 Dec. 1753, *Selected Letters*, pp. 258–9.
[2] *Grandison*, ii. 391.   [3] Ibid. iv. 70–1.
[4] Ibid., p. 214.

Now tell me freely—Do you think my guardian . . . would be displeased if matters were to come to something in time?—Three or four years hence, suppose . . .?[1]

She is still naïve but she is learning. It is very good for her to be left alone to manage things on her own, and have to decide for herself. The over-protected Clementina was not allowed to have her own emotions. The true devotee of *Grandison* wants to know if Emily does marry Beauchamp, but all the signs are that she will, and probably sooner than the time she here suggests. By the time she marries, she will be not only a good and charming woman, but also a fairly strong character (she could have been otherwise).

The Grandisons and Selbys are families in which personal development can take place. They are animate, allowing members to change, unlike the della Porrettas. Their harmony is achieved through allowing conflict to some degree as an alternative—they accommodate tension and discord as the Italian family does not. (This is reflected in the common tenor of their lives—Grandisons and Selbys tease each other, della Porrettas do not.) They provide an environment which enables the individual female to understand division within herself without being too frightened by it. And they recognize that, as Mrs. Shirley tells Harriet, 'Love . . . is a natural passion.'[2]

The vitality of the female characters in love with Sir Charles persuades us of his existence and importance, and the variety of character throughout the novel persuades us that the theme of love and courtship has been exhaustively discussed. For all the girls who fall in love with the hero—except Olivia, who is incorrigible and incredible—love is an educative experience. The novel is the only one which has (ostensibly) a male central figure, but he is static, and our attention is directed to the women around him. Their feelings are made vivid and interesting, and the rather stolid theme of the Christian hero is counterbalanced by the complex theme of love, so that we feel we have been reading a novel about passion rather than about morality. The kind of Christianity and hence the kind of world presented through Sir Charles suggests that all things work together for

[1] Ibid. vi. 294.   [2] Ibid. ii. 18.

good; then the conflict of love shows this is true in a far more interesting manner than the copy-book morality says. Richardson required a total theological background which entailed moral and social optimism before he could be optimistic about individual cases. He may have overdone the emphasis on 'chearful' Christianity, but the temptation to do so was the stronger after he had just said the opposite in *Clarissa*. The novel is not, however, a picture of placid happiness (it is doubtful if a novel ever has been or could be written on such a subject). It is optimistic in showing that happiness is possible. But the happiness in which Richardson is interested is the happiness of maturity, and, paradoxically, this fuller happiness of maturity is attainable only through some subtle kind of suffering. The suffering comes in self-recognition and self-division. To judge oneself at all is a kind of self-division. Falling in love, with its attendant possessiveness, anxiety, fantasies, jealousy (and the haunting suspicion of being somewhat absurd), entails some pain. Harriet's recognition of the irony of the situation, in her poignant cry that 'Love is a narrower of the heart', expresses a conflict within herself unknown before. It is in the middle of the novel when Harriet realizes her inner discord that she becomes truly important to us, and we realize why, in James's phrase, it is worth making such an 'ado' about her. All the heroines in *Grandison* (discounting Olivia but including Charlotte) become larger, more important personalities. Through their difficulties they achieve a finer union of heart and mind, sense and sensibility. Each becomes less egotistical, more capable of seeing the outer world and recognizing other people. This must be what George Eliot meant when she said of the novel 'The morality is perfect'.[1]

Because we know that the young women are all making the effort to leave the nest of ignorance and self-involvement, to grow up, we are able to accept the abundance of happiness and joyful domestic life without finding it cloying. Nothing is ever comfortably sluggish; within the domesticity we recognize a grace strenuously achieved. The heroines (each with her

---

[1] George Eliot to Sara Hennell, 13 Oct. 1847: 'Thank you for putting me on reading Sir Charles Grandison . . . I had no idea that Richardson was worth so much . . . The morality is perfect—there is nothing for the new lights to correct.' (*The George Eliot Letters*, ed. Gordon S. Haight, 6 vols., 1954–6, i, 240.)

qualities and limitations) are important: 'What in the midst of that mighty drama are girls and their blind visions? . . . In these delicate vessels is borne onward through the ages the treasure of human affections.'[1]

[1] George Eliot, *Daniel Deronda*, 4 vols., 1876, vol. i, chapter xi, p. 221.

XIII

'A Fiddle and a Dance': Patterns
of Imagery in *Sir Charles Grandison*

IN both *Pamela* and *Clarissa* we have observed Richardson's use
of cumulative imagery to convey the atmosphere of the novel
and much of the inner meaning of the story. In *Pamela I* the
instinctive life is suggested through the references to the
element of earth, and to simple domestic objects, to clothing
and food, which satisfy basic needs. Richardson's use of imagery
in *Clarissa* is more complex, rich, and varied; the images which
accumulate and reflect upon each other are powerful and disturbing symbols. In examining Richardson's use of this technique in *Grandison* we find that it differs again from the previous
novels. The question of the relation of nature and civilization,
which we find in *Pamela*, is here explored again, but in a
different way. The use of imagery is much less intense than in
Clarissa, more open and casual, demanding less from the reader.

Yet, many of the same images are used in *Grandison* and
Clarissa. Perhaps *Grandison* could be described as the obverse of
Clarissa. In the tragic novel, false courtship is consummated in
an act of hatred, and leads to the ceremony of the funeral. In
the last novel, true courtship leads to the ceremony of marriage,
to joy and fruition. What goes wrong in *Clarissa* is made right
in *Grandison*. The images used in *Clarissa* are given a new meaning and direction. As the strenuous Latitudinarian morality
is infused with a comic sense and optimistic spirit which the
author shows are appropriate to it, a new world is created for and
by the characters, in which a happy resolution of discord and
disorder is constantly shown to be possible.

One of the most striking examples of the difference between
the imagined worlds of these two great novels is found in the use
of animal imagery in each. The animal imagery in *Clarissa* is

harsh and frightening. Even the animals of farm and barnyard
are used to suggest ugliness, lust, or stupidity. The cock gives
the hen a grain of corn, a 'dirty pearl', so that he may tread
her.[1] The greedy, stupid Joseph Leman looks forward to his
marriage with Betty, his 'pretty Sowe', and the happy time to
come when they will keep 'the Blew Bore' as his master promises.[2] Images of predators abound; Lovelace is not only the
lion,[3] but also the spider who catches the fly.[4] Men can be
worse than animals: 'I would rather be a dog, a monkey, a
bear, a viper, or a toad, than thee', says Belford to Lovelace,
perhaps echoing Rochester.[5]
Man in general is an animal, and one of the worst of animals:

> Lords of the Creation!—Who can forbear indignant Laughter!
> . . . For what has he of his own, but a very mischievous, monkey-
> like, bad nature? Yet thinks himself at liberty to kick, and cuff, and
> elbow out every worthier creature: And when he has none of the
> animal creation to hunt down and abuse, will make use of his
> power . . . to oppress the less powerful and weaker of his own
> species!

Human beings are by nature cruel: 'There is more of the
Savage in human nature than we are commonly aware of.'[7]
Lovelace's treatment of women is of a piece with the 'sportive
cruelty' of boys in caging birds.[8] Man shares in the universal
savagery of creation. 'All the animals in the creation are more
or less in a state of hostility with each other', as Anna Howe
notices, illustrating her point with her own fable drawn from

---

[1] *Clarissa*, iii. 133. The image is perhaps suggested by John Gay's 'Before the
barn-door crowing', in *The Beggar's Opera*; (see 3rd ed., 1729, II. iv, Air xxiii, p. 25).
[2] *Clarissa*, iii. 247. Joseph's prospective marriage is strongly reminiscent of
Swift's description:

> They keep at Stains the old Blue Boar,
> Are Cat and Dog, and Rogue and Whore.

(*The Poems of Jonathan Swift*, ed. Harold Williams, 3 vols., 1937, 'Phillis, Or, the
Progress of Love', i. 225.)
[3] *Clarissa*, i. 257.   [4] Ibid. iii. 67.
[5]

> I'd be a Dog, a Monkey or a Bear,
> Or anything but that vain Animal
> Who is so proud of being rational.

(John Wilmot, Earl of Rochester, 'A Satyr against Mankind', *Poems on Several Occasions*, 1691, p. 89.)
[6] *Clarissa*, vi. 428–9.   [7] Ibid. iv. 15.   [8] Ibid., pp. 12–13.

the behaviour of her game chickens: 'Peck and be hanged said I . . . for I see it is the *nature of the beast*.'[1]

Most of the characters in the novel are in a state of nature as nasty and brutish as Hobbes imagines it. Without grace, man is left with his 'monkey-like, bad nature', an irredeemable Yahoo.

In *Sir Charles Grandison* also, animals are frequently used in simile and metaphor, but the tone is changed. True, at the beginning of the novel, something of the *Clarissa* pattern recurs. Men in relation to women are savages or beasts;[2] Sir Hargrave, the would-be abductor, uses Lovelace's metaphor of spider and fly.[3] However, after Sir Charles and the rest of the Grandison family appear, a gentler tone prevails. Sir Charles, describing his rescue of Harriet, comments on her throwing herself into his arms: 'Have you not read, Mr. Reeves (Pliny, I think, gives the relation) of a frightened bird, that, pursued by an hawk, flew for protection into the bosom of a man passing by?'[4]

The image is in effect the reverse of the image of the man with the caged bird that Lovelace uses, just as Sir Charles's treatment of Harriet is the reverse of Lovelace's treatment of Clarissa. After this point, animal imagery is used with suggestions of amusement and affection, instead of horror and disgust. Charlotte ridicules Lord G.'s 'collection of Butterflies, and other gaudy insects', but qualifies her raillery by a serious remark: 'I never saw a collection of these various insects, that I did not the more admire the Maker of them, and of all us insects, whatever I thought of the collectors of the minute ones.'[5] All creatures, including man, show forth the glory of God's creation to the enlightened eye. Such an attitude seems unremarkable, being so typical of its time, until we remember how much it differs from Richardson's picture of the world in *Clarissa*. Charlotte finds collectors a trifle absurd, but there is nothing ugly in the 'playful studies'. The cruelty involved in such collecting is not indicated (one wonders what Lovelace would have made of it).

Most of the animal imagery in *Grandison* emanates from Charlotte, the witty observer and tease whose comments connect the nobler attitudes and relationships of the central

---

[1] *Clarissa*, iii. 230.   [2] *Grandison*, i. 28; 92.   [3] Ibid., p. 250.
[4] Ibid., p. 213.   [5] Ibid., p. 351.

characters with the world of normal life. From her 'unromantic' standpoint we are given a view of a world somewhat absurd but agreeable, which is a suitable setting for the main comic action. Harriet compares Charlotte, with her love of teasing, to a kitten: 'it is not so much the love of power that predominates in her mind, as the love of playfulness: And when the fit is upon her, she regards not whether it is a China cup, or a cork, that she pats and tosses about . . .',[1] and Charlotte uses the same comparison in describing herself.[2] The emphasis is upon the kitten's playfulness; it is specifically stated that Charlotte does not act from love of power. The tone is strikingly different from that of Lovelace's reminiscence:

> I once made a charming little savage severely repent the delight she took in seeing her tabby favourite make cruel sport with a pretty sleek, bead-eyed mouse, before she devoured it. Egad, my Love, said I to myself . . . I am determined to lie in wait for a fit opportunity to try how *thou* wilt like to be tost over *my* head, and be caught again: How *thou* wilt like to be patted from me and pulled to me.[3]

The image of the caged bird, so frightening when used by Lovelace, becomes gentle and attractive in *Grandison*. Emily looks 'as sleek and as shy as a bird new-caught', when conscious of James Selby's admiration.[4] Charlotte uses the metaphor of the bird in the cage to express her rather sulky feelings about the married state: 'My Lord, to be sure, has dominion over his bird. He can choose her cage.'[5] The metaphor thus used is in the tradition of the discontented wife in stage comedy: Margery Pinchwife compares herself to 'a poor lonely, sullen Bird in a cage'.[6] But Charlotte is not a Margery. The comparison is not seriously meant; she says it to annoy her poor husband who, far from victimizing his wife, has to struggle to prevent her dominating him completely.

When Charlotte has settled into married life, and is expecting a baby, the image of a bird in a cage becomes that of the bird on the nest:

> These vile men! I believe I shall hate them all. Did *they* partake—

---

[1] Ibid. iii. 344.   [2] Ibid. v. 360.   [3] *Clarissa*, iv. 16.
[4] *Grandison*, iv. 214.   [5] Ibid., p. 196.
[6] Wycherley, *The Country-Wife*, 1675, iii. i, p. 32.

But not half so grateful as the blackbirds: They rather look big
with insolence, then perch near, and sing a song to comfort the poor
souls they have so grievously mortified. Other birds, as I have
observed (sparrows, in particular) sit hours and hours, he's and
she's, in turn; and I have seen the hen, when her rogue has staid
too long, rattle at him, while he circles about her with sweeping
wings, and displayed plumage, his head and breast of various
dyes, ardently shining, peep, peep, peep; as much as to say, I beg
your pardon, Love—I was forced to go a great way off for my
dinner—Sirrr-rah ! I have thought she has said, in an unforgiving
accent—Do your duty now—Sit close.—Peep, peep, peep—I will,
I will—Away has she skimmed, and returned to relieve him—when
she has thought fit.[1]

Charlotte starts her mock-complaint as if she were going to say
that the animal world is better than the human, but the scene
is a little parody of her own domestic life, with the meek,
apologetic male faced by the scolding wife. The birds are
attractive; the passage is a pleasant comic touch far removed
from the sinister implications of fables and animal comparisons
in *Clarissa*. The monkey image, earlier used in Charlotte's
slightly acid remarks on foolish men,[2] recurs at the end of the
novel: Charlotte refers to her baby as the 'little Marmouset'.[3]
There is a great distance between the vile 'monkey-like bad
nature' of humankind in *Clarissa* and this term of endearment.
There is no hostility between nature and reason in *Grandison*,
as there is between fallen nature and grace in *Clarissa*. We have
moved from the climate of Hobbes and Rochester to that of
Thomson's *Seasons*. The imagery of nature in *Pamela* (largely
earth and vegetation) authorises the health of instinctual life,
but does not suggest that nature is elegant. In *Grandison*, nature
is tractable, and civilization is the apotheosis of nature, not a
mask concealing the horror beneath.

In *Clarissa*, which deals so much with the relation of illusion
and reality, the image of dress, which becomes so strongly
connected with disguise, enforces the contrast between the
delusive and the real. The heroine in her undressing for death
has to put away the trappings of luxurious dress, and reject the
tempting world of appearance. In *Grandison* description of dress

---

[1] *Grandison*, v. 207–8.   [2] Ibid. i. 435; iv. 275.
[3] Ibid. vi. 231, 240.

indicates character: Aunt Nell wears juvenile pink and yellow ribbons,[1] Sir Rowland Meredith is arrayed in old-fashioned finery, and is innocently proud of his gold buttons.[2] This usage is a convention in novels of manners, including Richardson's earlier books. Dress is also used to indicate states of mind, as in all the scenes involving Clementina.[3] Indeed, in the scenes involving Clementina the symbolism is so obtrusive that the reader may feel that Clementina is forced upon him as a parallel to Clarissa. Actually, Harriet is the counterpart of Clementina, and the more interesting and intricate references to Harriet's dress are also symbolic, relating her to Clarissa by an almost exact contrast.

The masquerade scene near the beginning of *Grandison* is the only occasion in which the disguise theme, which figures so prominently in *Clarissa*, is of importance. The use of such a scene is a later version of an effect achieved earlier in *Pamela II*; in both descriptions he captures the pert badinage, and phantasmagoric atmosphere.[4] The relation of appearance to reality always fascinates Richardson; here there is a more optimistic contrast between the falsity of artifice and the truth of enlightened nature than anything in *Clarissa*.

It is suitable that Harriet, a country innocent and a romantic heroine, should appear as an Arcadian princess. We are given a lengthy description of her dress (chosen by her friends) which she dislikes for its gaudiness:

> They call it the dress of an Arcadian Princess: But it falls not in with any of my notions of the pastoral dress of Arcadia.

[1] Ibid. v. 57.   [2] Ibid. i. 105.

[3] Clementina at the height of her insanity dresses in black, with a black veil (ibid. iv. 142). When improving, she decides to wear colours, but displays 'fancifulness in the disposition of her ornaments' (ibid., p. 229). The interview with Sir Charles, in which she finally rejects him, is the substitute for the wedding she denies herself, and she appears in 'white satten' (ibid., p. 288). When recovered, and more independent, she is dignified, and 'charmingly dressed' (ibid. vi. 210).

[4] *Pamela*, iv. 95–7; *Grandison*, ii. 215. Richardson had never attended such an entertainment (see his letter to Mrs. Chapone, 11 Jan. 1751, *Selected Letters*, pp. 172–3). He might have been impressed by descriptions in the *Spectator*, and the moral attitude there is like his own. (*Spectator*, vol. i, number 8, pp. 35–8; also ibid., number 14, pp. 60–5.) Richardson, who never attended a masquerade, made the scene popular in the English novel; Fielding includes one in *Amelia* (vol. iii, book x, chapter ii, pp. 70–82) with the same disapproval, and Fanny Burney is obviously indebted to Richardson in her description of the masquerade in *Cecilia, or Memoirs of an Heiress*, 5 vols., 1782, vol. i, book ii, ch. iii, pp. 175–217.

A white Paris net sort of cap, glittering with spangles, and in-
circled by a chaplet of artificial flowers . . . is to be my headdress.

My shape is also said to be consulted in this dress. A kind of
waistcoat of blue satten trimmed with silver Point d'Espagne, the
skirts edged with silver fringe, is made to sit close to my waist by
double clasps, a small silver tassel at the ends of each clasp; all set
off, with bugles and spangles, which make a mighty glitter . . .

My petticoat is of blue satten, trimmed and fringed as my waistcoat. I am not to have an hoop that is perceivable. They wore not
hoops in Arcadia.[1]

Harriet is like an Arcadian princess, but the costume exaggerates and distorts her real personality, and conceals her true
freshness and innocence in ostentatiously calling attention to
them. The dress itself is in bad taste, reflecting no kind of truth,
historical or literary, and is contrived only for 'mighty glitter'.
It expresses the false luxury and inane pretension accepted by
a certain kind of empty-headed London society, the moral
average from which she is to be rescued. The heroine seems to
make an erroneous *début* into the wrong society, and is almost
initiated into sexual experience and married life with the wrong
partner. The colours of white, blue, and silver, even in this
garish dress, have 'a bridal appearance' (as Clementina later
says of her own white and silver[2]), and when Sir Hargrave
abducts and tries to marry her, her costume is a mockery of a
bridal gown. It is significant that she has this 'bridal appearance' when she first meets Sir Charles, although she is only
humiliated by recollecting the figure she made in 'that odious
Masquerade-habit', with her arms clasped about Sir Charles's
neck.[3]

At Colnebrooke, Harriet is relieved of everything that is
false and foolish. She has been rescued from the follies and
temptations of a world of artificial manners. Harriet says in
rapture 'I have fallen into the company of angels.'[4] Yet this
perfection is not isolated from the best that the world has to
offer, and virtue, in Grandisonian terms, is predominantly
social. The wedding, which combines love between individuals
with social responsibility, is the major symbol of the book, as
the funeral is of *Clarissa*. Clarissa moves from the false wedding

---

[1] *Grandison*, i. 172–3.   [2] Ibid. iv. 288.
[3] Ibid. i. 279.   [4] Ibid., p. 201.

(with Solmes, with Lovelace) to the true wedding, as the bride
of Christ. Harriet moves from the grotesque wedding nearly
achieved by Sir Hargrave to the true wedding, the union with
the 'godlike' Sir Charles, whose realm, however virtuous, is
most definitely of this world. Harriet's wedding is a reward for
an honesty of heart which has cast aside folly, affectation, and
pride, not only as presented by the world of the London masquerade, but also as inward temptations during the trial of her
love. Like Clarissa, and yet how completely differently, the
bride is her real and finest self: 'Harriet, as you shall hear, is
the least shewy. All in Virgin white. She looks, she moves, an
Angel.'[1] Colour and pageantry surround her in the wedding
procession:

As soon as the Bride, and Father, and Sir Charles, and Mrs.
Shirley, alighted, these pretty little Flora's, all dressed in white,
chaplets of flowers for headdresses, large nosegays in their bosoms,
white ribbands adorning their stays and their baskets; some stream-
ing down, others tied round the handles in true lovers knots;
attended the company; two going before; the two others here and
there, and every-where; all strewing flowers . . .[2]

There is a resemblance in the very contrast between Harriet
in her glory and Clarissa, who also appeared in virgin white,
simple and unadorned. There is pageantry surrounding Clarissa
too, in her last great procession in the hearse, and maidens
with flowers also surround her, to carry the coffin, and strew the
corpse.[3]

Riches multiply for Harriet, who after the simplicity of her
wedding day makes her first public appearance as a matron
'ornamented by richer silks than common, by costly laces, by
jewels'.[4] Sir Charles had made her a present, at their engagement, of costly jewels: 'The jewel of jewels, however is his
heart!'[5] She receives another gift of gems from her adopted
'father', Sir Rowland, including 'A costly diamond necklace
and ear-rings, a ring of price'.[6]

Clarissa sells her silks and laces to purchase her coffin, and
gives her jewels away. When she puts off the false glory of the
world, it means the spiritual dressing for death. Harriet puts
off the world's false glory only to put on the true glory the world

[1] Ibid. v. 367–8.   [2] Ibid., p. 376.   [3] *Clarissa*, viii. 76–7, 80–1.
[4] *Grandison*, v. 420.   [5] Ibid., p. 239.   [6] Ibid. vi. 64.

has to offer; she forsakes the tinsel only to be decked out in diamonds.

The 'house' image found in *Clarissa* is used in *Grandison* to quite different effect. In London, the Grandisons and their acquaintance live in St. James's and Grosvenor Squares, the new squares in the best area of town, far removed from the surroundings of Clarissa in her ill-fated sojourn in London. Mrs. Sinclair's brothel in Dover Street, Mrs. Moore's poky lodgings in Hampstead, the Smiths' cramped shop in Covent Garden—these are at a great distance, geographically and socially, from the environment of Harriet and Sir Charles. Clarissa's lodging in London was the pit of hell; Harriet, visiting the Grandisons in their town house, finds a foretaste of heaven in the exalted atmosphere of wealth, taste, and refinement.[1]

One of the most attractive houses in the novel is Selby-house, Harriet's home in Northamptonshire, a pleasant and unpretentious country residence. The room to which Harriet most often and most affectionately refers is the 'cedar-parlour', which suggests old-fashioned beauty, a comfortably rural elegance. This is the room for confidences. Near Selby-house is Shirley-manor, 'a fine old seat . . . with an estate of about *500 l.* a year round it.'[2] Its agreeable drawing-room is the setting for the young ladies in their 'vast hoops' sitting in the seats of the old-fashioned bow-window.[3] (It is here also that Sir Charles, to Harriet's admiration, refuses a chair and sits on the floor—as Richardson endeavours to make his oppressively majestic hero more boyishly engaging.[4])

Except in the description of Grandison Hall, Richardson is economical, making one detail (such as the cedar-parlour) do the work of a great deal of minute description. As always he is interested in showing movement in space; we see characters going from room to room, dining, taking tea, conversing,

---

[1] *Grandison*, i. 365.   [2] Ibid. iv. 219.   [3] Ibid. v. 168.

[4] Ibid., p. 169. There is an amusing echo of this scene in Mrs. Charlotte Smith's *Emmeline* (1788) when the Grandisonian hero Godolphin, meeting the heroine and her friend sitting on chairs on deck during a Channel crossing on a packet-boat 'threw himself on the deck at their feet', in order to converse—an exploit which sounds somewhat more painful than that of Sir Charles, who only 'threw himself at the feet of my Aunt and me, making the floor his seat'. (See Mrs. Charlotte Smith, *Emmeline*, ed. Anne Ehrenpreis, Oxford English Novels, vol. iv, ch. vii, p. 418.)

dancing, or seeking solitude in which to think and write. We admire the eighteenth century for its taste in architecture and furniture, and its love of the civilized and beautiful in ordinary life, but no novelist of distinction gave us just this sort of domestic atmosphere before Richardson. Jane Austen, who is also careful to let us know in what room a conversation took place, and to show us her characters' movements from solitude, or intimate discussion, into company, owes a debt to him. It is significant that her nephew mentions her knowledge of Richardson's novels in terms which intimate that she paid close attention to details of rooms and conversation in *Grandison*:

Her knowledge of Richardson's works was such as no one is likely again to acquire, now that the multitude and merits of our light literature have called off the attention of readers from that great master. Every circumstance narrated in Sir Charles Grandison, all that was ever said or done in the cedar-parlour was familiar to her; and the wedding days of Lady L. and Lady G. were as well remembered as if they had been living friends.[1]

Houses are important in all of Richardson's novels. There is a change from the first part of *Pamela I*, in which Mr. B.'s house is a prison, to the later part, and the sequel, in which houses are favourably described. The change is parallel to the change in setting from the prisons of *Clarissa* to the mansions of *Grandison*, although in neither of the two *Pamela* novels are the images as effective as in the two later books. The beautiful houses in *Grandison* provide more than merely a pleasant setting; they are outward and visible signs of the good life to be achieved.

On her marriage, Harriet becomes mistress of the largest and finest house of all—a mansion which has figured tantalizingly in the previous narrative, but which we do not see until Harriet goes to Grandison Hall as Lady Grandison. In these descriptions, as in a more ambitious painting on a larger canvas, we recognize effects previously sketched in *Pamela II*. Like her humbler sister, Harriet is exalted, her moral authority confirmed by her higher position.

Harriet, who admires the picture gallery at Grandison Hall, is very conscious that she has taken on a family heritage. Such an aristocratic house represents in miniature English life, its tradition and future. The house and some of the furnishings are

[1] J. E. Austen-Leigh, *Memoir of Jane Austen*, ed. R. W. Chapman, 1926, p. 89.

old, but the music room is a recent addition, and Sir Charles's scientific instruments and his collection of *objets d'art*—'pictures . . . of the best masters of the Italian and Flemish schools, statues, bustoes, bronzes'[1]—are innovations. Contemporary elegance and enlightenment achieved in harmony with an old and solid tradition is an eighteenth-century ideal which Grandison Hall exemplifies.[2]

The grounds, as well as the house, become important as a new setting for the characters, and we are often aware of the background, as in the charming glimpse of Clementina feeding the deer in the park.[3] This is a particularly pleasing moment, as Clementina in so much of the novel is not seen doing anything except meditate on her lot, and here she is unselfconscious, attending to something other than herself, and at one with the natural surroundings into which she has been released; there is something more constricting in the Porretta gardens, with their maze-like walks. Lucy describes house and grounds in detail as precise as if the reader were to draw a map. We know of the trout streams, cascade, and orangery; there are alcoves, temples, rustic seats, but the greatest attention is given to nature:

> The park itself is remarkable for its prospects, lawns and rich-appearing clumps of trees of large growth; which must therefore have been planted by the ancestors of the excellent owner; who, contenting himself to open and enlarge many fine prospects, delights to preserve, as much as possible, the plantations of his ancestors, and particularly thinks it a kind of impiety to fell a tree, that was planted by his father.[4]

Sir Charles agrees with Pope's dictum: 'In all, let Nature never be forgot.'[5] He is the opposite of the type of Sabinus' foolish son, 'Foe to the Dryads of his Father's groves'.[6] Sir Charles's

[1] *Grandison*, vi. 22.

[2] Richardson must have obtained the idea of Grandison Hall in fleeting views of such 'stately homes' as were then open to the public. So impressively has he depicted the gentleman's house of the period that the description of Grandison Hall is quoted as an illustration of the larger type of eighteenth-century country mansion. (See Geoffrey Webb, 'Architecture and the Garden', *Johnson's England*, vol. ii, ch. xviii, pp. 102–3.) There is gentle irony in the fact that Richardson, who lived most of his life in the inelegant suburban environment of Salisbury Court, is the author to furnish such an example of rural splendour.

[3] *Grandison*, vi. 280.   [4] Ibid., p. 25.
[5] Pope, *Epistle to Burlington*, l. 50.   [6] Ibid., l. 94.

care and prudence, as well as his love of beauty and respect for
the past, are seen everwhere:

> He will do any-thing that tends to improve the estate; so that it is
> the best conditioned estate in the county. His tenants grow into good
> circumstances under him . . . In a few years, improving only what
> he has in both kingdoms, he will be very rich, yet answer the
> generous demands of his own heart upon his benevolence . . .[1]

As a landowner, he represents everything his age admired:

> His Father's Acres who enjoys in peace,
> Or makes his Neighbours glad, if he encrease;
> Whose chearful Tenants bless their yearly toil,
> Yet to their Lord owe more than to the soil;[2]

like Pope's ideal, the Grandison house is an earthly paradise,
an example of what humanity can attain if man uses reason in
accord with nature.

   Within the novel, there is an overt comparison between the
moral ideal which Sir Charles represents, and the beauty and
order of his house and estate, in the passage in which Harriet,
after describing the beauties of Grandison Hall, touches on the
view of the estate: 'The gardens and lawn seem from the
windows of this spacious house to be as boundless as the mind
of the owner, and as free and open as his countenance.'[3] The
tone of the whole passage is not very different from that of
Fielding, in his description of Squire Allworthy's house and
estate, which concludes with the sight of Mr. Allworthy on the
terrace, overlooking his estate, with its lawn, lake, grove and
park,

> where the dawn opened every minute that lovely prospect we have
> before described to his eye. And now . . . in the full blaze of his
> majesty, rose the sun, than which one object alone in this lower
> creation could be more glorious, and that Mr. Allworthy himself
> presented; a human being replete with benevolence, meditating in
> what manner he might render himself most acceptable to his
> Creator, by doing most good to his creatures.[4]

In both novels, the gentleman's residence, with its well-kept
mansion and estate, is a symbol of nobility of mind which finds
its best expression in the social order. Tom Jones, when his

---

[1] *Grandison*, vi. 48.   [2] Pope, *Epistle to Burlington*, ll. 181–4.
[3] *Grandison*, vi. 24.   [4] Fielding, *Tom Jones*, vol. i, book i, ch. iv, p. 12.

innate nobility has been educated and enlightened by experience, returns to his true inheritance, Allworthy's house;
Harriet, after displaying her true goodness of heart during the
trials of her love, is rewarded by becoming mistress of Grandison
Hall.

Harriet's marriage is an entry into a larger world; she has
more happiness and more opportunity for giving happiness now
she is 'The declared mistress of this spacious house, and the
happiest of human creatures!'[1] Clarissa's 'enlargement' was in
death, and the 'house' she purchased was a coffin. Harriet is
given the kind of joy which was denied Clarissa. Her personality,
more amiable and less heroic than Clarissa's, finds its expression
on the plane of ordinary life at its best, and the best of ordinary
life is signified by the material beauty that surrounds her. The
rooms and furniture are minutely described by the delighted
bride; the appeal of the materials—'hangings . . . of beautiful
paper', 'crimson damask', 'crimson velvet, lined with white
silk'—is sensuously evoked.[2] Richardson uses such an unusually
detailed description of the house and grounds because he
wishes the estate to be a strong image at the end of the novel,
like a theme repeated in the major key at the close of a symphony. However, if he had not written *Clarissa*, he might not
have felt it necessary to dwell in such detail upon the picture of
earthly felicity. If Clarissa's 'house' had not been what it was,
he might not have desired to tell us so much about Harriet's
house. In this image, so differently used, and yet with points of
similarity (such as the furnishing in velvet and white silk), he
firmly establishes an acceptance of the world to counterbalance
the rejection of the world which is the resolution of *Clarissa*.

There is one very important image in *Grandison* which is not
found in *Clarissa*, a controlling metaphor for the world the
author wishes to create, suggesting the relation of passion and
reason, nature and art. Music is a major image in *Grandison*.
Richardson thought of his comedy of courtship in terms of
music, as can be seen in his jovial remarks to Hester Mulso:
'But will you have the story end with a fiddle and a dance: that
is to say with matrimony; or will you not? If you will, Harriet
must have her difficulties. If not, the dance may be the sooner
over, in order to make the happy pair shine in the matrimonial

---

[1] *Grandison*, vi. 19.   [2] Ibid., pp. 23–4.

life.'[1] Music and dancing, traditional elements of stage-comedy, are part of the novel's entertainment, and furnish comments upon the story.

Richardson's use of music here is slightly surprising when the attitude to music expressed in the *Pamela* sequel is considered. Playing and singing are there used to suggest the elegance of high life, and the atmosphere of harmony about the heroine, in a manner that anticipates *Grandison*.[2] But music is still viewed with a good deal of suspicion; it may be that the author's attitude to the refinements of high life changed slightly between the two novels. Pamela remarks upon the opera:

> If, Madam, one were all Ear, and lost to every Sense but that of Harmony, surely the *Italian* Opera would be a transporting Thing! —But when one finds good Sense, and Instruction, and Propriety, sacrific'd to the Charms of Sound, what an unedifying, what a mere temporary Delight does it afford! For what does one carry home, but the Remembrance of having been pleas'd so many Hours by the mere Vibration of Air, which being but Sound, you cannot bring away with you; and must therefore enter the Time passed in such a Diversion, into the Account of those blank Hours, from which one has not reap'd so much as one improving Lesson?[3]

Pamela's comment is not merely the commonplace of her time, a censure of the absurdity of operatic plots and *libretti*. At the heart of her statement is a criticism of the very nature of music: that it cannot instruct, but can only delight. Other arts can make direct moral comment; Richardson seems inclined to class music as a pleasure of the senses alone, and hence suspect in its nature. Music seems to negate language, the instrument of reason; while listening to it, the soul is morally inactive, which means that the pastime is, at best, a waste, and at worst, dangerous. Pamela's statement might lead one to believe that the author must have been totally insensitive to music, but this could well be a misinterpretation. When Pamela says that you can bring nothing 'away with you', she means that you have gained nothing that can contribute to your moral life. Richardson may have been as severe upon music as he is here in *Pamela* because he was susceptible to its charms.

In *Grandison*, music is presented favourably throughout;

---

[1] Richardson to Hester Mulso, 27 July 1751, *Selected Letters*, p. 187.
[2] e.g. *Pamela*, iii. 322–3.   [3] Ibid. iv. 89.

there is no suggestion that it is inimical to the moral life. On the contrary, an enjoyment of music is one of the expressions of the well-ordered soul. Musical allusions are also important in the novel's structure; many of the most important junctures in the action are signalized by detailed references to music, and it is often used to create atmosphere, and to suggest the major themes of the novel.

One of the functions of music is to establish an atmosphere of comedy, and this is its use in the first lengthy passage in *Grandison* involving a discussion of music and a musical event. In London, Harriet is inconvenienced by the attentions of two unwanted suitors: Greville, the rough country gentleman, and Sir Hargrave Pollexfen, the rakish gentleman of the town. On one awkward occasion, their visits to Harriet coincide, and music becomes the ostensible topic of a conversation in which each gentleman is determined to insult the other. Sir Hargrave, who has travelled, defends the quality of London entertainments, while Greville, who knows nothing of the matter, protests that performances abroad, particularly in Italy, are better. The vulgarity and stupidity of both parties are well presented in a humorous dialogue.[1] The comedy of the dialogue is well brought out, particularly in Greville's sulky riposte, 'Handel, Sir Hargrave, is not an Englishman.'[2] The discordant jangling of the two boors is emphasized by their argument upon music while they themselves, as Harriet notes, have no knowledge of it.

To soothe their discord, Harriet accedes to Greville's request: 'Music! if Miss Byron will give us a song, and accompany it with the harpsichord, I will despise all other harmony.'[3] She plays and sings two songs set by Galliard, 'Chloe, by all the pow'rs above' and 'The Discreet Lover'.[4] The lyrics of the first, approved by the gentleman, but not by Harriet, describe feminine inconstancy; the second describes the kind of love that Harriet approves, which is 'tender inclination'[5] rather than passion. The song is ironic in its relation to the main story; here Harriet is theorizing from inexperience, her heart still untouched. The kind of love which does eventually bring her 'the *lasting* joys of life'[5] will be unexpectedly disturbing, more

---

[1] *Grandison*, i. 157–60.   [2] Ibid., p. 158.   [3] Ibid., p. 160.
[4] Ibid., pp. 160–1.   [5] Ibid., p. 161.

ardent than the calm liking approved in the short lyric. This
moment captures the atmosphere of this period of her life before
she has met Sir Charles, and the music, like her feelings, is
light, cheerful, and detached. Harriet playing upon the harpsichord is a picture of all that is socially agreeable, but she is
more than this. At the beginning of the novel Greville describes
her: 'And have I not seen her dance? Have I not heard her
sing?—But indeed, mind and person, she is all harmony.'[1] At
the outset, Harriet's skill in music is connected with her harmony and grace of soul. Her playing is in itself a lesson in conduct, as Johnson says his 'Stella's' music could be:

> Mark, when the different notes agree
> In friendly contrariety,
> How passion's well-accorded strife
> Gives all the harmony of life;
> Thy pictures shall thy conduct frame,
> Consistent still, though not the same,
> Thy musick teach the nobler art
> To tune the regulated heart.[2]

Harriet is to seek 'the harmony of life'; after some discord,
when she is tried by the passions of love and jealousy, she is to
prove herself an example of the regulated heart.

When she meets the Grandisons, Harriet describes the
relationship among them as 'Such a family harmony'.[3] Their
emotional concord is expressed in their love of music. Charlotte
is a mistress of the art, as Harriet realizes when she hears her
idly playing before breakfast: 'She touched the keys in such a
manner, as shewed she could make them speak what language
she pleased.'[4] When Harriet visits the Grandisons at their house
in St. James's Square, the ladies entertain the company with
music. Charlotte, at her cousin's request, plays and sings
'Shakespeare's Cuckow', and 'with so much spirit and humour,
as delighted every-body'.[5] Lady L. plays 'one of Scarlatti's

---

[1] Ibid., p. 10.

[2] Samuel Johnson, 'To Miss — On her playing upon the harpsichord in a room hung with some flower pieces of her own Painting', ll. 29–36, first published in *The Museum* (number xviii, 22 Nov., 1756); see *The Poems of Samuel Johnson*, ed. David Nicol Smith and Edward L. McAdam., 1941, pp. 120–1.

[3] *Grandison*, i. 309.   [4] Ibid., p. 310.

[5] Ibid., pp. 365–6. Charlotte probably sang 'When daisies pied' to the setting of Thomas Arne, published in his first volume of Shakespeare songs in 1741.

lessons'.[1] Harriet herself is a trifle shy, but is soon called upon
to perform:

It is referred to you, my third sister, said Sir Charles . . . to favour
us with some of Handel's music: Mrs. Reeves says, she has heard
you sing several songs out of the Pastoral, and out of some of his
finest Oratorio's.

Come hither, come hither, my sweet Harriet—Here's his Alexander's Feast: My Brother admires *that*, I know; and says it is the
noblest composition that ever was produced by man; and is as
finely set, as written.

She made me sit down to the instrument.

As you know, said I, that great part of the beauty of this performance arises from the proper transitions from one different strain to
another, and one song must lose greatly, by being taken out of its
place; and I fear—

Fear nothing, Miss Byron, said Sir Charles: Your obligingness,
as well as your observation, entitle you to all allowances.

I then turned to that fine piece of accompanied recitative:

> Softly sweet, in Lydian measures,
> Soon he sooth'd his soul to pleasures.

Which not being set so full with accompanying symphonies, as
most of Mr. Handel's are, I performed with the more ease to myself,
tho' I had never but once before played it over.

They all, with more compliments than I dare repeat, requested
me to play and sing it once more.[2]

The characters define themselves by what they choose to play.
Charlotte's piece suggests wit and gaiety; Lady L.'s performance, her elegance and brilliance. Harriet performs a piece
by the composer whom the characters (and evidently their
creator) most admire. Richardson's description of this musical
evening is more than a mere reference to a fashionable and
innocuous pastime establishing the tone of high life. The author
wishes the reader to share the occasion as audience and to hear
in imagination the specific melodies involved. Richardson
could be assured that most of his readers would know *Alexander's Feast*, and would remember the music.[3] Harriet does not
choose one of the more stirring sections of the piece, but,
significantly, the part in which love is involved; the melody is

[1] *Grandison*, i. 366.   [2] Ibid., pp. 366–7.
[3] Handel's *Alexander's Feast* met with great success on its first performance in
1736 and had been repeatedly produced in public in the next decade.

as explicitly suggested to the reader as a novelist can suggest a particular air. Her choice indicates more than the fact that she is an accomplished young lady. Unconsciously she is expressing her own feelings, wooing Sir Charles with the music. This moment captures her early, less strained acquaintance with Sir Charles, new friendship finding expression in graceful entertainment, and in the tender, almost languishing melody (an air exploiting a full feminine voice, with its emotive changes from high to low soprano register) which is the manifestation of Harriet's new, half-understood emotions.

Handel's *Alexander's Feast* runs as a kind of *leit-motif* throughout the novel. It is sung again, in the little family concert after Charlotte's wedding:

> Mr. Beauchamp took the violin; Lord L. the bass-viol; Lord G. the German-flute; Lord W. sung bass; Lady L., Lady G. and the Earl, joined in the chorus. The song was from Alexander's Feast: The words,
>> *Happy, happy, happy pair!*
>> *None but the* good *deserves the fair*;
> Sir Charles, tho' himself equally *brave* and *good*, preferring the latter word to the former.[1]

Sir Charles's variation upon Dryden's words certainly seems unnecessarily priggish, although Lord G. could more justifiably be celebrated for virtue than for conspicuous valour. The original adjective is used to describe Sir Charles when the disappointed Greville quotes the couplet on relinquishing Harriet and giving her hand to the hero.[2]

Charlotte's wedding, which comes at an important juncture in the novel, is celebrated by a ball, of which Harriet gives a lengthy and detailed account:

> Lord G. began by dancing a minuet with his bride: She danced charmingly: But on my telling her so afterwards, she whispered me, that she should have performed better, had she danced with her brother. Lord G. danced extremely well.
> Lord L. and Lady Gertrude, Mr. Beauchamp and Mrs. Reeves, Mr. Reeves and Lady L. danced all of them very agreeably.
> The Earl took me out: But we had hardly done, when, asking pardon for disgracing me, as he too modestly expressed himself; he,

[1] *Grandison*, iii. 367–8.   [2] Ibid. v. 163.

and all but my cousins and Emily, called out for Sir Charles to dance with me.

I was abashed at the general voice calling upon us both: But it was obeyed.

He deserved all the praises that Miss Gran—Lady G. I would say, gave him in her Letter to me; and had every one's silent applause, while we danced; *so* silent, that a whisper must have been heard. And when he led me to my seat, every one clapt their hands, as at some well-performed part, or fine sentiment in a play . . .

Lord W. wished himself able, from his gout, to take out Miss Jervois. The Bridegroom was called upon by Sir Charles; and he took out the good girl; who danced very prettily . . .

Sir Charles was afterwards called upon by the Bride herself; and she danced then with a grace indeed! . . .

Once more he and I were called upon . . .

Sir Charles, when we had done, called me *inimitable*. The word was caught by every mouth, and I sat down with reason enough for pride, if their praises could have elevated me. But I was not proud. My spirits were not high—I fansy, Lucy, that Lady Clementina is a fine dancer.[1]

It must be admitted that Harriet's minute reporting is a bit like Mrs. Bennet's detailed summary of the assembly at Meryton: 'Then, the two third he danced with Miss King, and the two fourth with Maria Lucas, and the two fifth with Jane again, and the two sixth with Lizzy . . .'[2] But Richardson is the first important English novelist to use the details of drawing-room life and the trivial events of a ball to draw out his characters and carry the narrative. Because he had done this in *Grandison*, it was easier for Jane Austen to use the assembly and the ball at Netherfield, or the important ball at the Crown in *Emma*, about which we know almost every change of partner. In *Grandison* this episode marks a general change in the characters' situations, and tells us about their relationship to each other, even in small particulars; the reader can draw his own conclusions from the fact that Emily does not join in the general request that Sir Charles and Harriet should dance together (and Harriet's tone in speaking of Emily is somewhat patronizing). Charlotte is married, but still critical of her husband. Sir Charles is about to leave for Italy, and there is reason to

[1] *Grandison*, iii. 368–9.
[2] Jane Austen, *Pride and Prejudice*, ed. R. W. Chapman, vol. i. ch. iii, p. 13.

believe he will return as Clementina's husband. Harriet is about to return, rather sadly, to Northamptonshire. At the very moment she is impressing the company with her grace in dancing with Sir Charles, she is keenly aware that she is not to have him as a permanent partner. This contrast between a cheerful social occasion and the inward dissatisfaction or dejection of the heroine is used to effect by Jane Austen in most of her novels.

The sadness of Harriet's parting with Sir Charles is expressed in music. When he pays his last visit to the Reeves, he asks Harriet to play to him: 'He sung unasked, but with a low voice; and my mind was calmed.'[1] The more public farewell takes place at the dinner party in St. James's Square, to which the imperious Olivia and her aunt have also been invited. There is a little private recital, but Harriet cannot enjoy it as before.

Nobody was chearful after dinner but Sir Charles. He seemed to exert himself to be so. He prevailed on me to give them a lesson on the harpsichord. Lady L. played: Lady G. played: We *tried* to play, I should rather say. He himself took the violin, and afterwards sat down to the harpsichord . . . He was not known to be such a master: But he was long in Italy. Lady Olivia indeed knew him to be so. She was induced to play upon the harpsichord: She surpassed everybody. Italy is the land of harmony.[2]

The theme of the earlier argument between Greville and Sir Hargrave about the relative merits of music in Italy and England is reflected here, as an aspect of Harriet's unhappy feelings about the rival merits of herself and Clementina. Italy, where Sir Charles will wed the lucky Italian girl, now seems 'the land of harmony', and Harriet is left to feel discordantly miserable in England.

During the time in which Harriet and Sir Charles are parted, there is no more music from either of them. The images of music become associated with Charlotte, as a kind of comic comment on marital discord. Charlotte uses music to provoke her husband, as Harriet notices:

But hush! Here comes the man.—She ran to her harpsichord— Is this it, Harriet? and touched the keys—repeating,

[1] *Grandison*, iii. 411.   [2] Ibid., p. 412.

> Softly sweet, in Lydian measures,
> Soon she sooth'd—
>   Enter Lord G.

Lord G. Miss Byron, I am your most obedient servant. The sight
of you rejoices my soul.—Madam (to his Lady) you have not been
long enough together to begin a tune. I know what this is for—

Lady G. Harmony! harmony! is a charming thing! But I, poor I!
know not any but what this simple instrument affords me.[1]

The air from *Alexander's Feast*, the praise of love with which
Harriet responded to Sir Charles in an earlier scene, is now
used to quite different purpose as an expression of the domestic
quarrel. Charlotte is scarcely soothing her lover. The marital
discord, as it continues, is expressed in musical terms. Charlotte
gleefully reports: 'he attempted to hum a tune of contempt,
upon my warbling an Italian air. An opera couple, we! Is it
not charming to sing *at* (I cannot say *to*) each other, when we
have a mind to be spiteful?'[2] The theme of disharmony rises to a
dissonant *crescendo* in the scene where Lord G. takes his revenge,
and 'silenced, broke, demolished, my poor harpsichord'.[3] Only
after this do the couple make a reconciliation, sealed in their
visit to the Selbys' house, which is now in turn called (by
Charlotte) 'the land of harmony'.[4]

It is noticeable that the two main Italian sections of the novel
lack references to music. During most of these episodes Clementina is too distressed to be associated, as Harriet is, with joyful
song. The della Porrettas are, like the Selbys and the Grandisons,
called 'a family of harmony and love'.[5] But music-making is not
introduced to substantiate the metaphor, and the description
seems slightly ironic. The Porrettas are not really a family of
harmony like the Grandisons. Their seeming harmony is only
unison with no personal variation, no counterpoint as it were,
allowed. As soon as the youngest member of the family expresses
individuality, they are horrified, and the family harmony goes
out of tune. Grandisons and Selbys have recitals, allowing each
member of the family to express himself or herself in playing
and singing; they also have family concerts, at which members
play divers instruments. The idea of harmony including
variation, difference, is not originally congenial to the della

---

[1] *Grandison*, iv. 30–1.   [2] Ibid., p. 188.   [3] Ibid., p. 193.
[4] Ibid., p. 206.   [5] Ibid. iii. 143.

Porrettas, and this contributes to the inner disharmony in Clementina. Her temporary insanity indicates that there is less harmony in Italy among the Porrettas than in England even with that 'opera couple' the G.'s who are at liberty to express their discordance.

There is, however, a reflection of the dance motif in the description of Sir Charles and Clementina walking in the alleys of the Porretta gardens.[1] Their motion, as they go from and then towards each other, and bow and curtsy, is like a measure in a minuet. The pattern is repeated much later when Clementina meets her suitor, the Count Belvedere, in the grounds of Grandison Hall, and crosses the alley to meet him;[2] she is to take up the dance of courtship again, with a different partner.

After the middle of the novel, when the music is either muted or changed to discord, there is a pronounced change when Sir Charles returns to ask for Harriet's hand. A variety of songs and dances fills the last volumes; the section which deals with Sir Charles's courtship of Harriet and with the wedding is like a movement in *allegro*. When the hero and heroine are reunited, Harriet plays for Sir Charles again: 'I was once a little out in an Italian song. In what a sweet manner did he put me in! touching the keys himself, for a minute or two.'[3] Harriet's little musical fault is caused by her former unhappiness and suspense. Significantly, it is an Italian air that causes her difficulty; Italy has not meant harmony to her. Sir Charles restores the harmony of her spirit as well as that of her song.

Before the wedding, the Selby family entertain their guests with dancing and music of all kinds, from the playing of the violin to Mr. Selby's fox-hunting song.[4] The wedding day itself is full of music, beginning with a serenade and epithalamium,[5] and closing with the grand wedding ball. The ball, described by Lady G. with a close account of the various dances, and changes of partner,[6] is the counterpart of the dance at her own wedding. This time Harriet, a slightly nervous bride, does not dance so well, but her happiness is evident. Emily dances with Beauchamp; a new courtship is to begin for her.

The dance suggests not only patterns of courtship but also

[1] Ibid., p. 63.   [2] Ibid. vi. 307.   [3] Ibid. v. 103–4.
[4] Ibid., p. 352.   [5] Ibid., p. 370.   [6] Ibid., pp. 392–7.

the larger social harmony. This is implied when the dance at Grandison Hall introduces the new bride to her neighbours and establishes her in her new social duties in the atmosphere of 'decency, good order, mirth, and jollity',[1] and also in the allusion to the dance that Mrs. Shirley once led. 'The old Lady's lameness is owing, it seems, to a strained sinew, got in leading up a dance, not many years ago, proposed by herself, in order to crown the reconciliation which she had brought about, between a couple that had, till then, been unhappy . . .'[2] In *Pamela* or *Clarissa* the author might have used such an instance as an example of foolish pleasure, and of fit punishment for old age wasting time in frivolity. Here, the incident is meant to heighten our admiration for the lady, as proof of her benevolence and cheerful virtue. Mrs. Shirley, like Sir Charles, exercises the social virtue of reconciling neighbours, and promoting order and good will. She is, like Harriet, a bringer of harmony.

At Grandison Hall, spiritual and moral harmony are expressed in sensuous delight:

My dear Dr. Bartlett, said he, your soul is in harmony: I doubt not but all these are in order—'May I ask you, my Harriet?' pointing to the harpsichord. I instantly sat down to it. It is a fine instrument. Lord G. took up a violin; my Uncle a bass-viol; Mr. Deane a German flute; and we had a little concert of about half an hour.[3]

The family concerts as they are described in *Grandison* resemble the 'conversation pieces' in many paintings of the period. The musical motif in family portraits is found in Dutch paintings of the seventeenth century, but its use is most noticeable in French and English paintings of the eighteenth century. As in the novel, the musical motif in the painting has a meaning; it emphasizes the harmony of a family life maintained in elegance and order. There is a slight suggestion of Watteau about some scenes in *Grandison*. It was in this period that Philippe Mercier was appointed by Frederick, Prince of Wales, as his Court Painter, and met with great success in England with his paintings of family groups, musical parties, and *fêtes champêtres* in the style of Watteau. His paintings, such as *A Musical Family*

---

[1] *Grandison*, vi. 37.   [2] Ibid. v. 362.   [3] Ibid. vi. 27.

(Wilton House), depict graceful family harmony in a background of delicate and ordered landscape; reason, the passions,
nature are in harmony.[1] His portraits of another 'musical
family' in *Frederick Prince of Wales and his Sisters* (National
Portrait Gallery) shows not only the landscape of trees, roses,
and lawns, but also the beautifully ordered architecture of
Princess Anne's house at Kew (see Frontispiece). The whole
painting combines the images to be found in *Grandison* with
strikingly similar intent—although history leads us to believe
that 'poor Fred' and his family were unfortunately not as
harmonious as the Grandisons.[2] Mercier is certainly not a great
painter, but he exemplifies the spirit of the period in presenting,
with a certain charm, the beliefs of a class and an age; icono-
graphically, his works explain a good deal of what *Grandison* is
about. The debate on the rival merits of Italy and England,
often discussed in terms of their music and initiated in the
comic argument between Greville and Sir Hargrave, is given
its final answer. The Grandisonian world asserts itself in concord: 'Everything that *can* be adjusted, is.'[3]

The last music we encounter in *Sir Charles Grandison* is softer,
more intimate and informal than that which has gone before.
Lady G., that brilliant drawing-room performer, sings to her
own and her sister's babies in the nursery, and in her last letter,
almost at the very end of the last volume, she looks forward to
this employment: 'They are to crow at one another; and we
are to have a squalling concert. As it is Sunday, I will sing
an anthem to them. My pug will not crow, if I don't sing.

[1] See *A Catalogue of Paintings and Drawings in the Collection at Wilton House, Salisbury,
Wiltshire*, Compiled by Sidney, 16th Earl of Pembroke, 1968, pp. 70–1, and repro-
duction number 121, catalogue number 186.

[2] Another minor version of the domestic pastoral, suggesting the harmony between reason, the affections, and nature, is to be seen in the portrait of Sir Roger and
Lady Bradshaigh. Richardson obtained a copy to hang above his fireplace, and it
figures in the background of Highmore's portrait 'Samuel Richardson Author of
Clarissa' painted for the Bradshaighs (National Portrait Gallery). Sir Roger and
Lady Bradshaigh, in slightly romantic costume, are depicted on the lawn on their
estate; Sir Roger is standing by his chair; Lady Bradshaigh is sitting, fondling a pet
deer, and their imposing mansion is to be seen in the background. (There is a
rather charming incongruity between the sylvan deer and the very substantial
elbow chair which would appear to have been transported from the dining-room
or parlour.) The portrait was painted before *Grandison* was written; the inset picture
of the Bradshaighs suggests to us the novelist's aspiration to write about the life this
painting represents, an aspiration soon to be fulfilled.

[3] *Grandison*, vi. 314.

Yet I am afraid, the little pagans will be less alive to a Christian hymn, than to the sprightlier *Phillida, Phillida* of Tom Durfey.'[1] Romantic love is part of a cycle which includes marriage, child-bearing, and child-rearing; Harriet herself is about to have a child. The music for the children is a promise that the tradition of joyful order will not be broken. Out of custom and ceremony beauty will be born.

Mrs. Barbauld (among others) disapproves of the author's extending the novel beyond the wedding of Sir Charles and Harriet:

He . . . continued it a whole volume beyond the proper termination, the marriage of his hero, and having done so, he might . . . have gone on to the next point of view . . . till he had given the history of two or three generations . . . Sir Charles . . . would be improved by merely striking out the last volume, and, indeed, a good part of the sixth, where descriptions of dress, and parade, and furniture, after the interest is completely over, like the gaudy colouring of a western sky, gives symptoms of a setting sun.[2]

As far as the author's intention is concerned, certainly the interest is not completely over at that point. Striking out the last part of the novel would have left the theme incompletely fulfilled, and one major character, Clementina, abandoned to her unhappiness and imperfect maturity. Grandison Hall and the life there are meant to be established as the earthly paradise, where the free spirit can find virtue and happiness without losing freedom. Clementina's flight to London and eventually to Grandison Hall is justified in the event, as here she can be herself. Clementina is cured at Grandison Hall, a place of health, vitality, joy, and beauty like the images of earthly paradise—the garden of Adonis, Gloriana's court—in the works of a poet Richardson admired.[3] The spacious architecture, the Georgian lawns and parks, symbolic to that age of the perfect relation between man and nature, are appropriate images in a novel which conducts an optimistic examination of man's relationship to his own nature.

[1] *Grandison*, vi. 320–1 ('Durfey' misprinted 'Dufsey').
[2] Barbauld, 'The Life of Mr. Richardson', *Correspondence*, i. cxxxii–cxxxiii.
[3] For Richardson's admiration of Spenser ('What an imagination! What an invention! What painting! What colouring displayed throughout the works of that admirable author!') see his letter to Susanna Highmore, 22 June, 1750, *Selected Letters*, pp. 161–2; see also his letter to Lady Bradshaigh, 5 Oct. 1753, ibid., p. 246.

Grandison Hall represents Harriet's 'enlargement' not only materially and socially but morally; it is symbolic of the ordered formal growth of rational understanding and emotional sympathy. It becomes so for Clementina as well; her sympathies begin to emerge out of her unformed egotism. The passions of the heart are acknowledged, but they are not censured as sinful, or accepted as mere limitations. Love is not to be 'a narrower of the heart'. The three friends—Harriet, Sir Charles, and Clementina—ratify their friendship after the married couple have promised to visit Italy:

Promise me again, said the noble Lady. I, too, have marked the spot with my eye (standing still, and, as Sir Charles had done, looking round her) The Orangery on the right-hand; that distant clump of Oaklings on the left; the Villa, the Rivulet, before us; the Cascade in view; that Obelisk behind us—Be *This* the spot to be recollected as witness to the promise, when we are far, far distant from each other.

We both repeated the promise; and Sir Charles said (and he is drawing a plan accordingly) that a little temple should be erected on that very spot, to be consecrated to our triple friendship; and, since she had so happily marked it, to be called after her name.[1]

It seems fitting that this somewhat quixotic gesture of amity, a Renaissance theme in rococo form, with its slightly pagan touch should be introduced in the midst of an eighteenth-century park with all its ornaments. The code for which Sir Charles stands is that of 'The Christian hero', but what this code actually means is an upholding of the finest human and secular achievements, material and moral. However severe Latitudinarian virtue may seem, it looks to the world, and looks outward. Sir Charles is the ideal of his age in his toleration of Roman Catholics, Dissenters, even Jews (as long as all these, and the Anglicans too, behave themselves),[2] and in his rejection of boundaries between languages, nations, classes, and creeds. 'Friendship . . . will . . . make England and Italy one country.'[3]

[1] *Grandison*, vi. 313.
[2] 'I honour *every man* who lives up to what he professes,' he tells the rake Bagenhall who proclaims himself a Roman Catholic (ibid. i. 409). There are always moral riders to his statements of tolerance. The criterion of the value of belief seems to be its social utility, and social harmony is valued above religious zeal (ibid. iv. 242; v. 245). Dr. Bartlett reciting the 'Brachman's Prayer' seems to illustrate the universality of rational religion and aspiration for virtue (ibid. i. 357).
[3] Ibid. vi. 312.

Grandison Hall is not a retreat from the evils of a corrupt world; it is not suggested that the characters must barricade themselves within their castle of virtue. Sir Charles has visited the Continent; he and Harriet are to go to Bologna. Grandisons and Selbys travel in various parts of England, and the characters come from divers parts of Europe and the British Isles (Sir Rowland is Welsh, Lord L., Scots). The Grandisons take part in the society of their country neighbours, and Sir Charles will take his seat in Parliament. As in *An Essay on Man*, the circles of benevolence broaden outward. The implications of Clementina's temple lead us to the Romantic period, not only to the inward-looking sentimental nobility of Julie, St. Preux, and M. de Wolmar, but also to Schiller's *Ode to Joy* and Beethoven's Ninth Symphony.

A temple erected to the humane and secular virtue of Friendship seems a fitting culmination to the story. Pelagianism is a humanism. The morality for which Sir Charles stands does not seem oppressive because its inner meaning is expressed so positively in images as well as characters. Individual freedom can be achieved in this world, and the desire of the heart attained; this does not seem banal because the complexity of the search for both freedom and love is so fully expressed, the strains involved in growth so strongly emphasized, that they would seem overwhelming without the assurance that fulfilment is humanly possible, and the quest not absurd.

The world which Clarissa has to endure is cruel and bestial; things rank and gross in nature possess it merely, like the bouquet of dying weeds in the gaoler's room. Harriet's world is good at heart, and that goodness (which is not only moral virtue in the limited sense, but soundness, vitality, the forces of growth) will not be restricted or vanquished by circumstance, but is capable of fulfilment as ordered and beautiful as trees and cascade, park and mansion. The world of nature, the very animal world, is friendly and beautiful, as are the senses and passions. Senses and passions are not objects of dread; they do not always require what Pamela called 'good Sense and Instruction, improving Lessons', restraint through verbal exhortation. Intellect, passions, and senses are all satisfied in the celebration by music. It is fitting that music should be the dominant image, that the allusions to *Alexander's Feast*, which celebrate music's power to move the emotions, are allusions to Handel and not only to Dryden. It is not the least fitting image because it is true of the novel, as Harriet Byron said of Handel's piece, that 'great part of the beauty of this performance arises from the proper transitions from one different strain to another'. Our enjoyment of the book may depend on our appreciation of the delicate modulations and variations in the change of one key, as it were, to another, one movement to the next. Music suggests the joy of comedy, of love ending in marriage, and also the 'friendly contrariety' of the passions. Their 'well-accorded strife' gives 'all the harmony of life', both within the individual and in the social order. It is possible to learn 'to tune the regulated heart'. Heart and senses can be attuned because they are not at war with the intellect, or with Mansoul. It is true in all of Richardson's novels that 'Love is a natural passion',[1] but in *Grandison* this means something different from what it would have meant in *Clarissa*, because in the last novel 'passion' and 'nature' are already justified and saved.

[1] Mrs. Shirley to Harriet, *Grandison*, i. 18.

XIV

The Achievement of Samuel Richardson

> L'intérêt et le charme de l'ouvrage dérobent l'art de
> Richardson à ceux qui sont le plus faits pour l'apercevoir.
> Plusieurs fois j'ai commencé la lecture de *Clarisse* pour me
> former; autant de fois j'ai oublié mon projet à la ving-
> tième page; j'ai seulement été frappé, comme tous les
> lecteurs ordinaires, du génie . . .[1]

To his contemporary readers, Richardson seemed what he was, a genius in the art of fiction, and his novels were hailed as exciting creations of a new kind. He was one of the celebrities of the French Enlightenment at the end of the century—ironically, as he himself would have regarded this 'Enlighten-ment' as a spiritual darkening. One of his most appreciative readers was Denis Diderot, who, in the *Éloge de Richardson* (written on the occasion of the English novelist's death in 1761) expresses his admiration not only of Richardson the moralist, but also of Richardson the artist. He defends the importance of every detail, arguing that Prévost's translation and abridgement of *Clarissa* has cut a book which is admirable for its tightly woven pattern: 'Ici l'auteur ne fait pas un pas qui ne soit de génie.'[2] He appreciates the symbolic quality of *Clarissa*, as in the scene of Clarissa's return to Harlowe Place, and rebukes the translator for considering it a scene which could be omitted.[3] Diderot calls the author 'le poète Richardson',[4] and his novels 'trois poèmes de Richardson'[5]. In an image of his own, he con-veys his appreciation of what Richardson can reveal:

C'est lui qui porte le flambeau au fond de la caverne; c'est lui

<hr>

[1] Denis Diderot, *Éloge de Richardson, Œuvres complètes de Diderot*, 20 tomes, 1821, iii. p. 19. [2] Ibid., p. 26.
[3] Ibid., pp. 14–15. [4] Ibid., p. 21. [5] Ibid., p. 24.

qui apprend à discerner les motifs subtils et déshonnêtes, qui se cachent et se dérobent sous d'autres motifs qui sont honnêtes, et qui se hâtent de se montrer les premiers. Il souffle sur le fantôme sublime qui se présente à l'entrée de la caverne et le more hideux qu'il masquait s'aperçoit.[1]

Mme de Staël is less profound in her understanding of Richardson, but highly appreciative ('Elle a dit depuis que l'enlèvement de Clarisse avoit été un des événemens de sa jeunesse'.)[2] A humanist critic, she recognizes the importance of Richardson's kind of novel:

> Eh bien, sans approuver les opinions superstitieuses de Clémentine, l'amour luttant contre un scrupule de conscience, l'idée du devoir l'emportant sur la passion, sont un spectacle qui attendrit et touche ceux même dont les principes sont les plus relâchés, ceux qui auraient rejeté avec dédain un tel résultat, s'il avait précédé le tableau comme maxime, au lieu de le suivre comme effet.[3]

Not only was Richardson approved by intelligent critics; also, and more important, his influence on creative writers was immediate and widespread. His influence on the Continent during the thirty years after his death is apparent in three major Continental novels: Rousseau's *La Nouvelle Héloïse* (1761), Goethe's *Die Leiden des Jungen Werther* (1774), and Laclos's *Les Liaisons dangereuses* (1782).

The resemblances between the characters of *Clarissa* and those in Rousseau's epistolary novel have long been commonplaces of criticism. What is more interesting is the extent to which the emotional climate of the novel resembles that in Richardson's works, not only in *Clarissa*, but also in both parts of *Pamela*, and in *Grandison*. For Rousseau, Richardson had established the novel as a genre suitable for the philosopher, and quite distinct from the kind of fables and *contes* used by Voltaire. Moral and social themes could be discussed in and through the novel.[4] In the loose sense of a word loosely employed

[1] Ibid., p. 8.

[2] Mme Necker de Saussure, *Notice sur le caractère et les écrits de Mme de Staël*, 1820, p. 15.

[3] Mme de Staël, *Essai sur les fictions* (1795) in *Œuvres complètes*, 2 tomes, Paris, 1836, i. 71.

[4] Rousseau takes up some of the particular causes which Richardson had espoused. He deals with the iniquity of duelling (see *Julie ou la Nouvelle Héloïse*,

in Richardson's century, his novels have 'philosophic' overtones. One of the reasons for *Pamela*'s wide appeal was that
here a declaration of the equality of man is proved on the
pulses. Even though the heroine eventually marries into the
social Establishment, she and Mr. B. continue to act according
to conscience, not convention.

The element of unconventional perfection, so prominent in
Richardson—Pamela offers to release her husband from his
marriage; Clarissa makes a friend of Belford; Clementina and
Harriet become friends and Sir Charles builds a memorial to
the triumph of true hearts over jealousy—is taken to an extreme in Rousseau's novel. From the ordinary point of view,
the characters act quixotically, most remarkably in Wolmar's
invitation of his wife's former lover to Clarens. 'Tous les sentiments seront hors de la nature pour ceux qui ne croient pas à la
vertu.'[1] A delicate amity is the keynote; the difference between
separate characters and their views of what happens is not
exploited by Rousseau. Even more than Richardson, Rousseau
makes a careful distinction between what Richardson calls
'love of person' and 'love of mind'. Erotic love between the
virtuous is the delicate essence of friendship between man and
woman; it is like some beautiful rare plant growing on Alpine
slopes—few are able to mount those heights and find it in its
natural perfection.

All of Rousseau's major characters are good, conscientious
in the extreme; like Richardson's virtuous people they possess
high seriousness, but are unrelieved by wit or humour, certainly uncoloured by any of the grotesquerie in which Richardson abounds. (One is tempted to remark that if Clarissa were
transported to *La Nouvelle Héloïse*, she would be the wittiest
character present.) The tone and emphasis in the description
of the perfect community at Clarens recall the admiring por-
trayal of Pamela B. and her household, and Clarens is likewise

ed. René Pomeau, 1960, Ière partie, lettre lvii, pp. 127–35). He treats at length the
importance of a mother's role in the education of her children, as Richardson had
done in *Pamela II*. Both Pamela and Julie seek a way of education that is in accordance with nature, and deny that the child is reasonable from infancy (*Pamela*, iv.
308; *Julie*, Vième partie, lettre iii, p. 548). Both mothers entertain their children
with moral tales of their own devising (*Pamela*, iv. 436–42; *Julie*, Vième partie,
lettre iii, p. 568).

[1] Rousseau, 'Préface', *Julie*, p. 3.

a very close parellel to Grandison Hall. House and estate represent all that is fine and civilized, and the characters, 'la société des cœurs'[1] are, like the B.'s and the Grandisons, a society of the morally elect. The difference is that for Richardson, even when he most nearly approaches the ideas of the French *philosophes*, happiness is still consistent with living in the community at large and reforming it from within; for Rousseau, the whole social edifice requires to be rebuilt, and the ideal must be strictly severed from the real. His major characters are entirely free from human depravity, and the gross touch of the world is not allowed to come into contact with the sensitive plant.

La Nouvelle Héloïse had an important influence, of a kind which tended to diminish appreciation of Richardson's own achievement, and of Rousseau's as well. The *philosophe*'s novel led to curious imitation; writers turned to the Richardsonian type of novel as a vehicle for their doctrines. Thomas Holcroft's *Anna St. Ives* (1794) is a philosophic treatise after Rousseau and Godwin, with characters and plot blatantly lifted from *Grandison* and *Clarissa*. Anna is a Clarissa rendered philosophizing and self-confident; the hero, Frank Henley, is a revolutionary and a prig, with an incurable habit of delivering moral reproof, and lengthy instructions as to the evils of private property and superstition. His conduct is most unlike that of the 'atheist' of fiction half a century earlier—no Christian hero of Steele could be purer-hearted, more magnanimous, more courageous in declining duels and saving lives. We recognize Sir Charles in his Godwinian hat. Even the rake Coke Clifton, a villain drawn from Lovelace, is forced to capitulate and reform. Once he has seen the better path, he can no longer follow the worse. Rousseau's view that true love ennobles the soul becomes in Holcroft the Godwinian opinion that the relationship which ennobles the soul is not only superior to erotic love but designed to replace it (sexuality will eventually be reduced to the place it has in the life of Houyhnhnms). Tenderness of a responsible kind is to be founded on an Esteem located in arid intellectual regions not to be found on the *Carte du Tendre*.

Goethe's *Werther* develops entirely different aspects of the

[1] Rousseau, *Julie*, Vième partie, lettre ii, p. 529.

Richardsonian novel.[1] The irony of situation is developed, the intensity of emotion explored and admired for its own sake. Erotic love is here a major principle of life, but love, even and more especially between the good, is essentially destructive, and the hero almost voluptuously seeks death as a consummation of love. What is tragic in *Clarissa* verges on the morbidly self-indulgent in *Werther*. Goethe's example makes of the novel of letters a private *confessio*, an expression of intense self-communing—the natural development after this is into some kinds of poetry, not into further exploration of prose fiction. For the admirer of *Werther*, there is no novel to read after it; we had better forsake the 'poèmes de Richardson' for the poetry of Shelley and Byron. The limitation of *Werther*'s form, especially in the eyes of a later generation which desired to write of a wider world of manners, of characters, even of social events and politics, may have assisted in the decline of the popularity of the epistolary novel. Laclos's *Les Liaisons dangereuses*, a great and brilliant work by the novelist who best understood what Richardson was doing artistically in *Clarissa*, was, like Richardson's own novels, largely neglected in the nineteenth century. The neglect was not merely on account of Laclos's 'immorality' but also partly because the manner of narration had ceased to interest. For this change of taste, the extreme popularity of Richardson's novels may indirectly be responsible. The epistolary mode had been adopted by many imitators of Richardson who were not concerned with the deeper significance of Richardson's own work, and a surfeit of novels in letters created a disgust.

The most noticeable and direct influence of Richardson on major English literature was to come through *Grandison*

---

[1] Richardson's works were highly influential in Germany, affecting developments in the drama, as well as inspiring the first German novels. Prose tales in the epistolary mode, dealing with feminine sensibility, began to appear after *Pamela*. Gellert's *Leben der Schwedischen Gräfinn* (1747–8) can claim to be the first German novel, but it reaches a level no higher than the tales of Mrs. Haywood or Mrs. Davys. Sophie von La Roche attained some proficiency as a novelist; she uses the epistolary form (in a simple straightforward way) and endeavours to achieve the effects of Richardson's works, especially of *Grandison*. Sophie von Sternheim has some resemblance to Harriet (*Geschichte des Fräuleins von Sternheim*, 1771–2). Piety, courtship, and marriage are the themes of Sophie von La Roche. Her interest in characters' self-analysis was, as well as Richardson's own novels, an influence on Goethe's work.

rather than his earlier novels. The narration by letters became associated with the courtship tale as Richardson had developed it: *Evelina* (1778) is a most successful example. But young ladies could be shown entering society, observing manners, and falling in love, without sustaining themselves by constant sessions of letter-writing, and the novelist could tell their story without recourse to epistles. Jane Austen, who owes much, both directly and indirectly, to Richardson's novels, and especially to *Grandison*, flirted with the epistolary novel only in her juvenile stories. Material and perceptions deriving from *Grandison* went into a kind of novel for which the letter mode seemed but a cumbersome device. The real importance of what had been achieved by Richardson, especially in *Clarissa*, went unnoticed, and, before Richardson's own popularity had waned, the epistolary form was considered *passé*.

His reputation is fraught with the kind of ironies that sometimes bedevil a great artist. The strength of his own work was quickly eroded by his own influence. The meaning of his work became fragmented, chipped and quarried by successors and imitators, great and small. Isolated as he apparently was by rank and education from the intellectual and cultivated life of his own time, he had nevertheless anticipated the spirit of the coming age throughout Europe, touched an era as remote from the time of his birth as the distance which separates Tillotson and Dryden from Godwin and Goethe. To the Enlightenment he offered a new mode of didacticism, both rational and emotive, and a revolutionary quality which suggested the possibility of expressing a new message in fiction. To those of the Romantic period for whom ideological expression turned ultimately upon the inner working of the soul, he offered a mode of revealing psychological activity, and, for those at the Romantic extreme, a powerful image in the anarchic and fascinating Lovelace.[1] To the sentimentalist,

[1] The Lovelace figure recurs in European literature, a theme with variations. There are minor examples like Holcroft's Clifton and Sophie von La Roche's Mylord Derby, as well as Laclos's brilliant Valmont. Pushkin's verse novel *Evgeny Onegin* (1821–31) plays on the irony of Tatyana's mistaking Onegin, a kind of Lovelace, for a Grandison, as the references to Richardson from the beginning of the story point out. In Onegin we see the Lovelace type merged with the Byronic hero, with whom he has a close affinity. Byron himself played on responses to this type already present in his readers. Pechorin in Lermontov's *A Hero of Our Time* (1841) is a late-Romantic instance of the Lovelace type as Byronic hero. Charlotte

Richardson, in some ways so tough a thinker, apparently offered a justification for sentimentalism, and, to those interested in exploring the niceties of female manners in a sophisticated social world, he gave a new model for the story of the female *début*. Certainly none of these are bad things, and we would be grateful to Richardson for having pointed out paths for later novelists, such as Jane Austen, to tread, if he had done nothing else. But he had done something more, and it is distressing to think that a great writer can, once certain aspects of his work are explored and made use of by others, become neglected in favour of the later authors who have extracted single elements which once existed in a unique and vital combination. The work of a great artist, unlike the achievements of technology or science, is not rendered obsolete by later developments, although in the aftermath of his greatest novelty and influence there may be a temptation to think so. By 1830, the tedium of too many didactic rational novels, of too many minor stories of young ladies going into society, had created a surfeit, and the desire to peruse Richardson's own works, now uncomfortably suggestive of old-fashioned days, had diminished. He had served two generations as a master, almost as an idol, and idolatry and imitation distorted the view of his own work. His reputation eventually had to pay for this period of great popularity.[1] A writer of great importance to a certain time will almost inevitably be considered as the voice of that epoch alone, once time has advanced a little further. Social and intellectual movements, the literary modes and fashions of an age, perceptibly ebb into history, and with them, for a while at least, go the fame and achievements of that era's celebrities. The poetry of Pope, the novels of Scott, have undergone lengthy eclipse and recovered.

The terms of writers and critics of the late eighteenth century —'instruction', 'pathos', 'sentiment'—were frequently used by critics in a genuine effort to define Richardson's quality; the meanings of the terms were altered by time, but they were still

Brontë's Rochester is partly a modified Lovelace; it is interesting that she has given her hero the name of Lovelace's own predecessor in real life, the Earl of Rochester of fascinating memory, who undoubtedly provided inspiration for Richardson in drawing Lovelace.

[1] His reputation never underwent as great a decline in France as in England, however; the French have been his most consistent admirers.

applied by generations of critics after they had come to bear a pejorative sense. Nineteenth-century critics continue to repeat the stale language of criticism. Trollope feels constrained to praise the 'pathos' of *Clarissa*, but thinks 'the vehicle in which the narration is given is awkward and tedious'.[1] It is a relief to find someone like Hardy who, even while disliking Richardson, admires him for his understanding of structure and his artistic sense of form.[2]

Even when Richardson's reputation has been in darkest eclipse, his work viewed with scorn by academics and almost unknown to the general public, he has been generally appreciated by other novelists, from Balzac and George Eliot to André Gide and Angus Wilson. To say that Richardson is a 'novelist's novelist' is probably to do the author a disservice; such praise frightens off the ordinary reader with intimations of arcane mysteries of craft. Nevertheless, there is some truth in the phrase, but that a writer is admired by other authors (as Keats by other poets) should be taken as a sign that he has, not less, but more than usual to offer to the attentive common reader.

Ordinary readers, in all walks of life, were, after all, the first admirers of Richardson. To arrive at a fresh assessment of Richardson's achievement, the best starting-point could be the judgements of his immediate contemporaries, admirers of 'le poète Richardson' whose perception was not coloured by the prismatic division of Richardson's unity into various single hues. Richardson's contemporary admirers, from the enthusiastic Lady Bradshaigh to the intellectual Diderot, were accustomed to compare him to Shakespeare. Such a comparison, which is almost bound to be hyperbole, assisted in the decline of the author's reputation, when later critics could intimate that eighteenth-century taste was sadly wanting, and that an admiration for the writer which could be expressed by persons

[1] Anthony Trollope to E. S. Dallas, 22 Aug. 1868, *The Letters of Anthony Trollope*, ed. W. Bradford Booth, 1951, p. 383. It is the more surprising that Trollope should have been so dismissive, on the whole, of Richardson, whom at some points he resembles, especially in his sense of the eager fluctuations of the inner life, and his understanding of subtle moral strenuousness even in the quiet lives of women.

[2] Thomas Hardy, 'The Profitable Reading of Fiction', first published in *The Forum*, New York (March 1888); see Hardy's *Life and Art*, Essays Collected by Ernest Brennecke Jr., 1925, p. 70.

capable of such extravagant lapse is thus ridiculous in itself. Yet, in using this comparison, eighteenth-century readers were endeavouring to express something they felt about his work, the unity, massiveness, and diversity that it presented.

One of the things they did mean was that Richardson had created a variety of characters, each with his own voice and manner. It was noted at the time that readers discussed characters in Richardson's books, especially those in the two great novels *Clarissa* and *Grandison*, as if they were living people, some praising, others blaming the same character for the same actions; readers were excited to find that this could be so, that various people formed different impressions of the same character, as is true of common acquaintance in real life. Diverse folk diversely they said—that Clarissa is too prudish, too imprudent, obedient or rebellious, formal or extravagant. Charlotte is considered an arch-wife or an arch-wit, Harriet is selfish or self-abnegating, Clementina morally strong or morally weak. This variety of impression is open to readers, not because the author is deficient in drawing characters but because his dramatic personages are shown so fully. Like Shakespeare's characters, they present themselves, even their inmost selves, in all their complexity, without the godlike author as intermediary and controlling expositor. That such a bristle of possibility, such a fullness of meaning, could be created in the novel was a minor revelation, and contemporary readers were right to make such a to-do about it. The characters of the picaresque novels are animated but flat. The more moral a novel of any kind claimed to be, the more definitely the reader is usually assured about the exact nature of the characters. Fielding's great moral picaresque novels, deriving from the neo-classical tradition, possess the kind of characterization most powerfully displayed in the comic dramas of Ben Jonson. The difference between Shakespearian and Jonsonian characterization had long been recognized, so it is not unnatural that the English readers should have turned to Shakespeare for comparisons in expressing their sense of the difference between Richardson's kind of novel and that of Fielding and Smollett.

Another 'Shakespearian' quality is the mingling of tragic and comic material and attitudes within one work in such a manner that these elements reinforce each other. Even at the outset of his literary career, Richardson was experimenting in this way in *Pamela*, where the seriousness of sexual violence, and the even more important seriousness of the individual's right to freedom, no matter what the condition of social subjection, is fused with the comic spirit of the pastoral and mock-pastoral, and with sexual comedy. In *Clarissa* the violently tragic and the violently comic are inseparably mingled. Even in *Grandison* the threat of destruction, presented here as emotional self-destruction, looms large, and not only in Clementina; her major insanity is reflected in Harriet's jealousy which begins to manifest itself in the irrational ambiguities of her attitude to Emily. Because the threat, not of outward circumstance alone, but also of inward desires, is recognized, the full comic narrative is not felt as a mere arbitrary working of a love story from complication to solution.

Richardson's mingling of comic and tragic in *Clarissa* is masterly, and manifests a comprehension of tragedy beyond that of his age. Richardson rescued the concept of tragedy from the trappings of outworn technique. His own bourgeois tragedy is closer in spirit to Dryden than to the pathetic tales of Otway, Lillo, or Moore. It is no mere tale of misfortune in bourgeois life, but a deep and complex account of the growth and nature of consciousness doomed to enact its being under the perpetual threat of destruction. We do not have interludes of comic relief; the whole novel is about the absurdity of the hero and heroine's misunderstanding of themselves, each other, and their world. And absurdity manifests itself in violent comedy at the same time as tragic irony is most fully expressed.

The humour of Richardson may well give us pause. That there is humour in *Clarissa* was early recognized by Fielding, who, although he is so often made the stalking-horse for attack on the other novelist, admired the work:

> In all the Accounts which Loveless [*sic*] gives of the Transactions at Hampstead, you preserve the same vein of Humour which hath run through the preceding Volumes. The new Characters you Introduce are natural and entertaining, and there is much of the true Comic Force in the Widow Bevis. I have seen her often, and I Promise you, you have drawn her with great exactness.[1]

[1] Fielding to Richardson, 15 Oct. 1748, as quoted by A. D. McKillop in *The Early Masters of English Fiction*, p. 79.

As Fielding perceives, the humour here comes not mainly from the Widow Bevis herself, but emerges through Lovelace, who is a continual source of surprising comedy. The most important humour in the novel does not arise from minor characters like Joseph Leman or the Widow Bevis, or even the Harlowes with their sour comedy of domestic life. It is not even merely in Lovelace himself, although he is an arch-humorist, an inventive wit, imaginatively willing to dissolve and re-create, and to enjoy the process. The most vital comedy emerges from the conflict between the major characters, and it is in this context that Lovelace's wit has its full effect. Richardson flouts 'decorum' with artistic assurance; tragic irony and the comedy derive from the same source, in the characters' relation to each other and to their world.

At its most audacious, Richardson's humour plays upon the sexual relationship, the topic of all the novels. This humour is felt time and again throughout *Clarissa*, from the heroine's retort to her jealous sister, the taunt 'It is not my fault, Bella, if the *opportune* gentleman don't come!'[1] to the ingenious and convincing logic with which Lovelace elaborates his scheme for universal annual marriage and its beneficent effects (lowering the crime rate, satisfying the courts 'whether *spiritual* or *sensual*, *civil* or *uncivil*', and effecting 'A Total alteration for the better in the *morals* and *way of life* in both Sexes') in a parody of the formulas of social concern worthy of one of Swift's projectors.[2] Freedom of the will, sex, and death are the subjects of a humour which shades at one end of its spectrum into macabre and grotesque distortion, and, at the other, into a kind of metaphysical wit and baroque play of images. Richardson's humour can be a bit frightening; we may feel that within Samuel Richardson, master printer and family man, there was someone who laughed with demonic gusto at the deep absurdities of the human sexual condition. It would be easy to make him out altogether as a dark humorist, but it would be false. We cannot choose to ignore the sanity and gentleness which are also Richardson's and which play through the lighter iridescent shades of his comic sense. There is for instance, the earthy vitality of Pamela, or the innumerable gentle touches of fun in

---

[1] *Clarissa*, i. 314.
[2] Ibid. v. 292–6.

Grandison: Harriet making mouths in the glass, Charlotte toying with her diamond ring, 'sometimes putting the tip of her finger on it, as it lay upon the table, and turning it round, swifter or slower'.[1] The command of various kinds of comedy, not the repetition of one kind alone, gives Richardson some claim to an affinity with Shakespeare.

Although he deals with the passion of love, 'Venus toute entière à sa proie attachée', with a Racinian intensity, Richardson is English and Shakespearian enough to function best when dealing with an immense amount of material. In *Pamela II* he set out before he had matter enough, but in all the other novels he has acquired material, a vast quarry of characters, themes, intellectual and moral problems, from which to extract, design, and shape his intricate and harmonious edifice. As we have seen, Richardson drew upon a wealth of material, varying from novel to novel, in order to produce his original tales. The sources are in each case transformed into new meaning. Pamela is and is not the country maid of pastoral poem and pastoral comedy; *Clarissa* is more than a mixing of devotional literature with heroic tragedy and the incipient novel of love. With an imagination naturally, but not simply, symbolic, the author creates new layers of meaning, disturbs us with echoes and intimations. Thus material artistically almost static in Quarles and Wither and even in Taylor becomes kinetic in *Clarissa* where we share an inward world, a moving film of images superimposed on one another, ambiguous and frightening. The reader shares and struggles to understand, as the heroine struggles to understand, Clarissa's apparently solid but still-dissolving world; we are haunted as she is haunted by the possiblities of 'dress', 'wooer', 'will', 'house'. Richardson loves the enormous and complicated. He could comprehend the vast and attend to the minute. His love of a density of material enabled him to do what no other contemporary novelist and few dramatists of his age could do in organizing subplots without making them episodes. Anna Howe's relationship to her mother and Hickman, Charlotte Grandison's courtship and marriage are subordinated to the main design of their respective novels, while each is fully developed, self-consistent and progressive, and organically related to the main theme. The sense

---

[1] *Grandison*, ii. 167.

of thematic relationship between various strands of action is an unusually strong quality in Richardson, and may be one of the reasons why the novels evoked from contemporary readers the comparison with Shakespeare.

There is still another 'Shakespearian' quality in the novels which early readers may have obscurely felt or perceived. As we have seen, each of the novels is derived from different sources, and each achieves its design through quite different patterns of imagery. In each case imagery is organically related to characters and action, and the result is that, in reading the three major novels, the reader successively enters different worlds. The atmosphere, not merely the superficial setting but the moral atmosphere, changes from novel to novel. To say this is only another way of saying that Richardson changes his imaginative theology, as it were; moral and spiritual concern is always there, but in each novel he chooses a different view of man's relation to himself and to his fate. This is patently indicated by the references to different kinds of religious literature in *Clarissa* and *Grandison*, but these references only direct our attention to what the novel itself is saying in each case. *Clarissa*'s world is corrupt, brutish, and desperately mortal; the world of Sir Charles and Harriet and Clementina is benign, the correlative of a sophisticated humanist interpretation of the Christian ethic. *Pamela*, in its allusion to pastoral, fable and psalm, portrays a simpler world than is found in either of the other two major works; it is neither as evil as that of *Clarissa* nor as positively good as that of *Grandison*. It is a world of innocence; its earthy references suggest primary matter, crude energies in the process of transformation, like the heroine and even the hero, to a higher state of life. The differences between *Pamela*, *Clarissa*, and *Grandison* are almost as marked in their way as the differences between the worlds of *As You Like It*, *Hamlet*, and *A Winter's Tale* in their greater way. The capacity to alter imaginative vision with such thoroughness and effect is relatively rare, and the mark of a great literary artist.

Of course Richardson is most un-Shakespearian in his constant attention to one theme. Each novel is essentially concerned with the nature of sexual desire. Such consistent attention to one central problem is both a limitation and a source of strength. One of Richardson's favourite quotations was Dryden's line 'Love various minds does variously inspire', and this each of his novels illustrates. The various behaviour inspired by love is always for Richardson both psychologically and morally interesting. The novelist he most resembles is probably Henry James; in James's novels, too, love variously inspires various minds, and its inspiration manifests itself in the characters' diverse moral activity.

Richardson's concern with sexuality is inseparable from his imaginative moral concern. The event in his novels is always the inner event, which is necessarily in all respects a moral event. His study of the 'natural passion', the power of erotic love, is concerned with a creature whose acknowledgement of love, whether generous or mean, noble or vile, is indissolubly connected with a complex attitude to the nature of identity.

The force of love, the ardent desiring response to the being of another, also involves a response to and within the self, animates and concentrates the energies of the inmost spirit. The nature and processes of being, conscious and unconscious, which the normal patterns of existence would conceal, cannot then be ignored. These processes of being are forcefully transmitted to the rational mind, which must translate and interpret the significance within. The narrative form which Richardson discovered and exploited to the utmost artistic effect beautifully reflects this continuous and subtle work. The narrators become themselves in endeavouring to interpret the operation of being and in endeavouring to communicate their consciousness to others. The communication is important—how different the novels would be if they were written in, for instance, journal form. Conscious life is not writing a diary for itself; it is also concerned with relationship to other human beings, in knowing the relationship to other complex personal consciousnesses, and in defining and deciding its action in relation to the world of human life. Imperfections, even falsifications and distortions, inevitably occur in the difficult attempt to interpret and communicate consciousness. Each human being, good as well as evil, suffers from limitation of understanding; the single point of view (which is all each of us has) is a distorting view; all cannot be seen, or seen justly, from that perspective. No one is omniscient. Clarissa cannot know what Lovelace has done, or how he sees events, neither can he know what she thinks, what

is important to her. The process of interpreting inner impulse
and knowledge is also fraught with possibilities of error because
of the effects of will and desire, themselves inner forces which
cannot easily be interpreted. Pamela does not want to let herself know that she is in love, because too much would be threatened by that recognition. Interpretation and communication
can fail at times, even in characters so candid as Harriet and
Emily—can even break down under unexpected and severe stress,
as is the case with Clementina. The process of consciousness can
be transformed and falsified by a dominant organizing power of
imagination, as with Lovelace, whose interpretation of life is
a brilliant solipsism, refusing to communicate on any but its
own terms. The diversity of possible responses to being, which
Richardson saw, is expressed by the author in a variety of
styles, images, and effects, ranging from mannerist to baroque to
classical to romantic, one of these dominant in each novel, the
others always present.

Richardson's novels are great images of consciousness. They
express, in their divers ways, the fact that no one is merely
passive and static, that in the inmost recesses of being the consciousness is always alive and growing. Every person, even the
humblest servant-girl, is a consciousness involved in creating its
own nature and destiny at every moment. To refuse this great
work is impossible. To wish to refuse it, to desire not to be, as do
Belton and Mrs. Sinclair, is the sin against the Holy Ghost
which cannot in the nature of things be forgiven. Unconsciously
to attempt to evade the arduous and exciting task, as Clementina does, is an invitation to disaster. The possibility of error is
ever-present—very well, that too must be accepted. 'It is good
for me that I was afflicted', says Clarissa, who in her ultimate
maturing accepts both responsibility and mistake. Men and
women must face and explore the ironic connection and apparent incompatibility of the rapacious desire of love and the
knowledge of identity, which is the acknowledgement of the
nature of freedom, both of oneself and of others, of the beloved
object too, who is also subject.

We find in Richardson an expression of the spirit making
itself and its world, understanding both its nature and its
passion through that nature and passion. The strenuous drama
of inner event, the intensity and complexity of the experience

of living are reflected in the form of each novel as well as in the matter of the tale itself. Richardson's novels will always be of interest as long as we are concerned with the search for the reconciliation of love and freedom, and with how much may be endured in our quest for fulfilment.

Bibliography

FOR Richardson's novels I have followed the standard practice of using the Shakespeare Head edition; a truly satisfactory modern edition of the novels has yet to appear.

For works written before Richardson's novels, or at roughly the same time, I have been careful to choose editions of a date such that they might have been seen by the novelist. Where possible, I have endeavoured to use first editions; where this was not possible I have used the earliest edition I could obtain. A large exception has been made in the case of Fielding's novels, in which it seemed sensible, for the sake of the reader, to use the Shakespeare Head edition of his novels, as of Richardson's, and the readily obtainable *Shamela* edited by Martin C. Battestin.

For works written after Richardson's death, I have attempted to use satisfactory standard editions, or, where possible, good modern editions. In some cases, such as that of Fanny Burney's *Cecilia*, the only reliable edition is still the first. In such cases I have tried to go back to the first edition, but this was not always obtainable; as readers will realize, particular problems arise in the case of reference to minor works of Continental literature.

I. WORKS BY SAMUEL RICHARDSON

A. *Fictional Works:*

Æsop's Fables. With Instructive Morals and Reflections, Abstracted from all Party Considerations, Adapted to all Capacities; And designed to promote Religion, Morality, and Universal Benevolence, 1740.

Familiar Letters on Important Occasions, 1741; ed. Brian W. Downs, 1928.

Pamela, or Virtue Rewarded, 1740–1; Shakespeare Head ed., 4 vols., Oxford, 1929.

Clarissa, or, The History of a Young Lady, 1747–8; Shakespeare Head ed., 8 vols., Oxford, 1930.

The History of Sir Charles Grandison, 1753–4; Shakespeare Head ed., 6 vols., Oxford, 1931.

B. 1. *Richardson's Letters, and those of his Correspondents:*

The Correspondence of Samuel Richardson, ed. Anna Lætitia Barbauld, 6 vols., 1804.

Selected Letters of Samuel Richardson, ed. John Carroll, Oxford, 1964.

B. 2. Forster Collection, Victoria and Albert Museum, Richardson MSS., 48 E 5–48 E 10, vols. xi–xvi.

II. CRITICISM OF RICHARDSON'S WORKS

Anon., 'The Character of Sir Charles Grandison', *Gentleman's Magazine*, xiii (Nov. 1753), 512–13.

Diderot, Denis, *Éloge de Richardson*, in *Œuvres complètes*, 21 tomes, 1821, tome iii.

Eaves, T. Duncan, and Ben D. Kimpel, 'Richardson's Immediate Family', section v of 'Samuel Richardson and His Family Circle', *Notes and Queries*, n.s. xi (Oct. 1964), 362–71.

—— —— *Samuel Richardson, A Biography*, Oxford, 1971.

Golden, Morris, *Richardson's Characters*, Ann Arbor, Michigan, 1963.

Hornbeak, Katherine, 'Richardson's *Familiar Letters* and the Domestic Conduct Books', *Smith College Studies in Modern Languages*, xix (Jan. 1938), 1–29.

Konigsberg, Ira, 'The Dramatic Background of Richardson's Plots and Characters', *PMLA*, lxxxiii (Mar. 1968), 42–53.

—— *Samuel Richardson and the Dramatic Novel*, Lexington, Kentucky, 1968.

McKillop, Alan D., 'Samuel Richardson's Advice to an Apprentice', *JEGP*, xlii (1943), 40–54.

—— *Samuel Richardson Printer and Novelist*, Chapel Hill, North Carolina, 1960.

Sale, William L., *Samuel Richardson: Master Printer*, Ithaca, N.Y., 1950.

Scott, Sir Walter, 'Prefatory Memoir to Richardson', Ballantyne's Novelists' Library, vol. vi, 1824.

Sharrock, Roger, 'Richardson's *Pamela*: the Gospel and the Novel', *Durham University Journal*, lviii (Mar. 1966), 67–74.

Wendt, Alan, 'Clarissa's Coffin', *PQ*, xxxix (Oct. 1960), 481–95.

III. PLAYS

Anon., *St. Cecily: Or, The Converted Twins*, by 'E.M.', 1666.

Aston, Anthony, *Pastora: or, The Coy Shepherdess*, 1712.

Beaumont, Sir Francis, and John Fletcher, *Comedies and Tragedies Written by Francis Beaumont and John Fletcher Gentlemen*, 1647.

Cibber, Colley, *The Careless Husband*, 1705.

—— *The Double Gallant: or, The Sick Lady's Cure*, 1708.

Cibber, Theophilus, *Patie and Peggy; or, The Fair Foundling*, 1700.

Congreve, William, *Love for Love*, 1695.

Congreve, William, *The Way of the World*, 1700.

Crowne, John, *Sir Courtly Nice: or, It cannot Be*, 1685.

Dance, James, *Pamela*. A Comedy, 1742.

Dryden, John, *Tyrannick Love, or the Royal Martyr*, 1670.

—— *The Conquest of Granada by the Spaniards*, part i, 1672.

—— *Aureng-Zebe*, 1676.

—— and Nathaniel Lee, *Oedipus*, 1679.

—— *Don Sebastian, King of Portugal*, 1690.

—— *King Arthur, or The British Worthy*, 1691.

Farquhar, George, *The Inconstant: or, The Way to Win him*, 1702.

—— *The Recruiting Officer*, 2nd ed. [1706].

—— *The Beaux Stratagem* [1707].

Gay, John, *The Beggar's Opera*, 3rd ed., 1729.

Howard, Sir Robert, *Four New Plays*, 1665.

Johnson, Charles, *The Country Lasses: Or, The Custom of the Manor*, 1727.

Leanerd, John, *The Country Innocence*, 1677.

Lee, Nathaniel, *The Tragedy of Nero, Emperour of Rome*, 1676.

—— *Gloriana, or the Court of Augustus Cæsar*, 1676.

—— *The Rival Queens, or The death of Alexander the Great*, 1677.

—— *Mithridates, King of Pontus*, 1678.

—— *Cæsar Borgia; Son of Pope Alexander the Sixth*, 1680.

Lillo, George, *Silvia: or, The Country Burial*. An Opera, 1731.

Phillips, Edward, *The Chamber-Maid*, 1730.

Rowe, Nicholas, *The Faire Penitent*, 1703.

Shirley, James, *The Wittie Faire One*, 1633.

—— *The Traytor*, 1635.

Steele, Richard, *The Funeral: Or, Grief A-la-mode*, 1702.

—— *The Tender Husband: Or, The Accomplish'd Fools*, 1705.

—— *The Conscious Lovers*, 1723 ed.

Villiers, George, Duke of Buckingham, *The Rehearsal*, 1672.

Webster, John, *The White Divel, or, The Tragedy of Paulo Giordano Ursini, Duke of Brachiano, With the Life and Death of Vittoria Corombona the famous Venetian Curtizan*, 1612.

Wieland, Christopher Martin, *Clementina von Porretta*, in *Sämmtliche Werke*, 36 Bände, Leipzig, 1857, Band 28, pp. 91–199.

Woodes, Nathaniel, *The Conflict of Conscience*, 1581.

Wycherley, William, *The Gentleman Dancing-Master*, 1673.

—— *The Country-Wife*, 1675.

IV. NOVELS AND LETTER-WRITERS

[Alcaforada, Marianna], (work now attributed to Gabriel-Joseph de Lavergne de Guilleragues) *Lettres d'Amour d'une Religieuse Portugaise, écrites au Chevalier de C.* Dernière édition, augmentée . . . The Hague, 1696.

Austen, Jane, *The Novels of Jane Austen*, ed. R. W. Chapman, 3rd ed., 5 vols., 1932, and vol. vi, *Minor Works*, 1954.

Barker, Mrs. Jane, *The Entertaining Novels of Mrs. Jane Barker*, 2nd ed., 2 vols., 1719.

—— *A Patch-Work Screen for the Ladies*, 1723.

Breton, Nicholas, *A Poste with a Packet of Mad Letters*, 1633 ed.

Brown, Tom, *Lindamira*, 1702.

Burney, Frances, *Evelina, or A Young Lady's Entrance into the World*, 3 vols., 1778.

—— *Cecilia, or Memoirs of an Heiress*, 5 vols, 1782.

—— *Camilla: or, A Picture of Youth*, 5 vols., 1796.

Davys, Mary, *The Reform'd Coquet: or, Memoirs of Amoranda*, 1724.

—— *The Works of Mrs. Davys*, 2 vols., 1725.

Edgeworth, Maria, *Tales and Novels*, 10 vols., 1893.

Eliot, George, *Daniel Deronda*, 4 vols., 1876.

F., G., *The Secretary's Guide*, 1734 ed.

Fielding, Henry, *Joseph Andrews and Shamela*, ed. Martin C. Battestin, 1965.

—— *Novels*, Shakespeare Head edition, 9 vols., Oxford, 1926.

Gellert, Christian F., *Leben der Schwedischen Gräfinn von G***, in *C. F. Gellerts Sämmtliche Schriften*, 6 Theilen, Leipzig, Theil iii, 1840.

Goethe, Johann Wolfgang, *Die Leiden des Jungen Werther*, in *Goethes Werke*, 14 Bände, Hamburg, 1951, Band vi.

Haywood, Mrs. Eliza, *Love in Excess*, 1719.

—— *The British Recluse: or, the Secret History of Cleomira, Suppos'd Dead*, 2nd ed., 1722.

—— *Idalia, or the Unfortunate Mistress*, 1723.

—— *Lasselia; or the Self-Abandon'd*, 1724.

—— *Letters from a Lady of Quality to a Chevalier*, 2nd ed., 1724.

—— *The Surprize; or, Constancy Rewarded*, 1724.

—— *Secret Histories, Novels and Poems*, 2nd ed., 2 vols., 1725.

—— *The Tea-Table: or, A Conversation between some Polite Persons of both Sexes, at a Ladies Visiting Day*, 1725.

—— *The Fruitless Enquiry*, 1727.

—— *Love Letters on All Occasions*, 1730.

—— *The History of Miss Betsy Thoughtless*, 4 vols., 1751.

Holcroft, Thomas, *Anna St. Ives*, ed. Peter Faulkner, Oxford English Novels, 1970.

Johnson, Samuel, *The History of Rasselas, Prince of Abissinia*, in *Works*, ed. Arthur Murphy, 12 vols., 1823–4, vol. iii.

Kelly, John, *Pamela's Conduct in High Life*, 1741.

Laclos, Choderlos de, *Les Liaisons dangereuses*, in *Œuvres complètes*, ed. Maurice Allem, 2nd ed., Bibliothèque de la Pléiade, Paris, 1943.

La Fayette, Marie-Madeleine Pioche de la Vergne, Comtesse de, *La Princesse de Clèves*, Paris, 1678.

La Roche, Sophie von, *Geschichte des Fräuleins von Sternheim. Von einer Freundin derselben aus Originalpapieren und anderen zuverlässigen Quellen gezogen.* Herausgegeben in den Jahren 1771 und 1772 von C. M. Wieland. Ed. Dr. Fritz Brüggemann, in *Deutsche Literatur: Reihe Aufklärung*, 15 Bände, Leipzig, 1938, Band xiv.

Lennox, Mrs. Charlotte, *The Female Quixote*, ed. Margaret Dalziel, Oxford English Novels, 1970.

Lettres Portugaises *see* Alcaforada.

Povey, Charles, *The Virgin in Eden: or, The State of Innocency*, 1741.

Rousseau, Jean-Jacques, *Julie ou la nouvelle Héloïse*, ed. René Pomeau, Éditions Garnier Frères, Paris, 1960.

Rowe, Mrs. Elizabeth, *Friendship in Death; in Twenty Letters from the Dead to the Living.* To which are added *Letters Moral and Entertaining*, 4th ed. 'Corrected with Additions', 1736.

Scudéry, Madeleine de, *Clélie, Histoire Romaine*, 10 vols., 1660–1.

—— *Clelia, an Excellent New Romance* (parts i–iii translated by J. Davies; parts iv–v translated by G. Havers), 1678.

Sidney, Sir Philip, *The Countesse of Pembroke's Arcadia*, in *The Prose Works of Sir Philip Sidney*, ed. Albert Feuillerat, 4 vols, 1962–9, vol. i, 1962.

Smith, Mrs. Charlotte, *Emmeline the Orphan of the Castle*, ed. Anne Henry Ehrenpreis, Oxford English Novels, 1971.

Smollett, Tobias, *The Adventures of Roderick Random*, 2 vols., 1748.

Yonge, Charlotte, *The Heir of Redclyffe*, 2 vols., 1853.

V. POEMS

Carey, Henry, *The Poems of Henry Carey*, ed. Frederick T. Wood, 1930.

Dillon, Wentworth, Earl of Roscommon, *A Prospect of Death: A Pindarique Essay*, 1704. *See* Pomfret, John.

Draper, John W., ed., *A Century of Broadside Elegies*, 1928.

Dryden, John, *The Poems of John Dryden*, ed. James Kinsley, 4 vols., Oxford, 1958.

Fellowes, E. H., ed., *English Madrigal Verse*, 1920.

Johnson, Samuel, *The Poems of Samuel Johnson*, ed. David Nichol Smith and Edward L. McAdam, Oxford, 1941.

Norris, John, *A Collection of Miscellanies*, Oxford, 1687.

Pomfret, John, *A Prospect of Death: A Pindarique Essay*, 1704 (attrib. Roscommon).

Pope, Alexander, *The Poems of Alexander Pope*, Twickenham edition, ed. John Butt, 5 vols., 1950.

Quarles, Francis, *Emblemes*, 1635.

Roy, Claude, *Trésor de la poésie populaire française*, Paris, 1954.

Swift, Jonathan, *The Poems of Jonathan Swift*, ed. Harold Williams, 2 vols., Oxford, 1937.

Uvedale, Thomas, *The Death-Bed Display'd: With the State of the Dead. A sacred poem*, 1727.

Wilmot, John, Earl of Rochester, *Poems on Several Occasions*, 1691.

Wither, George, *A Collection of Emblemes, Ancient and Moderne*, 1634–5.

Young, Edward, *The Complaint. Or Night-Thoughts on Life, Death and Immortality. Night the Eighth. Virtue's Apology: Or, the Man of the World Answer'd*, 1745.

VI. RELIGIOUS, MORAL, AND SATIRIC PROSE LITERATURE

Allestree, Richard, *The Practice of Christian Graces. Or The Whole Duty of Man Laid down in a Plaine and Familiar Way for the Use of All*, 1658.

—— *The Gentleman's Calling*, Oxford, 1660.

—— *The Ladies Calling*, Oxford, 1673.

Anon., *Het groote Tafareel der Dwaasheid*, Amsterdam, 1720.

Anon., *A Present for a Servant-Maid: Or, the Sure Means of gaining Love and Esteem ... To which are Added, Directions for going to Market; also, For Dressing any Common Dish, whether Flesh, Fish, or Fowl. With some Rules for Washing, &c. The Whole calculated for making both the Mistress and the Maid happy*, 1743.

Bacon, Nathaniel, *A Relation of the Fearful Estate of Francis Spira*, 1653.

Bayly, Lewis, *The Practise of Pietie*, 11th ed., 1619.

Boyle, Robert, *Occasional Reflections upon Several Subjects*, 2nd ed., 1669.

Butler, Joseph, *The Analogy of Religion, Natural and Revealed, to the Constitution and Course of Nature. To which are added two Brief Dissertations. I. Of Personal Identity. II. Of the Nature of Virtue*, 1736.

Chudleigh, Lady Mary, *The Female Advocate; or, a Plea for the just Liberty of the Tender Sex, and particularly of Married Women. Being Reflections on a late Rude and Disingenuous Discourse, Delivered by Mr. John Sprint*, 1700.

Defoe, Daniel, *Religious Courtship: Being Historical Discourses on the Necessity of Marrying Religious Husbands and Wives only*, 1722.

Drexelius, Hieremias, *The Considerations of Drexelius upon Eternitie*, trans. Ralph Winterton, Cambridge, 1636.

—— *The School of Patience*, trans. R. S., 1640.

Gardiner, Samuel, *A Booke of Angling, or Fishing. Wherein is shewed, by conference with Scriptures, the agreement between the Fishermen, Fishes, Fishing of both natures, Temporall and Spirituall*, 1606.

Hervey, James, *Meditations Among the Tombs*, 1746.

Hooker, Richard, *The Works of that Learned and Judicious Divine, Mr. Richard Hooker*, ed. John Keble, 7th ed., 3 vols., Oxford, 1888.

L'Estrange, Sir Roger, *Fables, of Æsop and other Eminent Mythologists*, 1692.

S[ault], J[ohn], *The Second Spira: Being a fearful Example of an Atheist who had Apostatized . . .* , 3rd ed., 1693.

Savile, George, Lord Halifax, *The Lady's New-years Gift: or, Advice to a Daughter*, 3rd ed., 1685.

Sharp, John, *Fifteen Sermons Preached on Several Occasions By the most Reverend Father in God, Dr. John Sharp, late Lord Arch-Bishop of York*, 5th ed., 1722.

Sherlock, William, *A Practical Discourse Concerning Death*, 1689.

South, Robert, *Sermons Preached upon Several Occasions*, 4th ed., 5 vols., 1737.

Sprint, John, *The Bride-Womans Counsellor. Being a Sermon Preach'd at a Wedding, May the 11th, 1699 at Sherbourn, in Dorsetshire*, 1700.

Steele, Richard, *The Christian Hero: An Argument proving that no Principles but those of Religion are sufficient to make a Great Man*, 2nd. ed., 1701.

Swift, Jonathan, *The Prose Writings of Jonathan Swift*, ed. Herbert Davis and Irvin Ehrenpreis, 14 vols, 1939–68.

Taylor, Jeremy, *The Great Exemplar of Sanctity and Holy Life according to the Christian Institution*. Described in the History of the Life and Death of the ever Blessed Jesus Christ the Saviour of the World. With Considerations and Discourses upon the several Parts of the story, and Prayers fitted to the several Mysteries, 1649.

—— *A Funerall Sermon, Preached at the Obsequies of the Right Hon. and most vertuous Lady, the Lady Frances Countess of Carbery* (2 Samuel xix 14), 1650.

—— *The Rule and Exercise of Holy Living*, 1650.

—— *The Rule and Exercise of Holy Dying*, 1651.

—— *The Golden Grove*. A Choice Manual: Containing What is to be *Believed*, *Practised* and *Desired* or *Prayed for*; the *Prayers* being fitted to the several Days of the Week, 17th ed., 1690.

Tillotson, John, *Sermons on Several Subjects and Occasions*, 12 vols., 1742.

Tindal, Matthew, *Christianity as Old as the Creation, or the Gospel a Republication of the Religion of Nature*, 1730.

VII. HISTORICAL AND PHILOSOPHICAL WORKS

Burnet, Gilbert, *History of His Own Times*, 2 vols., 1724–34.

Chateaubriand, François René, Vicomte de, *Le Génie du Christianisme*, in *Œuvres complètes*, ed. M. Sainte-Beuve, 12 tomes, Paris, 1861, tome ii.

Cooper, Anthony Ashley, Lord Shaftesbury, *Characteristicks of Men, Manners, Opinions, Times*, 3 vols., 1711.

Hyde, Edward, Lord Clarendon, *The History of the Rebellion and Civil Wars in England, Begun in the Year 1641*, 3 vols., Oxford, 1702–4.

Locke, John, *The Reasonableness of Christianity*, 1695.

Mandeville, Bernard de, *The Fable of the Bees: or, Private Vices Publick Benefits*, 1714.

Nichols, John, *Literary Anecdotes of the Eighteenth Century*, 9 vols., 1812–15.

VIII. BIOGRAPHICAL AND AUTOBIOGRAPHICAL WORKS, AND PERSONAL LETTERS

Anon., *Some Authentick Memoirs of the Life of Colonel Ch—s, Rape-Master-General of Great Britain*. By an Impartial Hand, 1730.

Austen-Leigh, I. J. E., *Memoir of Jane Austen*, ed. R. W. Chapman, Oxford, 1926.

Delany, Mrs. Patrick (Mary Granville), *The Autobiography and Correspondence of Mary Granville, Mrs. Delany*, ed. Lady Llanover, 3 vols., 1861.

Eliot, George, *The George Eliot Letters*, ed. Gordon S. Haight, 6 vols., New Haven, Conn., 1954–6.

Goldoni, Carlo, *Mémoires de M. Goldoni*, 3 tomes, Paris, 1787.

Hawkins, Sir John, *The Life of Samuel Johnson, LLD.*, 1787.

Johnson, Samuel, *The Lives of the most eminent English Poets; with Critical Observations on their Works*, 4 vols., 1781.

Montagu, Lady Mary Wortley, *The Letters and Works of Lady Mary Wortley Montagu*, ed. W. Moy Thomas, 2 vols., 1893.

Necker de Saussure, Susanne, *Notice sur le caractère et les écrits de Mme de Staël*, Londres, 1820.

Sévigné, Mme de Robertin Chantal, *Letters of Madame de Robertin Chantal, Marchioness de Sevigné, To the Comtesse de Grignan, Her Daughter*, 2 vols., 1727.

Smith, John Thomas, *Nollekens and His Times*, 2nd ed., 2 vols., 1829.

Stanhope, Philip Dormer, Lord Chesterfield, *Letters Written by the Late Right Honourable Philip Dormer Stanhope, Earl of Chesterfield, to His Son, Philip Stanhope, Esq.: Late Envoy Extraordinary at the Court of Dresden*, 2 vols., 1774.

Trollope, Anthony, *The Letters of Anthony Trollope*, ed. W. Bradford Booth, 1951.

Villiers, George, Duke of Buckingham, *Miscellaneous Works, Written by his Grace, George Late Duke of Buckingham*, 1704.

Wilmot, John, Earl of Rochester, *Familiar Letters: Written by the Right Honourable John late Earl of Rochester and several other Persons of Honour and Quality*, 1697.

IX. WORKS ON ART

Antal, Frederick, *Hogarth and His Place in European Art*, 1962.

Combe, William, *The History of the Abbey Church of St. Peter's, Westminster, its antiquities and monuments*, published by Rudolph Ackermann, 2 vols., 1812.

Hagstrum, Jean H., *The Sister Arts*, Chicago, Ill., 1959.

Herbert, Sidney, 16th Earl of Pembroke, *A Catalogue of the Paintings and Drawings in the Collection at Wilton House, Salisbury, Wiltshire*, 1968.

Mâle, Émile, *L'Art religieux de la fin du XVIᵉ siècle, du XVIIᵉ siècle et du XVIIIᵉ siècle*, Paris, 1951.

Ripa, Cesare, *Iconologia o vero descrittione d'imagini delle virtv', vitii, affeti, passioni humane, corpi celesti, mondo e sue parti*, Padua, 1611.

X. ESSAYS

Addison, Joseph, and Richard Steele, *The Spectator*, ed. Donald F. Bond, 5 vols., Oxford, 1965.

Coleridge, Samuel Taylor, *The Literary Remains of Samuel Taylor Coleridge*, ed. Henry Nelson Coleridge, 2 vols., 1836.

de Staël, Mme (Anne-Louise, baronne de Staël-Holstein), *Essai sur les fictions*, in *Œuvres complètes*, 2 tomes, Paris, 1836.

Hardy, Thomas, *Life and Art*, Essays of Thomas Hardy Collected by Ernest Brennecke Jr., New York, N.Y., 1925.

Hazlitt, William, *Lectures on the English Comic Writers*, in *The Complete Works of William Hazlitt*, ed. P. P. Howe, 21 vols., 1930-4, vol. vi, 1931.

Mendelssohn, Moses, *Briefe die neueste Litteratur betreffend*, in *Gesammelte Schriften*, 7 Bände, Leipzig, 1843-5, Band iv, Theil 2, 1844.

Young, Edward, *Conjectures on Original Composition*, 1759.

XI. GENERAL HISTORICAL AND CRITICAL STUDIES

Allison, C. F., *The Rise of Moralism*, 1966.

Day, Robert, A., *Told in Letters*, Ann Arbor, Michigan, 1966.

Draper, John W., *The Funeral Elegy and the Rise of English Romanticism*, New York, N.Y., 1929.

King, Bruce, *Dryden's Major Plays*, Oxford, 1966.

McAdoo, H. R., *The Spirit of Anglicanism*, 1965.

MacCarthy, Bridget G., *Women Writers, their Contribution to the English Novel, 1621-1744*, Cork, 1944.

McKillop, Alan D., *Early Masters of English Fiction*, Lawrence, Kansas, 1956.

Martz, Louis L., *The Poetry of Meditation*, New Haven, Conn., 1954.

Parnell, Paul E., 'The Sentimental Mask', *PMLA.* lxxviii (Dec. 1963), 529-35.

Richetti, John J., *Popular Fiction before Richardson: Narrative Patterns, 1700-1739*, Oxford, 1969.

Turberville, A. S., *Johnson's England*, 2 vols., Oxford, 1933.

Van Ghent, Dorothy, *The English Novel: Form and Function*, New York, N.Y., 1953.

Watt, Ian, *The Rise of the Novel*, 1957.

Index

I. Richardson and the novels

RICHARDSON, SAMUEL

(a) Biographical detail

birth and education 2–6; 250
childhood 4–5
emotional life 7–10; 333
friends, home life, in middle age 286–7; 299; 304–5; 363
political views 3–4
self-portrait 9
social position 1–6; 297; 363
theatre, experience of 113
work as printer 5–6; 12

(b) SR on art of novelist

advice to other novelists 302–4
comments on own work:
— on atmosphere and setting 297–8
— on characterization 277; 286–7; 304
— on his own characters 265; 312–13; 327; 333; 335–6
— on narrative technique 4; 125; 277–8; 297
— on situations and themes 30; 107; 138; 255; 277

(c) SR's characteristics as novelist

technique:
— comedy and humour, SR's use of 33; 65; 68–9; 83; 90–1; 216–17; 222–31; 242; 253–5; 275; 279 ff; 343–4; 377–9
— creation of individual style for characters 27–8; 30–3; 61–3; 69; 130; 140–1; 284–92; 299–300; 304
— dramatic scenes, use of 65–6; 81; 90–1; 94; 119–20; 146–7; 279–85; 288–90; 301
— epistolary narration 11; 13; 29–34; 128–32; 183–6; 198; 277–80; 298–300; 313–15; 372–3; 381–2
— imagery 50–61; 67; 70; 81; 83–4;

91; 94–5; 152–3; 164; 184; 187–8; 216–40; 316; 340–67; 378–80
— sub-plot and subordinate themes, how managed 66; 78; 131–2; 183–4; 255–7; 279; 300–3; 313–14; 379–80
— transformation of source material 12–13; 32–3; 36; 43; 54; 137; 150; 153; 163–4; 307–9; 376–7; 379

views and general themes:
— Christian and spiritual view of life 34; 69; 94–5; 101–2; 106; 124–5; 153; 178–9; 182; 213–15; 239–40; 248; 267–73
— emphasis on personal consciousness, sacredness of identity 44; 69; 86; 104; 121–2; 126; 151–3; 164; 171; 191; 204; 320; 325; 329–31; 336–7; 360–1; 381–3
— exploration of experience rather than didacticism 12; 68–70; 86; 89; 94–7; 183–4; 257; 273; 310; 318–20; 337–9; 365–6; 376
— freedom, necessity of 11; 60; 95; 97; 104–5; 122–35; 207–8; 274–5; 311; 325; 366; 377
— moral views of sex 10–12; 54; 96–7; 104; 378; 380–3
— 'nature', 'passion', and civilization in novels 11–12; 50–8; 63; 67–70; 81–2; 97; 104; 106–7; 124–5; 263–4; 313; 337; 344–6; 350–2; 366–7; 381–3
— rebelliousness, unconventional response supported 60; 69–70; 94–7; 103; 183–7; 191; 273; 310–13; 318; 329–30; 370
— women, their position and SR's treatment of feminine characters 4; 8–9; 17–18; 24; 44; 48–50; 74; 86–9; 92–7; 103; 185; 231; 242; 245; 257; 271; 290–3; 310–11

Index 397

SIR CHARLES GRANDISON [h] minor
   characters [*cont.*]:
Maffei, Lady 359
Mansfield family 259
Mansfield, Miss 259; 294
Marescotti, Father 266; 322
Merceda, Solomon 260
Meredith, Sir Rowland 275; 284–6;
   300; 345
O'Hara, Major 263; 283–4
O'Hara, Mrs. (Mrs. Jervois) 284;
   294; 318; 334; 336
Oldham, Mrs. 260; 293
Olivia, Signora 264–5; 332–5; 337–
   8; 359
Pollexfen, Sir Hargrave 251; 260;
   262–3; 282–3; 302; 346–7; 354;
   363
Porretta, della, family 266; 318;
   320–1; 329–31; 337; 360
Porretta, Marchese della 321
Porretta, Marchesa della 321; 323
Porretta, Giacomo 265–6; 321
Porretta, Jeronymo 260–1; 323
Reeves family 284–5; 294; 310
Reeves, Archibald 282; 285

Salmonet, Captain 263; 283–4; 300
Selby family 337; 360
Selby, George 275; 294; 361
Selby, Mrs. 275; 294
Selby, James 336; 343
Selby, Lucy 302; 313; 335
Sforza family 321
Sforza, Laurana 302
Shirley, Mrs. 249; 275; 294; 337;
   362; 367
Singleton, Mr. 281; 293
Somner, Mr. 281
W., Lord 259; 293–4
Walden, Mr. 250; 281; 293
Williams, Lady Betty 281–2
Wilson 260
(j) *Sir Charles Grandison* compared with
   other SR novels
   with *Pamela I*: 49; 63–4; 66–7; 80–1;
      245; 309; 313; 340; 362
   with *Pamela II*: 78; 80–1; 97–8; 280–1;
      300; 309; 313; 345; 349; 353; 366
   with *Clarissa*: 13; 16; 25; 68; 245;
      257; 271–5; 277–9; 300–2; 305;
      309; 314; 318–20; 328; 340; 362;
      366; 377

II. General Index